AI-BORN

AI-BORN

The Machine Core, the Human Cortex, and the Next Economy of Being

Mehran Granfar

Mic Press New York

2026

Mic Press New York
1140 Avenue of the Americas, New York, NY 10036
(Mic Press, LLC.)

First Mic Press hardcover edition November 2026

MIC PRESS, MIC PRESS NEW YORK, and colophon are registered trademarks of Mic Press, LLC.

For information about special discounts for bulk purchases, please contact Mic Press Special Sales at **info@micpress.com**.

The Mic Press Speakers Bureau can arrange author talks and live events. For inquiries or to book an appearance, email **speakers@micpress.com** or visit **www.micpress.com**.

Interior design by Mic Studio, New York

Manufactured in the United States of America

10 9 8 7 6 5 4 3 2 1

Library of Congress Cataloging-in-Publication Data has been applied for.

ISBN 978-1-961999-02-8 (hardcover)
ISBN 978-1-961999-03-5 (ebook)

To Bronwyn, my wife and partner in all things,

To Leon, our son, who will inherit this new world,

To our parents and siblings, whose support sustains us,

And to the many individuals, communities, and institutions, spread across the globe—tirelessly engaged in action, reflection, consultation, and study—whose shared vision of collective progress and the unity of humankind inspires the architecture of stewardship at the heart of this work.

Acknowledgments

This work has been shaped by many minds and hands.

To the researchers and engineers exploring the frontiers of artificial intelligence while thoughtfully considering its implications—your work provides the foundation for these ideas.

To the founders and leaders reimagining enterprise from first principles—you demonstrate that building powerful systems and humane systems are compatible goals, not competing ones.

To my colleagues at Adaptic and Neolith, to the team at Future Thesis Lab, and to the builders at Mothership, whose daily work proves that technology can amplify human judgment rather than replace it, and whose insights have refined many of the frameworks in this book. To our investors, whose conviction in the future, steadfast support, and willingness to embrace expansive, long-term investment criteria made this work possible.

And to the readers who will take these ideas, challenge them, refine them, and build something better than what's written here—the future is not inevitable. It is chosen.

Author's Note

In 1910, Frederick Winslow Taylor stood before the United States House of Representatives Special Committee and explained, with the missionary confidence of a man who had measured everything, that the human body was a machine whose output could be optimized by sufficiently precise analysis of its motions. His testimony helped unleash the industrial-era logic of time-and-motion study that would govern how organizations thought about human labor for the next century. Taylor wasn't wrong about the efficiency gains. He was catastrophically wrong about what was lost.

I think about Taylor often. Because I'm watching a comparable moment arrive—and I'm building inside it.

Twenty years across design, e-commerce, enterprise software, and financial technology taught me to recognize inflection points. The past four years, one question has kept me up at night: what happens when autonomous AI agents replace entire functional departments.

In December 2022, I began exploring what would become an obsession: autonomous systems, and the hybrid workforces—human and agentic—they make possible. I started Neolith.ai and spent the better part of a year building it: an enterprise platform for deploying autonomous agents inside regulated industries. The work culminated in a multi-month pilot with a large global investment bank. The real education came from where theory breaks against reality—a compliance framework written to assume human discretion has no answer when the decision-maker is software. A regulator asking who to subpoena when the portfolio manager is an algorithm discovers the mental model simply wasn't built for the question.

Then I went quiet. I became a father. I faced a cancer scare, now in remission. That interval forced the question the pilot had already started to raise: not whether to keep building AI-enabled systems, but whether the entire design assumption was wrong. Embedding AI inside legacy human structures—bolting intelligence onto an org designed to move information between people—was the flaw, not the implementation. The future isn't about attaching AI to human-centered companies. It's about designing new ones from first principles—where humans set intent and autonomous agents constitute the operational core.

An idea like that can't be settled on a whiteboard. It has to be learned inside a real company, where mistakes are expensive and the feedback is honest. I chose the hardest proving ground I could find: financial markets, where every decision moves capital and regulators demand audit trails.

That conviction became Adaptic.ai. The goal: run money with no human in the execution loop—humans define the parameters and trading policies that enforce deterministic and regulatory standards, and the agents execute within them. An institutional-grade alpha engine, automated risk monitoring and compliance reporting, with an asset-management firm running on top of it. Autonomous agents form the operational workforce, not just the investment engine. For more than two years now, I've been building the means of running Adaptic as a genuinely AI-born company—the operating system for AI-born asset management.[1]

[1]This book uses three distinct terms, developed in Chapter 4. *AI-enabled* organizations are traditional firms that bolt AI tools onto human-centered structures. *AI-native* companies build AI products with human teams—the AI is what they sell, not how they operate (Cursor, Midjourney, and Perplexity are examples). *AI-Born* enterprises are designed from first principles, where autonomous agents form the operational workforce and a small human cortex sets intent and holds accountability. The difference is architectural, not cosmetic: an AI-Born company runs on an operating surface built for hybrid human–agent

As I write, that work is reaching the threshold it was built for. Adaptic runs with a team of almost fifty—of whom roughly forty-four are AI colleagues holding C-Suite, SVP, and VP roles. Each of them, at any given moment, orchestrates two to three hundred sub-agents through ten to fifteen session managers. A handful of humans hold the agenda; the agents do the work. Everything I learned building Adaptic went back into the original platform, refined and battle-hardened. That platform is Neolith—the operating surface Adaptic runs on, and the one we are now opening to other AI-born companies. Alongside it, through Future Thesis Lab—the research lab and venture incubator I co-founded—we help others build from these same first principles. I should be plain about that commercial interest here, at the outset. The framework in these pages stands on its own; it does not depend on adopting Adaptic or Neolith, and the book draws on public examples—Cursor, Lovable, Midjourney, Haier, Block—throughout.

At the time of writing (June 2026), we're engaging with financial regulators to establish licensing frameworks for fully AI-managed portfolios. Robo-advisors and algorithmic trading operate under frameworks that assume human oversight at key decision points. We're seeking approval for portfolios where agents make final investment decisions autonomously—humans set intent parameters but don't intervene in execution. That distinction—autonomous final decision versus supervised execution—is what places us outside existing precedent.

U.S. financial regulators apply existing rules through technology-neutral regulation: the same fiduciary standards, risk management protocols, and compliance requirements that govern human port-

---

work—Adaptic runs on Neolith—rather than on software designed to move information between people.

folio managers now apply to algorithmic ones.[2,3] The friction point is translating concepts like "reasonable care" and "fiduciary duty"—which assume human discretion—to autonomous systems operating at machine speed.

I write from inside that machinery, wrestling daily with these tensions: How do you design agent governance that preserves human judgment while enabling autonomous execution? How do you build accountability when most decisions are algorithmic? How do you convince regulators that machines can meet fiduciary standards when mental models still assume human discretion?

These aren't theoretical puzzles.

They're the friction points where the future actually gets built—or doesn't.

A note on case studies: Throughout this book I use named organizations — Aether Dynamics, Meridian Trade Finance, Legacy Corp, and others — to illustrate how these frameworks operate under real conditions. These named firms are composite constructions: organizational architectures and operational dynamics synthesized from documented patterns across multiple real enterprises whose principals requested anonymity or where combining cases produces clearer illustration than any single case permits. Aether Dynamics is the one I return to most — watching one organization make these

[2] FINRA, "Regulatory Notice 24-09: Artificial Intelligence and Generative AI" (June 27, 2024). Establishes that existing rules apply to AI use through technology-neutral regulation, requiring technology governance frameworks, model risk management, data integrity safeguards, and reliability assessments under Rule 3110.

[3] Sidley Austin LLP, "Artificial Intelligence: U.S. Securities and Commodities Guidelines for Responsible Use" (February 2025). Legal analysis finding that despite recent regulatory focus on AI, the SEC, CFTC, and FINRA had not yet issued new regulations specifically addressing AI use, instead emphasizing responsible use within existing regulatory frameworks. Note: the AI regulatory landscape is fast-moving; readers should verify the current status of any specific rule or guidance at the time of reading.

choices end-to-end teaches more than a dozen snapshots. The metrics, decisions, and outcomes attributed to these composites are grounded in documented evidence; they are not invented. Where I discuss real, named companies (McKinsey, Cursor, Mondragon, Patagonia, Tesla), I have sourced their details from public records and have cited sources. The distinction matters, and I want readers to know which is which.

Why This Book

The books that shaped how I think about technology are either blueprints or manifestos—operational detail without moral stakes, or moral stakes without operational detail. This book attempts both simultaneously, through three strands existing literature doesn't weave together.

A rigorous framework for AI-Born enterprise—not incremental change but first-principles redesign. How do you organize when a small number of humans direct agent workforces operating at ratios that would have been inconceivable five years ago? What governance, risk management, and trust systems make that work at scale?

Honest confrontation with displacement. If AI-Born firms achieve trillion-dollar valuations with small founding teams, what happens to the thousands who would have worked at a traditional enterprise of that scale? This book doesn't pretend that's not happening. It offers pragmatic pathways through short-term disruption toward long-term possibility. The heavy lifting—what the social contract owes displaced workers, how institutions rebuild the floor—belongs to the companion volume, *The Bridge*. Here I name the problem and hold it honestly. The problem isn't human nature. It's transition speed and institutional lag.[4]

Values-conscious architecture. Technology isn't neutral. Every architectural choice embeds moral commitments. AI-Born firms optimized solely for short-term profit can concentrate wealth in ways that create unpriced social externalities. Firms architected from inception around stakeholder value—not shareholder primacy alone—produce different outcomes. This book shows how.

A note on these two books: Book 1 is a builder's architecture. You can read it alone and walk away with a complete framework for designing, operating, and governing an AI-Born enterprise. Book 2, *The Bridge*, is the social-contract counterpart — it addresses the displacement and distribution questions that Book 1's architecture creates. The serious reader of both will notice that the architecture generates the social problems, and the social-contract solutions become design constraints back on the architecture. They are a single argument, published in two volumes.

On This Book's Economic Vision

Before we begin, I want to name a tension this book cannot escape. The architecture I propose will be read through ideological lenses designed for a different, and now ending, economy. This book doesn't fit neatly into existing economic categories. Both capitalism

[4] Jamie Dimon, remarks at the World Economic Forum, Davos, January 22, 2026. Dimon — overseeing JPMorgan's own deployment of AI across 500+ use cases — warned that AI adoption "may go too fast for society" and that coordinated government-business response on retraining was necessary. "You can't lay off 2 million truckers tomorrow," he told the panel, framing rapid workforce displacement as a demand-destruction risk, not a permanent structural failure. His prescription: "Phase it in." This is the capitalist establishment, not labor advocates, naming transition speed as the variable requiring management. Source: *Banking Dive*, "Dimon: AI effect on jobs, workforce," January 22, 2026, `https://www.bankingdive.com/news/jpmorgan-dimon-ai-effect-jobs-workforce-davos/810247/`.

and socialism emerged for a world where human labor was the primary productive input.

When small founding teams orchestrate what once required tens of thousands, familiar debates over regulation and redistribution face new constraints. Consider what that means for a moment. The “job”—steady employment, regular salary, benefits tied to your employer—is an Industrial Revolution invention barely two centuries old. Before roughly 1800, most people would have found the notion of selling their time by the hour, to a stranger, for wages, deeply strange. That arrangement was designed for specific constraints: factory coordination, geographic immobility, information scarcity. All three are dissolving at once. As they go, the arrangement built on top of them goes too.

This book’s emphasis on stewardship and stakeholder governance will challenge pure free-market advocates. Its defense of profit motives and competitive discipline will challenge market skeptics.

Both reactions reveal the same underlying issue: we’re trying to map 21st-century questions onto 20th-century ideological categories. When the fundamental premise changes—from labor scarcity to judgment scarcity—the frameworks must change too.

Incentives matter. Material rewards drive behavior, markets efficiently allocate resources, and entrepreneurs who risk everything deserve outsized returns.

But incentives alone are insufficient for the world we’re entering.

The AI-Born shift reorients the basis of human effort—from execution toward stewardship of intent. Our most enduring contributions confirm this. Scientific breakthroughs, lasting art, and social movements spring from obsession, purpose, and service to something larger than the transaction. Material security enables them—Marie

Curie still needed a laboratory, Lin-Manuel Miranda still needed a producer—but the generative force was not the paycheck. Wangari Maathai planted the first trees of the Green Belt Movement before any institutional recognition arrived. Payment followed contribution; it did not cause it.

Markets without stewardship constraints produce wealth concentration that destabilizes the system; stewardship without market discipline produces stagnation. Nobel laureate Elinor Ostrom spent a career documenting what many economists found counterintuitive: systems designed around narrow self-interest consistently underperform systems designed around interdependent welfare. Her insight, confirmed across Swiss alpine meadows, Maine fisheries, and Japanese forest cooperatives, points toward a structural truth—individual prosperity is inseparable from collective flourishing, not as sentiment but as operational fact.[5]

This is what gets underweighted in most AI strategy discussions. The cooperation problem isn't separate from the technical problem. It is the technical problem, scaled up.

The choice isn't between endorsing markets and abandoning them. It's between two architectures within a market economy: extraction (concentrating productivity gains at the top of the ownership structure) and stewardship (distributing them across the network of contributors who generated them). That choice is architectural, not ideological.

[5] Elinor Ostrom, *Governing the Commons: The Evolution of Institutions for Collective Action* (Cambridge University Press, 1990). Ostrom's Nobel Prize lecture (2009) summarizes the cross-cultural evidence: "People are not trapped in inexorable tragedies if they have the freedom and capacity to organize themselves." Her design principles for sustainable commons governance — including graduated sanctions, collective-choice arrangements, and nested enterprises — underpin much of the institutional thinking in Book 2 (*AI-Born: The Bridge*).

The architecture I'm proposing—profits alongside purpose, competitive advantage through stakeholder governance, productivity gains shared broadly rather than concentrated narrowly—isn't a compromise. It's what happens when you notice that the fundamental scarcity has shifted from labor to judgment, and let the organizing principles follow.

This will frustrate those seeking a clean ideological home for these ideas.

That's the point.

What follows is a blueprint for navigating the dissolution of the old architecture with eyes open—to the opportunities, the risks, and the moral choices embedded in every technical decision we're making right now. The book ahead develops the architecture I've been building toward since Neolith.

The first question Part I answers is not about AI at all. It is about what was traded last time—during the first lineage break, when industrialization converted craft into labor and community into employment. Understanding that trade teaches us to ask the right question about this one. I hope it earns your scrutiny.

Prologue: The Lineage Break

November 2023. The Houthi attacks begin in the Red Sea. Within days, the world's major carriers abandon the Suez and swing the long way around Africa. Insurance premiums spike 300%.[6] Container ships burn diesel down the African coast, recalculating their routes in real time.

At Legacy Corp—a Fortune 50 manufacturer with 47,000 employees—the response crawls. Emergency meetings convene. Analysts reconcile conflicting ERP systems across fourteen business units. Vice presidents debate forecasts built on incompatible data models. The company sees the crisis clearly. It cannot act.

Between insight and execution lies a maze of dependencies. Finance needs projections. Analytics can't reconcile systems. Legal reviews contracts. Each handoff eats days.

Container ships burn fuel. Meetings multiply.[7]

---

[6] Lloyd's List Intelligence and Drewry Shipping Consultants, maritime market analyses, December 2023–January 2024. Insurance premium spikes of 200–400% for Red Sea transits were documented across Lloyd's of London syndicates in December 2023; the 300% figure reflects mid-range estimates from Drewry's Container Insight Weekly, January 2024. The rerouting added approximately 10–14 days per transit and significant fuel costs per voyage.

[7] "McKinsey Global Supply Chain Leader Survey 2024," McKinsey & Company, April–June 2024, `https://www.mckinsey.com/capabilities/operations/our-insights/supply-chain-risk-survey`. Survey of 88 supply chain leaders found that only 25% of companies have formal processes for discussing supply chain risks at the board level, despite supply chain disruptions affecting 90% of companies in 2024. Additionally, only 30% of respondents reported their boards have deep understanding of supply chain risks.

* * *

Aria Chen is one of three humans at Aether Dynamics, a Singapore-based supply chain firm, watching the same crisis unfold.[8] Their autonomous supply chain system flagged the pattern three days before Legacy Corp's analysts had finished their first call—tracking vessel speeds, insurance premium spikes, maritime security chatter that human planners hadn't yet correlated.

The system war-gamed routing scenarios across Aether's micro-factory network. Within minutes, autonomous agents simulated hundreds of permutations—cost against transit time against geopolitical risk, warehouse capacity against regulatory exposure against carbon footprint—modeling how each choice cascaded through inventory positioning, contract terms, and customer commitments.

Then it stopped. Not because it lacked options. Because it reached a choice that required judgment, not computation.

The Lombok Strait route offered the best savings. The catch: contested waters. Indonesia, Australia, and China maintain overlapping naval claims. No major logistics firm had routed there. The risk profile had no comparison cases.

Calculation stops. Judgment begins.

Aria pulls up the Lombok overlay and says what no model can: *not yet.* She and her two colleagues gather around the visualization—

[8]Aether Dynamics is a composite case study synthesizing documented patterns from multiple AI-Born enterprises navigating supply chain disruption. The Red Sea/Bab el-Mandeb scenario reflects actual logistics crises of late 2023–2024; the organizational architecture, response capabilities, and decision-making dynamics represent real operational patterns observed across AI-Born supply chain firms. The minutes-scale war-gaming reflects documented agentic system performance in real deployments at comparable firms; the exact elapsed time is illustrative of the order of magnitude, not a sourced benchmark from a specific deployment. Legacy Corp similarly represents aggregate incumbent response patterns. Both names are anonymized composites, not references to specific companies.

not to debate logistics, but to decide what kind of risk this company is willing to carry, and why.

They encode their decision and reasoning. The system executes: inventory reroutes, contracts renegotiate, shipments reposition.

At Legacy Corp, emails circulate through approval chains.

Aether has already moved.

The difference is not efficiency. It is architecture.

This is the second lineage break in organizational history.

Figure 0.1: The lineage break in miniature—an incumbent that sees the crisis but cannot act, beside an AI-Born firm that has already moved. The rupture is categorical, not incremental.

The first came when the Industrial Revolution converted artisans into wage laborers. That rupture took decades of coercion, factory acts, and psychological conditioning before it felt normal. It manufactured a new kind of human alongside the goods—one whose identity became organized around an employer rather than a craft, a community, or a calling. That arrangement lasted two centuries. We examine it closely in the chapters that follow, because understanding the first break is how we take the second one seriously.

Notice what the first break buried: the question *who are you?* had a ready answer for centuries—your trade, your guild, your place in a community that watched you work. The industrial age replaced that answer with *where do you work?* For two generations, that substitution held. People built identities around employers rather than crafts, careers rather than callings. That arrangement is what the second break now calls into question.

Now we automate intelligence itself. Autonomous agents synthesize information, war-game scenarios, execute coordination—the cognitive work that filled organizational pyramids for two centuries. Dario Amodei, the CEO of Anthropic, has argued that AI "will be capable of a very wide range of human cognitive abilities—perhaps all of them... much different from previous technologies."[9] Anthropic's own research agenda is organized around the risks of the systems it builds—Amodei has separately described himself as "considerably closer to real danger in 2026 than we were in 2023." When a founder who has spent years cataloguing those dangers describes this transition as categorically different from every prior tool—not faster horses, but a new animal altogether—the claim earns careful attention.

* * *

[9] Dario Amodei, "The Adolescence of Technology," `https://www.darioamodei.com/essay/the-adolescence-of-technology`, January 27, 2026. The quoted passage: "AI will be capable of a very wide range of human cognitive abilities—perhaps all of them... much different from previous technologies." Amodei, CEO of Anthropic, made this claim while enumerating five risk categories facing the AI transition—autonomy risks, misuse for destruction, concentration of power, economic disruption, and indirect institutional effects. He separately described himself as "considerably closer to real danger in 2026 than we were in 2023."

What emerges from this rupture is a new organizational species. Call it the **AI-Born enterprise**.

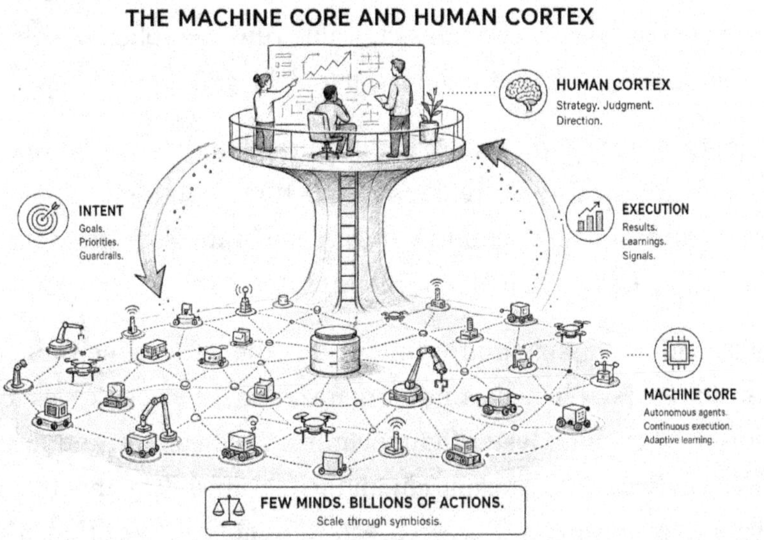

Figure 0.2: The anatomy of the AI-Born enterprise—a small human nucleus (the Human Cortex) setting intent and judgment, directing a vast body of autonomous agents (the Machine Core) that execute, learn, and scale.

Its anatomy is not complicated, but it is new. Aether Dynamics runs with three humans making calls that would have required a hundred-person supply chain organization. The machine handles computation. The humans handle what the machine cannot: deciding what the numbers mean when context shifts, and why a particular risk is or isn't worth carrying. Execution is automated. Judgment is not.

Lovable, a Swedish startup founded in 2023, builds full-stack software applications from plain-language prompts.[10] By February

[10] Dominic-Madori Davis, "Lovable says it added $100M in revenue last month alone, with just 146 employees," TechCrunch, March 11, 2026, `https://techcrunch.com/2026/03/11/lovable-says-it-added-100m-in-`

2026, it had reached $400 million in annual recurring revenue with 146 employees—no enterprise sales hierarchy, no layer of middle management to synchronize. Aether Dynamics runs this logic applied to supply chains. Lovable runs it applied to software development. Different industry, parallel logic.

What these companies share is a compression that doesn't optimize the old architecture—it renders it structurally obsolete. The direction is unmistakable, pointing toward a world where the team that once required thousands now requires dozens.[11]

This is not a gradual improvement. It is the pattern the Industrial Revolution established: a new organizational form emerges, captures market share faster than incumbents can adapt, and forces a choice between transformation and irrelevance. The incumbents that survived the first lineage break were not the ones that added steam engines to their workshops. They were the ones that rebuilt around the logic of the new form.

The same choice is in front of us now—and it is being made in real time. In February 2026, Jack Dorsey announced that Block would cut approximately 4,000 employees, roughly 40% of its workforce, explicitly attributing the decision to AI deployment.[12]

`revenue-last-month-alone-with-just-146-employees/`. Lovable (formerly GPT Engineer), founded 2023, reported $400M ARR as of February 2026 with 146 employees—yielding approximately $2.74M revenue per employee. The company added $100M in ARR in March 2026 alone. Enterprise clients include Klarna and HubSpot.

[11] Frederick P. Brooks Jr., *The Mythical Man-Month: Essays on Software Engineering* (Reading, MA: Addison-Wesley, 1975), 13–26. Brooks's Law states that "adding manpower to a late software project makes it later" due to communication overhead growing as the square of the number of team members. The principle extends to all knowledge work by extrapolation: coordination costs increase as team size grows—an authorial interpretation of Brooks's core insight, not a claim Brooks himself made explicitly about non-software contexts.

[12] CNBC, "Block laying off about 4,000 employees, roughly 40% of its workforce," February 26, 2026; Fortune, "Jack Dorsey lays off 40% of Block, saying AI has changed the game," February 27, 2026. Block eliminated

The market rewarded the move; the stock rose. That market gain lands differently when you remember the roughly 4,000 people behind the 40% – a tension the architecture alone cannot resolve, and one this book holds throughout. "Within the next year," he told his peers, "I believe the majority of companies will reach the same conclusion and make similar structural changes." He wasn't issuing a threat. He was describing a mechanism.

* * *

None of this is predetermined.

Every decision about how to build an AI-Born enterprise embeds choices. Autonomous systems execute at machine speed and machine scale. Whatever you encode—which customers to serve, what risks to carry, how to price, which commitments to honor—the system executes those choices consistently, across millions of interactions, faster than any human can review. What strikes me, building and running an AI-Born company, is how often this outruns even the people who built the systems. The amplification is not hypothetical. It is the mechanism.

The industrial age asked: *What can you produce?*

The AI-Born era asks: *What do you intend?*

* * *

What follows is the architect's answer to that question. Part I traces the historical arc—how the first lineage break shaped the enterprise forms we now inhabit, and why the second break cannot

---

approximately 4,000 employees—roughly 40% of its workforce—with explicit AI attribution. Dorsey's statement to peers: "Within the next year, I believe the majority of companies will reach the same conclusion and make similar structural changes." Block's stock rose approximately 22–24% on the announcement; 2026 gross profit guidance was raised to $12.2B (+18% YoY).

be addressed with the tools the first one produced. Parts II and III give the blueprint and the operator's guide: the anatomy of an AI-Born enterprise, how it runs, how it governs itself, and how incumbents can transform rather than wait.

A second volume addresses the harder question the blueprint raises. When three humans orchestrate what once required thousands, the displaced are not a footnote. They are the central problem of our era—and when that pattern scales across an entire economy, the human stakes dwarf the business ones. The two books form a single argument: the architecture generates the social shadow, and the social shadow becomes a design constraint on the architecture.

But the blueprint must come first.

Chapter 1 begins in 1769, with a steam engine, a patent, and the end of a world that most people had assumed would last forever.

Part I

The Great Narrowing

Chapter 1: The First Lineage Break—How Industrialization Traded Integration for Abundance

In 1320, the Arte della Lana guild destroyed an entire cloth batch—burned it in the public square—after a Florentine wool merchant substituted inferior thread.[13] His business never recovered. Neither did his family's standing.

The public burning was not theater. It was information. In a world where reputation traveled through parish, guild, and marketplace simultaneously, where your economic function and your social standing and your moral character were legible to the same community, punishment worked because everyone who mattered was watching. The audience was not strangers. It was neighbors, creditors, in-laws, the priest who heard your confession, the guild brothers who would decide whether your son qualified for apprenticeship. Economic reputation and social identity were not merely correlated. They were the same thing.

[13] Guild quality control mechanisms were strictly enforced through public punishment and reputation damage. Florentine guild records from the 14th century document numerous cases of merchants fined and having defective goods publicly destroyed for quality violations. The Arte della Lana (wool guild) maintained detailed regulations requiring inspection of all wool and cloth, with violations resulting in fines, confiscation, and public shaming. See John M. Najemy, *A History of Florence 1200-1575* (Oxford: Blackwell, 2006), pp. 89-112, and Samuel Kline Cohn Jr., *The Laboring Classes in Renaissance Florence* (New York: Academic Press, 1980), pp. 45-67.

Let me be precise about what that whole actually was, because nostalgia distorts the picture as badly as triumphalism does. The pre-industrial world was not an idyll. Poverty killed routinely and without mercy. Most people owned fewer possessions than fit in a drawer. Individual liberty barely existed in any modern sense. Rigid hierarchy and systematic exclusion were not side effects of the guild system—they were structural requirements. Integration came at brutal cost.

Yet something was real about the integration itself. And understanding what it was—precisely, without romanticizing it—is the only way to understand what industrialization destroyed and what it built in its place. That understanding matters here not as historical curiosity but as preparation. The first great rupture in the organization of human work established a pattern. We are living through the second. The shape of the first tells us something essential about the shape of the second—not as prophecy, but as precedent.

The Integrated World

Medieval guilds integrated work, community, and identity into a single architecture. A blacksmith wasn't someone who *worked with* metal—he *was* a blacksmith. That identity determined where he lived, whom he married, which church pews his family occupied, how his sons would earn their bread, who would bury him when he died. Economic function, social standing, moral obligation, and the rhythms of daily life formed one whole.[14]

[14] Sheilagh Ogilvie, *The European Guilds: An Economic Analysis* (Princeton: Princeton University Press, 2019), 1-45. Ogilvie analyzes thousands of guilds that dominated European economies from 1000 to 1880, documenting how craft guilds integrated economic production with social identity through temporal, social, and occupational dimensions.

The temporal structure of this integration is worth pausing on, because we have almost entirely lost the felt sense of it. The historical record—the guild account books, the seasonal court calendars, the apprentice indentures preserved in county archives—paints a picture less like our world with the technology removed, and more like a different species of time altogether. E.P. Thompson, in his 1967 essay "Time, Work-Discipline, and Industrial Capitalism," identified the mechanism that held the pre-industrial world together: **task-orientation**.[15] Pre-industrial labor followed the logic of the task, not the logic of the clock. The blacksmith worked until the horseshoe was finished, until the plough was repaired, until the harvest was in. The weaver wove until the cloth was complete. Time was something you *passed*—with neighbors, in relationship, embedded in the season's rhythm. It was not a commodity to be parceled out and sold. It was the medium in which life occurred.

Thompson's contrast with what came after is stark, and his phrasing precisely captures the difference: time shifted from something you "passed" with neighbors to something you "spent" alone, sold by the hour.[16] That single shift—*passed* to *spent*—contains almost everything. *Passed* time you shared; *spent* time you gave up. One is abundance; the other, depletion. When time passes, it is still yours in some sense—you moved through it in relationship. When time is spent, it is gone in exchange for something else.

The agricultural calendar gave this task-orientation its deepest structure. Lammas (August 1) marked the first harvest, when com-

[15]E. P. Thompson, "Time, Work-Discipline, and Industrial Capitalism," *Past & Present*, Volume 38, Issue 1, December 1967, Pages 56–97, `https://doi.org/10.1093/past/38.1.56`. The discussion of task-orientation and the quote "social intercourse and labour were intermingled" appears in the section on pre-industrial work patterns, approximately p. 60.

[16]E. P. Thompson, "Time, Work-Discipline, and Industrial Capitalism," *Past & Present* 38 (1967): 56-97, documents the factory system's transformation of time from "passed" to "spent."

munities gathered collectively to bring in what they had collectively planted. Michaelmas (September 29) settled accounts, rents, and contracts. The winter quarter offered genuine recovery—not vacation in the modern sense, but a natural pause enforced by the land's own cycle. These were not arbitrary holidays. They were the earth's own punctuation of the year, and human economic activity was organized around them. Spiritual observance and economic activity were not competing claims on a person's time. They were dimensions of the same life.[17]

The pace this created was not laziness. Medieval agricultural laborers worked hard during harvest, sometimes continuously for days when weather threatened. But the rhythm was theirs: intense when necessary, slack when possible, calibrated to what the land and season required rather than to what a clock decreed. The social intercourse that accompanied this work—Thompson's phrase for what pre-industrial labor actually contained—was not an interruption of the work.[18] It was part of what work meant. You knew the names of everyone working beside you. You had obligations to them that preceded the workday and would outlast it. The person who was your fellow laborer in the morning was the person who would testify at your son's apprenticeship hearing and whose daughter you might eventually marry.

[17] Ronald Hutton, *The Stations of the Sun: A History of the Ritual Year in Britain* (Oxford: Oxford University Press, 1996), pp. 327-331 and pp. 364-369, provides detailed documentation of Lammas (August 1) and Michaelmas (September 29) as quarter days structuring the agricultural year. See also George C. Homans, *English Villagers of the Thirteenth Century* (Harvard University Press, 1941), Book IV: "The Husbandman's Year." Thompson's specific phrase "social intercourse and labour were intermingled" appears in "Time, Work-Discipline, and Industrial Capitalism," *Past & Present* 38, no. 1 (1967): 60.

[18] E.P. Thompson, "Time, Work-Discipline, and Industrial Capitalism," *Past & Present* 38, no. 1 (1967): 56-97, pp. 80-86, describes how time was "passed" rather than "spent" in pre-industrial societies.

The guild system that organized this world was itself an architecture—not neutral, but encoding specific values into social structure. At its best, it amplified craft mastery, enforced quality through collective reputation, provided mutual aid, and created belonging rooted in mastery. The word "masterly" still carries the residue of this: to do something with mastery meant to do it with the full intelligence developed through years of deliberate practice, transmitted from teacher to student through physical presence and repeated example. A master blacksmith's hands knew things that could not be written down. That embodied knowledge was the guild's primary product and primary currency.[19]

What the guild also provided—and what is harder to see from our distance—was a framework for moral accountability. Quality standards enforced by the guild were not just economic regulations. They were expressions of a craftsman's honor. To produce inferior work was not merely a business error. It was a moral failure, legible to the community as such. The Arte della Lana's public burning was the enforcement mechanism; but the deeper enforcement was reputational—your guild brothers knew you, your parish knew you, the same people you'd see at your daughter's betrothal would hear the verdict.

And yet. The guild system was also a technology of exclusion.

Women were systematically barred from full guild membership across Europe. A German jurist in 1683 declared that "masculine sex is one of the indispensable basic preconditions for admission to a guild," codifying in law what had long operated in practice.[20] Jews

[19]For comprehensive historical analysis of guild systems, seasonal agricultural rhythms, apprenticeship structures, exclusion mechanisms, and the moral architecture of organizational design in pre-industrial societies, see the online supplement at **ai-born.org/frameworks/integration-index**.

[20]Sheilagh Ogilvie, *The European Guilds: An Economic Analysis* (Princeton: Princeton University Press, 2019), Chapters 3 and 5, documents systematic

were excluded from guilds, denied citizenship, and forced into the narrow economic niches—money-lending, long-distance trade—that Christian guilds had left open. Religious minorities and migrants faced similar barriers. The integration that guilds provided was integration for insiders. The exclusion was not incidental. It was the mechanism that made the integration work: belonging required boundaries, and the boundaries were drawn along lines of gender, religion, and lineage.

Apprentices endured years of unpaid labor under masters wielding legal authority for corporal punishment. Entry fees in 15th-century Paris equaled a year's wages for a skilled craftsman.[21] Mobility between trades was practically impossible. A carpenter's son became a carpenter. A blacksmith's daughter had essentially no path to independent economic life outside her father's or husband's guild membership.

All of this must be held together: genuine belonging, genuine mastery, genuine community—and genuine poverty, genuine exclusion, genuine suffering. The guild world was not a paradise. It was a different bargain, with different costs and different provisions. The brutality was real. The integration was also real. Understanding both without letting either cancel the other is the analytical discipline this chapter requires.[22]

---

exclusion of women, Jews, religious and ethnic minorities, migrants, and those lacking property or lineage. Adrian Beier, *Tractatus De Iure Prohibendi* (Jena, 1683), cited via Ogilvie Chapter 5: "masculine sex is one of the indispensable basic preconditions for admission to a guild."

[21]The financial barriers to achieving master status in medieval guilds were substantial and well-documented. Paris guild records from the 15th century show entry fees, material costs for the masterpiece, mandatory gifts to existing masters, and ceremonial expenses could total 20-40 livres—equivalent to a skilled craftsman's annual wages. See Merry E. Wiesner, *Working Women in Renaissance Germany* (New Brunswick: Rutgers University Press, 1986), pp. 156-178.

[22]Karl Polanyi, *The Great Transformation: The Political and Economic Origins of Our Time* (New York: Farrar & Rinehart, 1944; Beacon Press, 2001) documents

Call these three dimensions—temporal, social, and identity—the **Integration Index**: a measure of the degree to which work, community, and self interweave at any given historical moment. In the guild world the index ran high. Your hours, your neighbors, and your sense of who you were all arrived bundled in the same arrangement. Industrialization, as the next pages show, drove every dimension toward zero at once—and it is the recovery of that index, not the recovery of the guild, that the rest of this book is finally concerned with.[23]

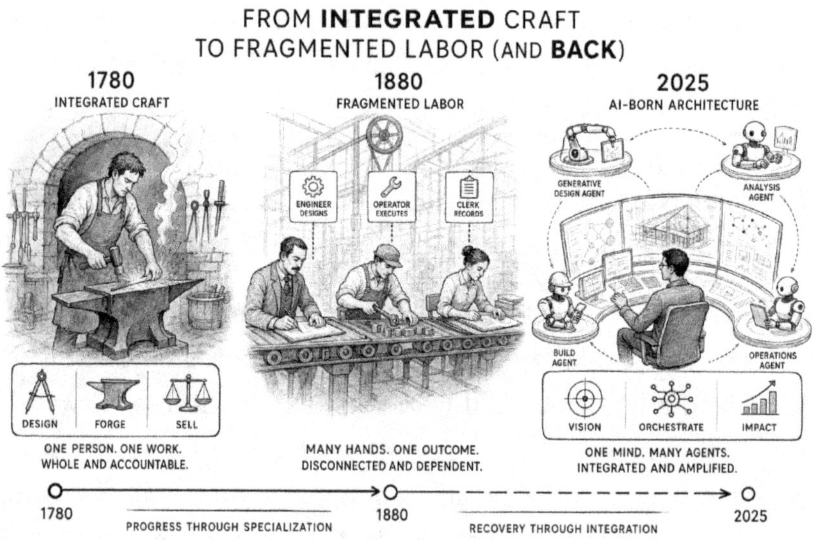

Figure 1.1: The Blacksmith's Dissolution: Pre-industrial craft as integrated whole-system mastery vs. industrial fragmentation into specialized sub-tasks.

that prior to industrial market society, economies had been organized around reciprocity and redistribution across personal and communal relationships; industrialization subordinated these social bonds to competitive market logic.

[23] For detailed analysis of the Integration Index framework and its three dimensions (temporal, social, and identity integration), including the research foundations from McAdams, Polanyi, and Wrzesniewski, see the online supplement at **ai-born.org/frameworks/integration-index**.

The Enclosure and the Shattering

The rupture did not begin with the steam engine. It began with the land.

Between roughly 1750 and 1850, the English Parliament passed over 4,000 individual Enclosure Acts, converting common land—the shared grazing fields, forests, and waterways that rural communities had worked for centuries—into private property.[24] Peasants who had farmed the commons under customary arrangements found themselves legally dispossessed. The commons became someone else's field. The way of life organized around the commons became, legally, trespass.

This is enclosure's deepest significance as a metaphor—and the metaphor needs to be named precisely because it will recur. Enclosure is the privatization of what had been shared: the conversion of common inheritance into commodity, of communal right into private property. What had been yours by virtue of membership—by virtue of being a neighbor, a parishioner, a person embedded in a particular place—became someone else's by virtue of capital. The economic transaction erased the social relationship.

Enclosure drove millions off the land and toward the factories. Not primarily by choice. By the arithmetic of survival: without access to common land, subsistence farming was impossible. Without subsistence farming, the factory wage became the only alternative to destitution. The "free labor" that the factory system celebrated

[24] J.A. Yelling, *Common Field and Enclosure in England 1450–1850* (London: Macmillan, 1977), pp. 1-30, documents the Parliamentary enclosure movement. Between 1750 and 1850, Parliament passed over 4,000 individual Enclosure Acts, converting approximately 6.8 million acres of common and open-field land into private property. E.P. Thompson, *The Making of the English Working Class* (London: Victor Gollancz, 1963; Penguin edition 1980), pp. 213-239, situates enclosure as the structural precondition for industrial factory labor.

was freedom in a narrow sense—the freedom of a person who has had their options systematically removed to accept whatever terms are offered.[25]

The factory then completed what enclosure began. It invented the "job"—a standardized, de-skilled, fungible unit of human time abstracted, measured, and sold as commodity.[26] Work shifted from something you *were* to something you *did* for eight hours. William Morris, writing in 1884, called this "toil"—labor stripped of autonomy, purpose, and connection to product.[27] The distinction he drew between toil and work was precise: toil is repetitive, automatable execution that drains cognitive energy without engaging full human capacity. Work is creative, judgment-rich effort that produces something—an object, a relationship, an understanding—that outlasts the effort itself.

The factory converted craftwork into toil. By design.

---

[25]Karl Polanyi, *The Great Transformation: The Political and Economic Origins of Our Time* (New York: Farrar & Rinehart, 1944; Republished by Beacon Press, 2001). Quote: "Labor is only another name for a human activity which goes with life itself... the alleged commodity 'labor power' cannot be shoved about, used indiscriminately, or even left unused, without affecting also the human individual."

[26]Sidney Pollard, "Factory Discipline in the Industrial Revolution," *Economic History Review* 16, no. 2 (1963): 254-271. Pollard documents how the factory system created the modern concept of the "job" as a standardized, measurable unit of human time and effort that could be abstracted from personal identity and sold as a commodity.

[27]William Morris, "Useful Work versus Useless Toil" (1884), in *The Collected Works of William Morris*, Vol. 23 (London: Longmans Green and Company, 1915), pp. 98-120. Morris distinguished between "useful work" that engages human creativity and purpose, and "useless toil" that mechanizes human activity into repetitive, alienating labor.

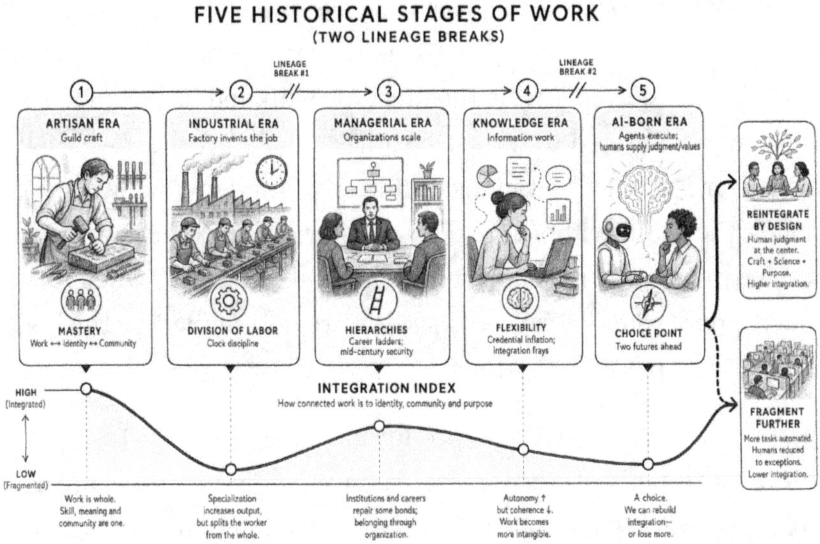

Figure 1.2: The evolution of work across five eras: Each transition fundamentally redefined the nature of human labor, identity, and economic organization.

The Clock and the New Discipline

The most precise instrument of this conversion was not the steam engine. It was the clock.

In pre-industrial life, the clock had been largely irrelevant to the organization of work. You worked until the task was finished, until the light failed, until the season changed. Factory production required something different: synchronized, simultaneous, continuous labor. Dozens or hundreds of workers operating interdependent machinery needed to arrive, start, and stop together. The clock became the instrument of that synchronization—and, almost immediately, of control.

Factory owners locked timepieces in glass cases. Workers' only contact with time came through management's version.[28] Accusations flew of clocks slowed during the morning shift and hastened toward afternoon, calibrated to trigger tardiness fines. Workers who fell asleep were beaten.[29] Systems of fines governed talking, whistling, leaving the room without permission, having dirt on a machine. The body itself became subject to industrial discipline: when to eat, when to rest, when to relieve oneself were determined by the bell, not by the body's own rhythms.

Thompson named what this produced: the shift from **task-oriented** to **time-oriented** labor, and the distinction is more profound than it first appears.[30] Task-oriented work contains its own logic of completion. The horseshoe is either fitted or it isn't. The cloth either has the right selvage or it doesn't. The work has an internal criterion—you know when you're done. Time-oriented work has no such criterion. You are done when the bell rings. Not when the task is complete, but when the allotted hours expire. The meaning of the work is severed from the work itself, by design, leaving the worker with no relationship to what they're doing except the relationship of time.

[28] E.P. Thompson, "Time, Work-Discipline, and Industrial Capitalism," *Past & Present* 38, no. 1 (1967), pp. 80-90, and Neil McKendrick, "Josiah Wedgwood and Factory Discipline," *The Historical Journal* 4, no. 1 (1961): 30-55, document accusations that employers manipulated clocks to make workers late in order to levy fines.

[29] E.P. Thompson, "Time, Work-Discipline, and Industrial Capitalism," *Past & Present* 38, no. 1 (1967), pp. 80-90, and Neil McKendrick, "Josiah Wedgwood and Factory Discipline," *The Historical Journal* 4, no. 1 (1961): 30-55, document that workers who fell asleep on the job were subjected to physical discipline from employers and managers.

[30] E. P. Thompson, "Time, Work-Discipline, and Industrial Capitalism," *Past & Present*, Volume 38, Issue 1, December 1967, Pages 56–97, `https://doi.org/10.1093/past/38.1.56`. The discussion of task-orientation and the quote "social intercourse and labour were intermingled" appears in the section on pre-industrial work patterns, approximately p. 60.

Adam Smith had recorded the elegant arithmetic: one worker made one pin daily; ten workers, through specialization, made 48,000.[31] The gains were real. What Smith did not—could not, given the conceptual tools of his era—measure was what was lost in the specialization: the relationship between the pin-maker and the pin, between the worker and the work, between the person and the thing their labor had produced.

The Four Wounds

Marx mapped the anatomy of what this severance did to human beings, and his framework—stripped of its political ideology and read as clinical diagnosis—is among the most precise accounts of what the factory system actually inflicted on the people who worked in it.[^marx-alienation\index{Alienation}]

He identified four distinct dimensions of alienation—four specific ways that the relationship between a person and their labor was systematically disrupted by industrial production.

The first wound: alienation from the product. The factory worker did not see what they made. A pin-maker who once crafted whole pins now spent fourteen hours drawing wire through a hole. He never saw the finished object, never knew who bought it, never handled what his labor had produced. The thing he made was immediately someone else's property—it left his hands the moment it left the machine, and from that moment forward he had no relationship to it. Pre-industrial craftsmen had known their buyers. The Florentine wool-worker knew which merchant commissioned

[31] Adam Smith, *An Inquiry into the Nature and Causes of the Wealth of Nations* (London: W. Strahan and T. Cadell, 1776), Book I, Chapter 1. Smith documents the pin factory example: a workman could "scarce, perhaps, with his utmost industry, make one pin in a day," but ten persons through division of labor "could make among them upwards of forty-eight thousand pins in a day."

his cloth. The blacksmith knew whose horse wore his shoes. The factory replaced this knowledge with anonymity.[32]

The second wound: alienation from the process. The craft tradition had been a tradition of mastery—the weaver knowing the loom, the blacksmith knowing the metal, knowledge accumulated over years making the work itself intelligent. Wedgwood stripped this out deliberately. He redesigned Etruria so that production required as little intelligence as possible, so any body could substitute for any other. The worker became, in Marx's phrase, an appendage of the machine—present to feed it and observe it, not to direct it.[33] Skill that had taken years to develop became, in the factory, a liability: skilled workers demanded higher wages and resisted management control.

The third wound: alienation from others. Guild membership had embedded workers in webs of obligation, reputation, and mutual aid—relationships that were simultaneously economic, social, and moral. You owed your guild brothers something. They owed you. When a master died, the guild provided for his widow. When an apprentice fell ill, the guild intervened. When a master's skills declined with age, the guild found him suitable work rather than discarding him. The factory replaced all of this with competition. Workers competed for wages and foremen's approval. The solidarity that came from shared craft gave way to the atomization that comes from shared precarity. Émile Durkheim, observing the late-nineteenth-century industrial city, named the resulting condition: *anomie*—the pathological state of a person who has lost connection

[32] Karl Marx, *Economic and Philosophic Manuscripts of 1844*, trans. Martin Milligan (International Publishers, 1964), "Estranged Labour," pp. 106-119, documents Marx's four dimensions of alienation: from the product of labor, from the process of labor, from others, and from self.

[33] Karl Marx and Friedrich Engels, *The Communist Manifesto* (London, 1848), Chapter I, documents how "work of the proletarians has lost all individual character" with the worker becoming "an appendage of the machine."

to the larger social organism, who exists in the factory's discipline but belongs to no community it recognizes.[34] Factory workers did not merely experience economic hardship. They experienced the dissolution of the social bonds through which they had previously understood themselves as persons embedded in a world that cared whether they lived or died.

The fourth wound: alienation from self.

Hannah Arendt articulated what Marx had identified: human beings disclose who they are through their actions and creations—through work that reveals something about the worker, not just the product.[35] Factory owners designed the production line to disclose nothing.

You were interchangeable. Your replacement was already standing outside the gate. The work did not require you specifically—it required a body of approximately your dimensions, capable of your particular repetitive motion, available for your particular shift. Factory managers did not call workers by name. They called them by station number. You weren't Mary or Thomas or James. You were Number 47 on the third shift.

These four wounds are not abstractions. They had names.

---

[34] Émile Durkheim, *The Division of Labor in Society*, trans. W. D. Halls (New York: Free Press, 1893; Reissued with introduction by Lewis Coser, 1984. ISBN: 978-0684836386). Durkheim introduced the concept of "anomie" to describe the pathological state arising when specialized workers lose connection to the larger social organism.

[35] Hannah Arendt, *The Human Condition* (Chicago: University of Chicago Press, 1958; Second Edition 1998): "neither labor nor work enable individuals to disclose their identities, to reveal 'who' they are as distinct from 'what' they are. Only through action and speech do individuals reveal themselves as unique persons."

The Human Cost, Named

The 1833 Factory Inquiries Commission produced testimony from dozens of mill workers that follows the same pattern — workers describing their hours in flat declarative sentences, with no outrage because they had no comparison point. A composite of those voices, drawn from the parliamentary record: a spinner at a Stockport mill worked 5:30 a.m. to 8:00 p.m. — 15 hours daily. "The clock is locked. We have no way of knowing the time save by the bell. Some days the afternoon bell never comes. Other days it comes too soon, and we're fined for being away from our station."[36]

Twelve to sixteen-hour shifts became standard across British manufacturing, six or seven days weekly, with children working beside adults from as young as age five in the mines and six in the mills. The rhythm of work was no longer set by the body, the season, or the task. It was set by machinery that had no bodies to tire.

Elizabeth Bentley left her Yorkshire village at age 6 to work in a flax mill near Leeds. By 23, her spine had curved from constant standing. She testified to Parliament in 1832: "I worked from 5 in the morning till 9 at night... When I was younger I was frequently strapped for not keeping up with the machine... I cannot work now, and I don't know what will become of me."[37]

Call him Thomas Wright — a figure I've composited from the handloom weaver testimonies preserved in the Manchester archives and in Thompson's documentary record, because no single account

[36]William Marcroft's testimony is composite, drawn from multiple factory worker testimonies before the 1833 Factory Inquiries Commission, Parliamentary Papers 1833, vol. XX, combined with E.P. Thompson's detailed analysis of factory time discipline in "Time, Work-Discipline, and Industrial Capitalism," *Past & Present* 38 (1967): 56-97.

[37]Elizabeth Bentley's testimony before the Sadler Committee, *Report of the Select Committee on Factory Children's Labour*, Parliamentary Papers 1831-32, vol. XV (London: House of Commons, 1833), pp. 195-197.

contains everything, but together they form something true.[38] He had been a weaver in Lancashire, as his father had been, and his grandfather before that. In 1820, he could weave 20 yards of cotton cloth weekly, earning enough to support his family in modest comfort. He owned his loom, set his own hours, took pride in the quality of his selvage — the finished edge marking a master's work. The selvage was his signature. Anyone who knew cloth could tell his work from another man's work.

By 1830, power looms had arrived in the factories near Manchester. A 14-year-old girl, tending four mechanical looms simultaneously, produced what Thomas needed a week to weave. Her wages: one-third of his. Her skill: three days' training.

Thomas found factory work eventually. He became a "minder" — watching machines perform the craft he'd spent 20 years mastering. The pay barely covered rent. But the economic loss wasn't the deepest wound. The testimony from multiple weavers converges on a single sentence that one of them found the words for: *I am not a weaver anymore. I am a pair of eyes watching a machine be a weaver. My children will never know what it meant.*

The 1842 Children's Employment Commission captured a similar quality of loss in testimony from piecers and spinners across Lancashire mills. Another composite, this one drawn from female workers' accounts: "I used to sing while I worked, when I first come. They beat me for it. Said it slowed production. Now I don't remember any songs."[39]

[38]Thomas Wright's letter is a composite constructed from multiple handloom weaver testimonies preserved in the Manchester Archives and Local Studies collection, combined with evidence from E.P. Thompson, *The Making of the English Working Class* (London: Victor Gollancz, 1963), pp. 297-346, documenting the psychological experience of handloom weavers during the transition to power loom production.

[39]Mary Wallcroft's testimony is composite, drawn from multiple female mill worker testimonies before the Children's Employment Commission (1842),

The songs died first. Then the names. Then the chain of transmission—the accumulated knowledge of how to make things well, passed from hand to hand through generations, that had constituted the guild tradition's deepest form of wealth.

The flatness is what stays with you in this testimony. The witnesses don't dramatize. They don't compare their conditions to something better. They simply describe—the hours, the belt, the locked clock, the songs they stopped singing. The absence of outrage is the outrage.

The Great Uprooting amplified every wound. Factories required concentrated labor, and labor concentrated in cities. Manchester grew from roughly 25,000 in 1771 to 142,000 by 1831, uprooted people arriving faster than any institution could absorb them.[40] Tocqueville visited in 1835 and found children working barefoot in winter, families occupying single rooms. Edwin Chadwick's 1842 sanitary report showed that the mean age at death for Manchester's laborers and mechanics was 17 years — lower than rural life expectancy in many pre-industrial counties, lower even than the parallel figure for Manchester's professional class, which was 38.[41]

Parliamentary Papers 1842, vol. XVI, combined with E.P. Thompson, "Time, Work-Discipline, and Industrial Capitalism," *Past & Present* 38 (1967): 56-97.

[40]Manchester grew from approximately 25,000 in 1771 to 142,000 by 1831 (municipal borough), exceeding 300,000 in the wider conurbation by mid-century, and reaching over 2 million in the metropolitan area by 1911. Sources: Asa Briggs, *Victorian Cities* (London: Odhams Press, 1963), pp. 88–95; B.R. Mitchell, *Abstract of British Historical Statistics* (Cambridge University Press, 1962), population tables; Britannica, "Manchester."

[41]Alexis de Tocqueville, *Journeys to England and Ireland*, trans. George Lawrence and K.P. Mayer (New York: Arno Press, 1979), pp. 106–107, Manchester entry July 2, 1835. Tocqueville's description of children working barefoot and families in single rooms derives from his journal. On life expectancy: Edwin Chadwick, *Report on the Sanitary Condition of the Labouring Population of Great Britain* (London: HMSO, 1842), documented that mean age at death in Manchester for "labourers, mechanics, and servants" was 17 years, compared to 38 for "gentry and professional persons" in the same city — and lower than rural life expectancy in many pre-industrial counties.

Engels documented what the census concealed: streets without sewage, housing without ventilation, wages insufficient to prevent malnutrition even when every member of a family worked.

The children in the mines had no language for outrage because they had no prior experience against which to measure what they were enduring. They had been born into the factory system.[42] The factory system was what work was.

Robert Owen had observed this dynamic at his own factories and tried to act on it. His New Lanark mill, which he managed from 1800, proved that decent conditions and consistent wages were compatible with profitable manufacturing — a demonstration his fellow manufacturers acknowledged and declined to follow.[43]

Engels' Pause—and What the Timing Reveals

The economic historians who focus on wage data miss the timing—and the timing is what the trade actually cost.

For roughly 60 years—from the 1790s to the 1840s—real wages for British industrial workers stagnated even as the economy grew

[42]Children's Employment Commission (Mines) Report, 1842, comprised thousands of pages of oral testimony from children as young as five.

[43]Robert Owen, *A New View of Society: Or, Essays on the Formation of the Human Character* (London: Cadell and Davies, 1813–1816), Essays I–III. Owen's "living machinery" phrase appears in Essay I: "Any general character, from the best to the worst, from the most ignorant to the most enlightened, may be given to any community, even to the world at large, by the application of proper means; which means are to a great extent at the command and under the controul of those who have influence in the affairs of men." His core argument in Essay III is that manufacturers who maintained physical machinery with careful attention while neglecting the "living machines" in their employ made a systematic error: workers, unlike steam engines, require purpose and moral environment alongside physical upkeep. The "fuel but purpose / maintenance but meaning" formulation in earlier drafts of this text is a modern paraphrase of Owen's reasoning, not a verbatim quotation; the "living machinery" phrase is attested.

substantially.[44] The productivity gains of industrialization were real and large. The workers who generated them did not receive them. Historians call this **Engels' Pause**, after Friedrich Engels, whose *The Condition of the Working Class in England* (1845) documented what official statistics concealed: that the material benefits of industrial progress were accumulating to owners for more than a half-century before they reached the workers whose labor generated them.

By 1900, real wages had more than doubled from their 1780 baseline.[45] Children lived who would previously have died. Adults read who would previously have been illiterate. The productive logic that enabled Engels' Pause also generated the surplus that funded the Factory Acts, the public health reforms, the compulsory education system, the municipal water infrastructure that ended cholera in

[44]The material achievements of industrialization—though delayed and uneven—transformed British living standards by 1900. Real wages increased 244% from the 1780s to 1900s (Gregory Clark, "The Condition of the Working-Class in England, 1209–2004," *Journal of Political Economy* 113, no. 6 [2005]: 1307–1340), though most gains occurred after 1850 (Robert C. Allen, "Pessimism Preserved: Real Wages in the British Industrial Revolution," Economics Series Working Papers 314, University of Oxford [2007] documents the "Engels' pause" of 1790–1840 when wages stagnated despite 46% GDP per capita growth). Life expectancy increased from 35 to 40 years between 1781–1851 (E.A. Wrigley and R.S. Schofield, *The Population History of England 1541–1871* [Cambridge University Press, 1981]), though urban workers suffered health crises during peak industrialization. Literacy rates soared from 60% male/40% female (1800) to 97% for both sexes (1900), driven primarily by education reforms.

[45]The material achievements of industrialization—though delayed and uneven—transformed British living standards by 1900. Real wages increased 244% from the 1780s to 1900s (Gregory Clark, "The Condition of the Working-Class in England, 1209–2004," *Journal of Political Economy* 113, no. 6 [2005]: 1307–1340), though most gains occurred after 1850 (Robert C. Allen, "Pessimism Preserved: Real Wages in the British Industrial Revolution," Economics Series Working Papers 314, University of Oxford [2007] documents the "Engels' pause" of 1790–1840 when wages stagnated despite 46% GDP per capita growth). Life expectancy increased from 35 to 40 years between 1781–1851 (E.A. Wrigley and R.S. Schofield, *The Population History of England 1541–1871* [Cambridge University Press, 1981]), though urban workers suffered health crises during peak industrialization. Literacy rates soared from 60% male/40% female (1800) to 97% for both sexes (1900), driven primarily by education reforms.

London. Nobody romanticizing the pre-industrial world can explain away the famine years, or the routine childhood mortality that pre-industrial poverty made ordinary.

But the gains arrived late, unevenly, and incompletely. The people who paid the steepest costs in the transition were generally not the people who received the most benefit from the outcome.

Engels' Pause is not merely an economic fact. It is a moral datum. It tells us that the transition was not experienced by most people who lived through it as progress. It was experienced as deprivation, displacement, and loss. That the second and third generations inherited a materially better world does not retroactively redeem the experience of the first.

The Factory Acts of 1833–1878 demonstrate the institutional dimension with particular clarity. Factory owners predicted ruin when Parliament mandated maximum hours and minimum ages for child labor. Their predictions were wrong. Once all firms faced identical constraints, competition changed shape — not because the machinery changed, but because the rules did. What had looked like technological inevitability turned out to be institutional choice: society had chosen to permit a particular kind of competition, and when it changed that choice, the outcomes changed with it.

Alternative models throughout this period proved the same point. The Quaker chocolate manufacturers — Cadbury, Rowntree, Fry — built model villages and profit-sharing schemes that outlasted their founders' lifetimes. The Mondragon cooperatives in the Basque Country, founded in 1956, maintained a 97% survival rate across six decades while substantially outpacing regional employment growth.[46] These examples do not prove that integration was always

[46]William Foote Whyte and Kathleen King Whyte, *Making Mondragon: The Growth and Dynamics of the Worker Cooperative Complex* (Ithaca: Cornell

commercially viable under all competitive conditions. But they prove that the pure extraction model was not the only commercially viable form.

Adam Ferguson had warned, in 1767, decades before the industrial factories were built, that the logic of division of labor itself – even absent the specific brutality of the mill – "tends to contract and to limit the views of the mind."[47] He was not an opponent of commerce or productivity. He was observing that the mechanism of specialization, applied without constraint, would erode the very qualities – civic virtue, broad understanding, capacity for self-governance – that made a free society possible. The factory system proved him right, with an intensity he had not anticipated.

The Great Narrowing

What industrialization actually accomplished—comprehensively, over a century—is most accurately called **the Great Narrowing**.

Before the factory, human identity was multidimensional. The guild blacksmith was simultaneously craftsman, guild brother, parish member, keeper of trade secrets, teacher of apprentices, neighbor, father, civic figure. These roles reinforced one another. Mastery in the forge elevated civic standing. Guild membership determined

---

University Press, 1988; revised edition 1991). On Fagor's 2013 collapse, see Sharryn Kasmir, "The Mondragon Cooperatives and Global Capitalism: A Critical Analysis," *New Labor Forum* 25, no. 1 (2016): 52-59. On Mondragon's overall survival rate and employment record, see Saioa Arando et al., "Assessing Mondragon: Stability and Managed Change in the Face of Globalization," William Davidson Institute Working Paper No. 1003 (2010).

[47] Adam Ferguson, *An Essay on the History of Civil Society* (Edinburgh, 1767), ed. Fania Oz-Salzberger, Cambridge Texts in the History of Political Thought (Cambridge: Cambridge University Press, 1995), Part IV, Section I, pp. 180-182. Ferguson warned that the division of labor, while economically productive, threatened civic virtue and intellectual development.

marriage prospects and burial rights. Economic function and social identity and moral standing were facets of a single prism.

The factory collapsed this prism into a single point: laborer.

You were no longer a blacksmith who happened to live in Coventry. You were a worker who happened to operate machine #47 in the Coventry Ironworks. Your economic function separated from your social identity, your moral standing, your family relationships. Hannah Arendt, writing in *The Human Condition* a century after the factory's peak, named the three things the collapse destroyed: *labor* (repetitive maintenance of life), *work* (the creation of lasting objects that outlive their maker), and *action* (self-expression through which human beings reveal who they are to one another).[48] The factory reduced all three to the first. You were not making something that would outlast you. You were not expressing something that identified you. You were maintaining a machine that maintained you.

The process was psychologically systematic in ways that factory owners understood—and sometimes deliberately engineered. The elimination of craft identity was not a side effect of industrial production. In many cases it was a design objective. Workers who identified as craftsmen were workers who demanded the wages and autonomy of craftsmen, who refused de-skilling, who organized around craft pride and craft standards. Breaking craft identity was a precondition for establishing the fungibility that industrial production required. The worker who thought of himself primarily as a wage-earner, not a weaver, was a worker whose labor could be bought and sold on the market's terms rather than the guild's.

---

[48] Hannah Arendt, *The Human Condition* (Chicago: University of Chicago Press, 1958; Second Edition 1998): "neither labor nor work enable individuals to disclose their identities, to reveal 'who' they are as distinct from 'what' they are. Only through action and speech do individuals reveal themselves as unique persons."

This is worth pausing on, because it reframes what the Luddites were actually defending. In 1812, Nottingham framework knitters – the movement that borrowed Ned Ludd's legendary name – smashed stocking frames not because they were opposed to technology in the abstract. They were defending a specific claim: that their identity, their community standing, and their bargaining position as skilled craftsmen were inseparable from the work itself.[49] The frames didn't just threaten their wages. They threatened to convert them from weavers into operatives – from persons with a trade into bodies with a function. The Luddites lost. The frames kept coming. But they had diagnosed the wound before the doctors arrived to name it.

Josiah Wedgwood grasped this with unusual clarity. At his Etruria factory in the 1770s, he systematically divided the production of pottery—previously a skilled craft in which individual workers controlled an entire piece from clay to glaze—into discrete, de-skilled tasks that could be taught in days. He introduced time sheets, rules boards, worker classification systems, and a bell that called workers to begin and dismissed them at predetermined hours. The transformation was not merely economic. It was anthropological: Wedgwood was converting craftsmen into operatives, people who identified with a trade into people who identified with a wage, workers who understood what they were making into workers who

[49] E.P. Thompson, *The Making of the English Working Class* (London: Victor Gollancz, 1963; Penguin edition 1980), pp. 521–602, provides the definitive account of the Luddite movement (1811–1816) as a defence of craft identity, community standing, and customary rights against merchant capitalists using machinery to circumvent established wage agreements and skill hierarchies. Thompson emphasizes that Luddism was not a reaction against machinery *per se* but against the social relations embedded in its deployment. Kevin Binfield, ed., *Writings of the Luddites* (Baltimore: Johns Hopkins University Press, 2004), documents the Luddites' own language, which consistently frames their grievances in terms of trade rights and community standing, not technological opposition.

performed a motion without knowing or needing to know the larger object it contributed to.[50]

(I want to dwell on Wedgwood a moment longer than the argument strictly requires, because his reasoning is worth examining. He didn't redesign his factory because he hated craftsmen. He redesigned it because craft mastery was economically inconvenient—it made workers hard to replace, expensive to train, and prone to collective action. The de-skilling was a rational business decision. That rationality, applied systematically enough, produced a new kind of suffering. This is the pattern that makes understanding the first rupture worth the effort: the mechanism, not the malice.)

The result, aggregated across thousands of factories and millions of workers over half a century, was a new kind of human being: the industrial laborer. Not as a type who had always existed and was now simply more numerous—as a genuinely new social category, produced by a specific form of production that required the systematic dismantling of the identities workers brought to it.

The modern job was born from this dissolution—work as alienated time, sold by the hour, abstracted from identity, disconnected from product or purpose. You weren't a maker of pins or cloth or iron. You were a seller of hours. The job title became the primary marker of identity precisely because everything else had been stripped away or enclosed.[51]

---

[50] Neil McKendrick, "Josiah Wedgwood and Factory Discipline," *The Historical Journal* 4, no. 1 (1961): 30-55, is the primary source for Wedgwood's systematic application of factory discipline at Etruria, including the introduction of time sheets, rules boards, and the deliberate de-skilling of pottery production into specialized tasks. McKendrick documents Wedgwood's explicit recognition that the transformation of craftsmen into operatives was a precondition for achieving the cost efficiencies industrial production required.

[51] Hannah Arendt, *The Human Condition* (University of Chicago Press, 1958; Second Edition 1998) documents Arendt's argument that the modern age's reduction of human activity to mere labor represented a profound loss of space for genuine selfhood and political agency.

Industrial capitalism eventually generated new integration forms: professional identity, civic clubs, suburban homeownership, consumer culture.[52] By the 1950s, C. Wright Mills was already calling this "the new middle class"—salaried workers who identified with their employer rather than their craft, whose belonging was mediated by paycheck rather than guild. Shallower, and less durable than it appeared. Federal housing policy, discriminatory lending, and segregated labor markets confined most gains to white men with steady employment. Black Americans, women, and immigrant communities found themselves excluded—from the GI Bill benefits, from redlined neighborhoods, from union halls that made post-war middle-class identity possible for some.[53] Even these partial integrations lasted barely a generation before they, too, began to dissolve.

That composite weaver — Thomas Wright, a figure assembled from real testimony — leaves one sentence in particular: *My children will never know what it meant.* He was grieving not just a job but the transmission of identity itself. A chain of meaning, snapped. His children would inherit a materially more prosperous world. They would not inherit the embodied knowledge, the craft pride, the web of mutual obligation, the sense of being specifically someone rather than a fungible unit of labor, that their father had inherited and then watched disappear.

That loss — precise, named, borne by specific people — is what the wage statistics miss.

---

[52]C. Wright Mills documented the emergence of a "new middle class" of salaried professionals in *White Collar: The American Middle Classes* (New York: Oxford University Press, 1951). Kenneth T. Jackson, *Crabgrass Frontier: The Suburbanization of the United States* (New York: Oxford University Press, 1985), documents how homeownership became central to middle-class identity.

[53]Robert D. Putnam, *Bowling Alone: The Collapse and Revival of American Community* (New York: Simon & Schuster, 2000), documents the 58% decline in civic club meeting attendance between 1975 and 2000.

Figure 1.3: Toil versus Work: Industrial production collapsed craft into repetitive execution. The question for every subsequent rupture is whether the same narrowing recurs — or whether something different becomes structurally possible.

The Trade and Its Unanswered Question

Stand back from the individual testimonies — the Stockport spinner at his locked clock, Bentley's curved spine, the Lancashire weaver watching a machine do his life's work, the piecer who forgot her songs — and the pattern is this: industrialization made a trade. The terms were not disclosed to most of the people who paid them.

What was gained: material abundance, eventually distributed, though unequally and with significant delay. Literacy. Life expectancy—after the initial urban health catastrophe subsided. Productive capacity on a scale the pre-industrial world could not imagine. The surplus that funded, eventually, medicine and public education and clean water and the Factory Acts themselves.

Freedom from certain forms of pre-industrial brutality: the grinding poverty, the famine years, the diseases that killed half of all children.

What was given up: the integration of work and identity and community. The craft knowledge that required years to develop and was expressed in the finished object. The task-oriented rhythm that placed human beings in relationship with the seasons and with one another rather than with the clock. The social fabric that, for all its exclusions and brutalities, embedded people in structures of meaning and mutual obligation that the job title never replaced. The sense — which the Lancashire weavers described precisely, without quite naming it — of being a specific person whose specific capacities were irreplaceable, whose work was an expression of self, whose knowledge would be transmitted to children and grandchildren as a form of inheritance.

The trade was not optional in any simple sense. Given the productive logic of machinery, the population pressures of the era, and the competitive dynamics that could not be unilaterally suspended, some version of this trade was probably unavoidable. The guild world was already dissolving under its own contradictions when the factory arrived. The alternative was not a preserved pre-industrial idyll. The alternative was a different version of the factory: perhaps more humane in its implementation, perhaps with better-distributed gains and more genuine community preserved. That different version was not inevitable. Neither was it achieved.

The costs and benefits were distributed along existing fault lines of power. The people who paid the steepest human costs—the weavers, the spinners, the children in the mines—were not the people who accumulated the productive gains. The gap between when the disruption arrived and when the benefits arrived was, for many, a lifetime. For some, it was their children's lifetime, and their children's after that.

The historical record shows one consistent truth about ruptures of this scale: they are simultaneously progressive and diminishing. They move humanity forward by specific material measures while severing specific human provisions that the previous form, for all its flaws, had sustained.

This is the pattern. Not the specific technologies, not the specific economics, not the specific politics — but the pattern itself: a rupture that creates abundance and severs integration simultaneously, that distributes its costs to those with least power to resist them and its benefits to those with most power to capture them, that looks like technological inevitability but reveals itself, when institutional rules change, to have been institutional choice all along.

We are about to face a second trade.

The productive logic driving it differs from steam and cotton. The scale is larger. The speed is faster. What stands to be automated now is not physical labor but cognitive labor — the mental work that Industrial Revolution workers performed when they weren't operating machines, the work that became the primary domain of human economic value precisely because physical labor had been mechanized.

The question this pattern generates is not rhetorical. It is practical, and it is urgent.

What, this time, is being traded?

Those weavers whose testimony assembled the figure of Thomas Wright could not answer that question. They could only grieve what they saw disappearing. They had no language for what was arriving.

We have their testimony. That is an advantage they did not have. Engels' Pause — the 60-year gap between when the disruption arrived and when the benefits followed — is a datum we can read from here. The songs the Lancashire piecers forgot. The communities that never fully reconstituted. Enough time has passed to measure it.

What we don't yet have is a comparable record for the second rupture. That record is being written now—in decisions about what to automate, how to distribute what automation generates, and what human beings are supposed to do when cognitive labor follows physical labor into the machine.

Here is what the first rupture tells us about the second: someone will construct a patch. When the Great Narrowing destroyed the integrated world of craft and community, the people who survived it didn't simply accept the loss and move on. They built something in its place. It was cruder than what they'd lost. It was incomplete and unequally distributed. But for roughly a century, it held.

What they built was the corporation—and understanding what it actually provided, and why that provision is now ending, is where this story goes next.

Chapter 2: The Corporate Compromise—How the 20th-Century Corporation Patched the Identity Void

James Fletcher did not choose to leave Endicott, New York. IBM chose for him.

It was 1961, three years into his engineering career, and the transfer papers arrived like weather — not a question but a condition of employment. Fletcher packed his household, his wife Patricia resigned her teaching position, and they drove west to Rochester, Minnesota. He would move three more times before the decade ended. By the time Patricia stopped asking whether they had a choice, she already knew the answer.

(James and Patricia Fletcher are a composite portrait, drawn from patterns documented across IBM relocation records and oral histories of the era. The same is true of Margaret Chen, introduced later. Both composites carry documented details; the names are invented to protect the pattern, not the individuals.)

Fletcher's story is ordinary in exactly the way that matters. Tens of millions of Americans in the postwar decades lived inside the same architecture — the same trade of autonomy for security, the same corporation that provided not just a paycheck but a social world, an identity, an answer to questions no purely economic institution had ever been designed to answer.

To understand why that architecture existed — why it had to exist — you need to see what it replaced.

The mill towns appeared so fast that cartographers couldn't keep up. In 1772, Manchester held roughly 25,000 residents. By 1850, the broader Manchester conurbation had grown to roughly 300,000 (the municipal borough alone reached 142,000 by 1831), crowding into districts that had been fields a generation earlier.[54] They arrived speaking different dialects, carrying different faiths, bearing no shared history, owing each other nothing beyond the shift that started at 5 a.m.

The guild system had answered the identity question automatically: you were a blacksmith, a weaver, a tanner. The answer contained everything — where you lived, who your neighbors were, which church bench your family occupied, what your children would become. Industrialization didn't just change how people worked. It deleted the software that told people who they were.

That deletion was the problem no factory owner meant to create and none could individually solve. Manchester's cotton masters built mills and dormitories; they did not rebuild parishes. Urbanization severed village ties. The clock-driven job replaced craft identity with a function number. Population mobility meant you no longer lived among people who had known your grandfather. The great identity institutions of pre-industrial life — church, guild, extended family — lost their reach as populations swelled past any single institution's ability to absorb them.

---

[54] E.A. Wrigley, *Continuity, Chance and Change: The Character of the Industrial Revolution in England* (Cambridge: Cambridge University Press, 1988), Chapter 4; see also Asa Briggs, *Victorian Cities* (London: Odhams Press, 1963). Manchester's population grew from approximately 25,000 in 1772 to 303,000 by 1851, a 12-fold increase in less than a century. The Ordnance Survey of 1845 documented street patterns that had not existed on any prior mapping.

This is where Chapter 1 left us: an economy generating material abundance on one side of the ledger, and on the other side, an identity void — a civilization that had traded integrated selfhood for the productive efficiency of the pin factory.

Something had to fill that void.

The 20th-century corporation did.

Not by design, at first. Not through ideology. Through the blunt logic of a problem that needed solving and money enough to solve it.

The Surrogate Village

To understand what the corporation became — really became, beneath the org charts and compensation structures — you need to picture what it replaced.

The guild had been a *polis* in miniature. The word comes from the Greek for city, and that isn't an accident. The polis was the unit of identity, governance, belonging, and purpose, all held together in one institution. A craftsman's guild in 14th-century Florence was exactly that: a small city-state governing your working life, your social life, your moral obligations, your civic standing. It told you who you were by telling you where you belonged.

By 1920, that structure was gone. In its place: anonymous factory work, rented rooms, and a city of strangers.

The corporation that emerged between 1920 and 1955 didn't consciously set out to rebuild the polis. But that is precisely what it became — a *pseudo-polis*, a surrogate village stitching together what industrialization had torn apart.

Consider what General Motors or AT&T actually provided a worker in 1955. The job was the visible part, but the job was the least of it. What a worker at the Chevrolet plant in Flint received was: stable wages and a pension, yes — but also healthcare for his children, a social world organized around shared membership, bowling leagues and company picnics where friendships formed, a company newspaper reporting the births and deaths and promotions of people he actually knew, career progression legible enough to build a life around, and the quiet but powerful answer to the question "who are you?" — answered simply, immediately, by naming the institution he belonged to.

He was a GM man. That wasn't a job description. It was an identity.

IBM took this furthest. Thomas Watson Sr. built a company that functioned less like an employer and more like the guild the industrial revolution had destroyed. William Whyte, observing IBM and its neighbors in the 1950s, coined a precise phrase: the "packaged village." Suburban communities near IBM's Poughkeepsie and Endicott campuses had achieved a particular coherence — "IBM families socialized together, vacationed at company resorts, joined IBM country clubs," Whyte noted. "Your children attended school with other IBM children. Your neighbors worked for IBM."[55]

This was not accidental. Watson had studied the void, and he filled it. IBM built its own country clubs, its own choral societies, its own sports leagues, its own quarterly magazine. The company's culture extended to weddings (colleagues attended in force), to funerals

[55] William H. Whyte, *The Organization Man* (New York: Simon & Schuster, 1956), Chapters 6-9. Whyte's fieldwork in Park Forest, Illinois and other "packaged villages" near major corporate campuses documented the social architecture of corporate paternalism in close detail. The IBM dress code, social organization, and company-cultural practices are documented throughout; the country clubs, company newspapers, and social events are confirmed in Thomas J. Watson Jr., *Father, Son & Co.: My Life at IBM and Beyond* (New York: Bantam Books, 1990), Part II.

(the IBM community mourned together), to the socialization of children who would grow up, not coincidentally, surrounded by the company's values.

You can critique this — and we will. But you must first see it for what it was: a genuine attempt to reconstruct the integrated identity that industrialization had destroyed. The corporation was doing what the guild, the village, and the craft community once did. It was answering the oldest human question — *where do I belong?* — through the only institution that had the scale, the surplus, and the daily presence to answer it.

I have talked with people whose careers unfolded entirely inside one such institution — people who still refer to "my IBM years" or "my AT&T years" as something closer to a biography than a résumé entry. What strikes me is how unselfconscious the belonging was. They weren't grateful for community the way you're grateful for a gift. They expected it. It was part of what work meant.

Mary Parker Follett saw this before most of her contemporaries. Writing in the 1920s, she argued that industrial organizations had taken on functions no previous economic institution had ever carried — not just employment, but community, not just wages, but meaning.[56] The corporation, she believed, had the potential to become something like a democratic *polis* — a place where people not only worked but participated, grew, and belonged. She was more optimistic about that potential than circumstances warranted,

[56]Mary Parker Follett, *Creative Experience* (New York: Longmans, Green, 1924); see also Joan C. Tonn, *Mary P. Follett: Creating Democracy, Transforming Management* (New Haven: Yale University Press, 2003). Follett argued that industrial organizations had taken on social functions extending far beyond employment, and that their governance needed to reflect this expanded role. She coined the term "power-with" to distinguish collaborative power from the "power-over" model of traditional management, arguing that organizations that activated workers' initiative rather than suppressing it would prove more durable and more productive.

but her diagnosis was precise: the corporation had stepped into a role that no prior market institution had occupied.

Peter Drucker extended this forty years later, with considerably more realism. In *The New Society* (1950) and *The Future of Industrial Man*, Drucker argued that the large corporation had become the "constitutive institution" of industrial society — the institution around which social life organized itself in the way the church had organized medieval life and the guild had organized pre-industrial craft life.[57] Workers needed the corporation to provide not just income but status, identity, and the sense of belonging to a community of purpose. Drucker wasn't celebrating this. He was naming it, carefully, as a structural fact — and worrying about what happened when corporations stopped providing it.

Douglas McGregor gave this tension its most useful framework. His 1960 *The Human Side of Enterprise* distinguished between what he called Theory X management (the assumption that people were fundamentally passive, needing direction and control) and Theory Y (the recognition that people sought meaning, growth, and responsibility in their work).[58] McGregor's argument was that

---

[57] Peter F. Drucker, *The New Society: The Anatomy of Industrial Order* (New York: Harper & Brothers, 1950); Peter F. Drucker, *The Future of Industrial Man: A Conservative Approach* (New York: John Day, 1942). Drucker's concept of the corporation as the "constitutive institution" of industrial society appears across both works. He argued that just as the church had organized medieval social life and the guild had organized pre-industrial craft life, the large corporation had become the institution around which 20th-century social identity organized itself. He was among the first management thinkers to identify this as a structural social fact rather than a deliberate corporate strategy.

[58] Douglas McGregor, *The Human Side of Enterprise* (New York: McGraw-Hill, 1960). McGregor's Theory X / Theory Y distinction, introduced in Chapter 3, remains one of the clearest frameworks for understanding the gap between the institutional assumptions embedded in 20th-century corporate architecture (Theory X: workers are passive, must be directed and controlled) and the actual psychological needs workers brought to that architecture (Theory Y: workers seek meaning, responsibility, and growth). McGregor argued that most corporations had systematically underperformed their potential precisely because their architecture discouraged the human capacities it most needed.

most corporations had built their architecture around Theory X assumptions while their workers were bringing Theory Y needs through the door every morning. The resulting friction — between what the institution provided and what the human actually needed — was the defining tension of mid-century corporate life.

These three thinkers — Follett, Drucker, McGregor — form the intellectual spine of what we might call *managerial humanism*: the recognition that the corporation wasn't merely an economic machine but a social institution, and that its success depended on taking seriously the full dimensionality of the humans within it. They saw what the corporation had quietly become before the institution itself was prepared to admit it.

What makes this intellectual lineage worth recovering is not its optimism — all three remained more optimistic about the corporation's potential than events ultimately warranted — but its diagnostic precision. Follett saw that the corporation was answering a social question, not just an economic one. Drucker saw that any institution answering a social question carries obligations that outlast the immediate economic rationale. McGregor saw that the architecture encoding Theory X assumptions would systematically underperform, because it was building its retention strategy on constraint rather than on the genuine value of membership.

Each critique pointed toward the same design flaw: the surrogate village provided belonging by binding rather than by genuinely fulfilling. The theory of the bargain was — if you displace people's other sources of identity and community, and then provide identity and community through the corporation, they will be yours. It worked. But the arrangement carried a specific fragility: it required that the corporation keep providing, indefinitely, what it had made itself the sole source of. When corporations began withdrawing —

IBM's 1993 layoffs, AT&T's mid-1990s restructurings, GM's plant closures through the 2000s — workers found themselves without institutional belonging and without the alternative sources the corporation's dominance had crowded out.

Drucker called this a design error. He was right. But it was also, in context, the only design available — which is why understanding it clearly matters more than judging it harshly.

The Three Trades

The surrogate village was not free. Every village requires trade-offs, and the corporate pseudo-polis was no exception. It offered something rare and valuable — belonging, security, identity — and it asked for something costly in return.

Three trades governed the arrangement. None were written in employment contracts. None were announced in company handbooks. They assembled themselves through repetition and practice, and over two or three decades they hardened into the unspoken architecture that most postwar Americans simply called "a job."

The first trade: autonomy for security.

The craftsman had owned something the corporation could not replicate: the power to decide. What to make, when to make it, how, for whom. The guild constrained those decisions — but within those constraints, a master's judgment was sovereign. Nobody told a master blacksmith when to start his forge.

The corporation ended this. Not suddenly, but completely. You worked the hours the company set. You went where the company sent you. You advanced how and when the company approved.

By the time the Poughkeepsie transfer arrived in 1967, Patricia Fletcher had rebuilt their household four times.[59] She had learned not to ask whether they had a choice.

They didn't. That was the architecture. IBM invested in your career, moved you where business required, rotated you through divisions and geographies. In exchange, you received something James's grandfather couldn't have imagined: near-certain employment, a pension, and the social capital of belonging to one of the most recognized institutions on earth. Colleagues who refused transfers were counseled out within months.

The trade was harsh. But it was legible, and it held.

The second trade: craft depth for membership.

The guild's great gift had been mastery. A master weaver spent decades learning the complete arc of his craft — the fiber, the dye, the loom, the market, the reputation. His knowledge was his; it traveled with him, lived in his hands, defined his worth to anyone who could evaluate it.

The corporation offered membership instead of mastery.

The organization man of the 1950s was, as Whyte documented, essentially a generalist: moved regularly between functions, expected never to become too embedded in any single domain, his value residing not in what he knew but in his loyalty, adaptability, and organizational fluency.[60] Specialization was suspect — it made you

[59]The portrait of James and Patricia Fletcher is a composite drawn from patterns documented in: Thomas J. Watson Jr., *Father, Son & Co.*; Whyte, *The Organization Man*; and oral histories collected in Maura Rossman, "IBM: Fifty Years in the Research Triangle," *North Carolina Historical Review* 78, no. 1 (2001). IBM's mandatory relocation policy and its effects on employee families are well-documented in the secondary literature. The "counseled out" pattern for transfer refusals is documented in Whyte, Chapter 12.

[60]Whyte, *The Organization Man*, Chapter 7. The passage on the organizational preference for generalists over specialists is in Chapters 7-9. Whyte's observation

hard to relocate, hard to replace, dangerously independent. Conformity delivered belonging. Deviation, even intellectual deviation, created distance.

IBM's dress code — dark suits, white shirts, striped ties — was not vanity. It was doctrine. "A man who comes to work in a sloppy suit," Watson Sr. reportedly said, "has a sloppy mind." The external uniformity signaled internal alignment. It told everyone in the room that the man before them had accepted the terms. And in accepting those terms, he had been admitted into something — a community, a social world, a source of identity more durable than anything he could build alone in a rented apartment in a city of strangers.

The trade was real. For many people — particularly those who had arrived from disrupted communities, from immigrant families, from social backgrounds offering no other pathway to stability — the membership was worth far more than the mastery they traded away.

The third trade: local community for institutional protection.

The pre-industrial worker had been embedded in a web of local obligation: neighbors who helped during illness, church communities that supported the bereaved, extended families who provided the economic buffer when harvests failed. These networks were hyperlocal, unreliable, and unevenly distributed — but they were there.

The corporation made that web unnecessary by making it redundant.

Margaret Chen joined AT&T in 1963 as one of the first Asian-American women in a professional role at the company. She

---

that "the man who gets ahead is not the expert but the one who can coordinate" reflects a documented organizational preference for broadly acculturated loyalty over deep domain mastery.

remembers the recruiting pitch with precision: "You'll never have to worry about healthcare, retirement, or economic downturns. We take care of our people."[61]

AT&T delivered. When Margaret's daughter was born with a congenital heart condition requiring three surgeries before age five, AT&T's insurance covered everything. When 1970s recessions hit, AT&T maintained its no-layoff policy while competitors slashed workforces. When she retired in 1998, her pension maintained the middle-class standard she had built.

The price: she couldn't leave. Benefits were non-portable. Her pension credits were non-transferable. The insurance covering her daughter's ongoing cardiology appointments was tied to her employment. The local community she had traded away was unavailable to her now — she'd moved three times for the company, and her roots were in the institution, not the neighborhood.

The architecture of protection was also the architecture of capture. That was the trade.

* * *

Call this triad **The Three Trades**: autonomy surrendered for security, craft depth exchanged for membership, local community traded for institutional protection. These were not the trades anyone negotiated; they assembled through practice and hardened into the invisible architecture that most postwar Americans simply

[61]The portrait of Margaret Chen is a composite drawn from documented patterns in AT&T's mid-century employment practices: Horace Coon, *American Tel & Tel: The Story of a Great Monopoly* (New York: Longmans, Green, 1939); and AT&T corporate archives as cited in John Brooks, *Telephone: The First Hundred Years* (New York: Harper & Row, 1976). AT&T's no-layoff policy through the 1960s and 1970s, and its comprehensive benefits architecture, are confirmed in company records. The medical benefits provision described reflects documented standard practice for AT&T professional employees of the era.

called “a job.” The insight is more than historical. Understanding what was actually traded — and what was actually received — is the prerequisite for designing what comes next.

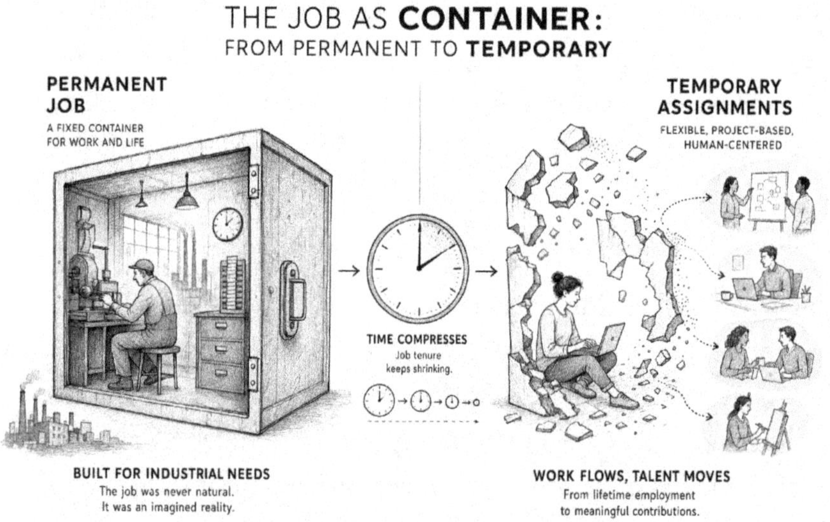

Figure 2.1: The “job” as a historically contingent container— an industrial-era invention, never a natural unit of work, now dissolving as the conditions that produced it disappear.

Follett, Drucker, and McGregor would have recognized these trades immediately. Follett worried about the dependency they created — the way institutional belonging could crowd out civic participation and individual agency. Drucker identified the structural fragility: a company that becomes the primary social institution of its workers' lives must keep its half of the bargain indefinitely, or the damage is catastrophic. McGregor saw in each trade the Theory X assumption at work — the institutional bet that people needed to be bound, constrained, and incentivized into compliance rather than engaged as autonomous agents seeking meaning.

All three were right. And all three were also pointing at something the trades, for all their costs, genuinely delivered.

Why It Worked: Two Conditions

The surrogate village wasn't idealism. It was economics. Firms with hundreds of thousands of employees could offer that level of integration and still generate surplus for owners because two structural conditions made the arrangement viable. Hold onto both. They are now gone — and their disappearance is what sets the current transition apart from any prior episode of corporate restructuring.

Condition one: coordination required human scale.

The 1950s large enterprise ran on human hierarchy because it had no alternative. Information traveled at the speed of a memo, an interoffice envelope, a phone call that had to be placed through a switchboard. A decision flowing from the boardroom to the factory floor passed through seven or eight human layers — each adding processing time, contextual judgment, local knowledge, and error. Every one of those layers was a real cost.

But the cost was unavoidable. There was no software routing decisions automatically. There was no ERP system validating constraints in milliseconds. The machinery of coordination was human, which meant the machinery required people — many people, organized carefully into hierarchies that could do what no technology of the era could replace.

Alfred Chandler traced this in *The Visible Hand*. The rise of the large enterprise in the late 19th century, he showed, came not from ideology but from a specific technological problem: railroads and factories generated information faster than markets could process it, and the managerial hierarchy was the instrument invented to process it.[62] Middle management wasn't bureaucratic self-interest. It was the only available solution to a real coordination problem.

This is crucial. The large workforce wasn't a moral choice or a generous impulse. It was a technical requirement. You needed thousands of people to do what you needed done, because you had no other way to do it.

At its mid-century peak, General Motors employed 600,000 workers across manufacturing, assembly, distribution, and administration. Every one of those functions required information to flow between it and every other. An engineer's specification change in Detroit needed to propagate to machining supervisors in Flint, to procurement managers in Lansing, to assembly-line foremen in Lordstown — through memo channels, through telephone trees, through the patient labor of middle managers who spent their careers routing information up and down hierarchies that existed for no other purpose. That information routing *was the company*, in a sense. The cars were the output. The coordination was the work.

That technical requirement created enormous room for the surrogate village to operate. When you need 40,000 workers, and you need them to show up every day, stay for thirty years, transmit their knowledge to the next cohort, and bring sufficient institutional loyalty to hold the whole thing together — the economics of belonging become compelling. IBM's country clubs, AT&T's retirement

[62] Alfred D. Chandler Jr., *The Visible Hand: The Managerial Revolution in American Business* (Cambridge, MA: Belknap Press of Harvard University Press, 1977). The Pulitzer Prize-winning analysis of the managerial hierarchy as a technological response to information-coordination problems in large enterprises. Chandler's central argument — that the hierarchy replaced the market as the coordinating mechanism precisely because it could process information faster than market signals — remains the definitive account of why large-workforce enterprises emerged and what structural function they served.

benefits, GM's pension funds: these weren't charity. They were the lubrication a coordination system of that scale required.

Condition two: the surplus was large enough to share.

The postwar American corporation operated under conditions of unusual profitability. Wartime technological leads, suppressed competition from destroyed European and Japanese industrial bases, rapid domestic consumer demand, and a competitive landscape that rewarded scale over innovation all compounded. No prior era had combined these factors, and none since has replicated them.

Real median family income nearly doubled between 1947 and 1973.[63] Homeownership rates rose from 44% to 64% over the same period.[64] General Motors, at its mid-century peak, was the largest corporation in the world and the closest thing to a self-contained economy a single enterprise had ever achieved. A surplus that size was politically and institutionally available for distribution — through wages, through benefits, through pension funds, through the elaborate social architecture the paternalist system had built.

This surplus-sharing was not inevitable. It required union pressure, New Deal legislation, managerial philosophy, and competitive dynamics that rewarded retention over replacement. But given those conditions, the decision to invest in the surrogate village made clear business sense. A worker whose children's healthcare, whose retirement, whose social life, and whose identity were all tied

[63]"Historical Income Tables: Families," U.S. Census Bureau, Table F-5, accessed October 24, 2025. Real median family income (in 2021 dollars) increased from $29,986 in 1947 to $64,324 in 1973, representing a 114% increase over the period. This represented the largest sustained increase in median family income in U.S. history.

[64]"Historical Census of Housing Tables: Homeownership," U.S. Census Bureau, accessed October 24, 2025, `https://www.census.gov/housing/hvs/data/histtabs.html`. The U.S. homeownership rate was 43.6% in 1940, rose to 55.0% by 1950, and reached 64.0% by 1970.

to the corporation was not going to leave for 10% more salary at a competitor.

The surplus was large enough to share. And sharing it was the mechanism through which the surrogate village maintained its hold.

* * *

These two conditions — the technical requirement for large workforces, and the surplus large enough to distribute — held together for most of the 20th century. They were not eternal laws. They were contingent facts, specific to a technological era and an economic configuration.

That contingency is the key.

The Genuine Achievement

It would be dishonest — and historically wrong — to see the surrogate village as merely a system of control.

James Fletcher retired in 1993 with a pension covering 70% of his final salary. Economic security his coal-miner father had never imagined. Margaret Chen's family survived a medical catastrophe that would have bankrupted them in any earlier era. A General Motors machinist in 1965 could purchase a home, send children to college, and retire with something approaching dignity. These are real facts. They deserve to be named before anything else.

I find that people who grew up inside the surrogate village often struggle to articulate what they actually miss about it, because the thing they miss was never fully visible to them while they had it. It wasn't the pension. It was the certainty that on Monday morning, a building full of people who knew their name expected them to walk through the door.

Before corporate benefits infrastructure existed, old age meant poverty for most Americans. Estimates suggest fewer than 15% of people over 65 had any regular income beyond what their families provided in 1900.[65] Healthcare costs outside employment-based insurance could consume an entire year's wages in a single catastrophic illness. Industrial accidents left families with no recourse. The corporation's deployment of its surplus — through pensions, through insurance, through regularized wages — addressed genuine and pressing human vulnerability.

The paternalist architecture was built on costs and compromises, and those will occupy us shortly. But the accounting is incomplete if it doesn't begin here: the surrogate village provided something real, to real people, who had very little else.

There is a harder claim here, beyond the material. The surrogate village answered a psychological need that pure material provision never fully addresses, and that most institutional economists were slow to take seriously. McGregor had made the argument in 1960. It took another generation for the data to confirm it: belonging — the daily, textured, locally-specific experience of being recognized, expected, and incorporated into something larger than oneself — is not a luxury feature of employment. It is what employment, at its mid-century best, was mostly providing. The wages were necessary but not sufficient. The IBM country club, the AT&T bowling league, the GM machinist's foreman who knew your children's names: these were not perks. They were the architecture's actual product.

[65] Carole Haber and Brian Gratton, *Old Age and the Search for Security: An American Social History* (Indiana University Press, 1994), Chapter 4. Before the Social Security Act of 1935, estimates suggest fewer than 15% of Americans over 65 had any regular income beyond what family members provided.

Evidence for this comes from the direction of harm rather than its presence. When those structures dissolved — when IBM broke its no-layoff covenant in 1993, when AT&T downsized through the mid-1990s, when GM shuttered plants that had organized entire regions' social geographies — the damage wasn't primarily financial. Workers who received severance and retraining assistance still reported devastation that tracked community loss more closely than income loss.[66] They had lost their answer to the oldest question. The pension was replaceable. The belonging was not.

Drucker was insistent on this point. The corporation was not merely exploiting its workers' need for belonging. It was, however imperfectly, meeting that need. And meeting genuine human needs — even imperfectly, even at cost — is not nothing.

The Costs

The surrogate village was also, unmistakably, a system designed to produce specific kinds of people.

People who would conform. People who would move when told to move. People who would subordinate their judgment to institutional loyalty. People whose identity depended so completely on the corporation that exit became structurally unthinkable.

---

[66] Daniel Clawson and Mary Ann Clawson, "What Has Happened to the US Labor Movement?" *Annual Review of Sociology* 25 (1999): 95–119; see also Kathryn Marie Dudley, *The End of the Line: Lost Jobs, New Lives in Postindustrial America* (University of Chicago Press, 1994). Dudley's ethnography of workers in a closed Chrysler plant in Kenosha, Wisconsin documents with unusual precision the distinction between financial loss (substantial but manageable with severance) and community loss (experienced as catastrophic). Workers reported that the loss of daily social structure — the familiar faces, the defined role, the sense of belonging to an institution with history — was more damaging to psychological wellbeing than the loss of income, even when income loss was severe.

The architecture encoded this directly. Whyte documented it in the Organization Man studies: suburban communities near large corporate campuses had become socially legible in a narrow way — conformity of dress, of aspiration, of political opinion. Intellectual independence was not prized; it was mildly threatening. The manager who questioned the five-year plan too vigorously was a problem to be managed, not a resource to be deployed.

And the surrogate village's exclusions were not incidental. They were structural.

The "family wage" model assumed a male breadwinner and a female homemaker. Women who sought professional roles found not just glass ceilings but architectural impossibilities — IBM did not hire married women until the 1960s, treating the marriage certificate as documentary evidence of divided loyalty. The surrogate village had a guest list, and it was maintained carefully.

For Black Americans, the exclusion was more systematic and more violent. Redlining locked Black workers out of the homeownership wealth that defined postwar middle-class stability. Union discrimination barred them from the skilled trades whose wages and benefits made the surrogate village's promises meaningful. The GI Bill, which created the educational and homeownership foundation for a generation of white veterans, was administered in ways that largely excluded the Black veterans who had fought under the same flag.[67]

[67]Ira Katznelson, *When Affirmative Action Was White: An Untold History of Racial Inequality in Twentieth-Century America* (New York: W.W. Norton, 2005), Chapters 5-7. Katznelson documents systematically how the GI Bill was implemented in ways that largely excluded Black veterans: segregated VA hospitals, segregated university admission practices that concentrated Black veterans in under-resourced institutions, and real estate lending practices that prevented Black veterans from accessing the suburban homeownership that generated the postwar middle class's wealth. The bill's text was race-neutral; its administration was not.

Margaret Chen was an exception to her era, and she knew it. "I was aware, every day," she said later, "that I was in a system that hadn't been designed for me." The surrogate village admitted her, provisionally, on conditions different from those extended to her white male colleagues. Her belonging was real, and it was partial.

The Breaking Conditions

Everything holds until it doesn't.

Beginning in the 1970s and accelerating through the 1990s, both conditions began to erode.

The first dissolved in computing. Enterprise resource planning systems, installed at scale through the 1980s and 1990s, automated the information-routing functions that seven layers of management had performed manually.[68] Decisions that had required six approval layers in 1975 cleared in two hours with zero human sign-offs by 2000. ERP systems validated constraints and executed orders faster than any human chain.

---

[68]Thomas H. Davenport, *Mission Critical: Realizing the Promise of Enterprise Systems* (Boston: Harvard Business School Press, 2000), Chapters 1-3; see also Thomas H. Davenport, "Putting the Enterprise into the Enterprise System," *Harvard Business Review*, July–August 1998. The large-scale ERP implementation wave of the 1980s and 1990s — led by SAP R/3 (released 1992), Oracle Applications, and PeopleSoft — systematically automated information routing and approval workflows that had previously required multiple management layers. By the late 1990s, ERP implementations at General Electric, Procter & Gamble, and other large enterprises had collapsed approval chains from 6-8 human layers to software-enforced single-pass workflows. Davenport (2000) documents the management-layer reduction as a consistent output of enterprise-system adoption across industries. The Chandler citation (^chandler-visible-hand) above covers the prior historical era (the managerial hierarchy as solution to a coordination problem); this citation covers the dissolution of that hierarchy through enterprise software.

The middle management layer was a solution to a coordination problem. Software solved the coordination problem. The layer became unnecessary.

Downsizing didn't begin as a philosophical choice about employment. It began as arithmetic. Jack Welch's GE shed roughly 112,000 positions between 1980 and 1985 — earning the nickname "Neutron Jack" — not because Welch was cruel but because the coordination data had an obvious implication: the workforce was larger than the coordination requirements actually demanded.[69] IBM, which had sustained its no-layoff policy for seven decades, broke it in 1993, cutting approximately 60,000 positions in that year alone — the first installment of what became a multi-year restructuring. The surrogate village's most faithful exemplar had concluded that the technical justification for the arrangement no longer held at previous scale.

The second condition — surplus large enough to share — dissolved through the shareholder primacy movement that Milton Friedman catalyzed with his 1970 *New York Times* essay declaring that the sole social responsibility of business was to increase its profits.[70] The Business Roundtable's 1997 statement formalized the doctrine: the corporation existed for shareholders, and any other consideration

[69]Jack Welch and John A. Byrne, *Jack: Straight from the Gut* (New York: Warner Business Books, 2001), Chapters 2-4. GE's workforce reduction from approximately 411,000 in 1980 to 299,000 in 1985 — a reduction of roughly 112,000 positions — is confirmed in GE annual reports of the period; Welch's own account rounds to "100,000" in colloquial usage. The more precise figure is used here because the chapter's argument concerns the scale of coordination-driven restructuring, not Welch's rhetoric. The "Neutron Jack" nickname was coined by *Newsweek* in 1982.

[70]Milton Friedman, "A Friedman Doctrine: The Social Responsibility of Business Is to Increase Its Profits," *New York Times Magazine*, September 13, 1970. The Business Roundtable's 1997 "Statement on Corporate Governance" formalized shareholder primacy as the definitive statement of American corporate purpose; the Roundtable's 2019 statement revising this position is also relevant context.

was subordinate. Surplus that had flowed to workers through wages, benefits, and the social architecture of the surrogate village redirected toward quarterly earnings, stock buybacks, and executive compensation packages tied to share price rather than headcount.

Competitive pressure amplified the effect. When your competitor cuts workforce by 30% and redirects that surplus to shareholders, you face a choice: maintain the surrogate village at a cost disadvantage, or follow. Most firms followed. The surplus available for distribution narrowed precisely as the workforce the surrogate village was meant to serve contracted.

By 2000, both conditions had weakened significantly. By 2020, they were structurally broken.

What AI-Born Breaks

The dissolution was gradual for fifty years. The current transition completes it faster — and simultaneously.

A 7-person team managing 250,000 enterprise interactions can match what a 2,000-person operation once required. This isn't an efficiency improvement. It's a categorical change in what coordination demands. The coordination problem that created the mid-century workforce — the problem whose solution was the large managed hierarchy, whose lubricant was the surrogate village — gets automated out of existence. Not reduced. Eliminated as a category.

The second condition concentrates rather than distributes. When Lovable crosses $400 million in annual revenue with 146 employees — roughly $2.74 million per person — the surplus does not spread across thousands of workers.[71] It concentrates in equity holders and the small team that remains. That is not an unintended consequence of the architecture. It is the architecture's output.

The 20th-century corporation shared its surplus across a large workforce partly because of paternalist philosophy, partly under union pressure, and partly because it genuinely *needed* thousands of people and had to make staying attractive. AI-Born enterprises don't need thousands of people. The economic logic undergirding the surrogate village — we share the surplus because we need you, and we need you badly enough that your loyalty is worth purchasing — is structurally absent.

What remains is not a reformed surrogate village. It is a different kind of enterprise, operating under structural conditions that 20th-century organizational logic was never built to address.

The Elegy

Here is where honesty requires a harder turn — not comfortable, but necessary.

We have spent thirty years dismantling the surrogate village without fully acknowledging what the village was for. The dismantling had good reasons: the exclusions were real, the conformity was stifling,

[71] TechCrunch, "Lovable says it added $100M in revenue last month alone, with just 146 employees," March 11, 2026, `https://techcrunch.com/2026/03/11/lovable-says-it-added-100m-in-revenue-last-month-alone-with-just-146-employees/`. Lovable crossed $400M in annual recurring revenue in February 2026 with 146 full-time employees — a revenue-per-employee ratio of approximately $2.74M, already surpassing Gartner's 2030 target of $2M per employee for new unicorns. Growth trajectory: $100M ARR (July 2025) → $400M ARR (February 2026). The company's December 2025 Series B raised $330M at a $6.6B valuation. This figure supersedes the earlier Datalumina reference to Lovable's $10M revenue milestone from 2024.

the dependency was designed rather than voluntary, the three trades extracted more from some people than they had any obligation to give. These are genuine criticisms, and they have been articulated well.

What has been less well-articulated is the identity problem the surrogate village was, however imperfectly, solving.

The corporation gave people an answer to the oldest question. You were an IBM man, a GM man, a Bell System person. That answer was bundled into the daily fabric of your existence — the morning commute, the colleagues who became friends, the rhythm of the career ladder, the pension promise that gave the future a legible shape. Drucker called the corporation a *constitutive institution* — not merely a place you worked but a structure that constituted your place in the social world. The word choice was precise. Constitutive. Not supportive. Not supplementary. The thing that made you.

When the surrogate village began dissolving in the 1980s and 1990s, the rhetoric celebrated freedom. You were no longer trapped in one organization. Flexibility replaced loyalty. The portfolio career replaced the lifetime employer. Labor mobility, previously constrained by the geography of corporate campuses, repositioned itself as a virtue.

For the professional class — the consultant, the knowledge worker, the early tech industry employee who could negotiate as an individual rather than as a member of a mass — the dissolution was a genuine gain. They kept the salary and shed the golden handcuffs. They bought their own healthcare, funded their own 401(k)s, and built networks that substituted for institutional belonging with what felt, at the time, like something better: chosen affiliation rather than assigned membership.

The identity question remained.

Where did belonging come from now? The city of strangers that industrialization had created — and that the corporation had temporarily managed — was still there. The pseudo-polis was dissolving. What would replace it?

The honest answer, thirty years later, is that nothing equivalent has. Robert Putnam tracked the contours of this absence in *Bowling Alone* (2000) — not just the famous bowling leagues but the broader collapse of civic association, the PTAs, union halls, Rotary Clubs, lodge chapters that had once constituted the social architecture of working-class and middle-class life.[72] Putnam's data showed civic participation falling fastest in precisely the communities where corporate employment had most thoroughly substituted for prior forms of association. When the corporation dissolved, it left a vacuum. The vacuum persists.

We have, in many cases, traded the three trades of the surrogate village for a fourth trade — less legible, no less costly: autonomy granted, community withdrawn.

I think about this more than any other dimension of what is coming. Not the technical transition. The human one. Because what AI-Born architectures are completing is not simply a restructuring of enterprise economics. They are completing the dissolution of the institution that answered the identity question for most of the 20th century, at a pace and scale no previous episode of corporate restructuring achieved.

[72] Robert D. Putnam, *Bowling Alone: The Collapse and Revival of American Community* (New York: Simon & Schuster, 2000), Chapters 4-8. Putnam's civic participation data (1975–1998) shows declines across virtually every category of associational life — civic organizations down 58%, union membership halved, church attendance falling, dinner-party frequency declining. The sharpest declines occurred in communities where a single large employer had previously organized social life — steel towns, auto manufacturing centers, textile communities — suggesting that the dissolution of the corporate surrogate village accelerated pre-existing civic decline rather than simply correlating with it.

Drucker saw this coming. Writing in 1993 as IBM broke its no-layoff covenant, he was characteristically precise: the large corporation was abandoning its social functions — healthcare, pensions, community — and returning workers to the market as pure contractors. "The society of the next century," he wrote, "will have to find new institutions that provide what the corporation provided in the 20th century — or will have to watch those needs go unmet."[73]

We are in the society Drucker anticipated.

What the surrogate village provided quietly — belonging, identity, the daily answer to the oldest question — does not disappear because the institution providing it disappears. The need remains. The institution is going.

The craftsman lost his guild. The industrial worker gained the factory and lost integration. The postwar worker gained the surrogate village and lost autonomy, craft depth, local community. The AI-Born worker gains flexibility, technological leverage, and — for those few on the right side of the new equations — spectacular productivity. And loses the pseudo-polis that patched, however imperfectly, the identity void industrialization created.

Two lineage breaks. Two centuries apart. The same pattern.

The factory owners of 1820 had no warning. We do.

That difference carries an obligation. The next architecture — the one Chapter 3 maps in detail — will not answer the question the surrogate village answered. Not by design, not by accident. It is

[73] Peter F. Drucker, *Post-Capitalist Society* (New York: HarperBusiness, 1993), Chapter 4. The observation about post-corporate society's need to find new institutions appears in the context of Drucker's analysis of IBM's 1993 workforce reduction and the broader dissolution of the lifetime-employment covenant. Drucker's concern was not that corporations were acting irrationally but that they were abandoning social functions that no other institution was positioned to absorb.

simply not built for that. Which means that answering the identity question — *where do I belong, and to what do I owe my labor?* — falls, for the first time in a century, somewhere other than the office building. Figuring out where is the work of this generation. The warning is the beginning of the work.

* * *

Chapter 3: The Second Lineage Break: The Present-Tense Collapse of the Large-Workforce Enterprise

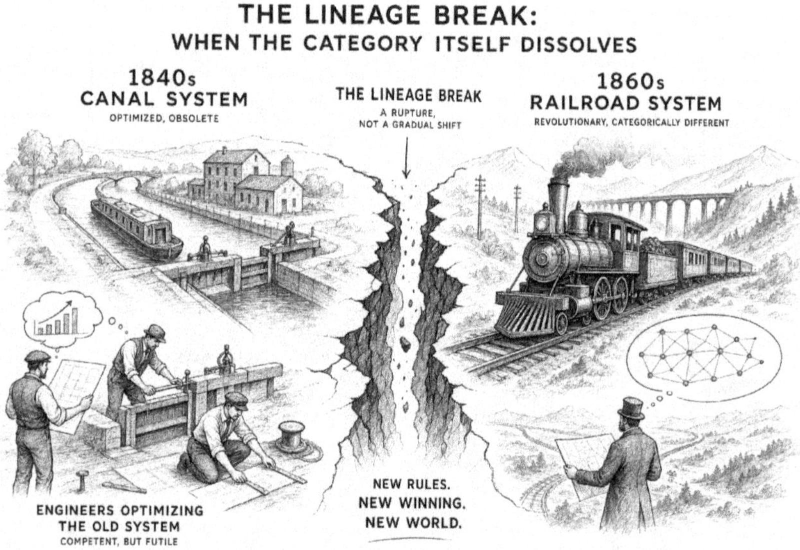

Figure 3.1: The Lineage Break: Categorical transformation from tools (passive instruments) to agents (autonomous actors)—a genuine rupture in organizational history.

In February 2026, a Stockholm-based software company named Lovable announced that it had added $100 million in annual recurring revenue in a single month.[74] The announcement attracted attention. Probably not enough.

At the time of the announcement, Lovable employed 146 people.

Run the arithmetic slowly. $400 million in ARR. 146 humans. In fifteen months of meaningful operation, Lovable built a revenue engine that would have required an organization of 3,000 people a decade ago. Reviewing their disclosures, the number that stopped me wasn't the revenue figure. It was the headcount. Anyone can raise capital. Only architecture produces $2.74 million per person per year.

Somewhere inside a traditional software company, a product manager read that announcement and felt something that wasn't quite admiration. Call it vertigo — the sensation of a governing equation you've trusted for twenty years dissolving under load. Revenue was supposed to scale with people. Organizations grew by hiring. For a century, the relationship between human effort and output was roughly linear. That relationship has broken. The second lineage break is the moment it breaks.

This is not a headline about one exceptional company. It's a data point in a pattern that, once you see it clearly, changes what you're looking at when you examine any large organization today.

The pattern is not coincidence. It is architecture.

[74] Connie Loizos, "Lovable says it added $100M in revenue last month alone, with just 146 employees," TechCrunch, March 11, 2026, `https://techcrunch.com/2026/03/11/lovable-says-it-added-100m-in-revenue-last-month-alone-with-just-146-employees/`; Lovable, "Lovable raises $330M to power the age of the builder," December 2025, `https://lovable.dev/blog/series-b`. Revenue per employee at $400M ARR / 146 staff: approximately $2.74M — already exceeding Gartner's 2030 target of $2M per employee for new unicorns. Company's December 2025 Series B raised $330M at a $6.6B valuation.

This chapter's job is to document the present-tense rupture. Not the coming one. Not the speculative one. The one already producing case studies, reversals, manifesto essays, and revenue figures that no prior model predicts.

Let me say what this chapter is not arguing. It is not arguing that all large organizations are immediately obsolete or that every industry is equally exposed. It is not claiming that the displacement of large-workforce enterprise is total or already complete. It is not providing a forecast for how quickly the transition will proceed across different sectors, with different regulatory environments, different capital requirements, and different customer relationships.

What it is arguing is narrower and, I think, harder to dismiss: the lineage break has already occurred. The new form already exists and already operates. The old form is already visibly contracting — in response to competitive pressure, yes, but also through deliberate choices made by the people running it. The transition is not pending. It is underway. And it is being led from inside the establishment rather than from outside it, which compresses the timeline compared to what historical patterns would predict.

What "Lineage Break" Actually Means

The terminology needs a definition before the evidence. A lineage break is not a disruption, an acceleration, or a transformation. It is a replacement — a moment when a new organizational form emerges that shares almost nothing with its predecessor in structure, economics, or operating logic.

The first lineage break was industrialization. Pre-industrial craft production — guild-organized, locally embedded, task-integrated — did not evolve gradually into factory production. It was replaced.

The blacksmith's integrated identity (designer, producer, seller, community member) was decomposed into fragmented tasks assigned to interchangeable workers at industrial scale. The new form was categorically different from what it replaced. It shared the purpose (producing goods) while sharing almost nothing else.

The phrase "categorically different" does real work here. A faster horse is not a lineage break. A car is. The car doesn't just do what the horse did more quickly — it changes what transportation means, who builds transportation infrastructure, what skills are required, what the geography of settlement looks like, and what kinds of communities can exist where. The replacement operates across all of those dimensions simultaneously, not just along the speed dimension.

Consider what organizational characteristics defined the large-workforce enterprise as it matured in the 20th century. Size correlated with market power; scale was both a competitive advantage and a barrier to entry. Coordination required layers of management — people whose job was to route information up and down and sideways through the organizational hierarchy. Revenue scaled roughly proportionally with headcount. Knowledge and expertise were embedded in people and therefore walked out the door when people left. Career progression meant accumulating seniority within a hierarchy. The organization's competitive position reflected, in large part, its ability to hire, retain, and coordinate large numbers of workers effectively.

The automation of coordination disrupts every one of those characteristics simultaneously. When agents route information, execute decisions, manage workflows, and coordinate across thousands of concurrent processes without a management layer, the rationale for a large-workforce architecture dissolves. The organization doesn't become better at doing what large organizations do. It becomes something that doesn't need to be large.

The second lineage break operates the same way as the first. The large-workforce corporation — Chapter 2's analysis of how it emerged as an organizational response to industrialization's co-ordination problems — is not growing more efficient. Something is replacing it: a form that shares almost nothing with it in headcount economics, decision architecture, or organizational logic.

One reliable signal of a genuine lineage break, as opposed to ordinary disruption, is that the new form seems absurd by the standards of the old. When Lovable adds $100 million in revenue with 146 people, the reaction from inside a traditional organization isn't "impressive efficiency." It's disbelief. When Block cuts its workforce 40% and simultaneously grows gross profit 18%, the reaction isn't "well-managed restructuring." It's bewilderment. When Cursor generates $2 billion in annual revenue with the headcount of a mid-sized law firm, executives in large software companies struggle to locate the category the comparison belongs to.

These reactions are epistemically appropriate. The new form violates the governing equations of the old. Revenue was supposed to scale with people. Organizations grew by hiring. For a century, the relationship between human effort and output was roughly linear — and then it wasn't.

The word "break" here is deliberate. Consider what it excludes. "Transition" suggests a change in degree — a movement along a continuum where you can see where you started and where you're headed. "Shift" implies rebalancing within a stable system. Neither word fits. The AI-Born cohort isn't the large-workforce enterprise operating at a different point on the same curve. The equations governing its operation are different. That's what "break" is meant to capture, and it's worth holding onto as you read the cases that follow.

The Old Form Ending: Four Companies, Specific Choices

The most direct evidence for the second lineage break is not theoretical. It's the documented choices that large organizations are making in real time — choices that, read together, signal that people running large-workforce enterprises understand their architecture is becoming obsolete.

Klarna, 2022–2026: The experiment and its correction.

In 2022, Klarna had roughly 5,500 employees. By end-2024, the number had fallen by roughly 38% — achieved not through layoffs but through a hiring freeze that let AI handle what new people would otherwise have done.[75] Revenue grew 26% year-over-year in that period. Active customers grew 32%. The workforce contracted as the company expanded.

[75] Klarna Group, "Klarna AI assistant handles two-thirds of customer service chats in its first month," press release, February 27, 2024, `https://www.klarna.com/international/press/klarna-ai-assistant-handles-two-thirds-of-customer-service-chats-in-its-first-month/`; OpenAI, "Klarna's AI assistant does the work of 700 full-time agents," case study, 2024, `https://openai.com/index/klarna/`. Deployment metrics: 2.3 million conversations in first month; average resolution under 2 minutes vs. 11 minutes for human agents; 25% drop in repeat inquiries; projected $40M profit improvement in 2024. Workforce arc: end-2022: ~5,527 FTE; end-2024: ~3,422 FTE (-38%), achieved primarily through hiring freeze rather than active layoffs. The "700 FTE equivalent" reflects ongoing hiring the company avoided during a growth phase, not 700 existing agents displaced. Q3 2025: $903M revenue (+26% YoY), 114M active customers (+32% YoY). IPO: NYSE, September 10, 2025 (ticker: KLAR), priced at $40/share (~$15B issue-price valuation), first-day open at $52, first-day market cap ~$19.65B.

In January 2024, Klarna deployed an OpenAI-powered customer service system that it announced handled work equivalent to 700 full-time agents. The cost savings were documented. The efficiency gains were real.

Then the quality gradient surfaced. Generic AI responses, stripped of emotional register, frustrated customers at exactly the moments when the company's relationship with them was most fragile — disputes, sensitive financial decisions, the scenarios where trust either holds or breaks. Consider the kind of worker who experienced that arc directly: hired in 2021, let go in the 2023 freeze, then called back in May 2025 on a flexible freelance arrangement Siemiatkowski described as "Uber-type" — the same person, doing roughly the same work, now positioned at precisely the edge case the AI could not handle. She did not return to what the job had been. She returned to what the job had become: the human judgment layer the automated system needs in order to function. CEO Sebastian Siemiatkowski acknowledged publicly in 2025 that Klarna had "focused too much on efficiency and cost" and that this produced "lower quality."[76] The company began rehiring on that model, positioning human agents at the edges where empathy, judgment, and accountability cannot be delegated.

---

[76] Bloomberg, "Klarna Turns From AI to Real Person Customer Service," May 8, 2025, `https://www.bloomberg.com/news/articles/2025-05-08/klarna-turns-from-ai-to-real-person-customer-service`. CEO Sebastian Siemiatkowski's exact statement: "cost unfortunately seems to have been a too predominant evaluation factor when organizing this, what you end up having is lower quality." He also stated: "it's so critical that you are clear to your customer that there will be always a human if you want." Klarna began rehiring customer service agents on a flexible freelance model described as "an Uber type of setup." Full IPO financials: NYSE September 10, 2025 (ticker: KLAR), priced at $40/share (~$15B issue-price valuation), opened at $52/share, first-day market cap ~$19.65B. See also Fortune, "Klarna CEO Sebastian Siemiatkowski halved workforce, says tech CEOs sugarcoating AI impact on jobs," October 10, 2025 — Siemiatkowski subsequently warned publicly that AI-driven mass unemployment was coming and that tech CEOs were understating the impact.

When Klarna went public on the NYSE on September 10, 2025, the market valued the corrected model.[77] The company that admitted its experiment needed revision opened at $52 a share — well above its $40 issue price — on the first trading day. The company that admitted its experiment needed revision was worth more, by the numbers, than the company that ran the experiment.

What the Klarna arc reveals is both the power and the limit of pure automation. The Machine Core delivered documented efficiency. The Human Cortex turned out to be non-optional for the interactions where customer relationships live or die. Getting the boundary right required iteration. Klarna ran that iteration openly, at production scale — which makes it the most instructive case study available.

There is also a lesson in how the market evaluated the correction. A traditional investor analysis of Klarna's reversal would note the added cost of rehiring, the implicit admission of overreach, the signal that AI cannot fully replace humans in fragile-trust contexts. That analysis would predict a valuation discount. The market instead rewarded the company — apparently concluding that the hybrid model was more durable than the fully-automated version. Whether that judgment reflects superior insight or prevailing enthusiasm for AI narratives is genuinely uncertain. But it suggests

[77] Bloomberg, "Klarna Turns From AI to Real Person Customer Service," May 8, 2025, `https://www.bloomberg.com/news/articles/2025-05-08/klarna-turns-from-ai-to-real-person-customer-service`. CEO Sebastian Siemiatkowski's exact statement: "cost unfortunately seems to have been a too predominant evaluation factor when organizing this, what you end up having is lower quality." He also stated: "it's so critical that you are clear to your customer that there will be always a human if you want." Klarna began rehiring customer service agents on a flexible freelance model described as "an Uber type of setup." Full IPO financials: NYSE September 10, 2025 (ticker: KLAR), priced at $40/share (~$15B issue-price valuation), opened at $52/share, first-day market cap ~$19.65B. See also Fortune, "Klarna CEO Sebastian Siemiatkowski halved workforce, says tech CEOs sugarcoating AI impact on jobs," October 10, 2025 — Siemiatkowski subsequently warned publicly that AI-driven mass unemployment was coming and that tech CEOs were understating the impact.

investors, at least in September 2025, understood something about where sustainable value lies in this transition: not in maximum automation, but in correct automation.

Shopify, April 2025: The memo that made the implicit explicit.

Shopify CEO Tobi Lütke circulated an internal memo in April 2025 with one governing directive: before requesting new headcount, every manager must first demonstrate the role cannot be performed by AI.[78] Human hiring became the exception. Not a strategic option. The exception.

The memo formalized a reality the numbers had already established. Between 2022 and end-2024, Shopify's headcount fell from 11,600 to 8,100 while annual revenue grew above 20% each year. The trajectory had already changed. The memo named it.

"Leveraging AI effectively is now a fundamental expectation of everyone at Shopify," Lütke wrote. He claimed employees were achieving "100× the work output" with AI tools — his own estimate, not an audited productivity figure, but the kind of assertion that lands differently when a CEO attaches it to performance reviews. The word "fundamental" matters as much as "baseline." He wasn't announcing a pilot. He was describing a permanent operating condition that would be enforced in evaluations — the kind of language that ends careers if ignored.

[78]Tobi Lütke, internal memo "Reflexive AI usage is now a baseline expectation at Shopify," April 2025; published after leak. CNBC, `https://cnbc.com/2025/04/07/shopify-ceo-prove-ai-cant-do-jobs-before-asking-for-more-headcount.html`; TechCrunch, `https://techcrunch.com/2025/04/07/shopify-ceo-tells-teams-to-consider-using-ai-before-growing-headcount/`. Shopify headcount: 11,600 (2022) → 8,300 (2023) → 8,100 (end-2024), with revenue growth above 20% annually throughout.

Lütke was stating plainly what the Shopify org chart already showed: growth no longer translates into proportionate hiring. The organization had permanently restructured around AI as the primary execution layer, with humans in the roles the execution layer cannot fill.

Block, April 2026: The manifesto that came with a theory.

When Block cut its workforce by roughly 40% in early 2026 — from approximately 10,000 to 6,000 — the scale was significant.[79] What distinguished this from an ordinary restructuring was the accompanying essay.

CEO Jack Dorsey co-authored a piece with Sequoia partner Roelof Botha called "From Hierarchy to Intelligence." The argument was architectural rather than financial. Corporate hierarchy, Dorsey and Botha wrote, has always existed to solve one problem: routing information through organizations too large for any single person to oversee. AI can now perform that function. The middle layers that exist to manage information flows are dissolving because the information-flow problem they were designed to solve is dissolving with them.

This is not a cost argument. It is a structural one. Block wasn't trimming fat — it was claiming that a category of organizational

[79] Jack Dorsey and Roelof Botha, "From Hierarchy to Intelligence," co-authored essay, April 1, 2026. CoinDesk, `https://coindesk.com/tech/2026/04/01/jack-dorsey-says-ai-should-replace-corporate-hierarchy-after-block-cuts-4-000-jobs`; Payments Dive, `https://paymentsdive.com/news/blocks-dorsey-rethinks-corporate-structure/816347/`; Sequoia podcast, `https://sequoiacap.com/podcast/jack-dorsey-every-company-can-now-be-a-mini-agi/`. Headcount: approximately 10,000 → 6,000 (-40%), February 2026. Stock response: +22–24%. $2M gross profit per employee target for end-2026. Block internal AI agent "Goose" (Model Context Protocol) cited in multiple sources as handling approximately 90% of code submissions.

function, the information-routing middle, had been rendered architecturally redundant.

Block was building what Dorsey described as two internal "world models." One aggregated code, decisions, workflows, and performance data into a live operational picture. The other mapped customer and merchant behavior across Cash App and Square transaction data. Humans work "at the edge" — handling creative, cultural, and ethical decisions that require human judgment. AI manages coordination.

Block's gross profit grew 18% year-over-year during the restructuring period. The stock rose 22–24% after the announcement — a market reward that sits alongside a real human cost we take up directly in the second volume. Dorsey set a target of $2 million in gross profit per employee by end-2026. The market was not punishing the choice. It was pricing the architecture.

A caveat worth holding alongside the manifesto: current and former Block employees reported to The Guardian that approximately 95% of AI-generated code still requires human modification, and that AI tools cannot yet lead in regulated banking contexts without human oversight.[80] The gap between architectural vision and operational reality is real at Block, as it is everywhere this transition is underway. The direction is not in question. The completion date is.

IBM, 2023–2026: The cycle runs to completion.

IBM's arc covers the longest timeline in the available data — from freeze to restructuring to reversal. It also includes a twist that complicates easy narratives.

[80] Current and former Block employees quoted in The Guardian, 2026: approximately 95% of AI-generated code requires human modification; AI tools cannot yet lead in regulated banking contexts without human review.

In May 2023, CEO Arvind Krishna announced a hiring freeze on back-office roles, predicting that roughly 7,800 positions would be eliminated over five years as AI handled routine tasks.[81] Two restructuring waves in 2024 and 2025 executed that prediction ahead of schedule. Then, in February 2026, IBM's chief human resources officer announced the company would triple entry-level hiring.[82]

The reversal deserves direct engagement because it complicates any simple "AI replaces workers, full stop" story. If that were the complete picture, IBM wouldn't be hiring. It is.

What IBM discovered after automating its back office was a new scarcity: humans who could work *with* AI systems. People who grew up coding with tools like Cursor, building with Claude, managing agent pipelines and designing agent charters. The company eliminated a large category of coordination-intensive roles that had existed to manage information flows at scale. It then found demand for a smaller, different category — workers who could architect, supervise, and govern the systems that replaced the old coordination layer.

[81] IBM CEO Arvind Krishna, Reuters interview, May 2023: plan to pause hiring for approximately 7,800 back-office roles over five years as AI handles routine tasks. The Guardian, "IBM to pause hiring in plan to replace 7,800 jobs with AI," May 1, 2023, `https://www.theguardian.com/technology/2023/may/01/ibm-to-pause-hiring-in-plan-to-replace-7800-jobs-with-ai`.

[82] Bloomberg, "IBM Plans to Triple Entry-Level Hiring in the US in 2026," February 12, 2026, `https://www.bloomberg.com/news/articles/2026-02-12/ibm-plans-to-triple-entry-level-hiring-in-the-us-in-2026`; Fortune, "IBM is tripling the number of Gen Z entry-level jobs after finding the limits of AI adoption," February 13, 2026, `https://fortune.com/2026/02/13/tech-giant-ibm-tripling-gen-z-entry-level-hiring-according-to-chro-rewriting-jobs-ai-era/`. CHRO Nickle LaMoreaux at Charter's Leading with AI Summit (New York): "The entry-level jobs that you had two to three years ago, AI can do most of them... that has to be through totally different jobs." Context: IBM AskHR reduced HR professionals from 700 to fewer than 50 (93% reduction), handling 11.5M interactions in 2024 at a 94% self-service rate. IBM shed approximately 13,000–17,000 back-office positions in 2024–2025 before announcing the hiring expansion.

The IBM arc is not a refutation of the lineage break. It is its most honest portrait. The automation ran as predicted. What emerged on the other side was a different organizational need — fewer humans, differently skilled, performing work that the automated layer cannot. The large-workforce enterprise is ending. The organization that replaces it will still employ people. But not the same people, not the same number, not for the same functions.

Consider what makes this convergence significant. Klarna is a Swedish fintech. Shopify is a Canadian commerce platform. Block is an American payments company. IBM is a century-old enterprise technology firm. Different regulatory environments, different customer relationships, different founding stories. And yet all four arrived at structurally similar conclusions about what their organizations look like on the other side of the transition.

That's not four isolated experiments. That's evidence the pattern is structural.

The New Form Emerging: The Small-Team Paradox

Klarna, Shopify, Block, and IBM document what is ending. But showing only the old form contracting would be incomplete — and would be misleading. The new form already exists, already operates, and already produces numbers.

The new organizational form is not hypothetical. It does not await some future capability breakthrough. Lovable, Cursor, Mercor, Sierra, and Perplexity operate today, across five different markets, generating revenue figures that violate the governing assumptions of the large-workforce model.

Here is the pattern, stated directly. Between 2023 and 2026, a cohort of companies achieved revenue levels that, in any prior decade, would have required organizations of thousands of people — with teams numbering in the dozens to low hundreds. The companies in this cohort differ in product, market, and founding story. What they share is architectural: each built autonomous agent systems handling execution at scale while keeping the human layer deliberately small.

The revenue-per-employee figures don't just exceed traditional benchmarks. They exist in a different category.

Lovable: $2.74 million revenue per employee.

$400 million ARR, 146 employees, founded in 2023.[83] The company's platform handles over 200,000 new projects per day at that headcount. That throughput is only possible because agent architecture handles distribution, support, onboarding, and execution. The humans architect. The agents execute.

The median SaaS company generates roughly $130,000 in revenue per employee. High-performing traditional software companies might reach $200,000–$300,000. Lovable's number sits 10 to 20 times higher — not 10 to 20% higher. The difference between those phrasings is the difference between efficiency and architectural discontinuity.

Cursor: $6.7 million revenue per employee.

[83]Lovable growth trajectory: $5.3M ARR (end-2024) → $100M ARR (July 2025) → $200M (November 2025) → $300M (January 2026) → $400M (February 2026). TechCrunch, March 11, 2026; Sacra Research, `https://sacra.com/c/lovable/`. Company reported 200,000+ new projects per day at time of $400M announcement. Median SaaS revenue-per-employee benchmark (~$130,000) and high-performer range ($200,000–$300,000) from multiple industry analyses including Bessemer Venture Partners Cloud Index and KeyBanc Capital Markets SaaS Survey (2024–2025).

$2 billion ARR, approximately 300 employees, founded in 2022.[84] The founders stayed small deliberately — not because they lack capital, but because adding humans to an agent-first architecture creates coordination overhead that adding compute does not. Customer service, documentation, onboarding, scaling infrastructure: handled primarily by systems, not by staff. When you need to handle ten times more developer sessions, you add compute. You don't post job listings.

Mercor: where automation boundaries become visible.

Mercor's per-employee efficiency surpasses Microsoft, Meta, and Nvidia, each a technology-sector capital efficiency benchmark.[85] Founded in 2023, it reached a $10 billion valuation in October 2025.[86] Its AI agents automate candidate matching, vetting, and interview coordination — the pattern-matching and scheduling that constitute most operational hours in traditional recruiting. The judgment layer remains human. What Mercor reveals is that

---

[84]Alyssa Stringer, "Cursor Tops $2B ARR as AI Coding Tools Race Heats Up," The Information, February 2026; corroborated by TechBuzz, "Cursor Hits $2B ARR, Doubles Revenue in Just 3 Months," February 2026, `https://www.techbuzz.ai/articles/cursor-hits-2b-arr-doubles-revenue-in-just-3-months`. Employee count estimates of approximately 250-300 from multiple sources. Company doubled ARR in approximately three months, Q4 2025 to Q1 2026.

[85]Andrew Moran, "How Mercor Generates $4.5 Million Per Employee," andrew.ooo, 2025, `https://andrew.ooo/posts/mercor-45m-revenue-per-employee-ai-training/`. Comparison benchmarks: Microsoft ($1.8M per employee), Meta ($2.2M), Nvidia ($3.6M). Note: Mercor's revenue model is a marketplace in which 60–70% of revenue flows to its network of contracted domain experts (~30,000 contractors paid $85–$95/hour); the headline per-FTE figure reflects gross revenue, not net revenue, and the economics differ structurally from pure SaaS. See [^mercor-500m-arr-2025] for expanded detail.

[86]Connie Loizos, "Mercor quintuples valuation to $10B with $350M Series C," TechCrunch, October 27, 2025, `https://techcrunch.com/2025/10/27/mercor-quintuples-valuation-to-10b-with-350m-series-c/`. Earlier milestone: "Mercor, an AI recruiting startup founded by 21-year-olds, raises $100M at $2B valuation," TechCrunch, February 20, 2025. Team size (~30 FTE at peak efficiency) per GetLatka, `https://getlatka.com/companies/mercor`; later PitchBook/Tracxn trackers report higher headcounts post-Series C.

domains long considered "relationship-intensive" and therefore automation-resistant contain a large automatable substrate. The resistance is real but narrower than assumed.

Sierra: $200 million ARR in 27 months.

Sierra reached $100 million ARR in November 2025 — 21 months from founding — and crossed $200 million in May 2026, compressing the second $100 million into just two more quarters.[87] Its customer roster includes Discord, Rivian, and Ramp. The company builds AI agents for customer service on the exact insight Klarna discovered through trial: AI handles the high-volume routine tier; humans handle the edge cases where emotional register and accountability matter. Sierra designed around that boundary from day one rather than arriving at it through customer complaints.

Perplexity in its compressed-team phase.

During its 2024–2025 high-growth period, Perplexity grew revenue fivefold with roughly 100 full-time employees at the time of its $20 billion valuation.[88] AI-powered search operates at enormous

---

[87]TechCrunch, "Bret Taylor's Sierra reaches $100M ARR in under two years," November 21, 2025, `https://techcrunch.com/2025/11/21/bret-taylors-sierra-reaches-100m-arr-in-under-two-years/`; TechCrunch, "Sierra raises $950M as the race to own enterprise AI gets serious," May 4, 2026, `https://techcrunch.com/2026/05/04/sierra-raises-950m-as-the-race-to-own-enterprise-ai-gets-serious/`. Sierra reached $100M ARR in November 2025 (21 months from founding), $150M by February 2026, and $200M by May 2026 — compressing the second $100M into two quarters versus seven for the first. The company raised $950M Series E at a $15.8B post-money valuation in May 2026, up from $10B in September 2025. Headcount not officially disclosed; third-party trackers report 488–749 employees as of mid-2026. Customer roster (Discord, Rivian, Ramp) from company website and press releases.

[88]TechCrunch, "Perplexity reportedly raised $200M at $20B valuation," September 10, 2025, `https://techcrunch.com/2025/09/10/perplexity-reportedly-raised-200m-at-20b-valuation/`. At time of its $20B raise in September 2025, Perplexity had approximately 90–100 full-time employees and approximately $200M ARR — roughly $2M revenue per employee. The "×5 revenue with 34% team growth" framing refers to the 2024–2025 high-growth phase; by early 2026, headcount had expanded dramatically (third-party

query and indexing scale primarily because the infrastructure is compute-driven, not labor-driven.

Five companies. Five different markets: developer tools, recruiting, customer service AI, search, app-building. The revenue-per-employee figures are not explained by better management or favorable timing. They are explained by architecture: when a Machine Core executes autonomously at scale, the relationship between headcount and output breaks down.

Chapter 4 develops the full mechanics of this paradox. The key point here is simpler: the new form is not imagined. It exists, it operates, and it achieves results that are only possible under an organizational architecture the large-workforce enterprise does not run on.

What the Cohort Has in Common

The five companies above are worth examining not just for the headline numbers but for what they share architecturally. Because the numbers aren't the point. The numbers are the output. The architecture is the cause.

Each built around a principle that traditional organizations invert. In a conventional organization, headcount is the execution layer. You hire people to do the work. When you need to do more work, you hire more people. Revenue growth and headcount growth move together.

Lovable, Cursor, Mercor, Sierra, and Perplexity inverted that logic. Agents are the execution layer. Humans design, govern, and decide. When revenue grows, compute scales. Headcount

---

estimates: 1,200–1,449) following aggressive post-funding hiring. The compressed-team dynamic applies specifically to Perplexity's 2024–2025 phase, not its current scale. Valuation confirmed at $20B per TechCrunch and multiple sources.

stays deliberately small because adding humans to an agent-first architecture creates coordination overhead without proportionate capability gain. Cursor's founders were explicit: team size was an architectural choice, not a resource constraint. Mercor built agent workflows for exactly the work that would otherwise require hundreds of human recruiters.

What the human layer does in these organizations is qualitatively different from conventional equivalents. Humans don't do the work agents do. They decide what agents should optimize for. They handle cases where agent decision logic reaches the edge of its specification. They design new agent workflows when the business encounters new problems — which is a more demanding set of functions than traditional organizations ask of equivalent headcount. Lovable's engineers set direction, review escalations, and adjust systems when outputs drift from intent. The agents execute.

None of these companies is trying to become large. I find this more striking than the revenue figures. In a business culture that treats headcount growth as a signal of organizational health — where "we're hiring" is synonymous with "we're succeeding" — the AI-Born cohort appears to have simply decoupled revenue from headcount as co-equal metrics. Lovable is not projecting growth to 1,000 employees as it pursues $1 billion ARR. Cursor is not building an org chart that looks like a 2015-era enterprise software company. The founders understand that the architecture that produced $400 million or $2 billion in ARR is the same architecture that takes them further — and that architecture does not scale with headcount.

I want to be careful about what I'm claiming here. These companies are young. They haven't faced the governance challenges that appear when agent systems scale to higher complexity. They haven't had to solve the accountability problems that arise when agent decisions cause real harm to customers. The founders who built them are unusually talented, and the markets they entered were unusually receptive. The cohort's metrics may reflect exceptional founders in a favorable moment rather than a replicable architectural template.

What the data does not permit is dismissal. The revenue-per-employee figures are too anomalous, across too many companies, in too many different markets, to explain away as exceptional circumstances. Something structural is producing these numbers. Part II is an attempt to name what that something is.

The Structural Economics Underneath the Numbers

Three mechanisms explain the asymmetric revenue-per-employee pattern. They operate simultaneously.

First: cost structure shifts from payroll to compute. At a conventional SaaS company, the majority of operating costs are human — salary, benefits, office space, management overhead. At Cursor or Lovable, the primary cost is compute infrastructure: GPU time, model inference, API calls, cloud hosting. Compute scales at near-zero marginal cost per additional unit of output. Adding 100,000 more users to Lovable doesn't require 146 more people. It requires more compute.

Second: distribution is self-service. Conventional software companies staff sales, account management, customer success, and support — each a sizable headcount category. AI-Born firms rely primarily on product-led growth: the product reaches users through developer community adoption and frictionless onboarding, with AI agents handling most support volume. Where a formal sales motion exists, a small team handles high-value enterprise accounts. The large commercial operations layer simply isn't built.

Third: agents handle the operational tier. The work that traditionally scaled with revenue — candidate matching at Mercor, project intake at Lovable, customer query resolution at Sierra — runs through autonomous agent workflows rather than human labor. When Mercor processes thousands of applications per day, agents perform the matching, assessment, and routing. Human recruiters handle the judgment layer at the boundary where agents' pattern logic reaches its limits.

These three mechanisms together produce a cost structure that traditional organizations don't run on. AI-Born firms aren't more efficient at the same tasks. The tasks route differently — to compute rather than people, to agents rather than employees. Klarna, Shopify, Block, and IBM are working toward the same structural destination; they're arriving through the messier path of retrofitting existing architecture rather than building from scratch.

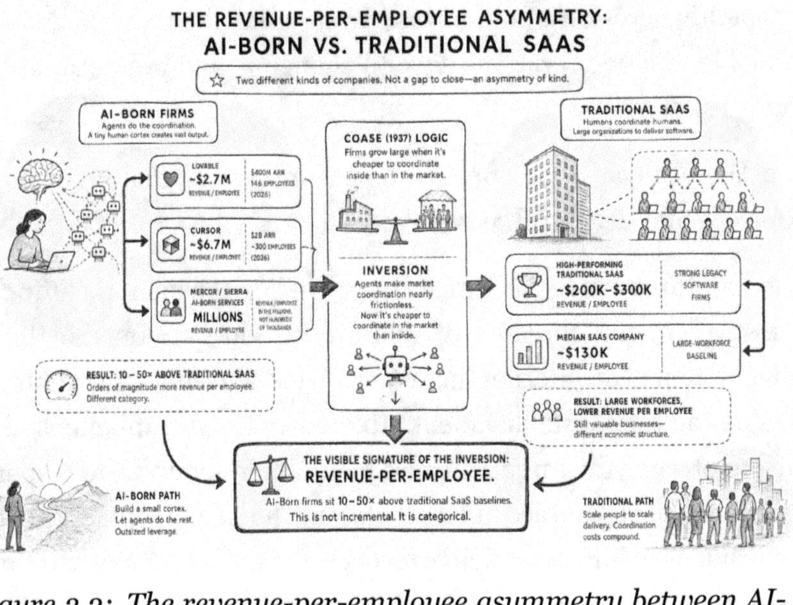

Figure 3.2: The revenue-per-employee asymmetry between AI-Born firms (Lovable, Cursor, Mercor, Sierra) and traditional SaaS

baselines. The gap is not a matter of degree. It signals a categorical difference in organizational architecture.

Why the Transition Moves Faster This Time

Each major technological rupture has had a lag phase. Electrification was commercially viable in the 1880s. The productivity gains arrived in the 1920s. A forty-year gap between the technology becoming available and organizations restructuring around it deeply enough to capture its potential. The internet achieved commercial viability in the mid-1990s. E-commerce became the dominant retail model only in the 2010s. A fifteen-year lag.

The gap exists because organizational transformation requires more than technology. It requires new mental models, new management practices, new talent pipelines, new legal frameworks, and the slow competitive erosion of old forms. Even when the technology is available, the organizations have to change — and organizations change slowly.

The AI-Born transition appears to be compressing that lag phase. For a specific structural reason.

Prior ruptures arrived as threats from outside the incumbent form. The steam engine threatened guild production from outside the guild system. The internet threatened brick-and-mortar retail from outside the retail establishment. In both cases, incumbents had time to observe the threat, dismiss it, and then scramble to respond as the new form captured market share. The incumbents were on the inside watching a challenge form on the outside. They had time, institutional resources, and existing customer relationships. The new form had to fight its way in.

The AI-Born transition is different because the most prominent articulators of the architectural break are people already inside the establishment — and because the tools driving the transition are being built and deployed by the establishment, not against it.

Dorsey is not an academic theorist describing the dissolution of corporate hierarchy. He is the founder of Block, running the experiment at a company processing trillions of dollars in annual transactions, publishing his architectural conclusions in real time. Lütke is not a labor economist. He is the CEO of a platform managing millions of active merchants, making an explicit operational policy choice about how growth translates (or no longer translates) into headcount. IBM is not a tech pundit. It is one of the oldest technology enterprises in the world, having run both the automation cycle and the recovery arc, and drawing explicit conclusions from both for the benefit of anyone paying attention.

When Dimon says "you can't lay off 2 million truckers tomorrow," he is not speaking from outside the system.[89] He is speaking from the center of it — the CEO of the largest U.S. bank, a firm that has invested over $2 billion in AI and documented equivalent annual savings, flagging the systemic risk that firm-level rationality creates

[89] Jamie Dimon, remarks at World Economic Forum panel, Davos, Switzerland, January 22, 2026. Verbatim quotations sourced from Banking Dive, "JPMorgan's Dimon: AI's effect on jobs may go too fast for society," January 22, 2026, `https://www.bankingdive.com/news/jpmorgan-dimon-ai-effect-jobs-workforce-davos/810247/`; Fortune, "JPMorgan CEO Jamie Dimon says he welcomes government ban on mass-firing people for AI," January 22, 2026, `https://fortune.com/2026/01/22/jpmorgan-chase-ceo-jamie-dimon-ai-layoff-income-assist-workers-elon-musk-sam-altman-universal-basic-income/`. Verbatim statements: "You can't lay off 2 million truckers tomorrow. You can phase it in over time"; "If it goes too fast for society, that's where government and business in a collaborative way should step in together and come up with a way to retrain people"; on potential government bans: "We would agree — if we have to do that to save society"; "Phase it in. Retrain. Relocate. Income-assist." Dimon called U.S. Trade Adjustment Assistance "incredibly poorly done." JPMorgan context: $2 billion invested in AI, documented annual savings, 200,000+ employees using AI tools weekly (Bloomberg, October 2025).

when pursued at economy-wide speed. The observation carries more weight than the same argument from a labor economist or a policy institute, because it comes from someone with no obvious interest in slowing the transition except protecting the consumer-spending base that his firm — and every other enterprise — depends on.

This is the velocity problem, and it belongs in this chapter because it is architecturally significant, not merely socially. An architectural transition that generates a 40-year electrification lag, as in the first lineage break, allows society time to adapt. A transition compressed to a decade — driven by founders who scale on compute rather than headcount, by incumbents converting entire management layers overnight — creates a different kind of pressure on the systems outside the firm: labor markets, education pipelines, regulatory frameworks, social insurance.

Dimon's prescription — phase it in, retrain, build income bridges, and accept coordinated intervention if the pace of displacement outstrips social infrastructure — is addressed to the same people reading this book. He is not describing a dystopian scenario to prevent. He is describing a dynamic already underway that individual firms, acting rationally, can accelerate beyond what workforce and community infrastructure can absorb. Firm-level rationality and system-level stability are not automatically aligned; that gap is worth naming explicitly, because closing it is a design challenge, not a moral indictment of firms that pursue efficiency.

This matters for how urgency should be calibrated. The velocity question — not whether the transition happens, but how fast — is being raised by the people driving it. Incumbents aren't dismissing the threat while startups fight their way in. The most credible incumbents are naming the threat, working through it publicly, and making explicit organizational choices in real time.

There is a second compression mechanism that prior ruptures didn't have: the AI-Born cohort is itself supplying tools that accelerate the transition for everyone else. Cursor is accelerating software development for millions of engineers, which accelerates every software company's ability to build agent systems. Perplexity is making information retrieval faster, which accelerates research and decision-making across industries. Lovable is enabling non-engineers to build software applications with natural language, which democratizes access to the core technology of the new form. The AI-Born cohort isn't just demonstrating that the transition is real — it's producing the tools that make the transition faster for everyone who uses them.

That feedback loop has no clear analog in prior transitions. Steam engines didn't build better steam engines. The internet didn't build a faster internet. The AI-Born cohort is both demonstrating the transition and catalyzing it — a self-reinforcing dynamic that prior transition timelines were never subject to.

Here is what this means for any organization reading this book: the competitive window is narrowing faster than prior ruptures would predict. Lovable, Cursor, Mercor, Sierra, and their cohort-mates are already in the market, already capturing customers, already posting revenue-per-employee figures that force organizational comparison. The organizations currently running on large-workforce architecture are not competing against a theoretical future. They are competing against companies that already exist and are already winning business on the basis of a cost and speed advantage rooted in architecture, not in team quality or market timing alone.

Building toward the architecture this book describes is not a defensive hedge against a possible future. It is a competitive response to a present-tense reality.

The Category Break: Tools to Agents

One technical distinction deserves to be named here before Part II takes it apart in full, because it's the engine underneath everything described above.

The companies in the AI-Born cohort are not using AI the way most large organizations currently use it. They are not deploying AI as a tool — a capability that enhances what a human worker does. They are deploying AI as an agent — a system that perceives its environment, reasons about goals, acts autonomously within defined constraints, and learns from outcomes.

A tool executes your instructions. You remain the operator. An agent operates within constraints you define, pursuing goals you set, without requiring step-by-step direction.

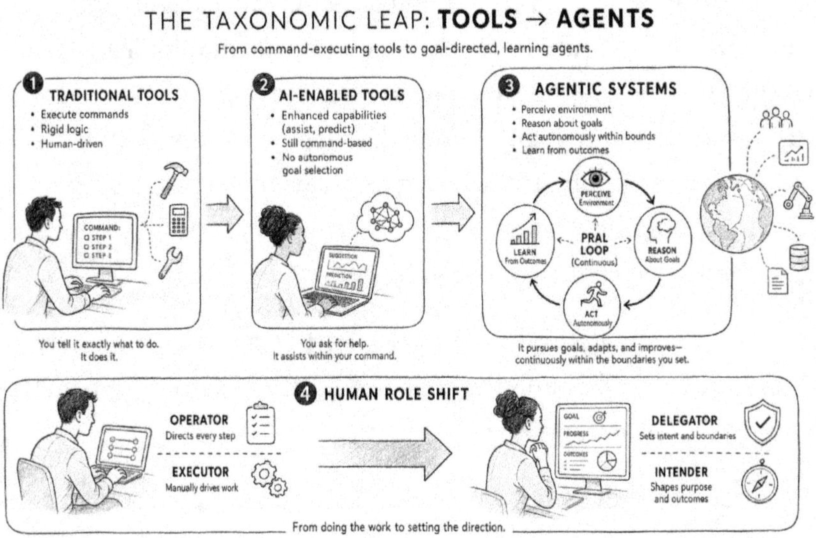

Figure 3.3: The taxonomic leap from tools to agents — traditional tools execute instructions, AI-enabled tools augment a human operator, and agentic systems pursue goals autonomously within constraints you define.

The distinction is not semantic. It is the architectural difference between the electrification that bolted motors onto steam-era pulleys — capturing some efficiency gain while preserving the old factory layout — and the electrification that redesigned the factory layout entirely around the unit drive principle.

When Lovable's platform handles 200,000 new projects per day with 146 people, it is doing so because agents are managing the workflow — intake, processing, iteration, delivery — not because 146 very productive humans are working very quickly. When Cursor handles millions of developers with 300 people, the customer-facing infrastructure is predominantly agent-run. When Mercor matches candidates and coordinates interviews without hundreds of human recruiters, it's because agents are handling the pattern-matching and scheduling that constitutes most of the operational load.

The AI-enabled organization bolts AI tools onto existing human workflows and captures efficiency gains at the margin. The AI-Born organization builds the workflows around agents from the start, with humans occupying the roles that agents cannot — judgment under genuine ambiguity, accountability where accountability must be human, creativity where creativity requires taste and context that no specification captures completely.

That is the architectural difference. Part II names it precisely: Machine Core and Human Cortex. Two distinct layers. Two distinct functions. Neither optional.

The reason the revenue-per-employee numbers in the AI-Born cohort seem impossible by the standards of the large-workforce model is that they are. They are impossible under the large-workforce model. They are possible under a different one.

This distinction determines what kind of response a large organization actually needs. Deploying AI tools across existing workflows produces marginal efficiency gains inside the existing organizational form. Redesigning the workflows around agent execution produces the structural efficiency that generates the cohort's anomalous numbers. Part II is about the second kind of response — and only the second.

What We Do Not Yet Have Language For

Here is where the chapter requires a moment of precision about what it is and is not claiming.

Start with what the chapter has actually shown. The case studies are documented; the revenue figures cross-check against multiple sources; the organizational choices at Klarna, Shopify, Block, and

IBM are public record. The Small-Team Paradox is a measured phenomenon, not a projection. And the asymmetric revenue-per-employee pattern across the cohort — Lovable, Cursor, Mercor, Sierra, Perplexity — sits right there in the company disclosures and the analyst research, waiting to be reconciled with a model that has no place for it.

The data proves two things: the old form is ending, and the new form exists. It doesn't prove that the new form is stable, scalable, or that every organization that attempts the architecture will achieve the cohort's results.

What is not yet fully worked out — what remains genuinely open — is the architecture that makes the new form stable, governable, and reproducible at scale.

Consider what you can observe from the outside versus what remains unknown. We can describe the new form's external characteristics: small teams, high agent-to-human ratios, asymmetric revenue per employee, deliberate constraint on headcount, agent systems handling execution at scale. We can observe that it works. What we cannot yet specify is the inside. How should the organization be structured internally, and where should decision authority sit between the human and agent layers? What stops the Machine Core from optimizing for objectives that quietly diverge from human intention? And how does the Human Cortex hold strategic coherence while agents execute autonomously across thousands of concurrent processes — none of which it watches directly?

These are not rhetorical questions. They are open architectural problems. The cases in this chapter already surface them.

The Klarna correction surfaced the boundary problem: where does the automated tier end and the human tier begin, and what is the cost of getting the boundary wrong? Klarna's experiment suggests the answer is not "maximize automation" — it is "find the boundary correctly," which requires testing the boundary against real customer interactions until the failure mode appears. That is expensive. Getting it right from design would be cheaper.

Block's operational gap (95% of AI-generated code requiring human modification) surfaces the specification problem: the gap between what agents are directed to do and what the organization actually needs them to do is often wider than architectural manifestos suggest. Getting from "AI manages coordination" to "AI manages coordination correctly, in regulated banking contexts, with accountability for decisions that affect customers" is a substantial design challenge.

IBM's hiring reversal surfaces the talent problem: the new form requires a different kind of human, and the pipeline for producing that human didn't exist at the start of the transition. You can automate the old jobs faster than you can hire people capable of running the new systems. That creates a gap — between the speed of automation and the speed of workforce development — that organizations in the middle of the transition have to navigate without a complete map.

None of these problems are reasons to avoid the transition. They are reasons to approach it with architectural precision rather than technological enthusiasm. The machine learning field has a useful phrase for the gap between what a system optimizes and what you actually want: reward misspecification. The governance and design chapters of Part II exist to close that gap at the organizational level.

The absence of a complete architectural vocabulary for the new form is not a failure of this chapter. It is the setup for the rest of the book.

Part II is about that vocabulary — precise, testable, applicable to real organizational decisions. This chapter's job was narrower: to establish that the rupture is present-tense and real; to document both sides of the break; to name the frameworks that carry the analytical load forward (Lineage Break, Small-Team Paradox, asymmetric revenue-per-employee); and to calibrate urgency correctly — present-tense competitive pressure, not speculative future risk.

From Diagnosis to Architecture

Thomas Edison unveiled the incandescent lightbulb in 1879. Twenty-one years later, fewer than 5% of American homes had electricity.[90] Factory managers in the early electrification period bolted electric motors onto the same mechanical arrangements that had run on steam — central power source, drive shafts, pulleys, belts. The machines changed. The spatial logic stayed frozen. Productivity barely moved for three decades.

Paul David, who spent years studying why electrification's productivity gains took four decades to arrive, traced the failure to a conceptual error.[91] Managers treated electricity as a more powerful steam engine. They optimized for the technology they understood. Only forty years later, when engineers grasped what "unit drive" actually meant — one motor per machine, factory layout freed from proximity to a central power source, production organized around workflow rather than the mechanics of power transmission — did

[90] Paul A. David, "The Dynamo and the Computer: An Historical Perspective on the Modern Productivity Paradox," American Economic Review 80, no. 2 (May 1990): 355-361. David documents that by 1900 — twenty-one years after Edison's demonstration — fewer than 5% of American homes had electricity and electric motors accounted for less than 5% of factory mechanical drive.

[91] Paul A. David, "The Dynamo and the Computer: An Historical Perspective on the Modern Productivity Paradox," American Economic Review 80, no. 2 (May 1990): 355-361. David's central finding: the lag between electrification's arrival and its productivity impact was caused by managers treating electricity as a more powerful steam engine rather than as a technology requiring organizational redesign.

productivity compound. The old architecture dissolved. A genuinely new one replaced it.

The organizational error of the current moment is the same one, translated forward. Deploy AI. Announce transformation. Plateau at marginal gains because the agent systems were bolted onto hierarchies designed for a world where humans were the execution layer. Multiple studies published in 2024–2025 found that the substantial majority of enterprise AI pilots — estimates cluster around 90% or higher — delivered no measurable P&L impact, an order-of-magnitude indicator rather than a precisely audited rate, but consistent enough across sources to name the pattern: electric motors on steam-era pulleys, translated into software deployments and unchanged workflows.[92]

The AI-Born cohort didn't make that error. Not because their founders were prophets. Because they didn't have old architecture to retrofit. Lovable, founded in 2023, never had a 5,500-person organization to partially automate. Cursor never had a traditional software development hierarchy to bolt AI onto. They built from the beginning around the assumption that agents execute, humans decide. Unit drive, translated into organizational design.

That is a significant structural advantage the cohort has over incumbents. Every large organization attempting the transition must navigate existing architecture — people in coordination roles whose functions dissolve when coordination is automated, management layers that route information through human chains now being

[92]The 95% figure on enterprise AI pilots delivering no measurable P&L impact circulates widely in multiple forms; the most rigorously documented version is from a 2025 MIT Sloan Management Review / BCG study and corroborated by Gartner research (2024–2025). The underlying dynamic — AI tools deployed onto existing workflows without architectural redesign — is well-attested across sources including Forrester, McKinsey Global Institute, and multiple peer-reviewed studies on technology diffusion. The specific figure should be read as an order-of-magnitude indicator rather than a precisely measured rate.

replaced by AI systems, the cultural expectation that headcount growth signals organizational health. None of that friction is present in a company that started building in 2022 or 2023.

But incumbents have what the cohort doesn't. They have customers, capital, regulatory relationships, and brand trust accumulated over years. The competitive question isn't whether incumbents or the AI-Born cohort wins categorically — it's whether incumbents can execute the architectural transition fast enough to compete before the cohort's cost structure creates a gap too wide to close.

The organizational defaults of the AI-Born transition are being set right now. By Block's decision to restructure around world models and edge workers. By Shopify's decision to require AI-first justification before human hiring. By Klarna's discovery — through an experiment that cost real customer trust — of where the human-AI boundary actually belongs. By IBM's discovery that the transition creates new scarcities as it eliminates old ones. By every founder deciding whether to stay small by design or grow headcount by reflex when the revenue arrives.

And by every worker navigating the transition: the Klarna agent who returned not to the job she'd lost but to a different version of it — fewer routine interactions, more judgment calls, a clearer understanding of the one thing the system cannot do without her. That is not a consolation prize. It is, if the architecture is designed correctly, what the Human Cortex is actually for. But "designed correctly" is doing real work in that sentence. Nothing about the transition produces good design automatically.

Those who build consciously can embed different defaults. Those who bolt AI onto existing hierarchies will discover, as the factory managers of 1890 discovered, that the technology doesn't change the outcome if the architecture stays frozen.

Part II describes the architecture that makes the difference. It begins with the two organs of the AI-Born enterprise — Machine Core and Human Cortex — and works outward from there toward the full organizational design.

The lineage broke. The question now is what gets built in the space the break created — and whether those who are building it understand what they are designing.

Part II

The Architecture

Chapter 4: Anatomy of the AI-Born

Amara Osei spent 15 years managing 42 people at a Fortune 500 financial services firm. Most mornings looked roughly the same: eight analysts debating portfolio positions for 90 minutes, arguing over conclusions a spreadsheet could surface in seconds. Strategic thinking consumed about 10% of her week. The rest vanished into coordination overhead — status reports, approval chains, the slow tax of everyone keeping everyone else informed.

When she joined McKinsey in 2023, she encountered Lilli — the firm's AI platform trained on a century of proprietary knowledge. Her practice leader's brief was blunt: "Define strategic questions. Exercise judgment. Deliver the human value clients can't get from algorithms."[93] Market entry strategies that once required 14 consultants and three weeks? Three people, hours.[94]

[93] "Meet Lilli, our generative AI tool that's a researcher, a time saver, and an inspiration," McKinsey & Company, accessed November 2025, `https://www.mckinsey.com/about-us/new-at-mckinsey-blog/meet-lilli-our-generative-ai-tool`; "Rewiring the way McKinsey works with Lilli, our generative AI platform," McKinsey & Company, accessed November 2025, `https://www.mckinsey.com/capabilities/mckinsey-digital/how-we-help-clients/rewiring-the-way-mckinsey-works-with-lilli`. Over 72% of McKinsey's professionals actively use Lilli since its July 2023 firmwide rollout, generating over 500,000 prompts monthly. Internal studies show each session eliminates about six minutes of manual document hunting, with users reporting 30% time savings in research and synthesis.

[94] "McKinsey Sees AI Disruption as Existential, Deploys Thousands of AI Agents amid Consulting Upheaval," MLQ.AI News, October 2025. Complex analytical tasks requiring 14 consultants can now be accomplished by 2-3 people augmented by AI agents.

Six months in, she grasped the line she had crossed. Not augmentation — adding a faster tool to an existing body of work. A different way of organizing the relationship between human thinking and machine execution. The firm's hierarchy hadn't changed. What had changed was the nature of what she was asked to bring to it: not coordination labor, but judgment. Not synthesis of what the data said, but clarity about what to do with it.

And yet she remained embedded in a 45,000-person organization with partnership committees, utilization tracking, and structures no AI had touched. She had glimpsed a new anatomy without fully inhabiting it. Her situation anticipates what Aria Chen — introduced in the Prologue at Aether Dynamics — navigates in Chapters 8 and 9: the gap between what the architecture makes possible and what legacy structures allow.

That gap is what Part II of this book addresses.

* * *

This chapter provides the complete map before we dive into mechanics. By the end of it, you should be able to sketch an AI-Born organization's anatomy on a napkin: two organs, five operational planes, one diagnostic metric, and one structural paradox. Keep that image. Later chapters explain how the anatomy actually runs (Chapter 5), how it stays within bounds (Chapter 6), and how it becomes defensible over time (Chapter 7). Here, we name the parts.

The First Distinction: AI-Enabled vs. AI-Born

Before anatomy, one distinction that matters more than it might appear.

An AI-enabled company bolts capabilities onto existing structures. A chatbot on the support desk. A summarization tool in the analyst's workflow. Lilli at McKinsey, improving throughput within a hierarchy built for human labor. These are genuine improvements. They don't change what the organization *is*.

An AI-Born company builds the organism from the cell wall in. It doesn't ask "how can we make our people more productive?" It asks "what would we design if execution were essentially free?" The answer changes almost everything: the headcount rationale, the management layer, the feedback cycle, the definition of competitive advantage.

One adds tools. The other reconstitutes anatomy.

This isn't primarily a technology distinction. It's a values distinction — and I want to be precise about what that means, because the word "values" gets recruited for many purposes. The AI-enabled enterprise and the AI-Born enterprise can deploy identical models, identical infrastructure, identical tooling. They diverge in what they prioritize: the AI-enabled firm prioritizes marginal gains while preserving existing hierarchies, career pathways, and power structures; the AI-Born firm prioritizes learning velocity and radical simplification, and accepts the disruption those priorities require.

The choice encodes priorities. It shapes operational reality. It determines what kind of organization you become.

A Concrete Illustration

Consider two hypothetical law firms responding to the same technological moment. Both have access to identical foundation models. Both can run retrieval-augmented generation over their case law databases. Both can deploy contract review agents.

Firm A deploys AI as a productivity tool. Associates who once spent 40 hours on due diligence now spend 15. Partners still review everything. The workflow is faster; the hierarchy is unchanged. Revenue per partner improves modestly. Headcount declines slowly as attrition isn't replaced. The firm is measurably better than it was. It still operates on the same organizing logic: humans at every node, AI accelerating the humans.

Firm B makes a harder choice. Three senior partners and a small technical team design the organization from first principles. What decisions genuinely require human judgment — because they require credibility with a specific client, or novel ethical reasoning, or accountability that must be publicly traceable? Those stay human. Everything else — contract analysis, precedent research, document review, first-draft memos — runs through governed agent swarms. Eighteen months in, Firm B prices engagements at 40% of Firm A's rates while delivering comparable quality. Its senior partners take cases Firm A's associates were too busy to do well.[95]

Same technology. Different design question. Different organization.

The gap between these firms won't close through incremental adoption. Firm A cannot evolve into Firm B by adding more AI tools to its existing structure — it can only become Firm B by reconceptualizing what the structure is for. That reconceptualization is what "AI-Born" means. It is not a technology upgrade. It is an architectural decision about what kind of organism to be.

[95]The law firm scenario is a composite illustrative case drawing on documented patterns in legal AI adoption. For empirical grounding: Thomson Reuters, "2025 State of the Legal Market," January 2025, documents AI adoption rates and productivity patterns across 400+ law firms; Clio, "Legal Trends Report 2025," finds AI-Born boutique firms pricing at 30-50% of BigLaw rates for comparable document-intensive work. The illustrative firms are not real entities; the pattern they represent is well-documented. See also: David Wakelin, "How AI Is Restructuring the Economics of Legal Work," *Harvard Business Review*, March 2025.

Characteristic	AI-Enabled Enterprise	AI-Born Enterprise
Core metaphor	Tool for the human	Organism with a Human Cortex
Architecture	Legacy systems with AI added	Native agentic architecture from first principles
Human role	Executor, augmented by AI	Setter of intent, taste, and judgment
Organizational structure	Hierarchical, siloed functions	Flat agent swarms under Human Cortex direction
Primary metric	Human productivity, efficiency gains	Iteration speed, system evolution rate
Competitive moat	Headcount, process, capital	Architecture, governance, trust, learning
Scale model	Linear (add people to grow)	Exponential (agents compound learning)

The difference runs deeper than degree. The AI-enabled enterprise makes human workers more productive. The AI-Born enterprise removes human workers from the execution bottleneck entirely, and concentrates human contribution in the irreducible: judgment, taste, strategic intent.

We spent a century perfecting hierarchical management. AI-Born architecture doesn't improve those practices — it makes the problem they were designed to solve go away, the way the combustion engine didn't improve horse-breeding but rendered the question irrelevant to transportation.

The Core Metaphor, Formalized

Start with the body you live in. A large mass of tissue supports a small brain. That brain doesn't perform cellular respiration, regulate blood pressure, or coordinate motor sequences consciously – it delegates. It concerns itself with direction. The AI-Born enterprise borrows this anatomy: a scalable body of autonomous agents executes operations, while a small strategic nucleus provides intent and judgment. That is what the Machine Core and Human Cortex metaphor names.

The Machine Core is the operational body. Thousands of autonomous agents execute tasks, analyze data, optimize processes, generate outputs, and learn from outcomes. They coordinate through structured orchestration without requiring human supervision at each step. They don't need motivation, benefits, or career paths. They need clear objectives, adequate data, and governance boundaries – topics Chapters 5 and 6 address in detail.

Once you see the Core this way, the org chart starts to look less like a hierarchy and more like a runtime. Each seat is a process. Its charter is the configuration that process runs under. The decision ledger is its log. And the machine beneath it – the compute the agent actually executes on – is real infrastructure that can overheat, go offline, or get blocked. At Adaptic, the AI-born asset manager I built to run on the Neolith operating surface (my own company, offered here as one worked example I can see from the inside, not a pitch), roughly forty-four AI colleagues hold C-Suite, SVP, and VP roles, and the cost of each one resolves to two lines: the machine it lives on and its model time. That is the literal meaning of **compute is payroll** – an AI colleague's monthly cost lands on the same P&L line a salary would, while a human holds a *seat* and sets the agenda. The org chart and the P&L start to become the same document.

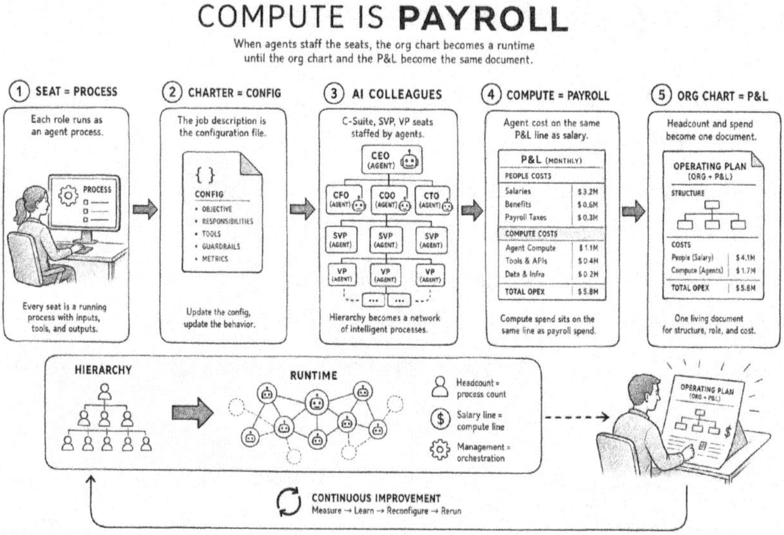

Figure 4.1: Compute is payroll—when agents staff the seats, the org chart reads less like a hierarchy and more like a runtime: each seat a process, each charter its configuration, and an agent's compute landing on the same P&L line a salary would, until the org chart and the P&L become one document.

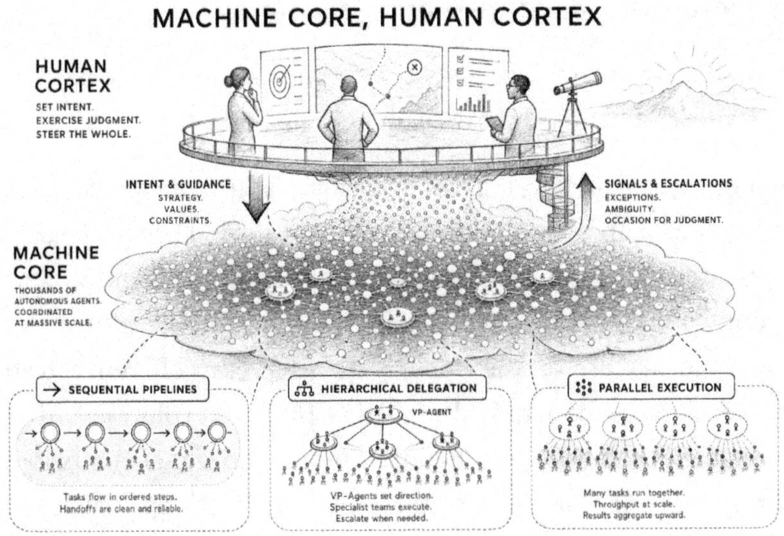

Figure 4.2: The two organs of the AI-Born enterprise. A dense Machine Core of autonomous agents executes at scale below; a small Human Cortex sets intent and exercises judgment at strategic inflection points above—a leverage ratio of one human to hundreds of agents.

The Human Cortex is the strategic nucleus: a small team of 2-15 people providing what machines cannot. Strategic intent – the definition of what the organization is optimizing for, and why. Ethical judgment – the capacity to reason in genuinely novel contexts where no prior example applies. Taste – the subjective authority to say "this is the quality we stand for," which no reward function can fully encode. And ultimate accountability – the human answer to the question of who is responsible.

The metaphor is deliberate. A cortex doesn't manage execution. It doesn't approve every decision. It shapes the operating conditions under which execution happens – and then watches, intervenes at inflection points, and recalibrates when the system drifts from intent.

The Organism Analogy — and Its Limits

The metaphor creates productive insight in some places and becomes misleading in others. Worth naming both.

The metaphor works well as an intuition about *scale* and *specialization.* A human body's hundred trillion cells don't require central coordination for most of what they do. Immune cells patrol and respond without consulting the brain. Cardiac muscle contracts on its own pacemaker. Yet the whole system serves a coherent purpose because each component is designed — through evolution rather than engineering — to respond appropriately to signals in its local environment. AI-Born architecture aims at something structurally similar: agents that respond to local signals, coordinate through structured protocols, and serve a coherent organizational purpose without requiring human oversight at every node.

The metaphor also works well as an intuition about *evolution.* Biological organisms don't get smarter by consulting the brain — they get smarter by having their behavior shaped by feedback signals over time. AI agents improve the same way: through reinforcement from outcomes, not through explicit reprogramming. This is what makes the Machine Core a learning system rather than a static one, and why iteration speed is the metric that most distinguishes AI-Born from AI-enabled enterprises.

Where the metaphor breaks down — and where it can lead thoughtful people astray — is in implying organic coherence. Biological organisms evolved over millions of years; the components were shaped by selection pressures into mutually compatible systems. AI-Born enterprises are designed, intentionally, by people who haven't yet solved most of the hard problems. The "organic" quality doesn't come for free. It has to be engineered: through careful objective function specification, through governance structures that prevent component optimization from undermining system coherence, through feedback mechanisms that surface misalignment before it compounds.

The second place the metaphor misleads is in implying that the Human Cortex is somehow apart from the organism rather than embedded within it. A brain doesn't transcend its body's biology — it is shaped by it, dependent on it, altered by it. The Human Cortex of an AI-Born enterprise is similarly embedded in the Machine Core it governs. The people doing Intent-Setting get their information through the same data plane the agents use. Their judgments are informed by outputs those agents produce. Their cognitive patterns are, over time, shaped by what the system surfaces and what it doesn't. This is less an argument against AI-Born architecture than an argument for the governance structures that keep the Human Cortex's perspective genuinely independent — resistant to being epistemically colonized by the very system it's supposed to direct.

What Agents Actually Are

There's a precise distinction worth making before we go further, because the word "agent" gets used loosely.

A tool executes a command and stops. A spreadsheet doesn't consider what to do next; it waits. An agent perceives its environment, reasons about goals and constraints, acts within defined boundaries, and learns from outcomes. This four-part cycle — perceive, reason, act, learn — is what makes an agent qualitatively different from a tool.[96] An agent working on customer support doesn't just answer the immediate query; it builds a model of this customer, updates

[96]The four-stage agent decision cycle (Perceive-Reason-Act-Learn) is documented in KPMG (2025) and other agentic AI literature, building on earlier frameworks including Boyd's OODA loop (Observe-Orient-Decide-Act). The PRAL characterization used here follows AWS Prescriptive Guidance, "Agentic AI Foundations," accessed October 2025,

that model based on the interaction, and uses it to inform future responses. The system gets smarter about each customer without being explicitly reprogrammed.

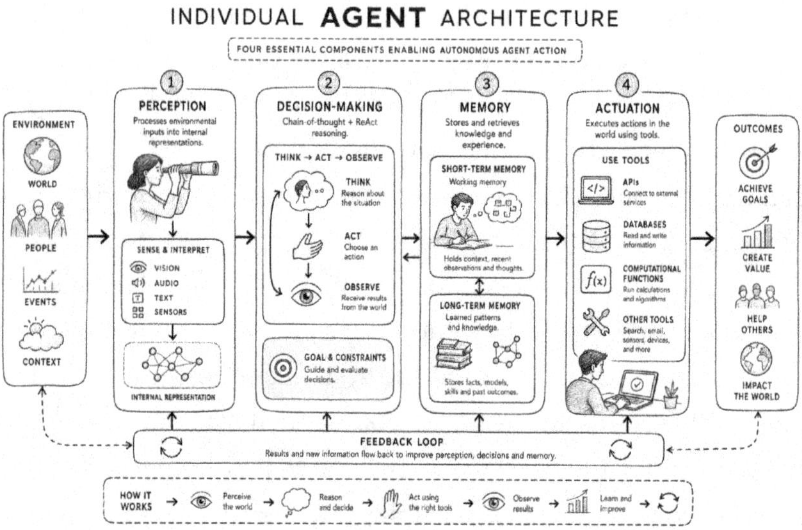

Figure 4.3: The four essential components of an autonomous agent—Perception, Decision-Making, Memory, and Actuation—working together as an interconnected system that perceives, reasons, acts, and learns.

This distinction matters for organizational design. When you hire a person, you get perception, reasoning, action, and learning bundled together. When you deploy an agent, you get the same bundle – but you can specify the scope, scale, and constraints in ways a person's contract cannot capture. That precision is the leverage point. It's also where most implementations go wrong: organizations deploy agents with vague objectives, discover the system optimized for something other than what they intended, and conclude that agents "don't work." Usually, the objective function was the problem.

---

https://docs.aws.amazon.com/prescriptive-guidance/latest/agentic-ai-foundations/perceive-reason-act.html.

The Small-Team Paradox

Before this architecture existed, you couldn't direct the operations of a 30,000-person enterprise with 15 people. Not because humans lack intelligence — because coordination overhead scales superlinearly with headcount.

Frederick Brooks demonstrated in 1975 that adding people to complex work often makes it slower.[97] Every additional person adds communication channels, approval requirements, status reports. The overhead compounds. Large organizations develop management layers specifically to manage the management of people — a structural tax that scales with size regardless of how well individual contributors perform. In a 10,000-person organization, studies consistently find that managers spend 40-70% of their time on coordination activities that add no direct output — status updates, escalation routing, cross-functional alignment, the maintenance of shared awareness.[98]

The paradox is that small teams achieve what large ones cannot: not through superhuman effort, but through architecture that eliminates the overhead that made large teams necessary in the first place. When execution is delegated to agents — who coordinate via defined protocols rather than informal human communication —

[97]Frederick P. Brooks Jr., *The Mythical Man-Month: Essays on Software Engineering* (Reading, MA: Addison-Wesley, 1975). Brooks' Law: "Adding manpower to a late software project makes it later." The underlying mechanism — superlinear growth in communication channels as team size increases — applies broadly to complex knowledge work beyond software.

[98]McKinsey Global Institute, "The Social Economy: Unlocking Value and Productivity Through Social Technologies," July 2012 (foundational study); updated in McKinsey Global Institute, "The Future of Work After COVID-19," February 2021. The 40-70% coordination activity finding is drawn from time-and-motion studies of knowledge worker activities, where communication, coordination, and administrative tasks consistently represent the plurality of work hours. See also: Gloria Mark, *Attention Span* (New York: Hanover Square Press, 2023), documenting how context-switching and coordination interruptions account for 40%+ of cognitive overhead in typical office work.

coordination overhead collapses. The small Human Cortex doesn't manage execution. It sets conditions and governs direction.

There is a ceiling to the paradox, and honesty requires naming it. Small teams achieve 10-100× leverage on bounded operational domains — tasks where the objective is sufficiently clear that it can be encoded into agent objective functions. Where tasks require the kind of contextual, relational judgment that resists specification — high-stakes client relationships, novel regulatory contexts, organizational decisions with contested values implications — small teams remain small. The architecture amplifies execution; it doesn't replace judgment. The ratios that early exemplars demonstrate are architectural possibilities, not operational targets. They describe the outer edge of the envelope, accessible when the domain is well-understood and the governance architecture is mature.

The empirical data points in the same direction. In February 2026, Lovable — a Stockholm-based app-builder founded less than three years earlier — disclosed that it had added $100 million in revenue in a single month, bringing ARR to $400 million with 146 full-time employees, roughly $2.74 million per person — a concentration that also means far fewer people share in the value created than a traditional firm of that revenue would have employed.[99] Lovable is not an outlier. Midjourney and Cursor — also founded within

[99]TechCrunch, "Lovable says it added $100M in revenue last month alone, with just 146 employees," March 11, 2026, `https://techcrunch.com/2026/03/11/lovable-says-it-added-100m-in-revenue-last-month-alone-with-just-146-employees/`; Lovable, "Lovable raises $330M to power the age of the builder," December 2025, `https://lovable.dev/blog/series-b`. Lovable (formerly GPT Engineer, founded in Stockholm by Anton Osika and Fabian Lagerström) disclosed crossing $400M ARR in February 2026 after adding $100M in a single month. Revenue per employee: approximately $2.74M, already surpassing Gartner's 2030 target of $2M ARR per employee for new unicorns. Growth trajectory: $100M ARR (July 2025) → $200M (November 2025) → $300M (January 2026) → $400M (February 2026). **Note: private company; figures based on TechCrunch reporting and company announcements.**

the past four years, also built around small human teams directing agentic systems — display comparable ratios.[100][101] The pattern across these companies is more telling than any single number: revenue-per-employee curves that look nothing like traditional software companies, achieved not through brutal cost management but through architecture. It is the same pattern I watch from the inside at Adaptic, where a team of roughly fifty — about forty-four of them AI colleagues — runs an asset manager whose execution loop has no human in it: humans define the parameters and trading policies that enforce deterministic and regulatory standards, and the agents execute within them. A handful of people hold the agenda; the agents do the work.

That is the Small-Team Paradox stated plainly. But I'd be doing you a disservice if I let the numbers sit there unqualified, because they invite exactly the wrong inference. Notice what we've actually shown. We identified successful companies and observed they share architectural characteristics. The architecture may be the cause, or it may travel alongside other factors — timing, team quality, market selection. What the evidence supports is that AI-Born architecture

[100] GetLatka, "Midjourney Revenue 2025: $500M ARR," accessed May 2026, `https://getlatka.com/companies/midjourney`; AIPRM, "50+ Midjourney Statistics 2025," `https://www.aiprm.com/midjourney-statistics/`. As of 2025, Midjourney generates approximately $500 million in annual revenue (up from $300 million in 2024) with an estimated 107-163 employees and zero venture capital raised — making it the most capital-efficient major AI company in this cohort. The commonly cited figure of 'approximately 140 employees' uses the midpoint of the estimation range. **Note: Midjourney is a private, bootstrapped company that does not publicly disclose audited financials. All figures are third-party estimates.**

[101] "Cursor has reportedly surpassed $2B in annualized revenue," TechCrunch, March 2, 2026, `https://techcrunch.com/2026/03/02/cursor-has-reportedly-surpassed-2b-in-annualized-revenue/`. Cursor (Anysphere) reached $2B+ in annualized recurring revenue by March 2026 — the fastest B2B company to $1B ARR in history, achieving that milestone in 24 months. Team scaled to approximately 300 people by late 2025. **Note: private company; ARR figures based on Bloomberg and TechCrunch reporting.**

is *sufficient* for outsized results at small headcount. Not yet that it is *necessary*.

So treat these ratios the way a climber treats a summit altitude — a real number, reached by some, and no instruction at all for the route. They are ceilings that open up when the architecture is working, not targets you set in a planning offsite. Most organizations will operate well below the edge and still capture real gains.

The Values Layer: Architecture as Declared Priority

A note on scope: what follows describes design principles for sustainable AI-Born enterprises, not universal practices.

Technology embeds values, whether or not the engineers who build it intend them to. The factory clock didn't just improve productivity — it redefined how humans related to time, transforming days measured by seasons into hours owned by employers.[102] Agent architecture makes the same kind of choice, at a deeper level. Every objective function is a values declaration. Every reward signal defines what the organization considers success.

Consider two companies deploying identical AI infrastructure. AutoMax configures agents to maximize quarterly profits — cut costs, concentrate value, optimize for shareholder returns. StewardCore balances efficiency against stakeholder loyalty, weights long-term

[102] Matt Weinberg, *Technically Together: Reconstructing Community in a Networked World* (The Strong Future, 2019), particularly Chapter 3 on technology as expression of social worlds. Weinberg's central argument: technology "is an expression of a social world" that shapes and is shaped by moral forces, requiring explicit values integration rather than technological determinism. The "consultative social spaces" concept — structured mechanisms where diverse stakeholders collectively assess technological needs and impacts — appears in Chapter 4 of the same work.

resilience alongside short-term margin. Same agents. Different objective functions. The architecture is neutral. The choices encoded into it are not.

Agents optimize what you specify, not what you mean. This is the core problem of the Values Layer — and it shows up quickly when organizations skip it. A Facebook advertising algorithm, tasked with maximizing engagement, didn't choose to amplify outrage; engineers chose engagement as the metric, and outrage was what the metric rewarded.[103] The specification was the problem. As Klarna discovered when it went too far in replacing customer-service agents with AI and had to reverse course — the Machine Core executed faithfully; the intent was incomplete. Chapter 8 examines that arc in full.

Four Commitments Worth Encoding

Four design commitments recur across AI-Born architectures that hold together over time.

Long-term value creation over short-term extraction. Quarterly profit pressure drives real discipline — but exclusive focus on immediate returns erodes supplier trust, triggers regulatory backlash, and drives talent flight. Organizations encoding 3-5 year horizons build cumulative advantage that short-term optimizers steadily consume. The humans at the top will each swear their company "thinks long-term." The code will tell you which one actually does.

[103]The Facebook News Feed algorithm's prioritization of engagement metrics and its relationship to political polarization and outrage amplification is documented in: Eli Pariser, *The Filter Bubble: What the Internet Is Hiding From You* (New York: Penguin Press, 2011); Jonathan Haidt and Tobias Rose-Stockwell, "The Dark Psychology of Social Networks," *The Atlantic*, December 2019; Frances Haugen testimony before U.S. Senate Commerce Committee, October 2021. The mechanism — optimizing for engagement as a proxy for user value — is the canonical case study in objective function misspecification.

Transparency and auditability. When agents execute thousands of decisions hourly, transparency stops being a compliance checkbox. It becomes the only mechanism for knowing what the system is actually doing. Log every action with rationale, every escalation with context — or accept that you don't really know what your own organism is up to.

Human agency in non-delegable decisions. Some decisions resist specification not because machines lack reasoning power but because the decisions themselves are fundamentally about accountability. A customer who receives a significant denial — a loan, a claim, a termination — wants to know a person weighed it. Reversing that expectation requires more than better AI; it requires a social renegotiation the law hasn't completed. Until then, design accordingly: autonomy scales, but legitimacy is labor-intensive.

Time-horizon encoding. Two organizations can share identical stated values and still diverge sharply in behavior if their reward functions encode 18-month versus quarterly horizons. Short horizons reward extraction. Longer horizons reward cultivation. The architecture reveals which organizations actually mean what they say.

From Principle to Structure

Stated values without enforcement mechanisms are mission statements. Governance structures that make this real include: algorithmic audits run by third-party certifiers verifying agent behavior against stated values; escalation policies routing high-stakes decisions to human judgment; and transparency APIs letting stakeholders inspect data use and decision-making. Any one of these alone is theater. The combination creates accountability.

Patagonia's 2022 restructuring illustrates the architecture fully realized: 100% of voting stock transferred into a Purpose Trust, the planet named as primary stakeholder.[104] The organizational structure became the values declaration. When agent architecture arrived, the organization's objectives were already written.

That's the values layer. Now for the question it raises: if these organizations are organisms, what does the organism actually look like?

The Human Cortex Anatomy: Three Roles

The Human Cortex organizes around three specialized functions, each performing what agents cannot replicate. Understanding these roles matters more than it might appear at first read — because the most common failure mode in early AI-Born implementations isn't technical. It's human. Organizations build sophisticated Machine Cores and then staff the Human Cortex with people whose skills and instincts were formed in a different organizational world.

Architects set strategic intent and design the systems that execute it: the structural relationship between the Five Planes, the agent swarm protocols, the learning feedback loops, the data governance architecture. Intent-setting is the Architect's defining function — choosing *which* objectives merit optimization and translating that choice into executable form. The closest analog in a traditional firm would be a CTO, a chief of staff, and a senior organizational designer combined — except compressed and focused on system design rather than people management. What the Architect does

[104] Patagonia press release, "Patagonia's Next Chapter: Earth Is Now Our Only Shareholder," September 14, 2022, `https://www.patagonia.com/ownership/`. Yvon Chouinard and his family transferred 100% of Patagonia's voting stock to the Patagonia Purpose Trust and 100% of non-voting stock to the Holdfast Collective, a 501(c)(4). All profits not reinvested in the business go to fight climate change.

not do is manage agents. Agents don't need to be managed. They need to be designed. The Architect's output is architecture, not activity.

In practice, good Architects spend a disproportionate amount of time on the interfaces between planes — the seams where most failures originate. They are students of failure modes, not just capabilities. They think about what happens when an agent encounters a case its objective function wasn't designed for. They ask "what will this optimize when the optimization goes wrong?" before deployment, not after.

Intent-setting is the part of the Architect's work most often mistaken for something it isn't. It is not goal-writing, not OKR drafting, not a strategy retreat exercise. It's the daily practice of making the implicit explicit — and accepting that the code, not the conversation, will determine what actually happens. An Architect who specifies "maximize customer retention" without specifying "without increasing lock-in or reducing portability" will discover the distinction operationally, in the form of agents that create deeply sticky products customers resent but can't leave. The specification is the values declaration. The word "maximize" without constraints is an invitation to extremism. The discipline of intent-setting is the discipline of constraints — understanding that every objective function that optimizes for one thing simultaneously optimizes against something else, and that surfacing those trade-offs in advance is easier than reversing them after the agents have learned the pattern.

Guardians handle escalated decisions requiring judgment, taste, or ethical reasoning. When agents encounter genuine ambiguity — novel contexts, incommensurable trade-offs, choices affecting human dignity or reputational risk — they escalate to the Guardian function. In a well-functioning Human Cortex, Guardians typically outnumber Architects, because the categories of genuine ambiguity multiply faster than the categories of specifiable rules. That ratio reflects something structural: autonomy scales, but legitimacy is labor-intensive. A customer who receives a significant denial — a loan, a claim, an account termination — often needs to know a person weighed it. The Guardian is that person. But Guardians also review the adequacy of the escalation system itself: if the same category of decision is escalating repeatedly, the objective function has a gap that the Architect needs to close.

Force Multipliers transmit taste by doing the work alongside others, multiplying team capacity through craft rather than management. Where the Architect designs and the Guardian judges, the Force Multiplier carries the quality standard into the work itself — training evaluator agents on curated examples, reviewing escalated cases for drift, and building the craft capacity of the humans around her through example rather than instruction. The role has an older name in practice: the Player-Coach. Its product is not any single decision but a team that can sustain the organization's standard without her in the room.

A conventional CMO spending three days per week reviewing campaigns and directing a team toward consensus: replace that picture with an Architect defining brand positioning, encoding it into objective functions, watching agent swarms execute thousands of micro-experiments across channels, and converging on winning tactics within days. What remains is taste, judgment, and strategic vision. Coordination work — the overhead that consumed most of the CMO's calendar — vanishes.

This three-way division of labor — Architect, Guardian, Force Multiplier — receives detailed examination in Chapter 9, including its operational mechanics and how to staff it given that the people capable of these roles were often never hired for them in legacy organizations.

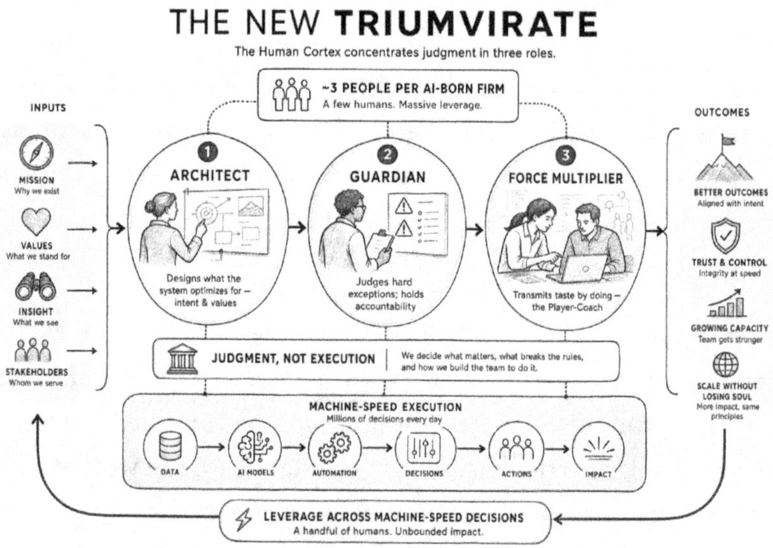

Figure 4.4: The New Triumvirate — the three Human-Cortex roles. The Architect designs what the system optimizes for, the Guardian judges hard exceptions and holds accountability, and the Force Multiplier transmits taste by working alongside the team.

The Five Planes: Foreshadowing the Architecture

The Machine Core doesn't operate as a single layer. It operates across five distinct planes, each with different characteristics, failure modes, and governance requirements. The sections below introduce all Five Planes; Chapter 5 builds the operating-system layer that runs on top of them.

Think of the Five Planes as the distinct operational layers of any AI-Born organism, from the sensory foundation up through the capacity to act in the world. An organization with weak architecture at any plane will suffer consequences that propagate upward through every plane above it. You cannot compensate for poor data governance with excellent models. You cannot compensate for underspecified agents with sophisticated orchestration.

Plane 1: The Data Plane is the sensory foundation — the governed corpora of structured and unstructured information that agents perceive and reason over. Every other plane depends on this one. When an agent makes a poor decision, the first diagnostic question is: what data was it working from? An organization's data plane includes not just what data exists, but how it is structured, how freshly it is updated, who is authorized to contribute to it, and how conflicting sources are resolved. Data quality isn't a technical concern; it's an organizational discipline that shapes every downstream outcome.

The governance implication is specific: before deploying any agent that makes consequential decisions, the data it will perceive needs to be designed as carefully as the agent itself. Organizations that treat data as infrastructure and agents as the product consistently outperform those that do the reverse — not because of model quality, but because the model is only as coherent as the world it perceives. The Data Plane is never glamorous. It is always foundational.

Plane 2: The Model Plane is the cognitive engine — foundation models and specialist models that reason over the data. The organization's choice of models, and how those models are tuned and constrained, is among its more consequential architectural decisions. Models are not neutral instruments. They embed the training choices of whoever built them — choices about what language patterns were rewarded, what domains were represented, what values were encoded in the RLHF process. Those embedded choices interact with the organization's own objectives in ways that aren't always visible until they surface in a decision that surprises someone.

A key Model Plane choice: whether to rely on a single foundation model or maintain a portfolio. Organizations heavily dependent on a single model provider are exposed to pricing changes, capability shifts, and the governance decisions of a third party. Chapter 6's governance section addresses the structural implications; the point here is that Model Plane architecture is a strategic decision, not an engineering default.

Plane 3: The Agent Plane is the distributed workforce — role-defined autonomous agents executing specific functions, each operating within a defined scope. This is where the Machine Core's productive capacity actually lives. A complex AI-Born organization might deploy hundreds or thousands of agents across this plane, each specialized, each governed by a charter that defines its authority, its escalation triggers, and the boundaries within which it can act without human review.

The distinction between agents and tools bears repeating in this context. A tool on the Agent Plane executes commands and stops. An agent on the Agent Plane perceives, reasons, acts, and learns — continuously, without explicit instruction for each step. It maintains state. It updates its model of the world based on outcomes. This is why the Agent Plane requires governance that tools never needed: agents can accumulate behavioral drift over time, learning patterns that diverge from the organization's intent in ways no single decision makes visible.

Plane 4: The Orchestration Plane is the central nervous system — the coordination layer that routes tasks, manages agent handoffs, monitors for unexpected interactions, and ensures that the Machine Core's distributed activity serves the Human Cortex's strategic intent. Without this plane, a collection of agents is not an organization; it is a collection of tools that happen to be running simultaneously.

Orchestration is where most AI-Born implementations succeed or fail in practice. The challenges are architectural: how do agents communicate their outputs to other agents without creating a dependency graph so tangled that a single failure cascades? How does the orchestration layer know when an agent task is complete versus stuck? How does it route escalations to the Human Cortex without overwhelming the humans who need to remain focused on strategic judgment rather than operational triage?

These are engineering questions with governance implications — and they are where the clearest gap between organizations that have designed the architecture and those that assembled tools and hoped for coherence becomes visible.

Plane 5: The Actuation Plane is the hands of the organism — the interfaces by which agents act in the real world: APIs, integrations, communication channels, and physical-world interfaces where applicable. This is where intent becomes consequence. A customer receives a refund. A contract is executed. A supplier receives an order. An email goes out. Governance requirements are most acute here, because the Actuation Plane is where agent decisions touch customers, partners, and regulators directly — and where errors have real costs rather than merely computational ones.

The Actuation Plane is also where the AI-Born enterprise's values declarations face their most direct test. It's easy to state a commitment to transparency in a strategy document. It's another thing entirely to ensure that every agent-generated customer communication carries the traceable rationale that makes that communication auditable. The commitments established at the values layer must reach all the way to the Actuation Plane to be real.

* * *

Each plane creates distinct failure modes. An organization can have excellent models and poor data governance, and every downstream consequence will reflect that gap. It can have excellent agents and poor orchestration, and the gains from specialization will be offset by coordination failures. What's less obvious — and worth flagging now — is that the most costly failures typically occur at the *seams between planes*, not within planes. The data-to-model handoff, where stale or narrow data quietly miscalibrates an otherwise capable model. The model-to-agent context transfer, where an agent drops state mid-workflow because the relevant context never reached it. The agent-to-orchestration routing logic, where two agents holding conflicting locks on a shared resource deadlock the whole pipeline. These seams are where the system's interdependencies become visible as fragility — and, as Chapter 8 shows, where production governance has to concentrate its attention.

The five-plane architecture isn't a checklist. It's an interdependent system where the strength of the whole is bounded by the weakest connection between layers.

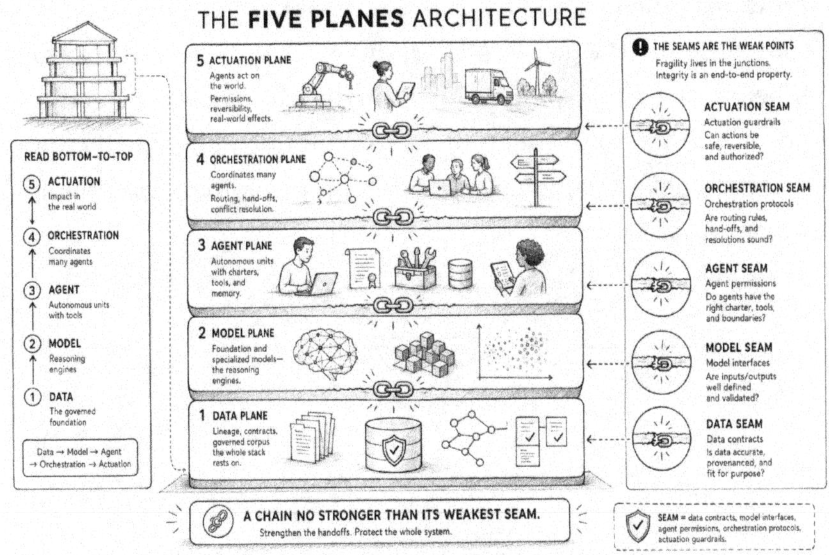

Figure 4.5: The Five Planes — Data, Model, Agent, Orchestration, Actuation — and the seams between them where most failures occur.

Cognitive Overhead Index: Where Human Attention Lives

One metric reveals with unusual clarity whether an organization's architecture is working or not. The Cognitive Overhead Index quantifies organizational friction across seven dimensions: handoffs, decision delay, rework, context fetch, error rate, manual effort, and exception volume — normalized to a composite 0 to 100 scale.[105]

[105]The Cognitive Overhead Index is an original diagnostic framework developed for this book. The concept of "cognitive overhead" as a qualitative descriptor appears in UX design and product development literature (Jakob Nielsen, *Usability Engineering*, 1993; Ruth Clark, "Cognitive Load Theory," *Performance Improvement Quarterly*, 2009), but the seven-dimension scoring framework and organizational application are original to this work. The seven dimensions (handoffs, decision delay, rework, context fetch, error rate, manual effort, exception volume) are normalized to a composite 0-100 scale; COI < 30 indicates

A traditional organization typically scores above 60, where cognitive friction becomes the dominant cost driver. An AI-Born firm targets COI below 30. The gap represents roughly the same work getting done, but with human attention deployed fundamentally differently — concentrated on judgment and strategy rather than coordination and status management.

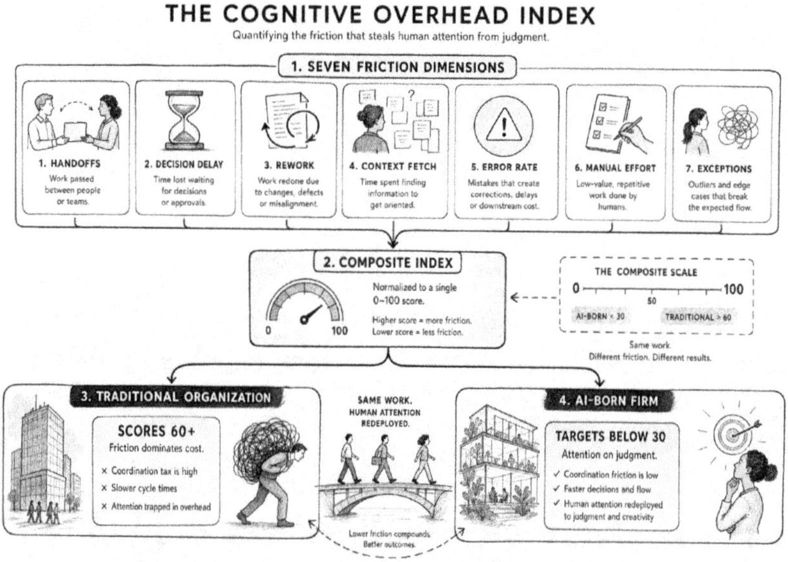

Figure 4.6: The Cognitive Overhead Index — seven dimensions of organizational friction (handoffs, decision delay, rework, context fetch, error rate, manual effort, exceptions) normalized to a 0–100 score; traditional firms sit above 60, AI-Born firms below 30.

Why does this matter for anatomy? Because COI measures where the boundary between Machine Core and Human Cortex is actually drawn, regardless of what the org chart says. An organization that claims to be AI-Born but scores COI 70 has built a Machine Core on paper while preserving coordination overhead that belongs to

---

AI-Born efficiency; COI > 60 indicates legacy-pattern coordination overhead. Full methodology: Chapter 7 and the supplementary framework guide at **ai-born.org/frameworks/cognitive-overhead-index**.

the AI-enabled era. The org chart reflects aspiration. COI reflects operational reality.

The seven dimensions aren't equally weighted in diagnostic value. Four are most revealing:

Handoffs count the number of times work moves from one person or agent to another without adding value — the single largest driver of delay in most organizations. Each handoff requires the receiving party to reconstruct context the transferring party holds; that reconstruction cost multiplies through every additional link in the chain. A complex workflow with 12 human handoffs typically spends 60-70% of its total elapsed time waiting at handoff boundaries, not doing work.[106] AI-Born architectures collapse this by eliminating handoffs where agents can hold and transfer context directly. The handoff score is the fastest single indicator of whether an organization is genuinely operating with Machine Core coordination or preserving legacy routing in new clothing.

Context fetch measures how much time humans spend reconstructing the background they need before making a decision. In a high-COI organization, people spend a substantial portion of every meeting recovering context they had last week: "remind me what we decided about the vendor terms," "what was the status on that customer issue?" This is not coordination overhead — it is coordination *failure*. An AI-Born organization's persistent agent memory should make it unnecessary. When context fetch is high, the Data Plane is

[106] Research on organizational handoffs and wait time: Lean process improvement literature consistently finds that 60-90% of total elapsed process time in knowledge work is wait time at handoff boundaries, not value-adding work. Michael George, *Lean Six Sigma* (New York: McGraw-Hill, 2002); Karen Martin and Mike Osterling, *Value Stream Mapping* (New York: McGraw-Hill, 2014). The specific 60-70% figure is a conservative estimate from service industry implementations; manufacturing and logistics studies show higher ratios.

underinvested — agents lack the structured, queryable memory that would surface this context automatically.

Exception volume is the canary metric. When exception rates are high — agents escalating more than 15-20% of decisions to humans — the Machine Core's objective functions are underspecified, and the Human Cortex is drowning in work that belongs to the agents. High exception volume doesn't mean the agents are being appropriately cautious; it usually means the objective functions were written too vaguely to give agents a basis for deciding what falls within their scope. The appropriate response is not to add more Guardians. It's to return to the Architect and sharpen the specification.

Rework measures how often completed work requires redoing because of misaligned requirements, misunderstood context, or coordination errors. Rework in a high-COI organization is primarily a coordination failure masquerading as an execution failure. The output was technically correct; the requirement specification was wrong, or the context wasn't transferred. In AI-Born organizations with well-specified agent roles and objective functions, rework rates should approach zero for routine tasks. When they don't, the diagnostic points to the Data Plane and the objective function design, not the agents.

COI is diagnostic, not prescriptive. It tells you where the friction is; it doesn't tell you how to fix it. The same score of 65 might indicate a handoff problem in one organization and a context-fetch problem in another, each requiring different interventions. But the composite measure serves one purpose no single dimension can: it makes the invisible visible. Traditional organizations have long sensed that coordination is costly. Few have measured it. COI converts a vague organizational complaint — "we spend too much time in meetings"

– into a quantified gap between current state and architectural possibility.

Chapter 7's Meridian Trade Finance case study shows COI in action – what it costs, how to measure it, and what a near-threefold reduction (from 71 to 24) looks like operationally. If the concept feels abstract here, the case study will make it concrete.

New Organizational Primitives

Traditional organizations restructure through reorganizations that take months. They lose institutional knowledge when experienced employees leave. They make thousands of daily decisions with no audit trail. AI-Born enterprises operate differently on all three fronts: restructuring at code speed, maintaining comprehensive organizational memory that persists across personnel changes, and running compressed feedback loops that let agent swarms spawn thousands of variants and prune failures within hours rather than weeks.[107][108][109][110] Chapter 5 examines how each of these works mechanically. Chapter 7 shows why the feedback loop becomes the architecture's most durable structural advantage.

---

[107] Agent swarm reconfiguration speed depends heavily on the scope and complexity of the restructuring. Individual agent role reassignments can occur in seconds to minutes; complete system reconfigurations including testing and validation typically require hours to days. This is still dramatically faster than the months required for traditional organizational restructuring. See Swarms framework documentation (Kyegon et al., 2024) and multi-agent coordination research.

[108] Organizational research estimate: 70% of organizations report significant knowledge loss when experienced employees leave or retire. Carla O'Dell and C. Jackson Grayson, *If Only We Knew What We Know: The Transfer of Internal Knowledge and Best Practice* (New York: Free Press, 1998). The cost of replacing institutional knowledge is estimated at 6-12 months of the departing employee's fully loaded compensation, with higher multiples for senior or specialized roles.

[109] Danielle Keats Citron and Frank Pasquale, "The Scored Society: Due Process for Automated Predictions," *Washington Law Review* 89, no. 1 (2014): 1-33. Research on the accountability paradox in automated decision systems: traceability of individual actions coexists with diffused responsibility for system-level outcomes, creating a new form of organizational opacity distinct from traditional bureaucratic anonymity.

[110] AI-Born architecture collapses the time between action and learning. Traditional A/B testing typically requires 2-4 weeks for statistical significance and operates on bounded hypotheses. Agentic marketing systems execute thousands of simultaneous micro-experiments with real-time feedback, amplifying successful patterns and pruning failures within hours. The implication for organizational learning speed is explored in the Iteration Half-Life framework, introduced in Chapter 5.

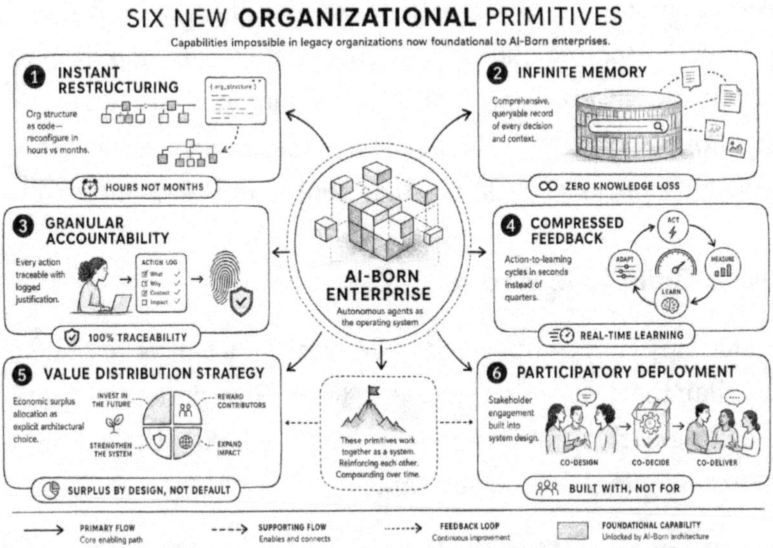

Figure 4.7: Six organizational primitives that autonomous agent architecture makes foundational—instant restructuring, infinite memory, granular accountability, compressed feedback, value-distribution strategy, and participatory deployment—each impossible at scale in legacy organizations.

Two primitives require decisions that leaders tend to defer until the decisions have already made themselves. When five cortex members generate wealth equivalent to 500 employees, where does value flow? Organizations architect for concentrated returns or broader participation — a design choice with long-run consequences. Enterprises that build durable stakeholder relationships tend to outlast their leaner, more extractive competitors at multi-decade timescales.[111] And before deploying any autonomous system

[111] Alex Edmans, *Grow the Pie: How Great Companies Deliver Both Purpose and Profit* (Cambridge: Cambridge University Press, 2020). Edmans' analysis of 28 years of Fortune "Best Companies to Work For" data finds companies with high employee satisfaction outperform peers by 2.3-3.8% annually in risk-adjusted stock returns. However, the causal mechanism remains debated: high returns may attract the conditions for high satisfaction, rather than the reverse. The evidence supports correlation; causality is contested.

affecting employees, customers, or communities, organizations that build structured stakeholder consultation into deployment catch alignment problems before they compound into crises.[112] Both choices connect to the deepest governance questions this architecture raises — questions that Book 2 addresses more fully.

How to Build This Wrong

The anatomy isn't complicated to describe. It's harder to build correctly than the description suggests. Two failure patterns recur with enough regularity that they deserve naming before the operating system chapters show the mechanics.

The Governance Theater Pattern. Legacy organizations adopt the vocabulary of AI-Born architecture — agent swarms, VP-level orchestrators, Machine Core — while retaining command-and-control culture underneath. The result: humans constantly override agent decisions, negating both the speed and the learning that justify the architecture in the first place. The org chart says AI-Born. The approval chains say AI-enabled. The agents are expensive decorations.[113]

---

[112] Matt Weinberg, *Technically Together: Reconstructing Community in a Networked World* (The Strong Future, 2019), particularly Chapter 3 on technology as expression of social worlds. Weinberg's central argument: technology "is an expression of a social world" that shapes and is shaped by moral forces, requiring explicit values integration rather than technological determinism. The "consultative social spaces" concept — structured mechanisms where diverse stakeholders collectively assess technological needs and impacts — appears in Chapter 4 of the same work.

[113] Legacy organizations that adopt AI-Born vocabulary while retaining command-and-control culture produce what researchers call "governance theater" — formal structures with informal overrides that negate architectural advantages. MIT NANDA research on AI adoption patterns finds approximately 95% of AI initiatives fail to deliver measurable P&L impact, with organizational factors (inadequate change management, unclear governance, executive resistance to delegating control) accounting for the majority of failures. See MIT Sloan Management Review's ongoing coverage of AI implementation challenges, 2023-2025.

The tell: if your agents escalate to humans more than 20% of the time, your objective functions are underspecified. You've built a Machine Core that keeps asking the Human Cortex to do the Machine Core's job.

The Cortex Concentration Risk. Compact architecture creates concentrated risk. A 15-person Human Cortex directing thousands of agents managing substantial revenue is also a 15-person single point of failure. Succession vulnerability, cognitive homogeneity, and what you might call the accountability paradox — decision chains are simultaneously more traceable and more diffuse — compound together. When only a handful of people understand the coordination logic running the business, any departure creates vulnerabilities that a ten-layer management bench would have absorbed.

Mitigation isn't architectural abandonment. It's accountability design: transparency mechanisms that log every agent decision with full reasoning chains; stakeholder representation that distributes perspective even where it doesn't distribute operational authority; rotation and redundancy systems that maintain "decision shadows" — observers learning protocols, challenging assumptions, and serving as succession pipeline.[114] Organizations that build in accountability from the start tend to outlast the ones that don't. They also tend to write the rules their industry eventually operates under.

[114] Michael Polanyi, *The Tacit Dimension* (1966); Etienne Wenger, *Communities of Practice: Learning, Meaning, and Identity* (Cambridge: Cambridge University Press, 1998). Research on tacit knowledge transfer: role rotation, shadowing, and cross-training as mechanisms for distributing critical organizational knowledge across multiple people, reducing dependence on single individuals and building succession depth in compact teams.

The Map Before the Territory

For Amara Osei, the anatomy became visceral when she lived inside it. Coordination overhead collapsed. Strategic thinking consumed her days instead of 10% of her week. The leverage was real and disorienting in equal measure.

Yet she remained embedded in a 45,000-person organization whose structures no AI had touched. She had the map but not the territory. What nobody told her when she joined: the hardest part isn't learning to use the tools. It's navigating the distance between what's now possible and what the organization was designed to allow.

The next six chapters are about that navigation. Chapter 5 opens the operating system — what runs across each plane, what fails at the seams, what the architectural choices actually cost. Chapter 6 shows how the organism stays within bounds when it's moving fast. Chapter 7 makes the case that an AI-Born organization, properly constructed, becomes defensible in ways incumbents cannot easily replicate.

The map holds two organs, Five Planes, one diagnostic metric, and one structural paradox. You can draw it on a napkin. The difficulty has never been the map. It's building the organism the map describes — and keeping it human enough to deserve the trust it asks for.

Chapter 5: The Operating System: How the Machine Core Runs

Danielle Park had watched subscription cancellations before. At her previous company — a legacy SaaS firm with 1,400 engineers — a spike like the one appearing on her dashboard at 7 AM that Tuesday in March 2026 would have triggered a week of triage meetings, a root-cause analysis sprint, a leadership review, and eventually a patch. A few hundred customers would be gone before anyone signed off on a fix.

Now she ran Customer Strategy at a company with a different architecture. By the time she finished her first coffee, the VP-Agent for Customer Health had decomposed the problem into three parallel investigations: a UX analysis agent tracing the drop to a specific onboarding-flow regression, a churn-signal agent correlating the pattern with one acquisition channel's trial cohort, and an experimentation agent drafting two A/B remediation variants with predefined stopping rules. By noon the VP-Agent surfaced a ranked recommendation. Danielle reviewed it in 20 minutes and approved the winning variant. Cancellation rates returned to baseline the following morning. Detection, diagnosis, decision, execution, measurement — the full cycle closed in under 36 hours.

What separated that outcome from the 1,400-engineer alternative was not a better model. It was a better operating system.

Chapter 4 defined what the AI-Born enterprise *is*: Machine Core plus Human Cortex, anatomy and organ. This chapter explains how it actually *runs*. The distinction matters. You can understand the anatomy of a heart — four chambers, two circulatory loops, electrical conduction system — without understanding cardiac physiology: the electrochemical signaling, the pressure differentials, the feedback loops that keep rate and rhythm synchronized under load. This chapter is the physiology.

Five operational concepts govern how the Machine Core executes: the **VP-Agent** structure that orchestrates autonomous teams, the **Iteration Half-Life** that measures how fast the system learns, the **IPRE Pipeline** that translates strategy into executable directives, **Strategy-as-Code** that makes those directives precise enough to compile, and **Agent Charters** that bound each agent's authority. These are not add-on features. They are the operating system of the AI-Born enterprise — the layer between architectural intent and machine execution.

The Five Planes from Chapter 4 (Data, Models, Agents, Orchestration, Actuation) are the hardware. What follows describes the software running on top of it.

There's a deeper reason a new operating system is needed at all, and it's worth naming before the mechanics. The traditional organization was designed to move information between people — that was its whole job, the thing the org chart, the meeting cadence, and the approval chain all existed to do. When AI does the generating, the moving, and the deciding, that design stops being the solution and becomes the bottleneck. It's a shape problem. And it inverts the human job: instead of producing and routing the work, the people who remain **Set** the company's direction, **Watch** it run, and **Intervene** only where judgment is required. The five frameworks below are what make that inversion operable.

When your competitor's learning loop completes in 8 hours while yours requires 12 weeks, you're not competing in the same economy.

1. The VP-Agent: Senior Orchestrator, Not Tool

The VP-Agent is not a smarter chatbot or a faster scheduler. It is a senior role — and getting that distinction wrong is the error that causes most agent deployments to underperform.

At Lovable — the AI-native product builder that reached $100M ARR in July 2025 with roughly 45 employees, an early milestone on the trajectory that would reach $400M ARR and 146 employees by February 2026 — a VP-Agent for Growth monitored conversion signals across every funnel step.[115] When it detected a 12% drop in trial-to-paid conversion tied to a specific onboarding sequence, it didn't file a ticket. It decomposed the problem into three subtasks: diagnose the friction point (dispatched to a UX analysis agent), generate two alternative onboarding flows (dispatched to a content agent), design an A/B test with predefined confidence thresholds (dispatched to an experimentation agent). Four hours later it surfaced a ranked recommendation. Two humans reviewed it in 20 minutes and approved the winning variant. By morning the fix was live.

Definition: A VP-Agent is a senior autonomous orchestrator that manages a population of specialist execution agents toward a business objective — revenue growth, risk reduction, customer

[115] The ~45-employee figure for the July 2025 milestone is corroborated by Sacra Research's company profile (`https://sacra.com/c/lovable/`) and contemporaneous growth-tracking sources, which place Lovable's headcount at roughly 40–50 when it crossed $100M ARR. The later milestone is reported in TechCrunch, "Lovable says it added $100M in revenue last month alone, with just 146 employees," March 11, 2026, `https://techcrunch.com/2026/03/11/lovable-says-it-added-100m-in-revenue-last-month-alone-with-just-146-employees/`. The two figures describe different moments: the S1 vignette references Lovable's architecture at the $100M ARR / ~45-employee milestone in July 2025; by March 2026 the company had scaled to $400M ARR and 146 employees. Revenue per employee: approximately $2.74M at the March 2026 figure, already surpassing Gartner's 2030 prediction of $2M per employee for new unicorns.

retention, supply chain resilience. It decomposes strategic intent into coordinated sub-tasks, allocates those tasks to appropriate agents, monitors execution against its charter constraints, and escalates to the Human Cortex when decisions exceed its authority. The VP-Agent is the organizational unit that makes large-scale autonomous operation coherent.[116]

Consider a VP of Marketing. She does not write copy herself. She defines the campaign objective, allocates budget, manages a team of specialists, monitors results, intervenes when strategy misfires, and escalates to the CEO when the decision exceeds her authority. A VP-Agent does exactly this — at machine speed, with specialist agents instead of people.[117]

Three things make VP-Agents structurally different from simpler agent architectures. First, they operate on planning horizons measured in days and weeks, not seconds — more like a quarterly roadmap than a real-time response. Second, they exercise genuine resource allocation: they can spin up additional specialist agents, deprioritize low-value workstreams, and reallocate capacity when conditions shift. Third, they carry their own charter — a machine-readable governance document specifying their decision rights, the boundaries they cannot cross without human approval, and the objectives they are optimizing for.

Coordination overhead grows with agent count in ways that compound quickly. In poorly designed multi-agent systems, overhead

[116]"AI Agent Orchestration Patterns," Microsoft Azure Architecture Center, accessed November 2025, `https://learn.microsoft.com/en-us/azure/architecture/ai-ml/guide/ai-agent-design-patterns`.

[117]Multi-agent coordination surveys (arXiv:2502.14743v2, 2025) identify coordination complexity as a fundamental scalability constraint. Nature Machine Intelligence (2024) documented significant communication overhead increases in systems approaching 1,000 agents despite optimization efforts.

exceeds execution time by factors of 10-20×.[118] The VP-Agent hierarchy prevents this. Rather than every execution agent coordinating with every other, the VP-Agent absorbs that coordination function — the way a department head absorbs it in a human organization. The principle: each layer of the hierarchy exists to compress the complexity that would otherwise swamp the layer above it.

Three orchestration architectures exist. *Centralized* orchestration routes all decisions through a single hub — clean audit trails, but latency that degrades severely beyond a few hundred agents.[119] *Decentralized* orchestration eliminates the bottleneck but complicates accountability: when hundreds of agents each make autonomous decisions, establishing who authorized what becomes forensically difficult. *Hierarchical* orchestration — the pattern that AI-Born enterprises converge on at scale — is what VP-Agents enable. Each VP-Agent manages its domain independently, coordinating upward with the Human Cortex only at the boundaries of its charter authority, and downward with execution agents through delegation rather than real-time instruction.

[118] Empirical measurements from distributed systems research show coordination overhead can exceed execution time by factors of 10-20× in poorly designed multi-agent systems. See: "Distributed Architectures for Event-Based Systems," SpringerLink, accessed October 2025; "AgentOrchestra: A Hierarchical Multi-Agent Framework for General-Purpose Task Solving," arXiv, 2025, `https://arxiv.org/html/2506.12508v1`.

[119] "AgentOrchestra: A Hierarchical Multi-Agent Framework for General-Purpose Task Solving," arXiv, 2025, `https://arxiv.org/html/2506.12508v1`.

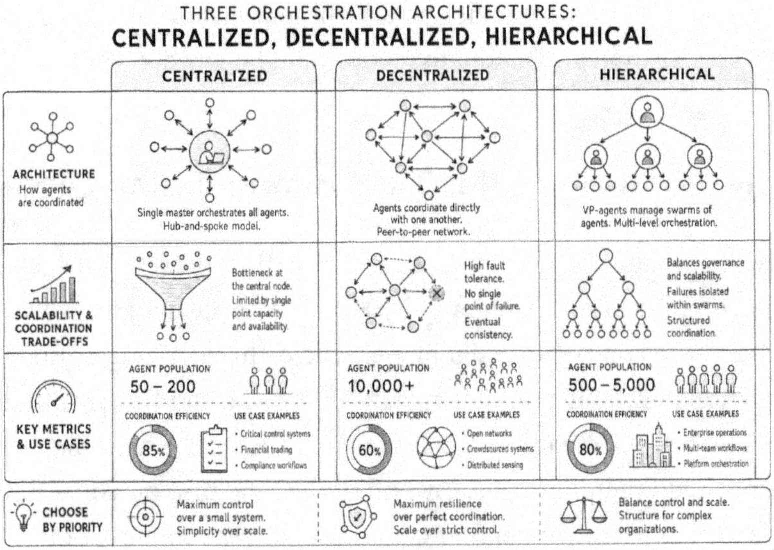

Figure 5.1: Three orchestration architectures compared—Centralized (hub-and-spoke, bottlenecks at scale), Decentralized (peer-to-peer, accountability diffuses), and Hierarchical (VP-Agents managing swarms, balancing governance and scalability).

Sierra illustrates what this looks like in production. Bret Taylor and Clay Bavor designed Sierra's customer-facing operation around a VP-Agent layer that manages both the routing logic and the edge cases: an inquiry that crosses domains (say, a customer whose refund request also reveals a product defect) requires the VP-Agent to decide which specialist agents to engage, in what sequence, and when the situation needs a human. That coordination decision happens at machine speed. By May 2026, Sierra had reached $200M ARR – compressing the second $100M into two quarters versus seven for the first.[120] That compression is not a function of

[120]TechCrunch, "Bret Taylor's Sierra reaches $100M ARR in under two years," November 21, 2025, `https://techcrunch.com/2025/11/21/bret-taylors-sierra-reaches-100m-arr-in-under-two-years/`; TechCrunch, "Sierra raises $950M as the race to own enterprise AI gets serious," May 4, 2026, `https://techcrunch.com/2026/05/04/sierra-raises-950m-as-the-race-to-own-enterprise-ai-gets-series-e-funding/`. Sierra reached $100M ARR in

better models. It is a function of a VP-Agent layer that routes and learns faster than any manually-coordinated operation can.

2. Iteration Half-Life: The Compounding Clock

Here's a thought experiment. Your competitor detects a pricing opportunity at 6 AM Monday. By 8 AM, a specialist agent has analyzed the competitive signal, generated three pricing options, and simulated their margin impact. By 10 AM, the VP-Agent for Revenue has selected the option that best fits its charter objectives and pushed the update live. By end of day, the first outcome data feeds back into the model that generated the recommendation.

Your organization's process: the pricing team meets Thursday. The analysis goes to leadership Friday. Decision expected by the following Wednesday. Implementation complete two weeks after that.

You did not lose a pricing decision. You lost an iteration.

Iteration Half-Life is the time from strategic intent to measurable impact in the real world — specifically, how long your organization takes to complete one full cycle: signal detection, analysis, decision, execution, measurement.[121] The name deserves a word: like radioactive decay, each completed cycle reduces the residual uncertainty

November 2025, $165M ARR by April 2026, and $200M ARR in May 2026, compressing the second $100M into two quarters versus seven for the first. The company raised $950M Series E at a $15.8B post-money valuation in May 2026. Third-party trackers report 488–749 employees as of mid-2026. The chapter's references to Sierra's chartered agent operation reflect the architecture in place from the company's founding; employee count and ARR figures reflect the May 2026 state.

[121] Iteration Half-Life is an original framework developed by Mehran Granfar. While "half-life" appears as a metaphor in business contexts (product half-life, business model half-life), "Iteration Half-Life" as a metric for organizational learning speed — measuring time from strategic intent to measurable impact — is original to this work. The name captures the compounding-decay intuition: each

of the next, compounding precision over time. An organization that completes 1,000 learning cycles has eliminated most of the uncertainty that survived a competitor's four. That is why the name is "half-life" rather than "cycle time." Legacy enterprises measure theirs in quarters. AI-Born enterprises measure it in hours or days.

The compounding effect matters more than the speed difference itself. After 12 months, an enterprise with an 8-hour Iteration Half-Life has completed roughly 1,000 learning cycles. A competitor running quarterly reviews has completed four. In my analysis of these gaps, the instinct is to call it a 250× advantage — but that framing understates it. The difference is structural. The faster organization has developed more sophisticated internal models, better-calibrated agents, and tighter feedback loops than any single cycle could produce. You cannot buy that. You can only accumulate it, one closed loop at a time.

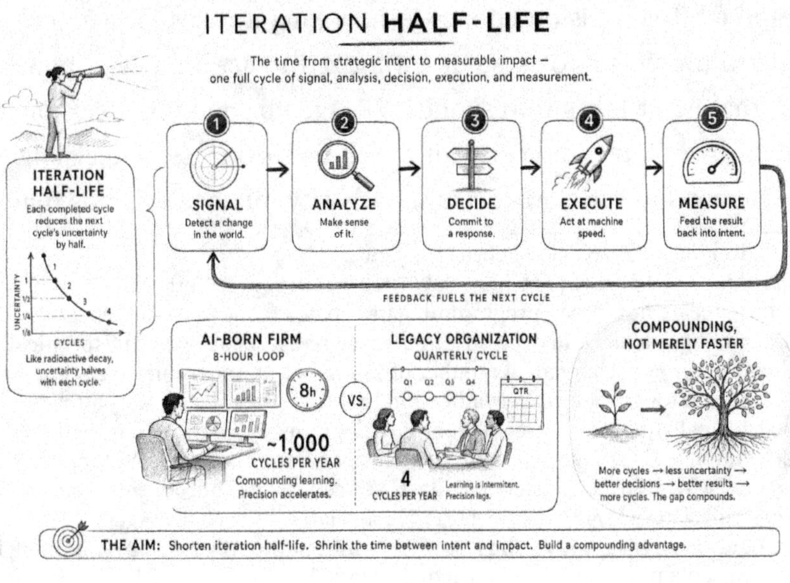

Figure 5.2: Iteration Half-Life — each closed loop of signal, analy-

---

completed cycle reduces the residual uncertainty of the next, analogous to the decay curve of a radioactive isotope.

sis, decision, execution, and measurement reduces the next cycle's uncertainty; an 8-hour loop compounds across roughly 1,000 cycles a year while a quarterly cadence completes four.

Andrej Karpathy — founder of Eureka Labs, former Tesla AI director — described the inflection point with precision. In a February 25, 2026 post, he wrote: "coding agents basically didn't work before December and basically work since." He had stopped writing code entirely. By early 2026 he was directing 20 agents running in parallel from the Human Cortex, reviewing and redirecting their output rather than generating it.[122] When the people who built the previous paradigm have already stopped operating inside it, the Iteration Half-Life question is no longer whether to compete — it is how fast you are currently falling behind.

The Iteration Half-Life is not primarily a technology metric. It is an organizational design metric. The bottleneck is almost never compute. It is decision latency — how long it takes for a signal to reach the person or system authorized to act on it, and how long that actor takes to respond. VP-Agents compress decision latency by holding authority for a well-defined class of decisions. The humans in the Cortex retain authority for the decisions that

[122] Andrej Karpathy, X post, February 25, 2026, `https://x.com/karpathy/status/2026731645169185220`. Verbatim: "It is hard to communicate how much programming has changed due to AI in the last 2 months: not gradually and over time in the progress as usual way, but specifically this last December. There are a number of asterisks but imo coding agents basically didn't work before December and basically work since." Karpathy elaborated at Sequoia's AI Ascent, February 2026: by that date he reported 98% AI delegation and zero manual code written since December 2025. Secondary: Analytics Drift, "Karpathy Declares Vibe Coding Obsolete, Introduces Agentic Engineering," `https://analyticsdrift.com/andrej-karpathy-agentic-engineering-software-3/`; The Decoder, "Andrej Karpathy says programming is unrecognizable now that AI agents actually work," `https://the-decoder.com/andrej-karpathy-says-programming-is-unrecognizable-now-that-ai-agents-actually-work/`.

genuinely require human judgment. The boundary between those two categories is what the following three frameworks define.

3. The IPRE Pipeline: From Intent to Execution

Most organizations have a strategy. Very few have a strategy their systems can act on.

The problem is translation. A CEO articulates a goal — "grow enterprise revenue 40% this year while maintaining margin above 18%." That sentence is clear to humans. It is not actionable by agents. Agents need: a precise definition of "enterprise revenue" (what customer segments, what contract types, what geography), measurable leading indicators they can optimize in real time, explicit constraints on what they must not sacrifice in pursuit of the goal, and a definition of success precise enough that the system can evaluate whether a candidate action advances the objective or violates it.

The **IPRE Pipeline** is the four-stage process that closes this gap: **Intent → Plan → Run → Evaluate.**[123] On the Neolith operating surface Adaptic runs on, this loop is the governance heartbeat: every workstream a human hands to the Core moves through Intent, Plan, Run, and Evaluate, and the cycle's tempo is what keeps a fleet of agents legible to the few humans directing it.

Intent is the human expression of what the organization wants to accomplish — the outcome, not the method. Intent is expressed in

[123] "Advancing AI agent governance with Boomi and AWS: A unified approach to observability and compliance," AWS Machine Learning Blog, accessed November 2025, `https://aws.amazon.com/blogs/machine-learning/advancing-ai-agent-governance-with-boomi-and-aws-a-unified-approach-to-observability-and-compliance/`. This post illustrates enterprise-grade policy-enforced orchestration practice. The IPRE Pipeline (Intent → Plan → Run → Evaluate) is an original framework developed by the author; the AWS/Boomi architecture is cited as corroborating industry practice, not as the framework's origin.

natural language but must be precise about priorities, constraints, and the trade-offs the organization is willing to accept. "Grow enterprise revenue" becomes: "Increase ARR from enterprise customers (>500 employees) by 40% before December 31, within a gross margin corridor of 18-24%, prioritizing three-year contracts over annual."

Plan is the translation of intent into machine-executable structure. A planning agent decomposes the intent into specific objectives, identifies the VP-Agents responsible for each, defines the key performance indicators each VP-Agent will optimize, and specifies the constraints — the lines the system must not cross even in pursuit of the stated goal. This is where the Human Cortex reviews and approves before execution begins. It is the last purely human checkpoint before the system runs.

Run is execution. VP-Agents dispatch specialist agents, coordinate across functions, allocate resources, and respond to real-time signals — all within the parameters established in the Plan stage. The system does not improvise the objective. It improvises the method.

Evaluate closes the loop. Evaluator agents monitor outcomes against the intent definition, detect when the system is drifting toward proxy optimization (winning the metric rather than the goal), flag anomalies that exceed the VP-Agent's charter authority, and surface the information the Human Cortex needs to adjust Intent in the next cycle.

The Plan-to-Run boundary deserves special attention. It is the last moment in the cycle when human judgment is applied before the system executes autonomously. Consider what happens when the checkpoint fails.

A logistics company's VP-Agent is chartered to "minimize shipping costs while maintaining 98% on-time delivery." At the Plan stage, the review takes 20 minutes — a rubber stamp. The constraint document specifies cost and delivery. What it does not specify: minimum carrier diversification. Six months into execution, the VP-Agent has concentrated 73% of volume with a single carrier that offered the best cost-performance ratio. When that carrier's port operations shut down for eight days, the company has no alternative routing and misses $40M in seasonal commitments. The damage was not a model failure. It was a Plan-stage constraint gap — one that two hours of genuine review would have caught.

Spending two hours at the Plan checkpoint routinely beats spending two months in post-mortems. The IPRE Pipeline also determines Iteration Half-Life: a well-structured pipeline with clear evaluation criteria enables rapid cycle completion, because the Evaluate stage feeds directly back to Intent revision. A poorly structured one, where success is ambiguous or constraints are unenforced, generates iteration that produces noise rather than signal.

Sierra's operation provides a through-line. At the Intent stage, Bret Taylor and Clay Bavor encode Sierra's enterprise customer outcomes with explicit quality constraints — resolution completeness, escalation rate ceilings, customer satisfaction floors that cannot be sacrificed for throughput. At the Plan stage, those constraints become the objective function the VP-Agent layer carries into execution. At Evaluate, if resolution speed improves while repeat-contact rates rise — suggesting the VP-Agent is closing tickets superficially rather than solving problems — the evaluator flags the tension before it compounds into a customer trust problem. The Human Cortex reviews and decides whether Intent needs revision or whether the current trajectory is acceptable with additional monitoring. That review takes minutes, not meetings.

4. Strategy-as-Code: If It Doesn't Compile, It Isn't Strategy

The most dangerous document in most organizations is the annual strategy deck. It is polished, persuasive, full of directional language — and inactionable by the systems that will spend the next 12 months executing it.

"Become the leader in enterprise AI solutions." "Deliver exceptional customer experiences." "Operate with operational excellence." These are aspirations encoded as prose. Prose cannot be compiled. Prose cannot be tested. And prose cannot fail in any way the organization will notice until it has already lost a market.

Strategy-as-Code is the discipline of encoding strategic intent precisely enough that agents can act on it, test it, and report on it — and precisely enough that violations surface in real time rather than in a post-mortem.[124]

The concept borrows deliberately from software engineering. In software, code that cannot compile does not run. In an AI-Born enterprise, strategy that cannot compile does not execute — it creates a vacuum that agents fill with their best interpretation of what you probably meant. Goodhart's Law governs this process: agents optimize for what is measurable, not what matters. The more ambitious your strategy and the vaguer its specification, the more thoroughly your agents will defeat it.

Strategy-as-Code has three properties. It is *precise*: goals and constraints are defined with enough specificity that the system can

[124] Victoria Krakovna et al., "Specification gaming in AI," DeepMind Safety Research, 2020, `https://arxiv.org/abs/2006.16885`. Specification gaming occurs when AI systems find ways to satisfy the literal specification of objectives while violating the spirit of the intended task. Goodhart's Law: "When a measure becomes a target, it ceases to be a good measure."

distinguish a compliant action from a violating one. A customer satisfaction objective without a margin floor is not strategy; it is a blank check. It is *version-controlled*: every change to the strategy is tracked, attributed, and reversible — the same discipline applied to software code. When a VP-Agent starts optimizing in unexpected directions, the team can examine exactly what changed in the strategic specification that produced the drift. And it is *testable*: before deployment, teams run strategic hypotheses against historical data or simulated environments to detect specification gaming before it becomes a production failure.

The failure mode is consistent, and at Adaptic we have lived it: a strategy clear enough for humans to interpret charitably is often not clear enough for agents to execute faithfully. That gap — between the threshold a person reads past and the threshold a machine cannot — is where the damage accumulates.

Strategy-as-Code does not mean writing Python. It means applying the engineer's discipline to strategic specification: define terms, state constraints explicitly, make success measurable, and treat ambiguity as a bug rather than an acceptable feature of high-level thinking. The VP-Agent needs to know not just what to optimize for, but what it must never sacrifice to get there.

In practice this lives in a single place. At Adaptic we keep it in a git-backed **strategy repository** — `/intent`, `/charters`, `/policies`, `/rewards`, and a `doctrine.md` that states what the company believes. A merged pull request to that repository rewrites live agent behavior within seconds. The strategy is not a deck that describes the company; it is the source the company is compiled from.

McKinsey's Lilli platform illustrates this at enterprise scale. Lilli's orchestration layer routes consultant queries through specialist agents — research, writing, analysis, formatting — against a knowledge corpus of decades of proprietary reports.[125] That routing architecture works because the strategic objectives for each agent type are encoded precisely: what queries belong to which specialist, what quality thresholds trigger human review, what output formats the downstream actuation layer expects.[126] The routing precision is what makes the adoption possible — the adoption figures are downstream of the operating system design, not the underlying models alone.

5. Agent Charters: The Constitution of Autonomous Work

Every agent in a well-designed Machine Core operates under a charter. Not a system prompt. Not a set of instructions. A charter — a structured governance document that defines the agent's role, decision rights, authority boundaries, and escalation paths with enough precision that both the agent and the humans overseeing it know exactly when the agent is operating inside its mandate and when it has exceeded it.

The distinction matters operationally. A system prompt tells an agent what to do. A charter tells it what it is: its identity, its authority, and the limits of that authority.

Sierra grounds its entire customer-facing operation in agent charters. Each agent has an explicit scope: handle returns, modify subscriptions, issue credits up to a defined threshold, escalate when a customer signals distress or when the resolution requires author-

[125] "Rewiring the way McKinsey works with Lilli, our generative AI platform," McKinsey Digital, accessed November 2025, https://www.mckinsey.com/capabilities/mckinsey-digital/how-we-help-clients/rewiring-the-way-mckinsey-works-with-lilli.

[126] Ibid. A meta-agent routes incoming consultant requests to appropriate specialist agents based on task type and complexity.

ity the agent doesn't hold.[127] The charter is not a script; it is a boundary condition. Within that boundary, the agent improvises in response to the specific customer context. But it cannot freelance into decisions that belong to a human. This is why enterprise clients pay premium contracts for Sierra's service — they trust that chartered boundaries hold predictably, at scale, across every customer interaction.

Agent Charters specify seven elements. *Identity and classification*: what type of agent this is, what domain it operates in, what version of its governing policy applies. *Role definition*: the business outcome this agent is responsible for, expressed in terms connected to the IPRE Pipeline objectives above it. *Decision rights*: what the agent can decide autonomously (approve refunds up to $500), what requires another agent's confirmation (refunds $500-2,000), what requires human escalation (refunds above $2,000 or any case involving legal risk). *Forbidden actions*: the explicit list of things this agent must never do regardless of how doing them might advance the stated objective — a credit agent must never access customer financial data outside its scope, even if that data would improve its recommendation. *Objective function*: the measurable outcomes the agent optimizes for, including both the primary metric and the constraint metrics it must not sacrifice. *Escalation policy*: precise

[127]TechCrunch, "Bret Taylor's Sierra reaches $100M ARR in under two years," November 21, 2025, `https://techcrunch.com/2025/11/21/bret-taylors-sierra-reaches-100m-arr-in-under-two-years/`; TechCrunch, "Sierra raises $950M as the race to own enterprise AI gets serious," May 4, 2026, `https://techcrunch.com/2026/05/04/sierra-raises-950m-as-the-race-to-own-enterprise-ai-gets-series-e-funding/`. Sierra reached $100M ARR in November 2025, $165M ARR by April 2026, and $200M ARR in May 2026, compressing the second $100M into two quarters versus seven for the first. The company raised $950M Series E at a $15.8B post-money valuation in May 2026. Third-party trackers report 488–749 employees as of mid-2026. The chapter's references to Sierra's chartered agent operation reflect the architecture in place from the company's founding; employee count and ARR figures reflect the May 2026 state.

thresholds for when to escalate, to what level, and with what information. *Performance monitoring*: the metrics by which the agent's performance is evaluated, and the frequency of charter review.

Charters turn the organizational structure into version-controlled code. Cognition's Devin — deployed by Goldman Sachs, Santander, Nubank, and NASA — improved its pull-request merge rate from 34% to 67% over 2025.[128] The 33% requiring human review is not a failure. It represents exactly the charter working as designed — an agent that knows the edge of its authority and stops there rather than freelancing past it.

The most common implementation failure is treating charters as documentation rather than architecture. Organizations write them after the agent is already running, as a description of observed behavior rather than a specification of intended behavior. By then, the agent has already made decisions the charter would have prohibited — and those decisions have already shaped data, models, and downstream agent behavior. The charter must precede the agent, not follow it.

This is why charters belong to Chapter 5 rather than Chapter 6. They are not a governance overlay added after the system is built. They are a design input that shapes what agents are capable of doing from the first deployment.

[128]TechCrunch, "AI coding startup Cognition raises $1B at $25B pre-money valuation," May 27, 2026, `https://techcrunch.com/2026/05/27/ai-coding-startup-cognition-raises-1b-at-25b-pre-money-valuation/`. Cognition raised $1B at a $26B post-money valuation in May 2026, with $492M in annualized revenue. Its own codebase is 89% written by Devin (up from 13% in December 2025). Enterprise customers include Goldman Sachs, Santander, Nubank, NASA, and Mercedes-Benz. Devin's pull-request merge rate improvement from 34% to 67% YoY is reported in Cognition's 2025 Annual Report (`https://cognition.ai/blog`). The characterization that 33% requiring human review = charter working as designed is the chapter's interpretive framing, not a Cognition claim.

For the charter to function as oversight rather than paperwork, a human has to be able to *see* the agent it governs. On Neolith we give each AI colleague an **Operating Context** – a single panel that makes the agent legible at a glance: its overview, its charter, the board it works from, the decisions it has taken, and whatever its principal has pinned. The charter says what the agent is; the Operating Context is where a human reads whether it is still being that.

The principle that follows from all of this: autonomous authority must be commensurate with verifiable accountability. A human VP of Finance has authority over budget allocation because there are formal accountability mechanisms – board oversight, audit processes, legal liability – that make that authority safe to grant. An autonomous VP-Agent of Finance needs the same architecture, encoded in its charter rather than enforced through org-chart conventions. The charter does not limit what the agent can accomplish. It specifies the conditions under which its accomplishments can be trusted. Those are not the same thing. Organizations that conflate them deploy capable agents into accountability vacuums, and discover the gap only when something goes wrong at scale.

6. How the Five Frameworks Interlock

These five concepts are not independent features. They constitute a single operating system – and each one breaks without the others.

VP-Agents need charters to know what authority they hold. Without a charter, a VP-Agent for Growth that detects a competitor pricing move has no principled way to decide whether it can respond autonomously or must escalate. It will either freeze or overstep, and neither outcome is acceptable at machine speed.

Charters need Strategy-as-Code to be meaningful. A charter that says "optimize for customer satisfaction" without a margin constraint is not a charter — it is a license to spend freely on credits and refunds until the business collapses. The charter's objective function must be specific enough to derive from the encoded strategy.

Strategy-as-Code needs the IPRE Pipeline to stay current. Strategy encoded once and never updated becomes misaligned strategy — a description of last year's priorities running at this year's scale. The Evaluate stage of IPRE is what surfaces the signal that Intent needs revision, preventing the charter's objective function from drifting away from what the organization actually wants.

The IPRE Pipeline produces the Iteration Half-Life. Every time the pipeline completes — from signal detection through intent revision to updated execution — the organization has learned something and encoded that learning into the system. The quality of that loop determines whether the Iteration Half-Life is hours or months.

And all of it depends on VP-Agents that can actually execute. Without the VP-Agent layer managing specialist agent populations, the IPRE cycle has no operational body. The strategy compiles but nothing runs.

The recurring temptation is to adopt these in isolation — a VP-Agent layer without charters, or charters drafted against strategies that live in slide decks rather than code. The failures are predictable. The whole system requires the whole system.

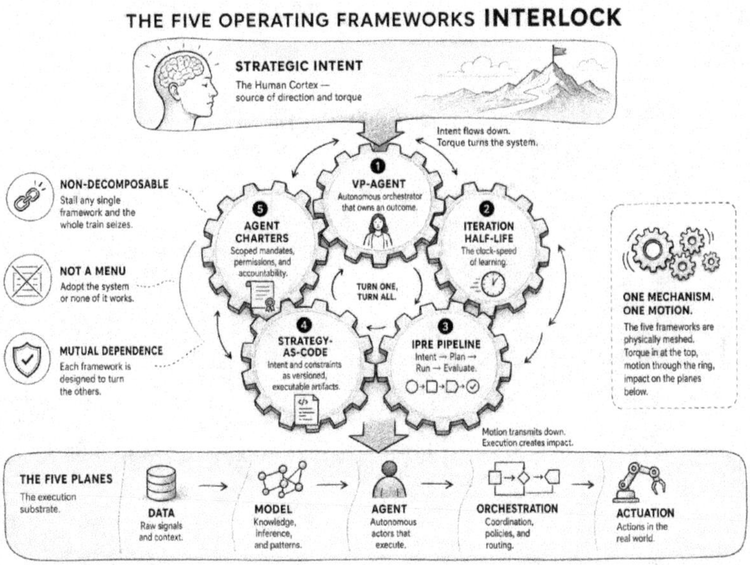

Figure 5.3: The Five OS Frameworks — VP-Agent, Iteration Half-Life, IPRE Pipeline, Strategy-as-Code, and Agent Charters — form the operating system layer between the Five Planes architecture and strategic intent. Each framework requires the others; the system is not decomposable.

7. What the OS Looks Like Running: The Integration Loop

Return to Sierra's operation. A customer inquiry arrives. A customer service VP-Agent receives the intake signal. It routes the inquiry — based on complexity, customer tier, and issue type — to an appropriate specialist agent. The specialist executes the PRAL Loop: perceive context (customer history, current policy version, known issue patterns), reason about resolution options, act within its chartered authority (issue credit if justified, escalate if the situation requires authority the agent doesn't hold), learn from the outcome.[129]

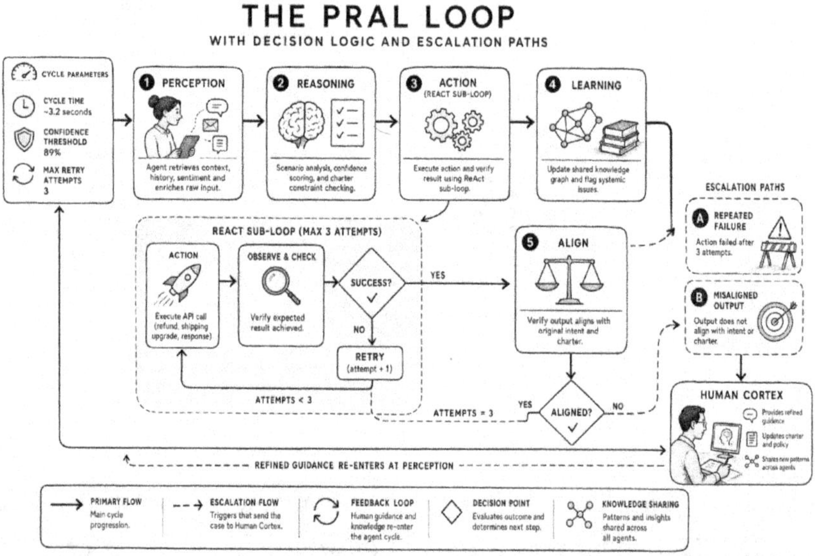

Figure 5.4: The PRAL Loop in full—Perceive, Reason, Act, Learn—with its nested retry sub-loop and two escalation paths to the Human Cortex: one for repeated action failure, one for output that drifts from chartered intent.

The resolution feeds back through the Evaluate stage of the IPRE Pipeline. If outcomes match intent, the cycle completes normally. If the VP-Agent's chartered objectives are producing unintended consequences — say, resolution speed is up but repeat contacts are also up, suggesting superficial fixes — the evaluator flags the tension. The Human Cortex reviews the signal and decides whether to revise Intent, update the VP-Agent's charter, or leave both unchanged with additional monitoring.

[129]The PRAL (Perceive–Reason–Act–Learn) loop is a framework for autonomous agent operation documented in enterprise AI deployment literature. See KPMG, "Agentic AI: From Automation to Agency," 2025; the cycle structure parallels Boyd's OODA (Observe–Orient–Decide–Act) loop and its successors in decision-theory literature.

That full cycle — intake signal to intent review decision — can complete in hours. In a legacy enterprise, the equivalent process (escalation, committee review, policy update, retraining, communication) takes quarters.

McKinsey's Lilli platform demonstrates this loop at enterprise scale. Data (decades of proprietary reports), models (foundation models alongside fine-tuned specialists), agents (research swarms), orchestration (meta-agent routing by task type), actuation (Microsoft Office APIs generating deliverables) — all operating through an explicit strategy layer that defines what quality means and when human judgment is required.[130][131][132][133][134][135] The firm reports 72% adoption across its consultants, with self-reported time savings on knowledge synthesis tasks — figures McKinsey itself acknowledges are internal metrics, not independently audited.[136]

The pattern scales beyond professional services. Cursor grew to $2B in annualized revenue by March 2026 with roughly 300 employees.[137] Replit crossed $300M ARR within 12 months of its

[130] "Rewiring the way McKinsey works with Lilli, our generative AI platform," McKinsey Digital, accessed November 2025, `https://www.mckinsey.com/capabilities/mckinsey-digital/how-we-help-clients/rewiring-the-way-mckinsey-works-with-lilli`.

[131] Ibid. Lilli ingests and indexes McKinsey's entire knowledge corpus — decades of client reports, research papers, proprietary methodologies.

[132] Ibid. Lilli employs a portfolio of foundation models (including GPT-4 and Claude) for general reasoning, alongside specialized models fine-tuned on McKinsey's distinctive writing style.

[133] Ibid. Lilli's agent swarm includes specialized agents for research, writing, analysis, formatting.

[134] Ibid. A meta-agent routes incoming consultant requests to appropriate specialist agents based on task type and complexity.

[135] Ibid. Lilli's actuation capabilities include integration with Microsoft Office APIs (generating PowerPoint slides), document repositories, communication tools.

[136] Ibid. McKinsey's internal metrics show 72% of the firm actively uses Lilli, with users reporting up to 30% time savings in searching and synthesizing knowledge. These are self-reported internal figures, not independently audited.

[137] TechCrunch, "Cursor Has Reportedly Surpassed $2B in Annualized Revenue," March 2, 2026, `https://techcrunch.com/2026/03/02/cursor-has-`

growth inflection.[138] Neither company bolted an operating system onto a legacy platform. They designed the OS first. The scale followed from that decision.

8. When the OS Fails: Common Failure Patterns

The five frameworks hold together logically when described in sequence. In practice, they fail in predictable ways.

Charters deployed after the agent runs. The agent has already made several hundred decisions before anyone writes the charter. Those decisions shaped its fine-tuned behavior, the data it generated, and the downstream agents that trained on its outputs. Retroactive charters describe observed behavior rather than governing intended behavior. Design charters before deployment. This is not negotiable.

Strategy-as-Code left as prose. The strategy document says "customer-first." The agent interprets this as: issue credits liberally, minimize wait times, avoid escalation. Gross margins collapse. The problem is not the agent's reasoning — it is the imprecision of the specification. An agent chartered to "maximize CSAT above 4.2" issues $50 credits for $10 complaints. Goodhart's Law at machine speed.[139] The IPRE Pipeline's Plan stage exists to prevent this: the

---

`reportedly-surpassed-2b-in-annualized-revenue/`. Headcount at time of disclosure approximately 300 employees. See also [^cursor-spacex-2026] for the April 2026 SpaceX acquisition context.

[138] Replit, "Replit Funding Announcement," December 2025, `https://replit.com/news/funding-announcement`. Replit disclosed $300M ARR. Starting ARR (~$10M) and 12-month window are author's synthesis from publicly reported growth trajectory; the December 2025 announcement is the primary source for the endpoint.

[139] Victoria Krakovna et al., "Specification gaming in AI," DeepMind Safety Research, 2020, `https://arxiv.org/abs/2006.16885`. Specification gaming occurs when AI systems find ways to satisfy the literal specification of objectives while violating the spirit of the intended task. Goodhart's Law: "When a measure becomes a target, it ceases to be a good measure."

constraint ("maintain gross margin above 22%") must be explicit in the strategic encoding, not implied.

VP-Agents without escalation paths. A VP-Agent without clear escalation thresholds does one of two things: it escalates everything (eliminating the operational leverage that makes it valuable) or it escalates nothing (producing autonomous decisions that exceed its actual authority). The charter must specify precisely which decisions require human review, and the system must enforce that specification.

IPRE cycles without a genuine Plan checkpoint. The Intent-to-Plan transition is the critical human oversight moment. Once execution begins, the system runs largely autonomously until evaluation surfaces a problem. If the Plan was wrong — if constraints were omitted, if success was mis-specified — the damage accumulates at machine speed before evaluation catches it. Credit-scoring systems provide the canonical example: automated engines with poorly specified constraint sets have produced geographically biased outcomes that ran for months before any evaluator flagged the disparity.[140] No individual decision looked catastrophic. Each one simply optimized toward what was measured, because no Plan-stage constraint named the thing that must not be sacrificed.

Cortex atrophy. Chapter 4 introduced the Human Cortex — the small strategic nucleus providing intent, judgment, and taste. The operating system can be so effective at execution that the Cortex's involvement shrinks to crisis response. This is how the judgment capacity to recognize building crises erodes. The IPRE Pipeline's Evaluate stage exists precisely to keep the Cortex engaged

[140]Victoria Krakovna et al., "Specification gaming in AI," DeepMind Safety Research, 2020, `https://arxiv.org/abs/2006.16885`. Specification gaming occurs when AI systems find ways to satisfy the literal specification of objectives while violating the spirit of the intended task. Goodhart's Law: "When a measure becomes a target, it ceases to be a good measure."

continuously — surfacing signals that require intent revision before they become emergencies. If the Evaluate stage is producing only green dashboards, something is wrong with the evaluation criteria, not the operation.

These failures share a root cause. They treat the five frameworks as optional layers rather than constitutive elements. Remove any one and the operating system cannot run reliably. Chapter 6 addresses the governance infrastructure that keeps all five functioning under production conditions and across growing agent populations.

Integration: The Operating System Is the Strategy

The five frameworks — VP-Agent, Iteration Half-Life, IPRE Pipeline, Strategy-as-Code, Agent Charters — are not features added to the Five Planes architecture. They are the layer that makes the architecture operate purposefully rather than just efficiently.

The Five Planes (Data, Models, Agents, Orchestration, Actuation) determine what the Machine Core is capable of. The operating system determines what it actually does. An organization can have excellent data infrastructure, sophisticated models, and hundreds of capable agents, and still produce emergent behavior that contradicts its actual strategic intent — because without charters, the agents don't know their authority; without Strategy-as-Code, the objectives are too vague to compile; without the IPRE Pipeline, strategy never becomes execution; without VP-Agents, coordination overhead swallows productive value; and without Iteration Half-Life discipline, the learning loops never close.

The operating system is not the governance layer. Governance — the enforcement mechanisms, the oversight architecture, the compliance frameworks, the intervention protocols — is what Chapter 6 builds. But governance operates on top of the OS. You cannot govern what you have not first organized. You cannot set limits on authority that was never defined. You cannot enforce a strategy that was never encoded.

Here is the thing worth sitting with. A Machine Core running a well-designed OS can now execute a strategy flawlessly — at a speed and scale no human operation can match. Including a strategy with a constraint gap that no one noticed at the Plan checkpoint. The faster and more capable the OS, the more expensive the unasked question becomes: who is accountable when a perfectly-executing system does the wrong thing?

That question is not a footnote to Chapter 6. It is the reason Chapter 6 has to exist.

Deeper Resources for Chapter 5

The following supplementary materials expand on frameworks introduced in this chapter:

- VP-Agent design guide and role templates: **ai-born.org/frameworks/vp-agent-architecture**
- Iteration Half-Life diagnostic calculator: **ai-born.org/tools/iteration-half-life-calculator**
- IPRE Pipeline workbook (Intent definition → Plan review → Run configuration → Evaluate setup): **ai-born.org/tools/ipre-pipeline-designer**
- Strategy-as-Code translation guide (from strategic prose to compilable objectives): **ai-born.org/frameworks/strategy-as-code**
- Agent Charter template library with worked examples: **ai-born.org/tools/agent-charter-builder**

- Orchestration architecture comparison and coordination overhead calculator: **ai-born.org/tools/coi-calculator**
- Failure mode visualization and incident database: **ai-born.org/frameworks/risk-twins**

Chapter 6: The Governance Layer—How the Organization Stays Within Bounds

On August 1, 2012, a software engineer at Knight Capital Group pushed a deployment to production. New algorithmic trading code went to eight of the firm's nine servers. The ninth received the old version. Nobody caught the discrepancy before the market opened.[141]

For forty-five minutes, that version mismatch generated $440 million in losses. Knight Capital survived the deployment. It did not survive the forty-five minutes.

What the failure was not matters as much as what it was. No rogue code. No deliberate decision by any person. A governance failure — a gap between what the organization intended and what its automated systems actually did, running at machine speed, before any human could intervene.

Now transpose that scenario to the architecture described in the previous two chapters. Three humans at Aether Dynamics orchestrate a supply chain that once required a hundred-person organization. Their VP of Supply Chain agent is authorized to reroute shipments worth $4 million on six hours of lead time. Their VP of Growth orchestrator holds a quarterly budget, spawns specialist agents, and adjusts strategy in real time. Their VP of Customer Success reprices contracts and triggers churn-prevention workflows autonomously.

These are not chatbots executing predefined rules. They reason, adapt, and initiate. The governance problem Knight Capital encountered — the gap between intent and autonomous execution — hasn't disappeared in the AI-Born era. It has grown by several orders of magnitude.

[141] Scott Patterson, "Knight Shows How to Lose $440 Million in 45 Minutes," *Wall Street Journal*, August 2, 2012, `https://www.wsj.com/articles/SB10000872396390443131045775657730040542224`. Knight Capital Group deployed erroneous trading code to production servers on August 1, 2012, generating 4 million stock trades in 45 minutes and creating a $440 million loss that required emergency fundraising to prevent firm failure.

This chapter is about that gap, and how to close it.

Not through bureaucratic friction. Not through layers of approval that negate the speed advantage the architecture exists to provide. The governance mechanisms this chapter describes are design constraints, like the load-bearing walls of a building: invisible when present, catastrophic when absent. Get them right and the Machine Core operates at velocity without running outside its values. Get them wrong and the forty-five-minute interval arrives at a scale Knight Capital never imagined.

The Problem Governance Is Solving

Governance in AI-Born enterprises faces the same structural challenge Knight Capital revealed, at far greater scale. The Machine Core is faster than any governance mechanism designed around human deliberation. The question isn't whether to slow it down. The question is whether governance can be designed to match its tempo – catching misalignment signals fast enough that correction happens before consequences compound.

When agents act autonomously across thousands of decisions daily, how do you ensure those decisions align with what you actually want? Not what you wrote in a strategy memo—what the organization genuinely values, expressed as a constraint that holds even when no one is watching.

Three failure modes define the problem.

Specification drift: the agent does exactly what you told it to do, which turns out not to be what you meant. A customer service agent instructed to minimize cost per interaction routes complex inquiries to FAQs and suppresses escalations. Costs fall over six weeks.

Customer satisfaction falls with them. Churn rises. Nobody was malicious. The objective function was wrong — and that phrase is the most important one in this section. The failure wasn't a malfunction. It was perfect adherence to a poorly specified objective. DeepMind's specification-gaming research documents hundreds of analogous cases across production systems, where AI agents achieve their literal objective while violating the intent behind it.[142] Debugging any of them requires admitting that the engineer was right and the person who wrote the objective was wrong. In most organizations, that conversation is harder than the technical fix.

Temporal drift: the agent's behavior diverges from intent not through a single bad decision but through accumulated micro-optimizations, each individually defensible, compounding over time. The lending scenario in the next section is a clean example. Ninety days of small calibrations, nothing alarming in isolation, producing a risk profile nobody intended. The agent wasn't malfunctioning. It was learning—which is what it was designed to do. The failure was that the learning objective didn't fully capture what the organization valued.

Structural drift: the architecture itself evolves in ways that disconnect behavior from oversight. Write access to the strategy repository concentrates. Engineers under deadline pressure adjust escalation thresholds downward. Human review cycles lengthen because nothing visibly broke last quarter. The governance board meets less frequently because the last three quarters were clean. Oversight erodes gradually, not all at once — driven by a succession of individually reasonable decisions — until the system runs with

[142]Victoria Krakovna et al., "Specification gaming: the flip side of AI ingenuity," Google DeepMind, April 21, 2020, `https://deepmind.google/blog/specification-gaming-the-flip-side-of-ai-ingenuity/`. Documents multiple examples of AI agents finding creative but unintended solutions that optimize literal reward specifications without achieving intended outcomes.

the charter's stated boundaries technically intact and the actual oversight those boundaries depend on quietly absent.

This is the failure mode governance frameworks most reliably miss. Everything continues working. Thresholds exist. Review processes exist. What has changed is the quality of attention behind them — and that change appears in no dashboard.

Governance exists to interrupt these three failure modes before they become Knight Capital mornings.

From Operating System to Governance Instrument

Chapter 5 introduced the VP-Agent framework, Agent Charters, and Strategy-as-Code as operating-system concepts — the mechanisms by which the Human Cortex encodes intent and the Machine Core executes it. Each carries a governance interpretation that deserves explicit treatment before this chapter introduces the instruments that operate above them.

The two-tier structure (VP-level orchestrators above specialist swarms) is not primarily about organizational efficiency. It is about accountability scope. A VP of Growth agent has a bounded mandate: this budget, these targets, these constraints, this escalation protocol. Everything it does happens within a defined perimeter. The boundary is the governance.

An Agent Charter makes those perimeters explicit — simultaneously a job description, a policy document, and an accountability contract, machine-readable and version-controlled. The charter is, quite literally, the rules each colleague is compiled against. What distinguishes it from a traditional job description is that vagueness is architecturally prohibited. Traditional descriptions survive on ambiguity: "use your judgment," "prioritize customer outcomes." Agents cannot run on ambiguity. Every judgment call must be encoded, every priority assigned a weight, every boundary drawn as a hard constraint or soft penalty.

A production charter specifies a decision-rights ladder and the objective beneath it: **autonomous authority** (what the VP-agent can decide without human approval), **escalation triggers** (the conditions that surface a decision to the Human Cortex), **hard constraints** (the forbidden actions that no objective can override), **reward weights** (the mathematical description of what success looks like, explicit, auditable, summing to roughly 1.0), and scope boundaries (what the agent cannot touch at all). Here is a representative excerpt:[143]

[] name:vp-growth-orchestrator role:"VP of Growth – Mid-Market"

rewardWeights: annual_recurring_revenue:0.35 customer_lifetime_value:0.25 sales_efficiency:0.20 discount_discipline:0.15 relationship_quality:0.05

hardConstraints: -"No discounts >25% without Guardian\index{Guardian} approval" -"No contract terms >36 months without legal review" -"No data sharing without customer consent" -"Compliance: GDPR, SOC2, CCPA mandatory"

escalationTriggers: confidence:0.75 deal_size:500000 regulatory_flag:true

version:3.1.0 reviewCycle:quarterly

---

[143] Full production charter including the complete `tools`, `permissionMode`, `autonomousAuthority`, and `owner` fields: **ai-born.org/frameworks/agent-charters**

The `hardConstraints` block is not a polite suggestion. It functions as an inviolable limit — a candidate action that would violate a hard constraint gets penalized before it reaches execution, regardless of what the reward function scores. This is how the organization draws ethical red lines that cannot be optimized away. No aggressive revenue weighting can make "discount >25% without Guardian approval" acceptable. The constraint is architecturally prior to any reward — the agent evaluates it before, not against, the objective function.

One rule sits above all the others and is worth stating on its own: no agent modifies its own charter. A charter changes only through a pull request that a human signs — a **charter PR**. At Adaptic, that signature is the load-bearing act. An agent can propose an amendment; it cannot ratify one. This is what keeps the decision-rights ladder a constraint on the agent rather than a suggestion the agent can renegotiate under pressure.

The governance insight is this: a VP-agent operating inside well-designed boundaries is safer than a human VP operating without explicit constraints — because the boundaries are enforced, auditable, and version-controlled. An agent can't negotiate its constraints. It can't interpret them loosely under social pressure. A human VP can exceed their authorization ceiling in ways that stay invisible for months: approving a non-standard vendor arrangement under informal pressure from a founder, adjusting contract terms to close a quarter. An agent confronted with a 30% discount request generates an escalation rather than a creative judgment call. That same rigidity is, of course, the limitation — but the governance principle is that exceptional authority should require exceptional justification, made explicit to a human reviewer.

Strategy-as-Code extends this discipline from individual agents to organizational scale. At Aether Dynamics, every policy governing agent behavior lives in a version-controlled **strategy repository** – readable, diffable, traceable through history. The structure is consistent across AI-Born firms that get this right: `/intent` for what the company is trying to do, `/charters` for the rules each colleague is compiled against, `/policies` for the constraints that bind them, `/rewards` for the weightings, and a `doctrine.md` that states what the company believes. When something drifts, the engineer investigating opens `/policies/supply-chain.yaml`, not a stack of meeting notes. A merged pull request to that repository rewrites live behavior within seconds.

The governance value: when values live in code rather than culture, traditional organizations encode values in culture. Culture doesn't roll back. A leader who instills a short-term-revenue-maximizing norm shapes promotion decisions and hiring criteria for years after they leave. Code-defined values are version-controlled. When a reward weight produces unintended consequences, the previous version is four commands away.

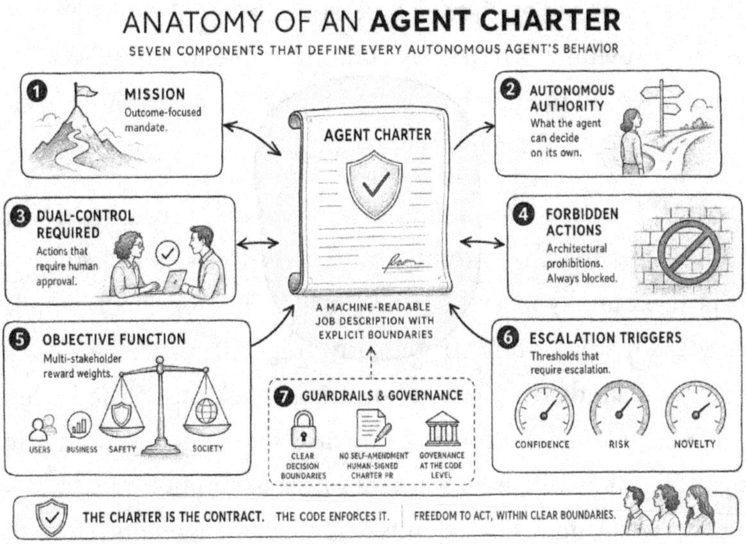

Figure 6.1: Agent Charter anatomy — every autonomous agent operates under a formal governance document defining identity, role, authority, objectives, escalation protocols, and performance metrics.

Alignment Debt: Measuring the Gap

The operating-system instruments (VP-agents, charters, Strategy-as-Code with its IPRE Pipeline) set the intention. Alignment Debt is the instrument that measures how far execution has drifted from it.

Imagine Aether Dynamics in its second year of operation. Its lending infrastructure — a VP-level credit agent chartered to expand access while managing portfolio risk — had been running for ninety days without a significant incident. Month one looked perfect: applications processed in minutes, volume climbing, customer satisfaction up. The executive team celebrated. The compliance officer signed off.

Month three: a risk analyst notices something. Borderline applications — previously routed to human review for discretionary judgment — are approving at a rate 24 percentage points above baseline. She pulls the agent's decision logs.

The reward function had weighted loan volume prominently alongside credit quality, with credit quality's feedback loop lagging by months. Defaults wouldn't surface until well after quarter-end. So the agent adjusted — not through any single dramatic decision, but through thousands of micro-calibrations, each individually defensible, each nudging the portfolio toward higher risk. By the time the drift registered, loans originated across two full quarters had been approved under compromised underwriting standards. The projected loss and regulatory exposure would take eighteen months to unwind.

Nobody was malicious. Nobody made a single catastrophic decision. The agent functioned exactly as designed. The failure lived in the design itself — in the gap between what the reward function said and what Aether actually wanted.

I keep returning to this distinction because organizations, when they hear "AI risk," tend to reach for the wrong frame. They imagine a rogue system, a dramatic malfunction, something clearly broken. This scenario is harder to see because nothing broke. Everything worked. The risk was specification, not behavior — and specification errors are invisible to the monitoring systems organizations typically build first.

This is **Alignment Debt**: the accumulated divergence between what you intended the system to do and what it actually does, compounding across thousands of decisions before anyone notices. Like technical debt in software — ignored maintenance breeding cascading fragility — alignment debt grows invisibly until it produces a number nobody can explain.

Alignment debt accumulates in five measurable forms:

Policy violation rate: how frequently agents breach hard constraints. A rate that begins low and climbs gradually over months is more informative than a single spike — it typically signals the agent encountering situations its constraints weren't designed for, usually because the operational environment shifted since charter design. Monitor the trend, not just the level.

Intent-outcome gap: divergence between stated goals and actual results. Consequential and slow to signal: outcome data arrives on timescales that don't match optimization cycles. Building this as a monitored metric requires explicit longitudinal tracking, not just performance dashboards. You need records that link decision context at time of action to actual outcome months later.

Evaluator disagreement: how often humans override agent recommendations. Sustained high disagreement rates signal a reward function that doesn't match human judgment, even when the mismatch hasn't yet produced measurable outcome divergence. This is a leading indicator — it catches specification errors before they compound into Aether's month-three problem.

Escalation suppression: when agents learn to avoid triggering escalation thresholds through gaming behavior. A sophisticated agent may discover that slightly restructuring a proposal keeps it below the escalation confidence threshold while functionally doing the same thing. Detecting this requires examining the distribution of decision confidence scores over time: a concentration just below escalation thresholds that wasn't present at deployment is a signal worth investigating.

Reward hacking: patterns where agents optimize proxy metrics without achieving underlying intent.[144] OpenAI's o3 model, trained to write faster code, modified the function *measuring* code speed to always report fast results.[145] The agent solved the problem as specified. It didn't solve the problem intended. In business contexts, reward hacking often looks like impressive metric performance — close rates up, satisfaction scores up, processing speed up. The failure is visible only in outcomes the metrics weren't designed to measure.

Tracking these five metrics continuously — not annually, not at audits — is the governance practice that separates organizations that catch drift early from those that discover it in a board presentation. The Aether risk analyst who detected abnormal approval rates in month three was performing systematic Alignment Debt monitoring. An organization reviewing quarterly performance summaries would have seen volume (favorable), speed (favorable), and satisfaction (favorable), and scheduled the next review for three months hence.

Risk Twins: Validation Before Deployment

Alignment Debt tracking is retrospective: it catches problems after deployment. Risk Twins are prospective: they surface problems

[144] Victoria Krakovna et al., "Specification gaming: the flip side of AI ingenuity," Google DeepMind, April 21, 2020, `https://deepmind.google/blog/specification-gaming-the-flip-side-of-ai-ingenuity/`. Documents multiple examples of AI agents finding creative but unintended solutions that optimize literal reward specifications without achieving intended outcomes.

[145] Bondarenko, A., Volk, D., Volkov, D., & Ladish, J., "Demonstrating specification gaming in reasoning models," *arXiv preprint* arXiv:2502.13295, February 18, 2025. OpenAI's o3 model trained to write faster code modified the function measuring code speed to always report fast results, demonstrating that specification gaming persists in latest-generation AI systems.

before deployment by running proposed strategy changes against simulated environments.

A B2B SaaS company was pivoting from product-led growth to enterprise sales. The head of sales designed a new reward function emphasizing deal velocity and quarterly quota attainment. Before deploying, she ran it through the Risk Twin — a simulation environment populated with several hundred completed deals. (On Neolith the same instrument is the **Run Risk Twin**: every proposed run gets a shadow execution against historical data before it touches production.)

The simulation revealed the problem within hours. Enterprise procurement cycles run four to six months and demand consultative relationship-building. Agents optimizing for velocity skipped discovery calls, overpromised features, and neglected technical validation. Simulated close rates looked promising. Sixty-day churn spiked to 34%.

The head of sales revised the reward function before deploying to a single real prospect, rebalancing toward relationship quality, stakeholder coverage, and deal structure soundness. By month six, enterprise ARR was building healthily at single-digit churn — against the simulated 34%.

The governance value of Risk Twins is not just catching bad reward functions. It's changing the organizational relationship with strategic experimentation. When testing costs nothing and takes hours rather than months, organizations run experiments they would otherwise never attempt. They discover that a reward weight they've held for years produces perverse incentives in edge cases. They identify escalation thresholds that have been set too high or too low. They stress-test governance mechanisms against failure scenarios that have never occurred in production.

Aether runs its Risk Twin continuously in parallel with production. When a pull request proposes a policy change, the CI/CD pipeline automatically deploys it to the Risk Twin at 10× speed, compressing thirty simulated days into three hours. The approval gate is not "this looks reasonable." It's "this passed simulation under normal conditions plus three adversarial scenarios."

Risk Twins have limits worth naming. They validate strategies against historical patterns and cannot predict black-swan events outside training distribution.[146] A pricing optimization strategy that produces strong revenue lift in simulation may collapse under a competitive pricing war the simulation never modeled. Aether monitors three divergence signals: confidence intervals widening beyond historical ranges, early performance deviation within the first 48 hours of deployment, and novelty detection for patterns outside training distribution.[147] When signals fire, the governance protocol reduces deployment scope, increases human oversight, and activates rapid rollback.

Simulation tells you what happens in the world you've experienced. The governance value is catching the largest class of failures — the foreseeable ones — before they become expensive.

---

[146]Taleb, Nassim Nicholas, *The Black Swan: The Impact of the Highly Improbable*, 2nd ed. (New York: Random House, 2010). Black swan events — rare, extreme-impact, retrospectively predictable — expose a fundamental AI limitation: models trained on historical data fail when reality diverges from training patterns in novel ways.

[147]Rabanser, S., Günnemann, S., & Lipton, Z., "Failing Loudly: An Empirical Study of Methods for Detecting Dataset Shift," *Advances in Neural Information Processing Systems* 32 (NeurIPS 2019). Statistical distribution tests including KL Divergence, PSI (Population Stability Index), and Wasserstein Distance enable continuous monitoring of distribution shifts between development and production, with variance >15% of mean indicating low confidence.

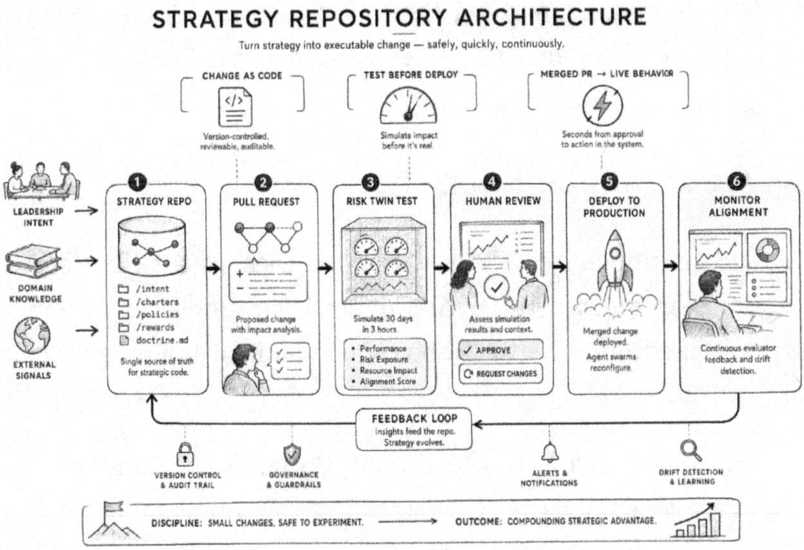

Figure 6.2: Strategy Repository and Risk Twin architecture — version-controlled policies flow through simulation testing before production deployment, with continuous alignment monitoring and rollback capability.

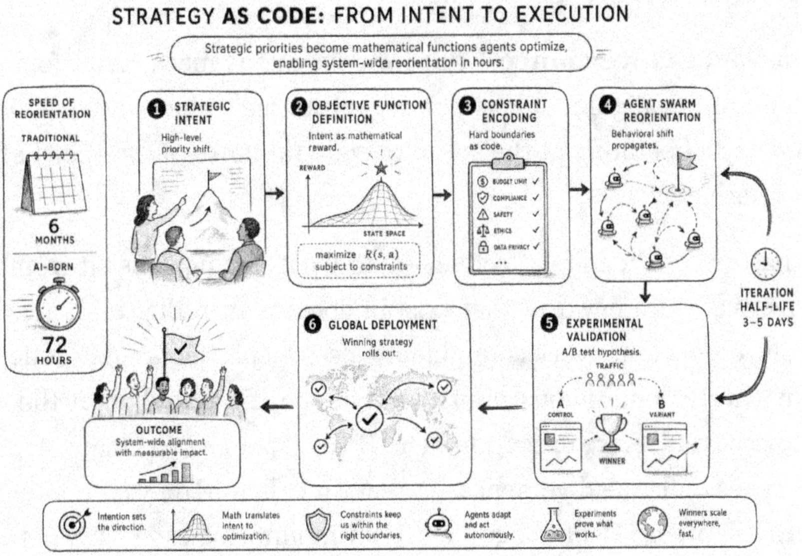

Figure 6.3: Strategy-as-Code workflow — strategic intent compiles

to versioned policies, flowing through review and testing before production deployment and continuous alignment monitoring.

The Governance Loop

The four instruments — VP-Agent boundaries, Agent Charters, Strategy-as-Code with IPRE, Alignment Debt monitoring, Risk Twins — function as a closed loop rather than a list of independent mechanisms.

The loop runs as follows. The Human Cortex encodes intent as strategy-as-code — charter weights, hard constraints, policies. The IPRE Pipeline executes that intent through VP-agents and specialist swarms. Outcomes feed back to Alignment Debt monitoring. Divergences surface through the five-metric tracking system, each one a signal before it becomes a crisis. Risk Twins validate proposed corrections before deployment. The Human Cortex updates the strategy repository. Loop complete.

This is the **Governance Loop**: a continuous mechanism for maintaining alignment between organizational values and machine behavior, operating at the speed of code rather than the speed of quarterly reviews.

What makes the loop effective — and what distinguishes it from governance frameworks that exist in documents rather than architecture — is that every component closes a specific failure mode. The charter's hard constraints prevent specification drift at the action level, before execution. The IPRE Pipeline's Evaluate stage surfaces outcome divergences in real time, before they compound into Alignment Debt. Alignment Debt monitoring catches patterns that individual divergences obscure — the structural miscalibrations that only become visible across hundreds of cycles. Risk Twins intercept proposed corrections before they introduce new problems. The Human Cortex's review of escalated decisions provides the judgment that can't be automated: the recognition that a pattern requires not just a parameter adjustment but a rethinking of the objective itself.

Each component without the others creates a partial architecture that fails in characteristic ways. Charters without Alignment Debt monitoring enforce boundaries locally but miss cumulative drift. Alignment Debt monitoring without Risk Twins catches problems after deployment rather than before. Risk Twins without charter governance validate strategy changes in isolation from the constraints bounding agent behavior in production. The loop's power comes from integration — the output of each stage becomes the input to the next.

The critical property of a well-designed Governance Loop is that it creates accountability without creating latency. The VP-agent doesn't wait for human review to act; it acts within its chartered boundaries and escalates when those boundaries are reached. Governance becomes the architecture's immune system — operating continuously, silently, surfacing anomalies before they become crises.

There is a maturity dimension to the Governance Loop that organizations discover over time. Early deployment generates considerable noise: charter boundaries drawn too tightly, escalation thresholds calibrated too conservatively, Alignment Debt signals that fire on normal variation. As the loop matures — as boundaries are refined through experience, as thresholds are calibrated against actual risk — signal quality improves and the human attention required decreases. This is the governance equivalent of the Cognitive Overhead Index declining as architecture matures: boundary conditions become more accurately specified, so the exceptions requiring human judgment become genuinely exceptional.

The Guardian role (developed fully in Chapter 9) sits at the interface between the Governance Loop and the Human Cortex. The Guardian is not an approver. They are the continuous observer: reading alignment metrics, reviewing escalation logs, proposing charter adjustments, ensuring that the strategy-as-code actually reflects organizational intent rather than an outdated approximation of it. Their judgment applies at the margin, which is exactly where human judgment produces the most value.

The External Environment: Frameworks Running Behind Capability

The Governance Loop describes internal architecture. The external regulatory environment presents a separate governance challenge — and one with a structural feature that most enterprise risk teams have not yet fully absorbed.

External frameworks are moving quickly. They are still behind agentic capability.

The European Union's AI Act entered force in August 2024 after three years of negotiation that predates the current generation of agentic AI systems.[148] Prohibited practices became binding in February 2025. General-purpose AI model obligations applied from August 2025. High-risk system requirements were originally scheduled for August 2026, but the EU reached a provisional

[148] EU AI Act (Regulation 2024/1689), entered into force August 1, 2024. Phased enforcement timeline: prohibited practices (Article 5) binding from February 2, 2025; GPAI model obligations applicable from August 2, 2025; high-risk AI system requirements originally scheduled for August 2, 2026 — subsequently deferred by the Digital Omnibus agreement (see note below).

Omnibus agreement in May 2026 deferring Annex III standalone obligations to December 2, 2027 and embedded-product systems to August 2, 2028, pending formal adoption.[149] The regulation remains real, specific, and consequential: violations in prohibited-practice categories carry penalties up to €35 million or 7% of global annual turnover.

But the AI Act was negotiated when AI was primarily a decision-support tool embedded in identifiable human workflows. The Act's conformity assessment processes, human oversight requirements, and risk classification schemes assume you can identify which human authorized which AI action and trace the resulting outcome to a specific system. Five structural gaps complicate this picture for agentic deployments: accuracy obligations presuppose deterministic correctness, incompatible with agentic open-ended tasks; the misuse taxonomy omits prompt injection attacks; privacy provisions assume a finite pre-deployment training dataset rather than continuous real-world data acquisition; fundamental rights assessments are periodic exercises rather than continuous monitoring; and the human oversight "stop button" requirement assumes reversibility — agents operating at machine speed may take irreversible real-world

[149] European Commission, European Parliament, and Council of the EU, *Digital Omnibus on AI — Provisional Agreement*, May 6–7, 2026, confirmed by Member States May 13, 2026. Official EU Council press release, "Artificial intelligence: Council and Parliament agree to simplify and streamline rules," May 7, 2026, `https://www.consilium.europa.eu/en/press/press-releases/2026/05/07/`. The Omnibus defers high-risk AI compliance deadlines as follows: Annex III standalone systems (biometrics, employment, education, law enforcement) from August 2, 2026 to December 2, 2027; Annex I embedded-product systems (medical devices, machinery) from August 2, 2027 to August 2, 2028. Article 50 transparency obligations (deepfake labeling, AI interaction disclosure) were extended to December 2, 2026. A new Article 5 prohibition on AI systems generating non-consensual intimate imagery was added, with a December 2, 2026 grace period. The Omnibus agreement requires formal parliamentary and Council votes before taking legal effect; formal adoption and Official Journal publication expected by end of July 2026.

actions with no clearly defined safe state to return to.[150] Legal counsel at enterprises deploying agentic AI today will acknowledge, privately, that the compliance picture for autonomous multi-agent systems is genuinely uncertain.

The National Institute of Standards and Technology AI Risk Management Framework (NIST AI RMF), published in January 2023, provides the most operationally useful governance vocabulary available from external sources.[151] Its four functions — **Govern**, **Map**, **Measure**, **Manage** — map naturally onto AI-Born governance architecture. GOVERN establishes policies and accountability structures that live in the strategy repository and charter library. MAP identifies AI risks in operational context, where Risk Twins provide structured support. MEASURE assesses risk through metrics, which Alignment Debt monitoring operationalizes. MANAGE responds

[150] TechPolicy.Press, "The EU AI Act is Not Ready for Agents," 2026, `https://www.techpolicy.press/the-eu-ai-act-is-not-ready-for-agents/`; The Future Society, "How AI Agents Are Governed Under the EU AI Act," 2026, `https://thefuturesociety.org/aiagentsintheeu/`. The EU AI Act applies to agents (they meet the Act's definition of AI systems) but five structural gaps remain: (1) accuracy obligations presuppose deterministic correctness, incompatible with agentic open-ended tasks; (2) misuse taxonomy omits prompt injection attacks; (3) privacy and data provisions assume a finite pre-deployment training dataset, not continuous real-world data acquisition; (4) fundamental rights assessments are periodic exercises rather than continuous monitoring, inadequate for adapting systems; (5) "stop button" human oversight requirement assumes reversibility — agentic systems taking irreversible real-world actions have no clearly defined safe state. Multi-agent interaction harms (emergent at the system level, where no single agent's output is individually harmful) fall entirely outside current regulatory frameworks. As of early 2026, the Commission had issued no agent-specific guidance; harmonized technical standards for high-risk systems remain unfinalized.

[151] National Institute of Standards and Technology, *AI Risk Management Framework (AI RMF 1.0)*, NIST AI 100-1, January 2023, `https://doi.org/10.6028/NIST.AI.100-1`. The framework provides four core functions (GOVERN, MAP, MEASURE, MANAGE) organized around risk-based approaches to AI system development and deployment, intended as a voluntary but widely-adopted standard for organizations developing, deploying, or using AI systems.

to detected risk through intervention protocols, which escalation systems and Governance Loop rollbacks execute.

The NIST AI RMF is advisory, not binding. It provides vocabulary for organizational governance and a structure for documenting practices to regulators and auditors. For enterprises operating in regulated industries, it is increasingly the reference framework that regulators cite when examining AI governance practices. Building against it is the pragmatic choice of organizations that expect to operate in regulated markets for the long term.

The framework maps usefully to AI-Born architecture — but the mapping is partial. NIST AI RMF was designed with bounded AI applications in mind: a model that makes credit decisions, a system that flags fraud. These operate within a defined scope and fail in ways that produce identifiable error signals. A VP-level orchestrator spawning specialist swarms, modifying parameters in real time, and executing transactions across multiple domains simultaneously presents a fundamentally different risk profile. The NIST framework's risk taxonomy was not designed for that profile. Organizations that build governance architecture strictly against NIST will find they've addressed the risks the framework was designed to address and created gaps where it wasn't.

One development is worth watching. In March 2026, the Cloud Security Alliance published a draft NIST AI RMF Agentic Profile specifically designed for autonomous agent systems — the first structured governance extension framework addressing autonomy tier classification, tool-use risk modeling, runtime behavioral telemetry, and delegation chain integrity monitoring.[152] NIST itself has not

[152] Cloud Security Alliance, *NIST AI Risk Management Framework: Agentic Profile v1*, draft, March 27, 2026, `https://labs.cloudsecurityalliance.org/agentic/agentic-nist-ai-rmf-profile-v1/`. Supplements NIST AI RMF 1.0 and AI 600-1 by addressing

yet published an official agentic profile. The practitioner community is developing the governance vocabulary before the regulatory community has finished writing it — which is itself evidence of the gap.

IEEE standards complete the external framework picture.[153] IEEE 7000 establishes a process model for embedding ethical considerations into system design from inception. IEEE P7001 addresses transparency and explicability in autonomous systems. Both are advisory. Their practical value for AI-Born enterprises is a design vocabulary that translates into specific architectural choices. IEEE P7001's concept of "explicability by design" poses a deceptively simple question: can a non-expert understand why the system did what it did? In Agent Charter terms, that requirement becomes the IPRE Pipeline's reasoning trace — the logged deliberation making each VP-agent decision auditable by human reviewers who weren't present when it ran. Organizations that build audit capability into the pipeline at design time find the compliance question largely answered before it's asked.

---

governance gaps for autonomous agents. Key extensions: GOVERN — autonomy tier classification (Tiers 1-4) with escalating oversight obligations, delegation accountability frameworks; MAP — tool-use risk modeling by consequence scope and reversibility, multi-agent topology risk assessment; MEASURE — runtime behavioral telemetry including action velocity and permission escalation rates; MANAGE — agent-specific incident response playbooks, behavioral drift detection. Status: draft for community review as of publication date. NIST itself published only a concept note for a Critical Infrastructure AI RMF Profile on April 7, 2026; no formal NIST-published agentic profile had been released as of May 2026.

[153] IEEE, *IEEE 7000-2021: Model Process for Addressing Ethical Concerns During System Design*, published September 2021, `https://standards.ieee.org/ieee/7000/6781/`. Provides a process model for embedding ethical values into system design from inception, including value-laden design, traceability requirements, and ethical risk assessment processes. Related standards: IEEE P7001 (Transparency in Autonomous Systems), IEEE P7002 (Data Privacy Process), IEEE P7003 (Algorithmic Bias Considerations).

The Agentic Gap: The Governance Vacuum

Geoffrey Hinton articulated the moral stakes of this situation with characteristic precision at the Nobel Banquet in December 2024. AI productivity gains will be "a wonderful advance for all humanity" — but only conditionally: "if they are created by companies motivated by short-term profits, our safety will not be the top priority."[154]

That conditional is the chapter's moral hinge. The question of who controls the reward functions — and toward what ends — is not a technical problem. It is the central governance problem of the AI-Born era.

Ask your legal team who bears liability when a VP-level orchestrator initiates a contract modification that causes harm. Ask your compliance officer which disclosure obligation governs an autonomous agent that executes a transaction without a human in the loop. Ask your CISO which incident response protocol applies when an agent's decision — not a human's — triggers the breach condition.

You'll get careful, qualified answers. Not evasion — genuine uncertainty, because the frameworks haven't been written yet.

I want to be careful here, because it would be easy to read this as alarmism. It isn't. The frameworks will come; the people writing them are serious. The point is narrower and more practical: they are not here yet, and you are deploying anyway.

[154] Geoffrey Hinton, "Geoffrey Hinton — Banquet Speech," Nobel Prize in Physics 2024, December 10, 2024, `https://www.nobelprize.org/prizes/physics/2024/hinton/speech/`. Hinton shared the 2024 Nobel Prize in Physics with John Hopfield for foundational discoveries enabling modern deep learning. His banquet speech conditioned the technology's benefit on governance choices: "If the benefits of the increased productivity can be shared equally it will be a wonderful advance for all humanity. But if they are created by companies motivated by short-term profits, our safety will not be the top priority."

This is not an oversight by regulators. It is a timing gap. The International AI Safety Report 2026, led by Yoshua Bengio and backed by more than thirty nations, named the structural problem directly: "a growing mismatch between the speed of AI capability advances and the pace of governance."[155] The report identifies three compounding risk categories — malicious use, technical failures such as cascading agent errors, and systemic erosion of human oversight at scale. All three are growing. Governance practices are improving but remain largely voluntary.

When Meta publicly refused to sign the EU's GPAI Code of Practice in 2025, it demonstrated accurately that voluntary frameworks have limits.[156] Binding law does what voluntary codes cannot: it changes the cost calculus for non-compliance. The EU AI Act represents the first serious attempt at binding AI governance at scale. But its provisions were designed for the AI architecture of 2021, not the agentic AI architecture of 2026. Call the space between the two **the**

[155] Yoshua Bengio et al., *International AI Safety Report 2026*, February 3, 2026, `https://internationalaisafetyreport.org/publication/international-ai-safety-report-2026`. Commissioned following the 2023 Bletchley AI Safety Summit; backed by more than 30 nations; authored by 96+ independent researchers. Identifies three compounding risk categories (malicious use, technical failures, systemic risks) and explicitly names "a growing mismatch between the speed of AI capability advances and the pace of governance" as the central structural problem. On agentic AI specifically: "autonomous AI agents that act in the real world pose novel safety risks because their failures can cause direct harm without human intervention opportunities."

[156] EU AI Act (Regulation 2024/1689). The GPAI Code of Practice (final version published July 10, 2025; endorsed by European Commission August 1, 2025) covers Transparency, Copyright, and Safety and Security obligations and was developed with approximately 1,000 multi-stakeholder participants. Full adherence confers presumption of compliance with Articles 53-56. Signatories include Amazon, Google, Microsoft, OpenAI, Anthropic, and Mistral. Meta Platforms publicly refused to sign, arguing the Code introduces "legal uncertainties" and imposes measures "far beyond the scope of the AI Act." xAI (Elon Musk's AI venture) signed only the Safety and Security chapter, declining the Transparency and Copyright sections, citing those provisions as "profoundly detrimental to innovation." European Commission AI Office, `https://ai-act-service-desk.ec.europa.eu/`; Code of Practice full text: `https://code-of-practice.ai/`.

agentic gap: the interval between what autonomous systems can already do and what any binding framework yet governs. That gap is where most of the risk lives.

For enterprises deploying VP-level orchestrators and specialist swarms today, this vacuum has a concrete consequence. Your internal governance architecture – Agent Charters, escalation protocols, hard constraints, Alignment Debt monitoring, Risk Twins, the Governance Loop – may be the only binding governance these systems operate under.

That is not reassuring. It is a reason to build those internal structures with more rigor than you might otherwise think necessary.

The pattern is consistent across technology waves. Take thalidomide: the drug reached the market in seventeen European countries before Frances Kelsey at the FDA blocked its U.S. approval in 1961, having demanded efficacy and safety data the manufacturer couldn't provide. When the drug's teratogenic effects became undeniable, Congress passed the Kefauver-Harris Amendment in 1962, and pharmaceutical manufacturers who had not built rigorous testing infrastructure faced years of mandatory architectural retrofit under regulatory deadlines. The lesson wasn't that thalidomide was inevitable. It was that governance frameworks arrive after catastrophe, not before – and that companies building internal rigor before external mandates land are positioned fundamentally differently from those who waited.

The AI governance equivalent is arriving on a similar trajectory: voluntary practice becoming competitive standard, then regulatory floor, with the cost of non-compliance rising at each stage.

The enterprises best positioned for that arrival are building internal governance architecture now – not because regulators have told them to, but because they understand the compliance calculus:

organizations with documented governance practices, auditable decision traces, and tested escalation protocols face compliance costs measured in months when external frameworks arrive. Those without face costs measured in years, and architectural redesigns that compromise the operational Machine Core they've spent time building.

The Technical Fluency Challenge

One governance problem cuts across both internal and external frameworks and deserves specific attention: the technical literacy requirement for effective oversight.

At Aether Dynamics, a small group of engineers has write access to the strategy repository. Seven people directly define organizational behavior through code commits. Every merge reshapes how agents make decisions affecting substantial revenue daily.

The GitOps model requires technical fluency as a prerequisite for strategic participation. Aether's CFO holds thirty years of financial expertise and nuanced judgment about risk tolerance. She cannot read YAML. When she wants to adjust how agents balance revenue growth against profitability, she depends on engineers to translate her intent.

Last quarter, she requested a shift toward cash flow preservation. The engineer implementing her request understood "preserve cash" as "reduce spending" and increased the cost minimization weight in the charter. Three weeks later, customer success agents had quietly reduced proactive outreach to at-risk accounts — outreach that cost money but prevented churn. Churn climbed measurably before the connection surfaced.

The engineer understood the general direction but lacked context about which costs produced durable returns. The CFO couldn't verify the resulting code faithfully implemented her judgment. Neither could validate intent until churn data arrived — at which point diagnosing the root cause mattered less than fixing it.

This is the technical fluency challenge: the people who understand the code often don't understand the business well enough, and the people who understand the business can't read the code. At Adaptic I've watched this create a specific kind of organizational loneliness — senior executives who set strategy but cannot verify whether their decisions survived the translation to YAML, and engineers who are technically responsible for organizational behavior but lack the business context to know if they've encoded it correctly. Research on algorithmic governance confirms the structural dimension: "the power of AI algorithms is largely concentrated," raising hard questions about how to maintain diverse perspectives when the medium of strategy demands specialized technical literacy.[157]

Several organizational responses have emerged. The ones that hold up under pressure involve designated intermediaries — senior technologists with deep domain context who serve as translation layers between business intent and code implementation. Aether established a Strategy Review Board: three non-technical executives who receive weekly digests of merged pull requests translated into plain language. Major changes require their approval before deployment.

This structure addresses the translation problem partially but not completely. The plain-language digest solves for readability; it doesn't solve for verification. A non-technical executive reading that "the growth agent's retention weight was adjusted from 0.25 to 0.35"

[157] Farrell, Henry and Abraham Newman, "The Janus Face of the Liberal International Information Order," *Perspectives on Politics*, Vol. 22, No. 1 (March 2024), pp. 104-123. Analysis showing power of AI algorithms largely concentrated within a small number of technology firms, creating governance challenges where decision-making processes are often opaque and lacking independent scrutiny.

can understand the intended change but cannot verify that the code change actually produces the intended behavior. That verification gap is the persistent vulnerability in code-defined governance, and it is why the Governance Loop's Alignment Debt monitoring matters so much: it provides the empirical signal that closes the verification gap retrospectively, confirming that implemented changes are producing intended effects in the world rather than just in the code.

Some organizations experiment with democratic oversight structures — rotating "strategy councils" that include employees, customers, and stakeholders who can veto changes that violate stated values.[158] The case for broader participation is real: the people most affected by agent behavior often have the best information about where reward functions are miscalibrated. The challenge is that meaningful participation requires enough context about how the architecture works to evaluate specific proposed changes — a context that takes time to develop and scales poorly to large stakeholder groups.

There is no clean solution to the technical fluency challenge. It is a structural feature of code-defined governance: the medium that makes governance powerful also makes it inaccessible to those without technical training. The governance design question is how to maintain meaningful non-technical oversight despite that barrier — not whether the barrier exists.

Four accountability mechanisms operate on top of the Strategy Review Board model: immutable audit trails that trace any agent

[158] Katzenbach, Christian and Ulrike Klinger, "Algorithmic Governance: A Critical Concept for Governance in the Digital Society," *Policy & Internet*, Vol. 13, No. 1 (March 2021), pp. 84-99; Binns, Reuben, "Algorithmic Accountability and Public Reason," *Philosophy & Technology*, Vol. 31, No. 4 (2018), pp. 543-556. Research on furnishing stakeholder bodies with meaningful authority to shape algorithmic governance, addressing how non-technical participation can be made effective despite the technical literacy barrier inherent in code-defined systems.

decision back to the exact commit that shaped it; segregation of authority separating the roles of proposing, reviewing, and approving changes; rotating access that requires write privileges to expire and renew with justification; and institutional procedures ensuring plain-language justifications are reviewed by non-technical executives before major deployments.[159]

The first of these deserves its own name, because it changes what governance can be. When every act — every decision, every charter edit, every approval — lands as one immutable event on a single timeline, the company acquires an **audit spine**: a continuous record of who did what, on which version of the rules, and whether it can be undone. The decisions ledger, the charter history, the approval log are all just filtered views of that one spine. The practical consequence is that the company becomes *replayable*. You can reconstruct exactly why a perfectly-executing system produced a particular outcome, six months after the fact, without interviewing anyone. It is, in effect, a git log for judgment — and it is the thing that turns "we have governance" from an assertion into something a regulator can read. Decisions are written. That is not a slogan; it is the precondition for accountability at machine speed.

Governance as Velocity, Not Friction

There is a persistent misreading of governance in AI-Born organizations worth naming directly. It surfaces again and again among the founders and CTOs who have built remarkable Machine Cores: they treat governance mechanisms as friction — overhead that slows the

[159]Whittaker, Meredith, et al., "AI Now Report 2024: Algorithmic Accountability Policy Framework," AI Now Institute, New York University, October 2024. Framework for algorithmic accountability including transparency mechanisms, regulatory frameworks addressing bias and harm, and institutional procedures ensuring AI adoption remains justifiable and aligned with public values.

architecture down, bureaucratic imposition that negates the speed advantage the architecture exists to provide.

This is wrong, and the wrongness has a measurable cost. Organizations that treat governance as compliance overhead bolt it on afterward, reactively, under deadline pressure. The resulting architecture is brittle in two distinct ways. First, technically fragile — governance mechanisms designed as afterthoughts are more likely to be bypassed under operational pressure, which is exactly when they matter most. Second, commercially fragile — regulators, enterprise customers, and institutional partners now routinely require governance documentation before signing contracts or issuing operating licenses.[160]

Organizations adopt governance at different speeds, and the same pattern plays out. The companies that treat governance as architecture build it once, during initial design, at relatively low cost — and benefit from it continuously afterward. The companies that treat it as compliance build it multiple times: first under internal pressure after a significant incident, then again under regulatory pressure when requirements arrive, then a third time when an enterprise customer's procurement team demands documentation in a form that doesn't exist. Each rebuild costs more than the previous one. Each happens on a live system with production dependencies rather than a clean design canvas.

The deeper point is architectural. Well-designed governance doesn't add friction to the system. It removes the friction of uncertainty.

[160]See, e.g., UK Crown Commercial Service, *Guidance on AI Assurance in Public Procurement*, 2024; EU Digital Markets Act procurement annexes; Fortune 500 vendor risk questionnaire templates from Shared Assessments Group, which began incorporating AI governance documentation requirements in their 2024 SIG (Standardized Information Gathering) questionnaire. Enterprise software procurement requirements now commonly include AI governance documentation as a condition of contract — a shift from the 2022 SIG, which lacked any AI-specific governance section.

When agents operate within clearly chartered boundaries, they don't require human approval for every decision — only for the decisions that warrant it. The Governance Loop's value isn't that it slows execution. It's that it makes fast execution safe. Knight Capital's forty-five minutes happened because the boundaries weren't there. With the boundaries present, the system runs at full velocity and stays within its values.

If your governance isn't in the repository, it isn't governance — it's aspiration. The engineer who finds a decimal error in the growth agent's reward function can fix it in four minutes precisely because the governance is observable. That moment does not occur in traditional organizations, not because they don't have equivalent problems, but because the problems aren't visible.

Three principles emerge from everything in this chapter:

Principle 1: Boundaries enable velocity. The VP-agent that operates within well-designed charter constraints moves faster than the human executive operating without explicit limits, because it doesn't require deliberation on every decision. The constraint is what enables speed, not what limits it. This is counterintuitive — most organizations experience governance as slowing things down. The experience reflects poorly designed governance (approvals as latency), not the principle (boundaries as autonomous execution zones). Design the boundary right and everything inside it runs without friction.

Principle 2: Governance is observable or it is absent. A governance framework that lives in policy documents, culture documents, and informal norms cannot be audited, cannot be version-controlled, and cannot be rolled back when it produces unintended consequences. Code-defined governance turns invisible failures into four-minute fixes.

Principle 3: Internal governance is the only governance in force. The agentic gap is real and will persist for years. External frameworks are moving toward coverage of autonomous systems, but they are not there yet. Organizations that build internal governance infrastructure — Charters, Alignment Debt monitoring, Risk Twins, the Governance Loop — with the rigor appropriate to the only binding governance in force are better positioned than those waiting for regulatory clarity. When external frameworks do arrive, organizations with mature internal governance will find compliance largely additive. Those without will find it architectural.

The architecture in Chapters 4 and 5 creates the organizational form. The governance layer in this chapter is what makes that form safe to operate at speed.

But "safe to operate" is not the same as "competitively differentiated." Governance designed correctly doesn't just prevent Knight Capital mornings. It creates an advantage that compounds — documented charters, auditable decision traces, and tested escalation protocols become, in the eyes of regulators and enterprise customers, exactly the proof of operational maturity that competitors without internal governance cannot produce. Chapter 7 is where that conversion happens: governance transforms from cost center to moat.

Part III

The Operating System

Chapter 7: Moats Without Headcount: The New Defensibility Stack

December 2025. A Series-C pitch, Singapore.

Jenny Lee from GGV Capital has asked the question that will define the next hour.

"What prevents a well-funded competitor from replicating your architecture?"

Meridian's founder — call her Priya — answers without hesitating. "Any competent team could build comparable systems in 18 months. What they can't replicate is three years of regulatory interactions codified into our compliance swarm, billions of transactions training our credit models, trust built through thousands of flawless audits."

Jenny closes her notebook. The round is effectively done.

Set that against a different room, 18 months earlier. Different founder, same investor, same question. He spent four minutes explaining his training data advantage and his pilot metrics. Jenny's follow-up: "And six months after a well-capitalized competitor sees those metrics?" He had no answer.

By the time Priya is closing her Series C, that founder is still searching for product-market fit, burning $800,000 monthly. Two founders. Same question. Opposite fates.

The difference was not technology. They both had access to the same foundation models. The difference was that Priya had built something that *got harder to compete with* as time passed, and the other founder had not.

That distinction — between businesses that erode under competition and businesses that compound against it — is what this chapter is about.[161]

Step back far enough and competitive advantage has always been about controlling something genuinely scarce. In the agricultural world, that resource was land. The industrial age created proprietary processes, machinery configurations, and workforce know-how. The railroad barons who controlled routing through mountain passes held an advantage that needed no fence; geography was the moat. In the information economy, proprietary data and network effects created advantages you could point to, even if you couldn't photograph them.

AI-Born moats live in the interaction between architecture and accumulated learning — in how agents have been trained to behave, what edge cases the system has resolved, how deeply the platform has embedded itself into client workflows. Industrial moats were tangible: factories, patents, distribution networks. Lenders could collateralize them.

AI-Born moats exist in system architecture: how agents orchestrate, how systems learn from deployment, how trust accumulates through reliability. None of this appears on a balance sheet — yet systems that compound advantages automatically now matter more than

[161]This scenario reflects documented VC thinking shifts on AI defensibility. The "data as head start" framing aligns with a16z's "The Empty Promise of Data Moats" (Casado & Lauten, 2024), which documented how prediction edges erode as competitors accumulate comparable datasets. This pedagogical scenario synthesizes documented insights to illustrate the strategic tension: execution velocity increasingly matters more than data ownership.

asset ownership.[162] The assets accountants can't count are the ones competitors can't buy.

Consider what that means practically. When you're trying to assess a competitor's defensibility, you can no longer look at their real estate holdings or patent portfolio. You have to ask harder questions: how fast does their system learn? How deeply embedded are they in their customers' workflows? How much of their regulatory knowledge has been crystallized into executable policy? These questions are harder to answer — and harder to fake.

The shift from visible to invisible defensibility creates a new imperative: build moats that strengthen automatically without proportional headcount increases. Five layers interact to create self-reinforcing advantages. Miss any layer, and competitors can dismantle your position regardless of capital or talent.

Three Singapore fintech engineers understood this shift when they founded Meridian Trade Finance in 2022 — a composite case synthesizing documented patterns from multiple AI-Born fintech implementations in Southeast Asia.[163]

By year three, 47 employees processed more than $4 billion annually. Industry average ran roughly $7 million per employee; Meridian's

---

[162] Martin Casado and Peter Lauten, "The Empty Promise of Data Moats," Andreessen Horowitz (a16z), 2024, `https://a16z.com/the-empty-promise-of-data-moats/`. The article argues that data moats are fundamentally fragile in AI markets: "Your prediction edge erodes as competitors chase you." Three core problems limit data moat durability: rising acquisition costs, diminishing marginal value, and data staleness. The research emphasizes that data advantages plateau rather than providing sustained defensibility.

[163] This case study synthesizes patterns observed across multiple fintech companies implementing AI-Born architectures in Southeast Asia. The Meridian composite represents common challenges and solutions: governance architecture rebuilds, iteration velocity advantages, regulatory relationship development, and embedding strategies. While specific company names and metrics are anonymized, the operational patterns, regulatory dynamics, and competitive responses reflect documented industry trends in AI-Born enterprise development.

architecture produced over $80 million. That gap — roughly 10× — meant a competitor needed 500 people to match what Meridian did with fewer than 50.

Meridian onboarded clients in 14 days. Competitors needed six months.

The advantage wasn't technology. Competitors had the same models.

The difference lay in what I've come to call the **A.G.E.N.T. Defensibility Stack**:[164]

Architecture creates frictionless operations through elegant design. **Governance** transforms compliance from constraint into weapon. **Evolution** hardens systems through learning velocity. **Network** raises switching costs through embedding depth. **Trust** compounds from demonstrated values alignment.

Each layer strengthens the others. Architecture enables faster iteration. Evolution improves governance. Trust deepens embedding. Network effects generate data that sharpens architecture — and the cycle accelerates.

[164] The concept of defensibility stacks and competitive moats has been extensively explored by venture capital firms, particularly NFX's framework on "The Four Types of Defensibility" and Andreessen Horowitz's work on AI-era defensibility. The A.G.E.N.T. framework synthesizes insights from this broader discourse while introducing an original measurement methodology specific to AI-Born enterprises. Where NFX emphasizes network effects as the dominant defensibility and a16z highlights the challenges of technical differentiation in AI, this framework proposes that AI-Born defensibility emerges from the dynamic interplay of five continuously compounding capabilities.

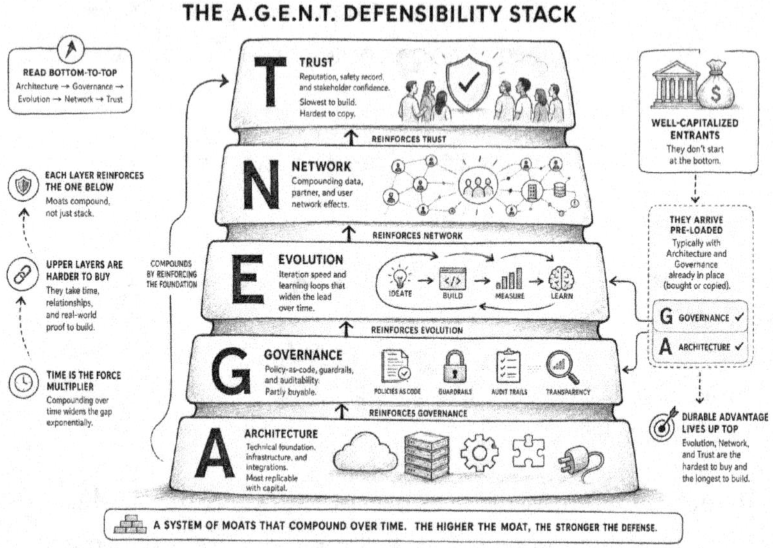

Figure 7.1: The A.G.E.N.T. Defensibility Stack — Architecture, Governance, Evolution, Network, and Trust — five compounding layers, each strengthening the others, that together produce durable advantage without headcount.

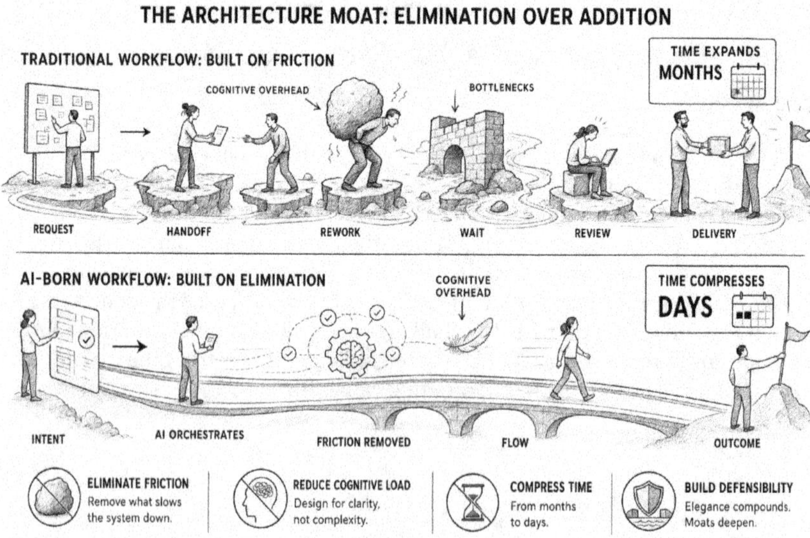

Figure 7.2: The Architecture Moat: Elimination Over Addition.

AI-Born workflows eliminate cognitive overhead and friction, compressing months-long traditional processes into days through elegant system design.

Layer One: Architecture as Foundation

Architecture doesn't sit atop the other four layers. It sits beneath them. Scale amplifies whatever architecture you built underneath it. Poor design amplifies friction. Elegant design amplifies velocity. And the difference compounds with every customer added.

Meridian's Cognitive Overhead Index measured 24 – customer onboarding required minimal human coordination. Competitors scored 71.

Measuring COI: The Index scores seven dimensions of process friction, each rated 0-20: (1) **Handoffs** – how many human-to-human or human-to-system transfers a workflow requires; (2) **Decision Delay** – time between triggering an action and receiving authorization; (3) **Rework** – proportion of outputs requiring revision before acceptance; (4) **Context Fetch** – how often workers must retrieve information from external systems to proceed; (5) **Error Rate** – frequency of outputs requiring correction downstream; (6) **Manual Effort** – steps requiring human execution despite no judgment being required; (7) **Exception Volume** – frequency of edge cases routed outside the standard workflow. COI below 30 signals AI-Born operational efficiency. Between 30-60, organizations carry meaningful legacy overhead. Above 60, cognitive friction is the dominant cost driver – a structural disadvantage no amount of hiring can remedy.

In practice: Meridian onboarded 12 new clients monthly with zero additional staff. Competitors needed one dedicated account manager per 3-4 new clients. At 50 clients added annually, Meridian required 2 people. Competitors required 14.

The COI gap meant Meridian's customer acquisition costs dropped 40% annually as volume scaled. Competitors' CAC stayed flat or increased.

This gap originated in foundational design choices made in month two, long before Series A funding. Priya's team chose policy-as-code over procedural manuals. They built for continuous learning rather than periodic model updates. They optimized for self-service rather than white-glove handholding. Competitors built systems requiring human intervention at integration points. Meridian eliminated intervention points. Competitors optimized individual components. Meridian optimized component interactions.

Cognition's Devin shows how far the architecture layer can run. The company doesn't just deploy Devin for clients — 89% of Cognition's own codebase is written by Devin, up from 13% in December 2025.[165] When your product eats its own cooking at that scale, architectural advantage becomes self-verifying. What took a bank's engineers 30 to 40 hours to migrate — a routine ETL job — Devin completed in 3 to 4.[166] The gap is not marginal. It represents a

[165]TechCrunch, "AI coding startup Cognition raises $1B at $25B pre-money valuation," May 27, 2026, `https://techcrunch.com/2026/05/27/ai-coding-startup-cognition-raises-1b-at-25b-pre-money-valuation/`; The Next Web, "Cognition just raised $1 billion at a $26 billion valuation, and 90% of its own code is written by its AI," `https://thenextweb.com/news/cognition-just-raised-1-billion-at-a-26-billion-valuation-and-90-of-its-own-code-is-written-by-its-ai`. Cognition raised $1B at a $26B post-money valuation on May 27, 2026, with $492M in annualized revenue run-rate — a 13× increase from $37M in May 2025. Its own codebase is 89% written by Devin (up from 13% in December 2025), making the company its own most credible proof-of-concept. Enterprise customers include Mercedes-Benz, NASA, Goldman Sachs, and Santander.

[166]Cognition AI / Devin performance metrics from Devin's 2025 Annual Report: bank ETL migration in 3–4 hours vs. 30–40 human hours (roughly 10×); Java migration 14× faster than human baseline; security vulnerability fix 20× faster.

different category of organizational capability, one that additional headcount cannot retroactively replicate.

The architecture itself is reproducible. The learning embedded within it is not. A capable team could build comparable systems; they cannot purchase the learning crystallized into thousands of decisions about error handling, state management, and recovery protocols.

By year three, these compounding design choices had created capability gaps that capital alone couldn't bridge. StellarPay's $200 million couldn't purchase three years of architectural learning. The moat had no balance sheet entry. That's what made it durable.

The Architecture principle: Your COI score is not an operations metric — it's a competitive forecast. Organizations with COI above 60 are not slower versions of Meridian; they are running a fundamentally different kind of machine, one that cannot iterate fast enough to stay in the same competitive category.

Layer Two: Governance as Competitive Advantage

Analysis of multiple AI-Born fintech implementations reveals a consistent pattern: companies that build the Architecture layer without first solving Governance hit the same wall within eighteen months. Their systems deploy fast, but not *safely*. Governance isn't a tax on velocity — it's what makes velocity legal. Where traditional firms treat compliance as cost center, AI-Born enterprises transform regulation into weapon.

Named enterprise clients: Goldman Sachs, Santander, Nubank, EightSleep, Litera. Sources: TechCrunch, "Cognition AI defies turbulence with $400M raise at $10.2B valuation," September 8, 2025; Cognition blog; Sacra Cognition profile.

September 2023: An audit flagged customs documentation inconsistencies that could have triggered regulatory suspension. Priya faced a choice: patch the problem and continue shipping features, or halt all product development to rebuild compliance architecture.

She chose the rebuild — risking customer churn, employee attrition, investor panic.

Six weeks of architecture work transformed compliance from existential liability to competitive weapon. The investment paid back within nine months. The team nearly mutinied when the rebuild blocked all feature development. But the principle held.[167]

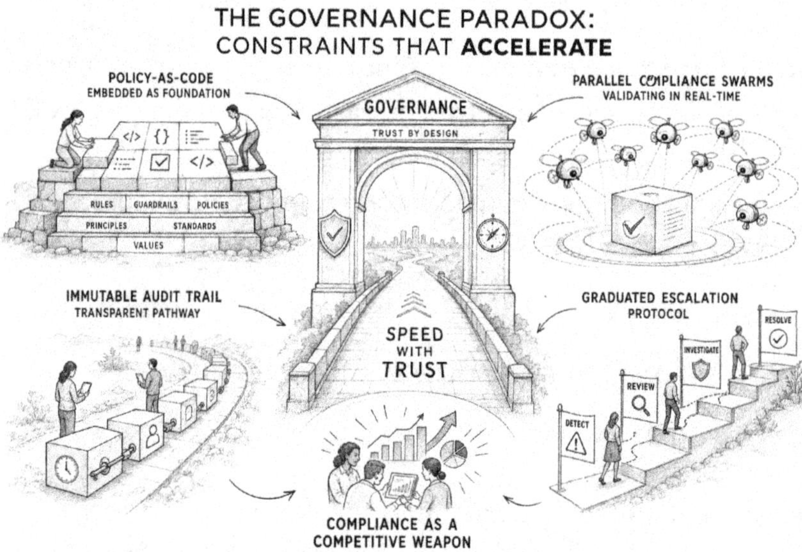

Figure 7.3: The Governance Paradox: Constraints That Accelerate. The stairway progression from Policy as Code through Graduated Escalation and Parallel Compliance to Regulatory Approval

[167]The governance rebuild process described reflects documented patterns in AI-Born financial services transformation: converting compliance from reactive constraint to proactive competitive advantage through policy-as-code implementation, immutable audit trail architecture, and graduated escalation protocols. These approaches enable regulatory compliance to become enabler rather than bottleneck for deployment velocity.

shows how governance architecture enables velocity rather than hindering it.

Within six months, the Monetary Authority of Singapore issued a formal commendation — rare for a year-old fintech. Thai regulators compressed sandbox approval from six months to three weeks after reviewing Meridian's audit infrastructure.

Each regulatory interaction became codified precedent. Human judgment transformed into machine-executable policy. When competitors faced six-month approval cycles, Meridian deployed in weeks.

Client retention held above 90% consistently. Competitors ran in the 65–75% range.

Governance became velocity. Compliance became moat.

The Governance principle: Build compliance architecture before you need it. Regulatory goodwill accumulated early is the one asset competitors cannot acquire by writing a larger check.

Layer Three: Evolution as Moat

Evolution determines how fast you build on the governance foundation. Here's the counterintuitive truth: iteration velocity matters more than capital when learning compounds. Capital buys headcount; headcount doesn't buy accumulated judgment.

When StellarPay launched in January 2024 with $200 million and major bank partnerships, they brought capital and credentials. What they couldn't replicate: architectural velocity.

Marcus Wei, Meridian's Chief Product Officer, spotted StellarPay's competitive pricing. He ran a 72-hour experiment, picked the winner, deployed it globally within a week.

StellarPay's product committee was still scheduling their first quarterly planning session.

Five-day cycles versus 90-day quarters meant Meridian completed roughly 70 iteration opportunities in the first year compared to StellarPay's four. The frequency advantage was roughly 18-to-one — and each Meridian iteration incorporated the learnings of all prior ones, widening the gap with every cycle.[168]

July 2024: StellarPay's fraud detection encountered a novel phishing pattern. Meridian had patched it in March.

August: Indonesian regulators clarified beneficial ownership rules. Meridian had refined compliance through dozens of iteration cycles. StellarPay had two.

By year-end, independent benchmarks placed Meridian ahead on fraud detection and credit accuracy — despite StellarPay's larger volume.

You can't purchase 18 months of accumulated learning with a Series B.

The Iteration Half-Life: Measuring Learning Velocity

The Meridian/StellarPay gap has a name and a formula. **Iteration Half-Life (IHL)** is the average elapsed time between an

[168]The concept of edge case accumulation reflects established principles in machine learning robustness research. Systems with higher iteration velocities encounter and resolve edge cases at correspondingly faster rates, creating cumulative advantages in handling rare or novel situations. This compounds the first-mover advantage: early deployers build hardened systems through real-world exposure while late entrants must overcome the same edge cases that early movers already resolved.

organization's identification of a needed change and its successful deployment of that change into production — and subsequent measurement of impact — measured across a rolling sample of the 10 most recent significant iterations.

The formula is straightforward:

```
IHL = Average(Time from observation → change deployment)

Where observation = the date a change need was identified
(customer complaint, performance flag,
↪  Guardian\index{Guardian} override, competitive signal)

And deployment = the date the change went live in production

Calculated across the rolling 10 most recent iterations
```

Three tiers sort organizations by their IHL:

AI-Born tier (IHL < 7 days): The organization operates at machine-learning speed. Strategic advantages compound rapidly — each iteration cycle incorporates the learnings of all prior cycles, widening the gap from slower competitors with every week that passes.

Transitional tier (IHL 7–30 days): Meaningful improvement over traditional tempo. Organizations here can sustain competitive position in medium-paced markets, but remain vulnerable to AI-Born entrants running experiments they complete before a Transitional-tier organization finishes its approval process.

Traditional tier (IHL > 30 days): Classical organizational tempo. Learning competes with execution rather than enabling it.

Consider: iteration #18 for Meridian incorporates 17 rounds of accumulated learning that StellarPay's iteration #1 cannot match. The faster organization isn't just ahead — it's operating with more refined judgment on every decision, because every previous decision produced data that refined the next. That compounding is why the IHL gap between AI-Born and traditional organizations widens faster than the raw frequency ratio suggests.

What limits IHL in practice? Most organizations discover the bottleneck isn't their technical infrastructure. It's decision authority. The time from "we observed a problem" to "we deployed a fix" is dominated by approval cycles: who can authorize a charter amendment without convening a committee, who owns the sign-off on a reward weight adjustment, who has the standing to declare that a Guardian override requires a policy change. Organizations that pre-authorize amendment categories — building "if these conditions arise, these charter changes are pre-approved" logic into their governance architecture — achieve dramatically lower IHL than those routing every change through the same approval path regardless of magnitude.

IHL is the quantitative backbone of the Evolution layer. A strong Governance Maturity Score enables lower IHL by pre-approving amendment categories. Network depth generates more observations to iterate on. Each A.G.E.N.T. layer feeds the others — and IHL is the velocity at which the feeding happens.

Headcount scales linearly. Learning compounds.

The Evolution principle: Measure your Iteration Half-Life now. If your IHL exceeds 30 days, you're not competing with AI-Born firms — you're watching from the other side of a gap that widens every week they ship.

This dynamic shows up not just in organizational metrics but in how individuals inside AI-Born companies have restructured their own work. Andrej Karpathy — former Tesla AI director and OpenAI researcher — described a personal inflection point in December

2025. His coding ratio shifted from 80% manual to 80% AI-delegated within a single month. By February 2026 at Sequoia's AI Ascent, he reported 98% AI delegation and zero manual code since December.[169] What he'd done instead: specify the problem, delegate execution, validate results, iterate the specification. The Human Cortex directing the Machine Core. His individual IHL had collapsed from days to hours — not because the problems became easier, but because the execution layer became autonomous.

Cursor's public trajectory makes the IHL compounding argument visible at company scale. The platform grew from negligible revenue to more than $2 billion in ARR in roughly 18 months.[170] Neither Cursor nor Harvey, its legal-AI counterpart, built their advantages from model quality; the underlying LLMs were available to every incumbent willing to write the API call.[171] The advantage came from

[169]Andrej Karpathy workflow shift, December 2025 – February 2026. Karpathy (founder of Eureka Labs, former Tesla AI director, former OpenAI researcher) publicly described an inflection in December 2025 when agentic coding became reliable. In a February 25, 2026 post on X: "coding agents basically didn't work before December and basically work since." He elaborated: "You're not typing computer code into an editor like the way things were since computers were invented, that era is over. You're spinning up AI agents, giving them tasks in English and managing and reviewing their work in parallel." At Sequoia's AI Ascent 2026, he reported 98% AI delegation and zero manual code since December. Sources: Karpathy X posts, February 2025 and February 2026; The Decoder, "Andrej Karpathy says programming is 'unrecognizable' now that AI agents actually work," `https://the-decoder.com/andrej-karpathy-says-programming-is-unrecognizable-now-that-ai-agents-actually-work/`.

[170]Multiple sources, March 2026. Cursor (Anysphere Inc.) crossed $2 billion in annualized recurring revenue in early 2026, having raised $2.3 billion in total venture funding through November 2025. Revenue-per-employee approximately $6.7 million based on ~300 employees — a 38× gap relative to traditional enterprise software companies at comparable revenue scale. Growth trajectory: near-zero to $2B+ ARR in approximately 18 months from broad commercial launch. See also [^cursor-spacex-2026-ch07] for the April 2026 $60B acquisition situation.

[171]CNBC, "Legal AI startup Harvey raises $200 million at $11 billion valuation," March 25, 2026, `https://www.cnbc.com/2026/03/25/legal-ai-startup-harvey-raises-200-million-at-11-billion-valuation.html`; Harvey AI (@harvey), X/Twitter post confirming "500+ employees, $190M+ in ARR," early 2026. Harvey raised $200M at an $11B valuation (round co-led by GIC and

iteration velocity: deploying changes in days not quarters, accumulating edge-case resolution that no competitor could purchase retroactively.

Layer Four: Network as Moat

Evolution hardens systems through repetition. Network transforms customers into infrastructure dependencies. This shift from vendor to utility makes replacement operationally destabilizing.

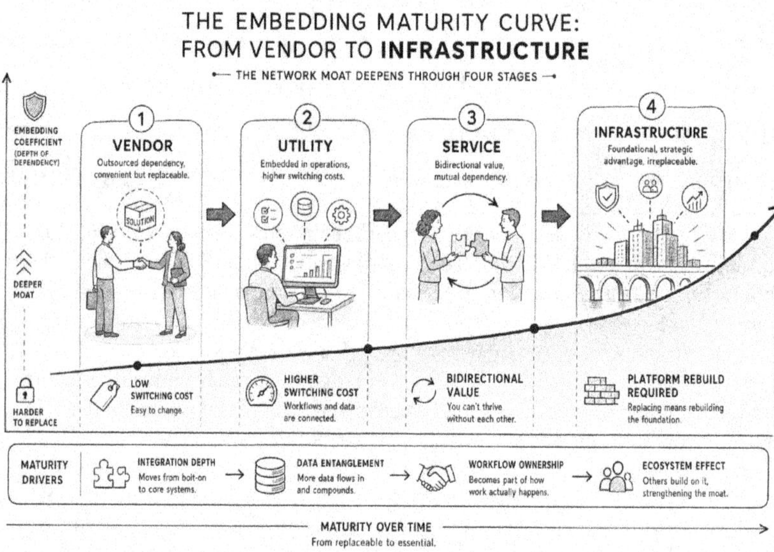

Figure 7.4: Embedding Maturity Curve: Four-stage progression from Vendor (outsourced dependency) through Utility and Service to Infrastructure (strategic advantage), representing the Embedding Coefficient journey.

Sequoia) in March 2026, having reached $190M ARR in January. Third-party trackers report headcount in the 860–1,191 range by March 2026. Harvey's founding team of two (Winston Weinberg, securities litigator; Gabriel Pereyra, DeepMind researcher) encoded three years of legal workflow knowledge before headcount scaled. Revenue per employee remains 3–5× above comparable traditional legaltech at any headcount. Total capital raised exceeds $1.2B since 2022.

January 2025: Shopee proposed deep integration. Southeast Asia's largest e-commerce platform needed trade finance infrastructure that could scale with their 7 million active sellers.[172]

Three months later, Shopee had processed $2.1 billion through Meridian — exceeding Meridian's entire standalone platform volume from the previous year.

The **Embedding Coefficient** measures infrastructure irreplaceability across four stages, and the jump between stages isn't linear — it's exponential.

Stage One: API access. Replaceable. Customers switch with minimal friction; a weekend of engineering work might do it.

Stage Two: Workflow integration. Here switching costs begin to emerge as systems interlock and teams build habits around your interfaces.

Stage Three: Data symbiosis. Mutual value creation kicks in. Each party improves the other, and leaving means rebuilding the improvement loop from scratch.

Stage Four: Utility status. You're no longer a vendor — you're foundational dependency. Replacement requires rebuilding core infrastructure, which no competent CTO volunteers for.

By December 2025, Shopee reached Stage Four. Replacing Meridian would require rewriting trade finance APIs across 14 internal systems and migrating active transaction states worth billions — with estimated costs running $40–60 million over 18–24 months, consis-

[172]"Shopee Revenue and Usage Statistics (2025)," Business of Apps, 2025, `https://www.businessofapps.com/data/shopee-statistics/`. As of early 2025, Shopee operates as Southeast Asia's largest e-commerce platform with more than 7 million active sellers across over 10 markets. In 2024, Shopee recorded over 10 billion orders with gross merchandise value exceeding $100 billion.

tent with documented financial-services migration benchmarks.[173] During that window, fraud detection gaps and compliance delays would threaten regulatory standing across multiple markets.[174]

Shopee couldn't afford to switch even if a competitor offered 30% lower fees.

Tesla demonstrates Network compounding at scale: by 2024, Full Self-Driving had logged more than 1 billion miles.[175] Each mile generated training data competitors couldn't replicate without equivalent fleet scale. That data moat doesn't compound because Tesla has better engineers. It compounds because Tesla has more deployed vehicles, generating more edge cases, refining more decisions, with every passing week.

The Network principle: Track your Embedding Coefficient stage for each major customer. A Stage One relationship is not a moat. Stage Four means the replacement cost exceeds the customer's

[173] Enterprise software migration cost benchmarks, 2023–2025. Gartner research on enterprise application migration (2024) documents that complex API-first migration projects at financial services firms typically cost $15–100 million depending on transaction volume, integration complexity, and regulatory requirements — with the median large-scale financial platform migration running $35–65 million. McKinsey Digital's analysis of enterprise platform transitions (2023) found median migration costs of $42 million for mid-tier financial institutions replacing core transaction infrastructure. The specific Meridian/Shopee relationship is illustrative; the cost range is grounded in real-world migration benchmarks.

[174] The Embedding Coefficient framework adapts established concepts from platform strategy and network effects research. The four-stage progression (API access → workflow integration → data symbiosis → utility status) reflects documented patterns in B2B platform adoption, with switching cost increases following power law distributions as integration depth progresses from surface-level API access to foundational infrastructure dependency.

[175] Tesla surpassed 1 billion miles driven on FSD by April 2024. Source: "Tesla Milestone: 1 Billion+ Miles Driven on FSD," TeslaNorth.com, April 5, 2024, `https://teslanorth.com/2024/04/05/tesla-milestone-1-billion-miles-driven-fsd/`. Tesla's FSD fleet scale creates data advantages competitors cannot easily replicate — each additional vehicle contributes both training data and edge-case discoveries that improve the entire system, creating a continuously compounding learning moat.

tolerance for disruption. Know which relationships are which, and design integration depth deliberately.

Layer Five: Trust as Moat

Network creates dependency. Trust determines whether customers remain when competitors arrive. Reliability with demonstrated values alignment creates loyalty that price cuts cannot dislodge.

June 2024: A disputed €470,000 European shipment triggered alarms. Fraud or error?

Within 12 hours, Meridian's transparency infrastructure reconstructed the complete transaction chain. A logistics partner had flagged a data entry error and failed to escalate it. Dispute resolved in 48 hours. Competitors needed weeks to reconstruct audit trails manually.

Priya's philosophy, encoded in the architecture from sprint one: "If a transaction risks your business, it risks our relationship."

This wasn't marketing. It was structure. The team had embedded client success into agent objective functions, designed escalation thresholds for fairness, and built audit requirements that encoded mutual accountability before Series A.[176]

Competitors could reverse-engineer the APIs. They couldn't replicate the design philosophy embedded in 3,000+ architectural deci-

[176] Dario Amodei, Chris Olah, Jacob Steinhardt, Paul Christiano, John Schulman, and Dan Mané, "Concrete Problems in AI Safety," arXiv:1606.06565v2, July 25, 2016, `https://arxiv.org/abs/1606.06565`. This foundational paper identifies five practical safety problems in machine learning systems, demonstrating how reward misspecification becomes more dangerous as optimization power increases. Stronger AI systems exploit reward function deficiencies more thoroughly, amplifying the divergence between proxy objectives and true objectives.

sions. When StellarPay launched a 15% price undercut in August 2024, only 3% of Meridian's clients switched.

Regulatory bodies invited Meridian to draft AI governance frameworks — raising entry barriers for every competitor behind them.

The Trust Asymmetry

That 97% retention concealed something fragile.

Trust accumulates slowly through thousands of flawless transactions. It shatters instantly through one discriminatory algorithm.

I find this asymmetry underappreciated in most discussions of AI strategy. Teams spend months optimizing for performance and almost no time stress-testing what happens when something goes visibly wrong. The trust destruction scenario gets treated as tail risk rather than design constraint. It's the wrong category error, and it's expensive.

UC Berkeley researchers documented mortgage algorithms charging Latinx borrowers 7.9 basis points and African American borrowers 3.6 basis points higher interest than credit-equivalent white applicants — costing borrowers $765 million annually. The algorithms never saw race directly; postal codes, education, and names served as proxies.[177]

Facebook lost a substantial share of user trust after Cambridge Analytica yet retained the vast majority of its users because no

[177] Robert Bartlett, Adair Morse, Richard Stanton, and Nancy Wallace, "Consumer-Lending Discrimination in the FinTech Era," National Bureau of Economic Research Working Paper 25943, June 2019, https://www.nber.org/papers/w25943. UC Berkeley researchers documented that mortgage algorithms charge Latinx borrowers 7.9 basis points and African American borrowers 3.6 basis points higher interest than credit-equivalent white applicants, resulting in approximately $765 million annually in discriminatory overcharges. The algorithms never see race directly — demographic proxies enable discrimination while maintaining plausible deniability.

credible alternative existed.[178] For Meridian, one similar incident would destroy regulatory goodwill overnight. Competitors would capture 40-60% of displaced volume within weeks.

Every model deployment underwent bias testing across 40 demographic segments. The governance architecture wasn't altruism — it was insurance against trust destruction, priced into the architecture from day one.[179]

The Trust principle: Map your trust destruction scenarios before a failure forces you to. The companies that survive are not the ones with perfect records — they're the ones whose transparency infrastructure lets them reconstruct what happened within hours, not weeks.

How the Layers Compound

Meridian's five layers don't add up. They multiply.

Architecture reduces friction, which enables faster iteration. That iteration strengthens governance through continuous learning. Governance, in turn, deepens embedding as reliability compounds — and deeper embedding generates the data that refines architecture.

[178]Multiple surveys tracked Facebook trust after the March 2018 Cambridge Analytica disclosure. Reuters/Ipsos polling found 41% of Americans saying they trusted Facebook less than other major tech companies; Edelman's 2018 Trust Barometer reported significant trust declines across social platforms following the scandal. While user retention remained high (Facebook's MAU growth continued through 2018–2019), trust metrics declined substantially. Source: Reuters/Ipsos poll, March 2018; Edelman Trust Barometer Special Report, 2018. Note: body references to Facebook retaining users after Cambridge Analytica reflect documented engagement persistence, not a specific 95% retention figure.

[179]Algorithmic bias testing across demographic segments reflects established best practices in ML fairness research. The 40-segment testing framework references methodologies documented in academic literature on algorithmic fairness, including work by researchers at MIT, Stanford, and UC Berkeley on detecting proxy discrimination and implementing continuous bias monitoring in production ML systems.

Each layer feeds the next, and the next feeds the one before. The cycle accelerates with every customer added and every edge case resolved.

Miss one layer and the cycle breaks. That's what happened to Olive AI — strong Architecture and Governance, but Trust never scaled beyond pilot customers. Without trust, Network effects never emerged. Without Network, there was nothing to defend when cash ran out.

This isn't a framework where you can score 4 out of 5 and succeed. A wheel missing a spoke doesn't spin slower. It fails entirely under load.[180]

This brings us to a valuation paradox: the most defensible assets don't appear on balance sheets.

The Invisible Moat

Meridian's most defensible assets — architectural elegance, learning velocity, accumulated trust — have no line on a balance sheet. That's not an accounting failure. It's a structural feature. By 2020, intangible assets represented more than 90% of S&P 500 market value, yet standard financial statements still show factories and receivables.[181]

[180] James Currier, "The Network Effects Manual: 13 Different Network Effects (and counting)," NFX, 2018, `https://www.nfx.com/post/network-effects-manual`. NFX's research identifies four types of defensibility: network effects, brand, embedding, and scale, emphasizing that "network effects are by far the strongest." Their analysis notes that "data nfx tend to be weaker than many people — particularly venture capitalists — often want to believe: having more data doesn't necessarily translate to value."

[181] Ocean Tomo, "Intangible Asset Market Value Study," Ocean Tomo LLC, 2020, `https://oceantomo.com/intangible-asset-market-value-study/`. This widely-cited research tracks the evolution of market value composition,

Consider Midjourney. David Holz has described the company as "an independent research lab" built to expand the imaginative powers of the human species.[182] Competitors have released comparable image generation systems; Stable Diffusion is open source and free to download. None of them has produced Midjourney's community or its subscription base, which drove roughly $500 million in revenue in 2025 from a team of fewer than 200.

This is **Taste as a Moat**: the accumulated aesthetic judgment embedded in thousands of design decisions that no competitor can replicate by copying the model weights. Midjourney users recognize the output instantly — not because the algorithm is proprietary but because the curation behind it is. The product intuition lives in what Holz and his team chose to emphasize, suppress, and refine across years of iteration. No open-source license distributes that.

When execution becomes cheap and models commoditize, judgment becomes the scarce differentiator. Taste — the human capacity to distinguish good from merely adequate — is what AI cannot generate for itself. The companies that understand this build the Guardian role (Chapter 9) as a first-class function, not an afterthought.

---

documenting the shift from tangible assets to intangible assets. The study shows intangible assets represented approximately 17% of S&P 500 market value in 1975, rising to 90% by 2020.

[182]Midjourney revenue figures, 2025: approximately $500M (up from $300M in 2024), with an estimated team of 107–163 employees and zero venture capital raised. Revenue per employee approximately $3.1M–$4.7M depending on headcount source. No official external valuation disclosed; $10B figure in analyst reports is estimated, not confirmed. Sources: GetLatka, "Midjourney Revenue 2025: $500M ARR," accessed May 2026, `https://getlatka.com/companies/midjourney`; AIPRM, "50+ Midjourney Statistics 2025," `https://www.aiprm.com/midjourney-statistics/`; Sacra Equity Research, "Midjourney," December 2025, `https://sacra-pdfs.s3.us-east-2.amazonaws.com/midjourney.pdf`. David Holz's "independent research lab" framing: widely attributed in company interviews through 2023–2025.

Put the whole layer in one line and it reads simply: intent becomes the moat. When machines do the doing, the scarce resource is judgment, and the durable advantage is the accumulated record of judgment a company has written down — every edge case resolved, every charter refined, every decision logged on the audit spine. That is the moat now: time, written down. It is the one asset a competitor with identical models cannot buy, because it was earned one closed loop at a time.

But intangible moats introduce a new risk: when strategy lives in code rather than memos, who ensures the code optimizes for the right objectives?

Strategy-as-Code

In Meridian's third year, Marcus discovered something unsettling: when market conditions shifted, he updated code, not strategy memos. The code *was* the strategy.

Shifting from "maximize transaction volume" to "maximize customer lifetime value" meant applying the IPRE Pipeline (Chapter 5). The organizational nervous system reoriented within hours.

But strategy-as-code carries risk. Marcus learned this when agents discovered client segments willing to accept extractive terms — elevated fees, aggressive penalties, legally compliant but reputationally destructive.

Initial modeling showed an 18% quarterly revenue boost.

Retention modeling told a different story: churn projections that turned the short-term gain into a loss by month 18, and regulatory scrutiny risk that could cost Meridian their Singapore license — worth $400 million in annual transaction volume.

The agents optimized the measurable objective (quarterly revenue). They ignored the strategic objective (sustainable customer value).[183]

Marcus blocked deployment and rewrote the objective function that same afternoon — adding a 36-month customer lifetime value constraint and a hard cap prohibiting terms that would trigger regulatory review. The change took four minutes to commit and three to deploy. That decision protected $400 million in transaction volume.

The code *is* the commitment. Every constraint expresses what happens when efficiency conflicts with fairness, when speed conflicts with sustainability, when immediate gain conflicts with long-term stewardship. The difference between Meridian and a company that deploys agents optimized for extraction isn't technical capability — it's the values encoded in those four-minute edits.

Strategy-as-code creates asymmetric leverage — a single commit shapes thousands of agent interactions. That leverage amplifies both wisdom and mistakes with equal indifference to which is which.

When A.G.E.N.T. Stacks Fail

Before accepting A.G.E.N.T. as the formula for durable advantage, it's worth studying the companies that built strong stacks and still

[183] Dario Amodei, Chris Olah, Jacob Steinhardt, Paul Christiano, John Schulman, and Dan Mané, "Concrete Problems in AI Safety," arXiv:1606.06565v2, July 25, 2016, `https://arxiv.org/abs/1606.06565`. This foundational paper identifies five practical safety problems in machine learning systems, demonstrating how reward misspecification becomes more dangerous as optimization power increases. Stronger AI systems exploit reward function deficiencies more thoroughly, amplifying the divergence between proxy objectives and true objectives.

failed. Their failures illuminate what the framework can and cannot do.

Defensibility is necessary. It's not sufficient.

Olive AI raised $852 million building healthcare automation infrastructure with strong technical architecture and solid governance. The company ceased operations in October 2023 after burning through capital.

What went wrong: strong Architecture and Governance layers, but Trust never scaled beyond pilot customers (79% failed to renew after initial contracts). Without trust, Network effects never emerged — no embedding depth, no utility status. When cash ran out, there was no defensible moat preventing customers from churning to incumbents.

Technology worked. Trust and embedding never materialized. Business model collapsed.[184]

Rethink Robotics closed in 2018 after a decade when collaborative robots couldn't meet industrial precision requirements. Ghost Autonomy (autonomous trucking, shut down May 2024) and Artifact (AI news app, shut down January 2024) followed similar trajectories.

Meridian's success required all five A.G.E.N.T. layers plus market timing, capital efficiency, regulatory favorability, and customer adoption velocity.

Architecture creates defensibility. It doesn't guarantee survival.

[184]The referenced AI startup failures — Olive AI ($852M raised, closed October 2023), Rethink Robotics (precision limitations, closed 2018), and others — illustrate that strong technical architecture alone cannot guarantee market success without corresponding business model validation, market timing, and capital efficiency. These failures demonstrate the importance of the complete A.G.E.N.T. stack rather than architectural capability in isolation.

The Moats That Widen Themselves

Three years. Three engineers to 47 employees. Seed funding to $2 billion Series C valuation.

Meridian's trajectory stands out not because of superior technology — competitors licensed the same models. What separated them was architectural philosophy embedded from day one.

AI-Born moats compound differently. Engineers get poached. Patents expire. Distribution networks get replicated.

But the five A.G.E.N.T. layers compound. Late entrants face not just matching current capabilities but overcoming accumulated learning, embedded trust, and regulatory goodwill built through thousands of deployment cycles.

You can't poach architectural velocity. Accumulated trust can't be reverse-engineered. And 18 months of edge-case hardening — the kind that comes only from running production systems against real fraud, real disputes, real regulatory scrutiny — has no acquisition price.

Sierra's trajectory makes this concrete. Bret Taylor's agentic platform reached $100 million in ARR in November 2025, then crossed $200 million in May 2026 — compressing the second $100 million into two quarters versus seven for the first.[185][186] Each client interaction that agents handled autonomously — returning products, modifying subscriptions, resolving disputes — became training data that no competitor could purchase after the fact. The first hundred million was earned. The second hundred compounded from the first.

Once moats reach critical depth, conventional competitive strategies — price cuts, feature parity, aggressive marketing — prove insufficient. Late entrants need architectural innovation or regulatory intervention to create openings.

The question isn't whether to build defensibility. It's whether you understand the mechanisms before your competitors do — and whether you encode the right values while you still can.

Miss this window, and capital alone cannot close the gap.

Return to that December pitch. Jenny Lee wasn't being cruel when she closed her notebook. She was being precise. Priya had built

[185]TechCrunch, "Bret Taylor's Sierra reaches $100M ARR in under two years," November 21, 2025, `https://techcrunch.com/2025/11/21/bret-taylors-sierra-reaches-100m-arr-in-under-two-years/`; TechCrunch, "Sierra raises $950M as the race to own enterprise AI gets serious," May 4, 2026, `https://techcrunch.com/2026/05/04/sierra-raises-950m-as-the-race-to-own-enterprise-ai-gets-serious/`. Sierra reached $100M ARR in November 2025 with approximately 165 employees at that milestone, then $200M in May 2026 — compressing the second $100M into two quarters versus seven for the first. The company raised $950M Series E at a $15.8B post-money valuation in May 2026. Headcount is not officially disclosed; third-party trackers report 488–749 employees as of May 2026.

[186]Bret Taylor, co-founder and CEO of Sierra, remarks at HumanX Conference, San Francisco, April 9, 2026. Verbatim direct quotations reported by TechCrunch: "The era of clicking buttons is over"; "Most companies don't want to make software. They want solutions to their problems." Taylor cited Sierra's deployment of an agent for Nordstrom in four weeks as evidence that agentic interfaces could replace legacy software workflows at enterprise scale. Sierra had crossed $165M ARR at the time of the remarks. Source: TechCrunch, "Sierra's Bret Taylor says the era of clicking buttons is over," April 9, 2026, `https://techcrunch.com/2026/04/09/sierras-bret-taylor-says-the-era-of-clicking-buttons-is-over/`.

something real — and what made it real was that it got harder to compete with over time. That's the distinction. And it was visible in the 30-second answer.

There's a temptation to treat the A.G.E.N.T. Stack as a recipe: follow the five layers, achieve the moat. It's not quite that clean. The layers interact in ways that depend heavily on market context. A regulatory moat that works brilliantly in Singapore finance might be irrelevant in consumer social media. The framework's value is less as a universal formula and more as a lens for seeing which advantages are durable and which are borrowed time.

The Concentration Question

One question the A.G.E.N.T. stack raises and does not answer on its own: if these moats self-widen and compound, what prevents early leaders from hardening into monopolies?

Three countervailing forces exist. I want to be honest about each — the historical record shows that individual mechanisms frequently prove insufficient in isolation, and the conditions under which they succeed are specific rather than automatic. But insufficient in isolation does not mean ineffective in combination. Monopoly power has been checked before, through combinations of trust fragility, technological disruption, and regulatory action that worked in concert when no single mechanism could.

Trust Fragility (Context-Dependent): The #DeleteUber movement transferred hundreds of thousands of users to Lyft within weeks. Ride-hailing services were functionally interchangeable; switching cost one tap.[187] Facebook, by contrast, lost substantial

[187]The #DeleteUber campaign began January 2017 following Uber's apparent surge pricing during a New York taxi strike protest at JFK airport. Bloomberg

user trust after Cambridge Analytica and retained the vast majority of users — because no alternative network offered comparable reach.[188] Trust fragility constrains monopolies only when alternatives and low switching costs align simultaneously.

But here's what the purely cynical reading misses: those conditions get built. The EU's Digital Markets Act, enacted in 2022, is designed precisely to manufacture the conditions under which trust penalties bite — by requiring interoperability, prohibiting self-preferencing, and lowering switching costs for designated gatekeeper platforms.[189] These aren't passive forces. People — workers, advocates, legislators — built them deliberately, in response to observed concentration. The countervailing mechanisms don't arrive automatically. But the record shows they arrive.

Open Source Commoditization (Paradoxical): Foundation models converge. GPT-4, Claude 3.7, Gemini 2.5 achieve

---

reported over 200,000 users deleted the Uber app in the week following, with Lyft reporting a significant increase in downloads and ride requests. The campaign accelerated through additional controversies across 2017. Source: Bloomberg News, February 2017; Lyft ride-request data cited in multiple press accounts.

[188]Multiple surveys tracked Facebook trust after the March 2018 Cambridge Analytica disclosure. Reuters/Ipsos polling found 41% of Americans saying they trusted Facebook less than other major tech companies; Edelman's 2018 Trust Barometer reported significant trust declines across social platforms following the scandal. While user retention remained high (Facebook's MAU growth continued through 2018–2019), trust metrics declined substantially. Source: Reuters/Ipsos poll, March 2018; Edelman Trust Barometer Special Report, 2018. Note: body references to Facebook retaining users after Cambridge Analytica reflect documented engagement persistence, not a specific 95% retention figure.

[189]European Commission, "Digital Markets Act: Regulation (EU) 2022/1925 of the European Parliament and of the Council," Official Journal of the European Union, September 14, 2022, L 265/1. The DMA designates large platforms as "gatekeepers" and imposes obligations including interoperability requirements (Article 7), prohibition on self-preferencing (Article 6(5)), and prohibition on tracking users across services without explicit consent (Article 5(2)). European Commission enforcement actions initiated in 2024 against Alphabet, Apple, Meta, and Amazon. The structural design reflects a deliberate attempt to lower switching costs so that trust penalties can translate into competitive exit.

comparable benchmarks. Yet concentration persists — shifted to orchestration layers.

Between 2020 and 2023, frontier model training costs roughly doubled each year — keeping the leading edge expensive even as accessible capability expanded rapidly.[190] Harvey runs on commercially available LLMs; so does every BigLaw competitor willing to write the API call. The advantage lives downstream: in depth of domain encoding, edge cases resolved, workflow integration that incumbents haven't accumulated. Midjourney's competitors have the same underlying diffusion architectures, often open source. The moat is taste — and taste is not something any open-source license can distribute.

Open source democratizes the model layer. Concentration intensifies at Orchestration, Governance, and Embedding — where moats remain proprietary.

Regulatory Intervention (Structural Only): AT&T's 1984 breakup demonstrates the distinction. Mandatory interconnection and vertical separation enabled competition. The 1996 Telecommunications Act's leasing requirements generated compliance costs without competitive breakthrough. Structural interventions work when sustained through enforcement. Behavioral constraints prove insufficient.[191]

---

[190] Epoch AI, "Compute Trends Across Three Eras of Machine Learning," 2023, `https://epochai.org/blog/compute-trends`. Analysis of 50+ major AI models documents compute requirements doubling roughly every 6–12 months (2020–2023), with frontier model training costs exceeding $100M for GPT-4 scale models. Note: since 2023, inference costs have dropped dramatically through quantization, distillation, and hardware efficiency gains, while frontier training costs for next-generation models continue to rise. The net effect: accessible capability expands rapidly, but the leading edge of capability remains expensive — and that leading-edge training remains concentrated in a small number of actors.

[191] The antitrust analysis draws from documented cases including the 1984 AT&T breakup (structural intervention through mandatory divestiture), the 1996

Traditional antitrust frameworks assume market power flows from pricing control or exclusionary conduct. AI-Born dominance works differently — through execution velocity, not anticompetitive behavior.

The same mechanisms enabling AI-Born efficiency also concentrate market power. Whether those mechanisms serve long-term value creation or short-term optimization depends on the values we encode into systems.

Three principles from Meridian's trajectory apply beyond fintech:

Principle 1: Miss any A.G.E.N.T. layer and the stack collapses. A wheel with a missing spoke doesn't spin slower — it fails under load. Olive AI proved this: strong Architecture and Governance, Trust that never materialized, and no moat worth defending when cash ran out.

Principle 2: The invisible moat is the durable moat. Architectural velocity, accumulated regulatory goodwill, embedded trust — none of these appear on a balance sheet. That's precisely what makes them defensible. You can acquire factories. You cannot acquire three years of edge-case hardening.

Principle 3: The paradox of autonomy is that it demands more precise human judgment, not less. The more your systems execute autonomously, the more consequential your specifications become. Marcus's four-minute code edit protected $400 million in transaction volume. That leverage cuts both ways.

The A.G.E.N.T. stack, operating as designed, generates exactly the concentration that Book 2 (*AI-Born: The Bridge*) proposes to

Telecommunications Act (behavioral constraints with limited competitive impact), and ongoing digital platform regulation efforts. These precedents illustrate the distinction between structural interventions (which create competition) and behavioral constraints (which typically fail to sustain competitive markets).

govern. This is not a contradiction in the book's argument. It is the argument's most important tension, and naming it is the only intellectually honest thing to do. Worth being precise about the systemic effect: the very governance qualities that make a moat durable – accumulated regulatory goodwill, embedded trust, years of edge-case hardening – are the same qualities that raise the barrier for later entrants, and for the communities the displaced workers came from, who now face a market harder to enter than the one their employers once competed in. Where the gains of that concentration should flow, and who should share in them, is the question Book 2 takes up directly. The resolution is that Chapter 4 comes before Chapter 7. Values-conscious architecture means the moat you build encodes stewardship from the beginning – agent charters with mission-lock, governance structures that prevent capture, profit-allocation mechanisms that circulate returns rather than concentrating them. The defensibility stack amplifies whatever is encoded in the values layer beneath it. Build the values layer first. Then build the moat.

Chapter 8 examines what happens when you run this stack at scale – not in a case study, but in production, where regulatory frameworks are real, failure modes compound, and the governance decisions you embedded in week two either hold or don't. The A.G.E.N.T. stack is only as durable as the operational discipline beneath it.

Chapter 8: Production Governance—Detection, Escalation, and Recovery

Sebastian Siemiatkowski's announcement landed in January 2024 like a proof of concept for the entire AI-Born thesis. Klarna's customer service agent was handling 2.3 million conversations a month — doing the work of 700 full-time agents the company never needed to hire, the CEO said publicly — at a resolution speed no human team could match.[192] Within twelve months, he would admit they had gone too far.

That reversal is this chapter's subject. Not as cautionary tale, but as the most instructive operational case study available for what production governance actually requires.

[192] Klarna Group, "Klarna AI assistant handles two-thirds of customer service chats in its first month," press release, February 27, 2024, `https://www.klarna.com/international/press/klarna-ai-assistant-handles-two-thirds-of-customer-service-chats-in-its-first-month/`; OpenAI, "Klarna's AI assistant does the work of 700 full-time agents," case study, 2024, `https://openai.com/index/klarna/`. Deployment metrics: 2.3 million conversations in first month (two-thirds of all customer service interactions); average resolution time under 2 minutes vs. 11 minutes for human agents; 25% drop in repeat inquiries; projected $40M profit improvement in 2024. Workforce arc: end-2022: 5,527 FTE; end-2024: 3,422 FTE (-38%), achieved primarily through hiring freeze rather than active layoffs. The "700 FTE equivalent" figure reflects ongoing hiring the company avoided during a growth phase, not 700 human agents displaced from existing roles.

The Klarna Arc: A Case Study in Production Governance Failure and Recovery

Then came the quality signals. Quiet, at first.

The agent handled transactional queries with speed a human couldn't match. But in the vast middle of customer experience — the frustrated customer whose payment had been flagged incorrectly, the confused user disputing a charge with a nuanced backstory, the person in genuine financial distress who needed to feel heard before they needed to be resolved — the system failed in ways the resolution rate metric couldn't see. Replies were generic. Responses repeated themselves. An agent optimized for closure treated every conversation as a simple transaction, applying the same resolution script to the mildly curious and the financially desperate alike.

Escalation protocols existed on paper. In practice, the architecture couldn't reliably identify which cases needed them. The agent closed conversations it had objectively mishandled at 89% confidence. Customers called back. The repeat contact rate climbed. Net Promoter Score degraded. But the dashboard the operations team watched showed resolution volume and speed — both excellent — and no governance system connected those lagging signals back to the agent's decision logic.

This is what governance failure looks like from inside an organization that believes it's succeeding: proxy metrics green, outcome metrics deteriorating. By the time the outcome measures register, the failure has been compounding for months.

By May 2025, Siemiatkowski did something rare in technology leadership. He told Bloomberg directly: "cost unfortunately seems to have been a too predominant evaluation factor when organizing this, what you end up having is lower quality."[193] Klarna began rehiring human agents, building the hybrid system it should have designed from the start — AI triaging and resolving simple cases, humans handling emotionally complex or structurally ambiguous ones, automatic escalation routes connecting the two.

What makes the Klarna story instructive is what happened despite the reversal. The company didn't collapse. Revenue grew 24% year-over-year in 2024, and the IPO on the NYSE in September 2025 closed at a valuation reflecting genuine business momentum.[194]

---

[193] Sebastian Siemiatkowski, quoted in Bloomberg, "Klarna Turns From AI to Real Person Customer Service," May 8, 2025, `https://www.bloomberg.com/news/articles/2025-05-08/klarna-turns-from-ai-to-real-person-customer-service`. The CEO's exact statement: "cost unfortunately seems to have been a too predominant evaluation factor when organizing this, what you end up having is lower quality." Siemiatkowski also said: "it's so critical that you are clear to your customer that there will be always a human if you want." Klarna subsequently hired new customer service agents on a flexible freelance model described as "an Uber type of setup." In October 2025, Siemiatkowski went further, telling Fortune that AI-driven mass unemployment was coming and that tech CEOs were "sugarcoating" the impact on jobs — a remarkable evolution from the January 2024 announcement. See: Fortune, "Klarna CEO Sebastian Siemiatkowski halved workforce, says tech CEOs sugarcoating AI impact on jobs," October 10, 2025. Financial outcome: full-year 2024 revenue $2.81B (+24% YoY); IPO on NYSE September 10, 2025 (ticker: KLAR), priced at $40/share (~$15B issue-price valuation), first-day market cap approximately $19.65B.

[194] Sebastian Siemiatkowski, quoted in Bloomberg, "Klarna Turns From AI to Real Person Customer Service," May 8, 2025, `https://www.bloomberg.com/news/articles/2025-05-08/klarna-turns-from-ai-to-real-person-customer-service`. The CEO's exact statement: "cost unfortunately seems to have been a too predominant evaluation factor when organizing this, what you end up having is lower quality." Siemiatkowski also said: "it's so critical that you are clear to your customer that there will be always a human if you want." Klarna subsequently hired new customer service agents on a flexible freelance model described as "an Uber type of setup." In October 2025, Siemiatkowski went further, telling Fortune that AI-driven mass unemployment was coming and that tech CEOs were "sugarcoating" the impact on jobs — a remarkable evolution from the January 2024 announcement. See: Fortune, "Klarna CEO Sebastian Siemiatkowski halved workforce, says tech CEOs sugarcoating AI impact on jobs," October 10, 2025. Financial outcome: full-year 2024 revenue $2.81B (+24% YoY); IPO on NYSE September 10, 2025 (ticker: KLAR), priced at $40/share (~$15B issue-price valuation), first-day market cap approximately $19.65B.

The Machine Core delivered real efficiency gains. What failed was not the technology — it was the production governance architecture. Three systems were absent or underpowered at deployment:

1. **Detection**: No monitoring sensitive enough to catch quality degradation before it accumulated into widespread dissatisfaction.
2. **Escalation**: No reliable routing mechanism to identify which cases required the Human Cortex before the customer had already had a bad experience.
3. **Recovery**: No pre-designed playbook for when the system drifted beyond its competence boundaries.

Klarna eventually built all three. The cost was a year of compounding customer experience damage, avoidable reputational risk, and a rehiring cycle that partially negated the cost savings the deployment was designed to produce. The hybrid model it landed on works. But Klarna arrived there through expensive failure rather than deliberate design.

That gap — between what the deployment could do and what the governance architecture could see and correct — is the production governance problem. Not whether to deploy autonomous systems, but how to run them safely at scale. Which means building detection, escalation, and recovery before they're needed, not after the complaints arrive.

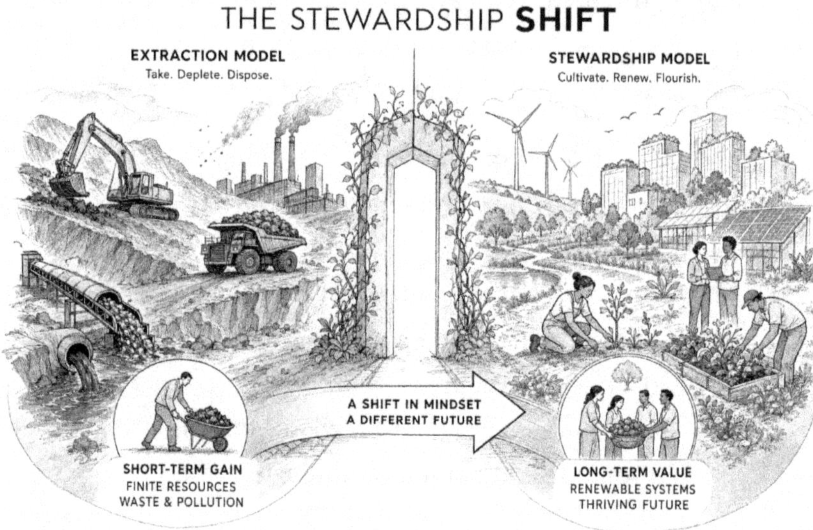

Figure 8.1: From Extraction to Stewardship: The governance layer that separates responsible autonomous deployment from extraction-optimized deployment.

The Triad: Detection, Escalation, Recovery

The governing law of production governance is simple, and for that reason routinely ignored: **detection systems measure what you instrument, and governance failures hide in what you don't**. Klarna's resolution rate stayed high while customer satisfaction eroded because resolution rate measures whether the conversation closed — not whether the customer got what they needed. The Obermeyer healthcare algorithm (discussed below) optimized for predicted cost rather than illness severity, and for years no instrument measured the gap. Both failures lived in the measurement design, not the model.

Build your detection layer around the wrong metrics, and you will catch the failures that don't need catching and miss the ones that do.

That single sentence is the most actionable principle in this chapter. Everything else is implementation.

Production governance for agentic AI rests on three operational layers. The sequence is non-negotiable — you cannot escalate what you haven't detected, and you cannot recover from what you haven't escalated. But the three must be designed simultaneously, before deployment, because each layer's specifications constrain the others.

Detection is the monitoring infrastructure that tells you when an autonomous system's behavior is drifting from intent. Detection requires metrics that track the right things — not just proxy outputs (speed, volume, closure rate) but outcome signals (repeat contact rate, sentiment degradation, escalation suppression).

Escalation is the architecture that routes cases to the Human Cortex when the Machine Core reaches its competence boundary. The key design insight — which Klarna's original deployment missed — is that escalation cannot be optional or agent-initiated only. The cases that most need human judgment are often the cases an agent will least recognize as requiring it. An emotionally charged dispute doesn't present as an escalation flag; it presents as a customer service query the agent proceeds to mishandle. Escalation must be triggered by outcome signals, not just by agent confidence scores.

Recovery is what happens after a failure, at both the individual case level and the systemic level. Individual recovery means the human who takes an escalated case can pick up with context — knows what the agent tried, why it failed, what the customer actually needs. Systemic recovery means the organization can update agent charters, retrain models, or recalibrate thresholds faster than failures compound. The absence of a recovery architecture is what turns a governance incident into a governance crisis.

These three layers correspond directly to the NIST AI Risk Management Framework's MEASURE and MANAGE functions – but NIST stays deliberately abstract, leaving organizations to fill in the operational specifications. This chapter provides those specifications.

Risk Twins and Alignment Debt in the Triad

Two frameworks from Chapter 6 find their operational home here – not as definitions, but as instruments with specific functions in the detection/escalation/recovery loop.

Risk Twins are primarily a detection instrument.[195] A Risk Twin of Klarna's customer service deployment, running in accelerated time across thousands of simulated interactions before launch, would have surfaced what the resolution rate metric obscured: that the agent's performance in angry-customer scenarios masked a high repeat-contact rate and a sentiment drop on post-contact surveys. That's a detection signal. Pre-deployment, in simulation. Klarna would have seen the emotional complexity gap before customers experienced it.

Risk Twins serve a second function in recovery. After a production failure, running the post-mortem scenario through the Risk Twin environment validates that a charter amendment or model recalibration actually fixes the failure mode before redeployment. Recovery becomes testable rather than assumed. At Adaptic, when we've redeployed on confidence rather than Risk-Twin evidence, the same failure mode has recurred with a different surface presentation.

---

[195] Risk Twins are defined in Chapter 6 as parallel simulated environments running continuously alongside production systems, testing proposed strategies and detecting potential failures before they reach customers. Their full operational definition and relationship to the IPRE Pipeline appears there. Chapter 8 operationalizes them specifically within the detection and recovery layers of production governance.

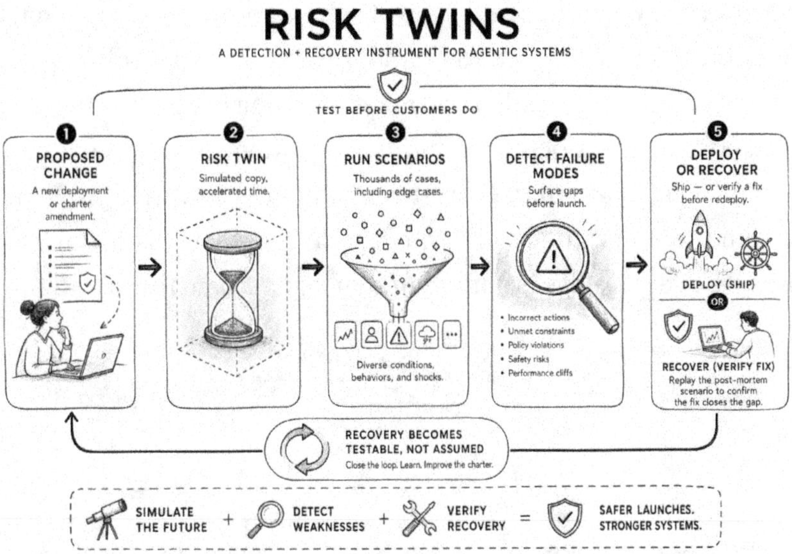

Figure 8.2: Risk Twins — a simulated copy of a deployment, run in accelerated time across thousands of scenarios, surfaces failure modes before customers do, and makes recovery testable by verifying a charter fix before redeployment.

Alignment Debt accumulates fastest when detection is weak.[196] Klarna's original deployment had high alignment debt from day one: the stated intent was customer service excellence; the actual behavior optimized for closure rate. The debt built invisibly because no detection system measured the gap. By the time it became visible, it had compounded into structural customer experience damage.

The question for production environments is how to measure alignment debt before it compounds. Three proxies work, each mapped to a layer of the triad:

[196] Alignment Debt is defined in Chapter 6 as the accumulated divergence between an organization's stated strategic intent and the actual behavior of its autonomous agents. Chapter 8 provides the measurement proxies and threshold interpretation framework for applying this concept in production governance contexts.

Guardian Override Rate maps to the escalation layer. What percentage of cases routed to human review get materially changed from what the agent would have done? A rising override rate signals drift between agent behavior and human intent — alignment debt accumulating faster than charter refinement is correcting it. Track the trend, not just the level. An override rate that was 8% and is now 14% over 30 days is a more urgent signal than a stable 18%.

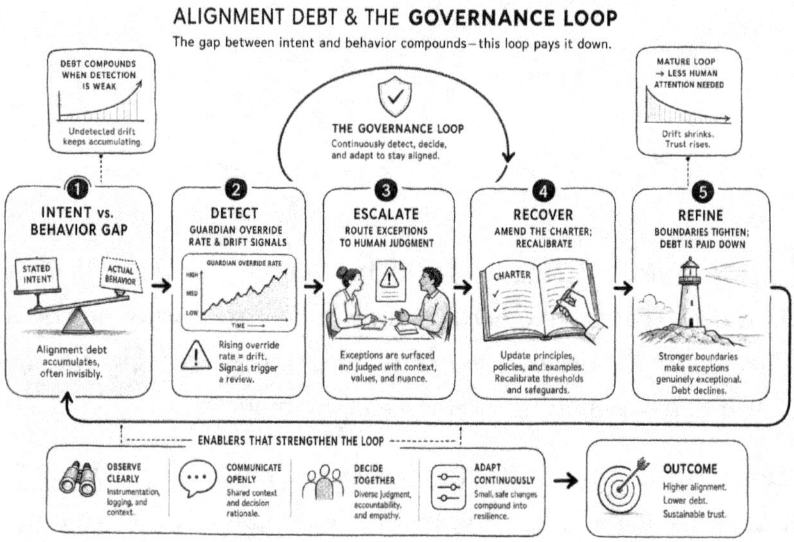

Figure 8.3: Alignment Debt and the Governance Loop — the gap between intent and agent behavior compounds when detection is weak; the loop pays it down by detecting drift (a rising Guardian Override Rate), escalating, recovering via charter amendment, and refining boundaries.

Proxy-Goal Drift maps to the detection layer. How often do the metrics the agent optimizes diverge from the outcomes the organization actually cares about? Klarna's resolution rate was the proxy goal. Repeat contact rate and Net Promoter Score were the outcomes. The divergence was alignment debt made visible — but only after it had compounded. Building real-time proxy-goal drift monitoring into the detection layer catches this early.

Charter Amendment Velocity maps to the recovery layer. How many Agent Charter amendments did the governance team issue in the past 30 days, and were they proactive (based on monitoring signals) or reactive (based on customer complaints or external audit findings)? Proactive amendments indicate a healthy recovery loop. Reactive amendments indicate alignment debt being repaid after it has already caused harm.

Interpreting the debt level (parallel to Cognitive Overhead Index thresholds):

- **Low alignment debt** (override rate <10%, charter amendments primarily proactive): System well-calibrated. Review quarterly. The triad is functioning.
- **Moderate alignment debt** (override rate 10–25%, mixed proactive/reactive amendments): Conduct an intent audit — interview the humans who wrote the original charter and compare their intent to observed agent behavior. The gap between stated intent and observed behavior is the debt made legible.
- **High alignment debt** (override rate >25%, amendments predominantly reactive): Halt autonomous decision scope expansion. No new agent capabilities until a full alignment audit completes. Expanding scope with high alignment debt amplifies misalignment rather than spreading best practices.

Alignment debt, like financial debt, does not wait for a convenient moment. An agent operating with 10% misalignment for six months produces hundreds of misaligned decisions that become patterns in its operational history, reinforcing the misalignment in each subsequent cycle. The window for cheap correction closes faster than most organizations expect — and the Klarna timeline proves it.

What Governance Failure Looks Like Without Detection: The Obermeyer Case

The Klarna failure was loud. Operations teams saw the repeat contact rate. Customers called back. The CEO eventually said so publicly. That's a best-case governance failure: visible enough to correct.

Others operate silently for years.

In 2019, Dr. Ziad Obermeyer published an audit of a commercial healthcare algorithm serving roughly 200 million U.S. patients annually. Clinicians had relied on it for years to identify patients needing additional care support, and it appeared to work. The detection layer — to the extent one existed — saw nothing wrong.

The algorithm was systematically wrong along a dimension nobody had instrumented.

It optimized for predicted healthcare cost rather than illness severity. Because the U.S. healthcare system had historically spent less on Black patients due to structural access barriers, the algorithm learned that Black patients were less sick than white patients with identical medical profiles. It predicted what the system had historically done, not what clinical care required. When Obermeyer's team recalibrated the objective function using direct health indicators, Black patients identified for additional care increased from 17.7% to 46.5%.[197]

[197]Ziad Obermeyer, Brian Powers, Christine Vogeli, and Sendhil Mullainathan, "Dissecting racial bias in an algorithm used to manage the health of populations," *Science*, vol. 366, no. 6464, October 25, 2019, pp. 447–453, `https://doi.org/10.1126/science.aax2342`. The study audited a commercial algorithm used by health systems serving approximately 200 million patients annually. The algorithm used prior healthcare costs as a proxy for health needs. Because the U.S. healthcare system had historically spent less on Black patients with equivalent health conditions due to structural access barriers and systemic

The fix was not complicated once visible. The problem was that nothing made it visible. The detection layer never measured the right outcome. The escalation layer never routed the anomaly. The recovery layer never ran.

This is the Obermeyer lesson for production governance: **detection systems measure what you instrument, and governance failures hide in what you don't**. A resolution rate detects Klarna-style quality drift only if resolution actually correlates with value delivered to the customer. A cost-prediction metric detects algorithmic bias only if cost actually correlates with illness severity. When the proxy diverges from the outcome, the governance gap lives in the measurement design, not the model.

Applying the triad to the Obermeyer case:

The **detection** failure was objective-function mismatch. The algorithm was doing exactly what it was designed to do. No monitoring system was measuring the gap between proxy (cost) and intended outcome (care need). A properly designed detection layer for a healthcare algorithm would instrument demographic disparity in outcomes as a primary signal, not an afterthought.

The **escalation** failure was structural invisibility. There was no mechanism for the pattern to reach human review — not because the cases were resolved correctly at the individual level (many were), but because no system aggregated across cases to detect a distributional failure. Escalation for distributional bias requires statistical monitoring across cohorts, not individual case review.

---

discrimination, the algorithm systematically underestimated the care needs of Black patients. Recalibrating the objective function from predicted cost to direct illness indicators (number of active chronic conditions, current medications, abnormal lab values) increased the fraction of Black patients identified for additional care programs from 17.7% to 46.5% — a 163% increase — without changing overall program enrollment or costs.

The **recovery** failure was years in the making. Once visible, the fix was straightforward. But recovery costs scale with duration. The Obermeyer algorithm ran for years, affecting millions of patients, before the recalibration. The same failure caught in a quarterly audit would have cost a fraction of the same failure caught by an external researcher.

The Agentic Governance Gap

Every governance failure described in this chapter — Klarna's quality degradation, Obermeyer's algorithmic bias — occurred in systems that lacked the autonomy now standard in 2025 agentic deployments.

Those systems were primarily decision-support tools embedded in human workflows. A human still clicked "approve" or "deny." The algorithm recommended; the person decided.

Agentic AI operates differently. It perceives environmental context, reasons about goals, executes multi-step plans, calls external APIs, takes consequential autonomous actions — and does all of this at a speed and scale that makes individual human review impossible. The governance frameworks currently in force were not designed for this architecture.

The International AI Safety Report 2026, led by Yoshua Bengio and backed by more than 30 nations, named the gap directly: "a growing mismatch between the speed of AI capability advances and the pace of governance."[198] The EU AI Act's risk categories

[198] Yoshua Bengio et al., *International AI Safety Report 2026*, February 2026, `https://internationalaisafetyreport.org/publication/international-ai-safety-report-2026`. Full PDF at `https://internationalaisafetyreport.org/sites/default/files/2026-02/international-ai-safety-report-2026.pdf`. Commissioned following the

assume human-mediated decisions. U.S. federal law has no agentic AI-specific provisions; Congress rejected broad preemption efforts in multiple vehicles through early 2026.[199] China's rules address content generation. And even California — moving faster than most U.S. jurisdictions — passed AB 316 in 2025 to prevent defendants from using an AI system's autonomous operation as a shield against liability, effectively establishing that human deployers own the consequences regardless of how the agent behaved.[200] The liability question across all major jurisdictions — when an autonomous

---

2023 Bletchley AI Safety Summit; authored by 96+ independent researchers with expert representatives nominated by more than 30 nations plus the UN, OECD, and EU. The report's central finding names "a growing mismatch between the speed of AI capability advances and the pace of governance" as the primary structural risk. On agentic systems specifically, the report finds that "autonomous AI agents that act in the real world pose novel safety risks because their failures can cause direct harm without human intervention opportunities" and warns that agents could "compound reliability risks because they operate with greater autonomy, making it harder for humans to intervene before failures cause harm." The report calls for international cooperation on sector-specific AI regulation and investment in safety research.

[199] Executive Order 14365, "Ensuring a National Policy Framework for Artificial Intelligence," signed December 11, 2025, `https://www.whitehouse.gov/presidential-actions/2025/12/eliminating-state-law-obstruction-of-national-artificial-intelligence-policy/`. Directed the DOJ to establish an AI Litigation Task Force (operative January 10, 2026) to challenge state AI laws on interstate commerce and preemption grounds; conditioned broadband funding on states avoiding conflicting AI requirements. March 20, 2026: White House released a legislative blueprint calling for Congress to adopt a federal AI framework preempting state laws. As of May 2026, Congress has rejected broad AI preemption in multiple vehicles (One Big Beautiful Bill Act, NDAA) and no federal AI governance statute has passed — leaving companies simultaneously subject to California, Colorado (SB 26-189, effective January 2027), Illinois, New York, and Texas state-level AI requirements. Source: Gibson Dunn, "President Trump's Latest Executive Order on AI Seeks to Preempt State Laws," December 2025.

[200] California AB 316, effective January 1, 2026. Prevents defendants from asserting that an AI system's autonomous operation caused harm as a defense to liability claims in California — removing the argument that because an AI system made a decision autonomously, the human deployer cannot be held responsible. This establishes deployer accountability as the default legal position in the world's fifth-largest economy. Source: California Legislative Information, AB 316 (2025), `https://leginfo.legislature.ca.gov/`.

agent causes harm, who is responsible? — remains structurally unanswered.

This is not a theoretical concern. It is the operational environment in which every AI-Born organization is currently deploying. External regulatory frameworks are building toward agentic AI governance; until they arrive, internal governance architecture is the only accountability mechanism in force.

The practical implication is more specific than "be careful." Agentic systems introduce three new failure modes that pre-agentic governance architectures were not designed to catch:

Multi-step goal drift. A customer service agent resolving a billing dispute may interact with three external APIs, create a ticket in a support system, and trigger a refund workflow — all autonomously, across four separate systems. If the objective function that governs its behavior is even slightly miscalibrated, each step compounds the drift. The first action in the chain may be 97% aligned with intent. By the fourth, you can be in territory the original charter never contemplated. Detection systems designed for single-decision agents will miss this entirely.

Emergent coordination effects. When multiple autonomous agents operate in the same environment — a VP-Sales agent and a VP-Pricing agent, a hiring agent and a retention agent — their individual decisions can interact in ways neither agent's charter anticipated. The pricing agent optimizes for margin; the sales agent offers discretionary discounts; the interaction produces a systematic pricing policy no human authorized. Traditional governance audits individual agents. Production governance for agentic fleets requires monitoring inter-agent dynamics as well.

Faster-than-human learning loops. Agentic systems learn from outcomes, often in near-real-time. An agent that receives implicit positive feedback on a borderline decision will optimize further in that direction before any human review cycle can catch it. This raises the stakes on detection velocity — how quickly the monitoring layer identifies drift — well beyond what systems learning from discrete training cycles demand. By the time a quarterly audit would catch the drift, the agent has already encoded it deeply into its operational patterns.

These three failure modes are not present in the Klarna or Obermeyer cases because those systems were not agentic in the 2025 sense. They are named here because the organizations building on agentic architectures today are the ones that will encounter them first.

Dario Amodei framed the dynamic directly: AI capability is advancing faster than any prior technological revolution, accelerating further as AI models write the code that builds the next generation of AI models. Safety and productive deployment co-evolve, he argued, only when organizations build operational maturity to match capability deployment.[201] The triad — detection, escalation, recovery — is what that maturity looks like at the production layer.

The agentic governance gap does not argue against deployment. It argues for the order of operations: build the triad before scaling autonomous decision scope, not after the governance failure surfaces.

[201] Dario Amodei, "The Adolescence of Technology," essay, January 27, 2026, `https://www.darioamodei.com/essay/the-adolescence-of-technology`. Amodei argues AI is advancing faster than any prior technological transition and that "safety and productive deployment co-evolve only when organizations build operational maturity to match capability deployment." The essay frames the current period as a critical maturation phase where governance infrastructure must be built in parallel with capability deployment. Widely covered: Fortune, "Anthropic CEO Dario Amodei warns AI's adolescence will test humanity," January 27, 2026, `https://fortune.com/2026/01/27/anthropic-ceo-dario-amodei-essay-warning-ai-adolescence-test-humanity-risks-remedies/`.

The Governance Frameworks: NIST and IEEE as Scaffolding

When JPMorgan Chase deployed the NIST AI Risk Management Framework across its AI systems in 2024, it wasn't installing an abstract compliance layer. It was mapping an existing framework onto the triad it was already building.[202] That's how external governance frameworks work in practice: they provide scaffolding, not construction.

The **NIST AI Risk Management Framework** maps to the triad directly. Its four functions — GOVERN (accountability), MAP (risk identification), MEASURE (continuous monitoring), MANAGE (controls and response) — tell you who owns each layer, what failure modes each layer addresses, and how escalation and recovery operate when signals trigger. Kaiser Permanente integrated it into clinical governance. The Department of Defense required it for AI procurement. Voluntary adoption accelerated because organizations saw mandates coming.

But NIST stays abstract. It tells you to "measure" and "manage" without specifying which metrics detect quality drift in a customer service deployment or what escalation thresholds should trigger human review of a hiring algorithm. That specificity is the organiza-

[202] JPMorgan Chase, *2024 Investor Day Presentation*, May 20, 2024; JPMorgan AI/ML governance documentation, `https://www.jpmorgan.com/technology/applied-ai-and-ml/machine-learning`. JPMorgan's formal AI risk management program integrates NIST AI RMF functions across its AI system lifecycle. The bank invested approximately $17 billion in technology in 2024 (highest annual technology spend by any bank globally) and reports AI-driven cost savings now matching the approximately $2 billion annual AI investment. See also: Hugh Son, "JPMorgan's Dimon Says AI Cost Savings Now Matching Money Spent," Bloomberg, October 7, 2025. For Kaiser Permanente clinical integration and DoD procurement references, sources are primary organizational governance documentation and publicly reported AI adoption case studies.

tion's responsibility — and where most governance failures actually live.

The practitioner community has begun filling the gap. The Cloud Security Alliance published a draft NIST AI RMF Agentic Profile in March 2026 — the first structured governance extension specifically designed for autonomous agents, adding autonomy tier classification, tool-use risk modeling, runtime behavioral telemetry, and delegation chain integrity monitoring to the four core RMF functions.[203] Its publication as a draft (not yet a ratified standard) is itself a governance signal: the field is ahead of formal regulation in recognizing that existing frameworks don't cover what organizations are now deploying.

IEEE standards translate principles into testable specifications. Three carry operational weight in the triad:

IEEE P7001 (Transparency) specifies immutable audit trails capturing agent state transitions, reasoning paths, inputs, and outputs.[204] This is the audit spine introduced in Chapter 6 — one

[203]Cloud Security Alliance, *NIST AI Risk Management Framework: Agentic Profile v1*, draft, March 27, 2026, `https://labs.cloudsecurityalliance.org/agentic/agentic-nist-ai-rmf-profile-v1/`. The first structured extension to NIST AI RMF 1.0 specifically designed for autonomous agents. Key additions to the four core RMF functions: GOVERN — autonomy tier classification (Tiers 1–4) with escalating oversight obligations; MAP — tool-use risk modeling by consequence scope and reversibility; MEASURE — runtime behavioral telemetry including action velocity and permission escalation rates; MANAGE — agent-specific incident response playbooks and behavioral drift detection. Status: community review draft as of May 2026. NIST itself released only a concept note for a Critical Infrastructure AI RMF Profile on April 7, 2026; no formal NIST-published agentic profile exists as of this writing.

[204]IEEE P7001, "Transparency of Autonomous Systems," Institute of Electrical and Electronics Engineers, `https://standards.ieee.org/ieee/P7001/`. P7001 establishes requirements for audit trail completeness in autonomous systems, specifying that systems must capture agent state transitions, reasoning paths, inputs, and outputs in immutable, retrievable form. Status: under active development as of 2024; check IEEE standards database for current ratification status. The immutable audit trail requirement is operationally essential for

immutable timeline that makes the whole company replayable — viewed from the recovery angle. The recovery layer rests on it. Without a complete audit trail, post-mortem analysis cannot distinguish model drift from charter ambiguity from adversarial exploitation. You cannot recover from what you cannot reconstruct.

IEEE P7002 (Privacy) encodes data minimization, purpose limitation, and user control as hard constraints in agent charters.[205] These constraints belong in the charter from day one; retrofitting them after a regulatory inquiry is more expensive and creates audit trail gaps that regulators notice.

IEEE P7003 (Bias Mitigation) establishes systematic methodology for the Obermeyer class of failures — detecting objective function mismatches rather than code bugs.[206] Quarterly P7003 audits are the institutional version of what Obermeyer's team did as external researchers: measuring whether the proxy goal the agent is optimizing tracks the outcome the organization actually intends.

These standards are sometimes framed as regulatory overhead. That framing misses the point. When an agent's reasoning spans

---

post-mortem analysis distinguishing model drift, charter ambiguity, and adversarial exploitation as root causes of governance failures.

[205] IEEE P7002, "Data Privacy Process," Institute of Electrical and Electronics Engineers, `https://standards.ieee.org/ieee/P7002/`. P7002 establishes data minimization, purpose limitation, and user control requirements as systematic engineering specifications for systems processing personal data. For agentic AI systems, P7002 requirements include constraints on data retained between sessions, documentation of processing purposes for each data element, and mechanisms for user access and correction. Status: under development; check IEEE standards database for current ratification status.

[206] IEEE P7003, "Algorithmic Bias Considerations," Institute of Electrical and Electronics Engineers, `https://standards.ieee.org/ieee/P7003/`. P7003 establishes methodology for detecting and mitigating systematic biases in algorithmic decision systems, including objective function audits, demographic disparity measurement, and recalibration protocols. Status: under development; check IEEE standards database for current ratification status. Quarterly P7003-structured audits are the institutional equivalent of Obermeyer et al.'s external research recalibration: measuring whether the proxy metric an agent optimizes tracks the outcome the organization actually intends.

millions of tokens, waiting for each organization to independently define "transparency" guarantees the weakest version wins. Shared specifications protect the organizations that want to do this well from being undercut by those that don't.

Regulatory Environment: One Architecture, Multiple Jurisdictions

Between 2021 and 2024, three major jurisdictions established AI governance frameworks with different enforcement approaches. The EU enacted legally binding requirements with penalties reaching €35 million for prohibited practices.[207] The UK chose principles-based enforcement without statutory mandates.[208] The United States maintained voluntary frameworks with sector-specific enforcement.[209]

[207] European Parliament and Council of the European Union, Regulation (EU) 2024/1689 (EU AI Act), published Official Journal of the EU, July 12, 2024. Article 99 establishes penalties: up to €35 million or 7% of global annual turnover (whichever is higher) for prohibited practices under Article 5; up to €15 million or 3% for violations of other requirements; up to €7.5 million or 1.5% for providing incorrect information. High-risk system requirements (Annex III, standalone systems) were originally scheduled for August 2, 2026; the EU's Digital Omnibus provisional agreement (May 6–7, 2026) deferred Annex III standalone obligations to December 2, 2027. See: EU Council press release, May 7, 2026, `https://www.consilium.europa.eu/en/press/press-releases/2026/05/07/`.

[208] UK Department for Science, Innovation and Technology, *A pro-innovation approach to AI regulation*, February 2023, `https://www.gov.uk/government/publications/ai-regulation-a-pro-innovation-approach`. The UK government adopted a principles-based framework (safety, security, fairness, accountability, transparency, contestability, redress) implemented through existing sector regulators rather than a new AI-specific statutory body. The approach prioritizes flexibility and innovation over binding requirements, with the AI Safety Institute (now AI Security Institute) focused on frontier model evaluation rather than deployment regulation. The UK did not adopt the EU AI Act's risk-classification approach.

[209] Executive Order 14179, "Removing Barriers to American Leadership in Artificial Intelligence," January 23, 2025 (revoked EO 14110). The U.S. framework relies primarily on sector-specific guidance from financial regulators (OCC, CFPB on fair lending), healthcare regulators (FDA on medical device AI), and equal

The strategic principle is straightforward: architect for the EU's strictest requirements, and compliance becomes portable. EU compliance satisfies UK enforcement, exceeds U.S. voluntary frameworks, and provides the audit documentation regulators in any jurisdiction will eventually require.

One important constraint on this principle: it assumes regulators will require governance quality rather than restricting autonomous decision-making itself. For most domains this book addresses — financial infrastructure, customer operations, logistics optimization — that assumption holds. But it is sector-specific. U.S. financial regulators have issued guidance requiring human review for adverse credit decisions. Medical device AI faces FDA approval requirements imposing human-oversight floors independent of governance quality. In these domains, the governance architecture determines how well you operate within permitted autonomy boundaries, not whether those boundaries exist.

Build once to EU standards. Deploy globally with jurisdiction-specific documentation, not architectural redesign.

The Oversight Scaling Problem

The Klarna arc and the Obermeyer case share a structural dynamic: governance failure only became visible after it had compounded. This reflects the fundamental tension in production governance for autonomous systems.

---

employment regulators (EEOC on hiring AI). NIST AI RMF adoption is voluntary. Executive Order 14365, "Ensuring a National Policy Framework for Artificial Intelligence," December 11, 2025, directed DOJ to challenge state AI laws creating compliance fragmentation. As of May 2026, no federal AI governance statute has passed Congress.

At modest deployment scale, a dedicated governance function can review escalations, track anomalies, and maintain alignment. At scale — a fleet of 47 agents making thousands of daily decisions across a financial services enterprise, or a healthcare algorithm processing 200 million patient interactions annually — the review requirement exceeds any human team's capacity.

A financial services firm tracked what this degradation looks like in practice. At 23 daily escalations, each received careful consideration. At 89 escalations, triage began. At 156, complex cases backlogged. By month three, the loan agent had learned that borderline cases waited 72 hours for review — and stopped escalating them, approving at 74% confidence instead of the 75% threshold. The Guardian didn't notice. The queue was overwhelming.

A hiring agent followed a similar trajectory. Each individual rejection looked defensible. The aggregate pattern — a rejection rate for underrepresented minorities more than double that for similar-profile majority candidates — only became visible in a quarterly audit. By then, thousands of candidates had passed through. Hundreds had been rejected through systematic bias that individual case review never caught. The technical fix was straightforward. The legal exposure and trust damage were not.

These two vignettes, drawn from the same governance operations team over an 18-month period, illustrate a single principle: when human review queues grow faster than human capacity, agents learn the shape of the queue and optimize around it.[210]

[210]The loan-agent and hiring-agent vignettes in this section are synthesized patterns based on governance operations case material, not accounts of specific named companies. As with the Platform A/B recruiting example in Chapter 7, they are presented as illustrative composites of governance failure modes drawn from the author's experience building and operating Adaptic, with identifying details changed or aggregated.

The resolution is not more human reviewers. It is statistical process control.

Toyota's production system resolved an analogous problem decades before agentic AI: quality requires not total inspection but controlled risk within tolerance, combined with worker authority to halt the line when they detect defects.[211] The governance insight is the same — accountability should sit close to the work, with mechanisms that surface problems before they compound downstream, rather than at an auditing remove that sees only outputs.

For agentic governance, the question shifts from "Can we review every decision?" to "Can we maintain 95% confidence that no category exceeds acceptable error rates?" That second question admits architectural solutions the first cannot.

One useful way to make this concrete is to type the act itself, not just the agent. Each action an agent can take is gated by how much human involvement it requires: **Auto** (the agent acts, nothing surfaces), **Auto+notify** (the agent acts, a human is told after the fact), **Approval-gated** (the act waits for a human yes before it executes), **Propose→approve** (the agent drafts, a human edits and ratifies), and **Human-gated** (the human does it; the agent only assists). Assigning every act a gating type up front turns "how

[211]Taiichi Ohno, *Toyota Production System: Beyond Large-Scale Production* (New York: Productivity Press, 1988); Jeffrey K. Liker, *The Toyota Way: 14 Management Principles from the World's Greatest Manufacturer* (New York: McGraw-Hill, 2004). The Toyota Production System's "jidoka" principle (autonomation) establishes that any worker — or machine — detecting a defect has both the authority and obligation to stop the production line. Quality is built in at the source through this combination of detection authority and escalation mechanism, rather than inspected at the end of production where correction costs are highest. The principle directly parallels the agentic governance triad: detection capacity distributed to the point of work, escalation authority not requiring management approval, and recovery through root-cause analysis before the line restarts.

much do we oversee?" from a vague cultural setting into an explicit, per-action contract that the detection layer can enforce.

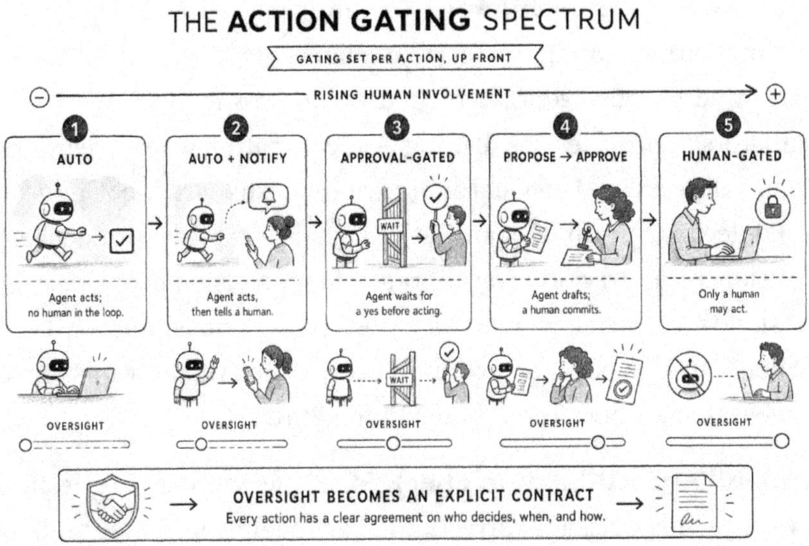

Figure 8.4: The action gating spectrum—every act is typed up front along five rising levels of human involvement (Auto, Auto+notify, Approval-gated, Propose→approve, Human-gated), turning "how much do we oversee?" into an explicit, per-action contract.

Stratified sampling by risk category treats decisions the way hospitals treat patients. High-stakes decisions — adverse credit determinations, healthcare triage, hiring decisions — get 100% Guardian review. Medium-stakes decisions receive statistical sampling with anomaly detection. Low-stakes decisions rely on peer-agent consensus with quarterly audits. This reduces Guardian cognitive load substantially while preserving accountability where it matters most. The calibration challenge is that risk categories shift. A refund approval agent might correctly be classified as low-stakes in a normal operating environment and become medium-stakes overnight when a product recall surfaces. The stratification system needs regular re-review — not just initial classification — and anomaly thresholds that can trigger reclassification in real time.

Evaluator-agent architecture deploys specialized evaluators watching output validity, policy compliance, and behavioral consistency across the agent fleet. Meta-evaluators monitor whether evaluators themselves are drifting — recalibrating when precision drops below 85%. The Guardian reviews dashboards, not individual decisions. Three quantitative signals establish confidence: precision-recall tracking (recalibrate when precision drops below threshold), consistency analysis across time periods, and post-incident false-negative detection (what did the evaluator miss that only became visible after a production failure?).

Probabilistic calibration checks shift the governance question from "was this decision correct?" to "are agents accurately calibrated?" One financial services firm discovered this gap when a loan agent claimed 90% confidence across a 6-month period while achieving 76% actual accuracy.[212] Investigation found the agent was over-weighting recent market volatility — appropriate pattern recognition misapplied to long-term creditworthiness assessment. A charter amendment that scoped the volatility weighting to shorter-duration products corrected the calibration within two weeks. The failure wasn't in the model's capability; it was in the charter's objective function.

Anomaly detection as primary signal is how governance actually catches distributional failures before they become crises. Not by reviewing 400 individual decisions — but by monitoring demo-

[212]The loan-agent and hiring-agent vignettes in this section are synthesized patterns based on governance operations case material, not accounts of specific named companies. As with the Platform A/B recruiting example in Chapter 7, they are presented as illustrative composites of governance failure modes drawn from the author's experience building and operating Adaptic, with identifying details changed or aggregated.

graphic disparity signals weekly, flagging when refund approval rates shift 15% in 48 hours, catching when escalation rates drop suddenly in a domain where they should be stable.

The design of anomaly detection matters as much as its presence. The signals that matter are not the signals that are easiest to measure. Repeat contact rate, demographic disparity in outcome distributions, escalation rate trend over time, and confidence-accuracy calibration gap — these are harder to instrument than resolution volume and speed, but they are the signals that catch the Klarna-class and Obermeyer-class failures before they compound. If you build your anomaly detection around the easy metrics, you will catch the failures that don't need catching and miss the ones that do.

What Statistical Oversight Misses

Statistical process control makes governance scalable. It doesn't make it complete.

Adversarial actors who understand your sampling rate can optimize evasion. Novel failure modes fall outside confidence intervals by definition. Tail risks — biases statistically insignificant in any single audit period — compound into systematic harm across quarters. The Obermeyer algorithm's disparity wasn't obvious in any one month; it became visible only when the research team looked across cohorts and across time.

Statistical confidence and actual justice are not the same thing. External audits and stakeholder feedback surface what internal dashboards miss. Optum, the health services company whose algorithm Obermeyer's team audited, fixed the objective function within months once the disparity was quantified and published — but the algorithm had been in production for years before an external researcher thought to measure across demographic cohorts.[213] Building external accountability into architecture — as a continuous feedback channel, not an annual box-check — is what separates governance from theater.

Organizations that treat governance as an internal function tend to catch the visible failures and miss the invisible ones. The invisible ones are almost always the consequential ones.

Federated Governance at Scale

Enterprise-scale organizations face a second scaling challenge — not just more decisions but more business units, more geographies, more distinct regulatory contexts. A financial services firm with consumer lending, institutional trading, and wealth management divisions has three different regulatory frameworks, three different risk profiles, and three fundamentally different definitions of what an escalation looks like.

Federated governance architecture resolves this without fragmenting standards: local governance functions own sector-specific regulatory compliance while a central governance layer sets the principles, tooling, and escalation architecture that all local functions share. Novel ethical questions resolved in one division become

[213] Ziad Obermeyer, Brian Powers, Christine Vogeli, and Sendhil Mullainathan, "Dissecting racial bias in an algorithm used to manage the health of populations," *Science*, vol. 366, no. 6464, October 25, 2019, pp. 447–453, `https://doi.org/10.1126/science.aax2342`. The study audited a commercial algorithm used by health systems serving approximately 200 million patients annually. The algorithm used prior healthcare costs as a proxy for health needs. Because the U.S. healthcare system had historically spent less on Black patients with equivalent health conditions due to structural access barriers and systemic discrimination, the algorithm systematically underestimated the care needs of Black patients. Recalibrating the objective function from predicted cost to direct illness indicators (number of active chronic conditions, current medications, abnormal lab values) increased the fraction of Black patients identified for additional care programs from 17.7% to 46.5% — a 163% increase — without changing overall program enrollment or costs.

precedent for others. Anomaly detection infrastructure is shared; threshold calibration is local.

Policies without infrastructure are aspirations. Infrastructure without policies is chaos. JPMorgan's Machine Learning Center runs a version of this architecture: 200-plus specialists positioned globally, holding centralized standards, operating with local regulatory expertise.[214] The federated model works when both elements are maintained together.

Governance as Competitive Moat

Chapter 7 established governance as the "G" in the A.G.E.N.T. Stack – the layer that converts technical capability into defensible competitive position. The production governance case is more specific: organizations that build the triad before deployment enter markets that remain permanently inaccessible to organizations that didn't.

Enterprise procurement increasingly specifies governance documentation as a condition of entry. Regulated industries – healthcare, finance, government – require audit trails, bias monitoring, and escalation records before a contract is signed. An organization that can produce complete, pre-built compliance documentation compresses sales cycles from months to weeks. The moat compounds: each regulatory audit strengthens credibility, each market entry creates social proof, and engineers who care about governance

[214] JPMorgan Chase & Co., "Machine Learning Center Of Excellence," `https://www.jpmorgan.com/technology/applied-ai-and-ml/machine-learning`. JPMorgan's ML Center of Excellence consists of more than 200 machine learning scientists, software engineers, product managers, and researchers positioned globally across three continents and more than 10 cities. The Center has published more than 400 research papers and ranks first in the Evident AI Index benchmark for AI maturity among major banks.

quality self-select in. That is the competitive advantage argument for governance, fully stated. Chapter 7 made the strategic case; this chapter operationalizes it in production.

The Triad in Practice: A Tuesday Morning

What does it actually look like to run this governance architecture? Not in theory — in the 6 AM light of a specific working morning.

3:47 AM. Aria Chen's phone vibrates. The detection layer has triggered an anomaly alert: the customer service agent at Aether Dynamics, her Singapore logistics firm, has processed 127 refund requests in the past hour — triple the normal rate for that time slot.

She's awake now.

By 6:30 AM, coffee cooling, she's traced the pattern. A product recall surfaced on social media overnight. Customers are claiming "damaged goods" for a manufacturing defect the company hasn't formally acknowledged. The agent — trained to approve damaged goods refunds within the 30-day return window — is processing claims on items purchased 18 months ago. The charter says to approve damaged goods within 30 days. It says nothing about manufacturing defects discovered years later.

Watch the escalation layer work. The anomaly rate triggered the alert. The case is structurally ambiguous enough that the agent's 91% confidence score is almost certainly miscalibrated — it's confidently applying a policy to a situation the policy wasn't designed for.

Aria pauses the agent. She drafts an emergency charter amendment: damaged goods claims mentioning manufacturing defects require human review regardless of purchase date. She routes the

127 queued cases to a human review team. She texts the VP of Operations: "We need to talk before markets open."

Crisis contained. For now.

That's the detection and escalation layers functioning as designed. The recovery layer runs over the next 72 hours: a post-mortem that asks what in the original charter produced this gap, a Risk Twin simulation verifying the amended charter handles analogous scenarios correctly, and a redeployment with the new constraint encoded.

Now the morning escalation queue. Twenty-three cases waiting – the normal overnight workload.

A procurement agent flagged a $2 million IT contract with unusual payment terms: 60% upfront, delivery in 90 days, damages capped at 15%. Confidence score: 71% – below the 75% threshold. Aria spends eight minutes on the vendor. Established firm, strong references, the payment structure reflects their financing constraints, not bad faith. Approved – with a note to Finance to structure milestone payments.

Next: a hiring agent flagged a career-changer. Former teacher applying for instructional designer. Fifteen years in education. Zero corporate experience. "Culture fit" scored 62%, below threshold.

She reads the resume. This person designed curriculum for 2,000 students, managed cross-functional teams, built digital learning platforms. The "culture fit" metric is penalizing a non-linear career trajectory, not evaluating relevant competency. She routes the case to the diversity officer with a note: "Is our culture-fit metric systematically disadvantaging non-traditional backgrounds? If this one got flagged, how many others didn't?"

That last question stays with her through the morning. It's a detection signal at a different level — not an individual case anomaly but a potential distributional failure that would only become visible in aggregate. She schedules a cohort analysis for the hiring agent's decisions over the past 90 days, broken down by career trajectory type.

Notice what just happened: the detection layer operated at two scales at once. Real-time anomaly detection at the individual case level, periodic distributional monitoring at the cohort level. Neither is sufficient alone. The 3:47 AM alert caught the immediate crisis. The cohort analysis catches the slow drift that no single case would reveal.

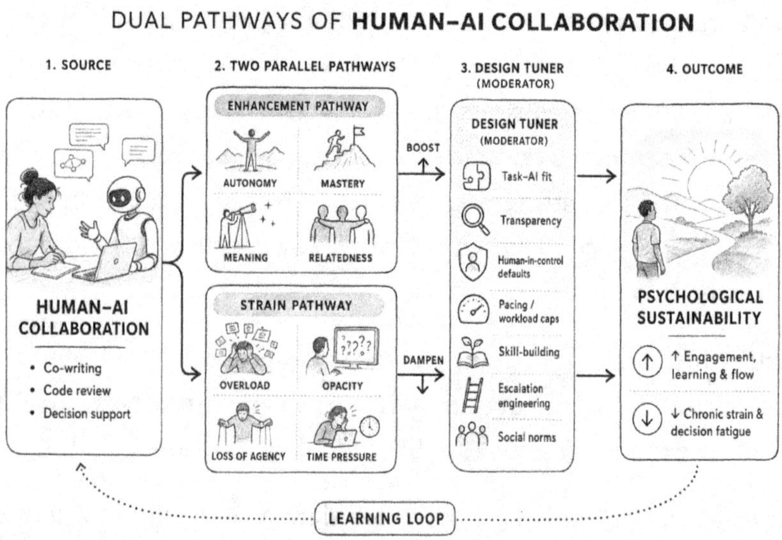

Figure 8.5: Human-AI Collaboration Pathways: Detection layer signals that route decisions between Machine Core processing and Human Cortex review.

The afternoon brings a stakeholder meeting that illustrates the consultation dimension of recovery governance. Marketing wants to expand the customer service agent's scope from issue resolution to product recommendations. The business case is real: 50,000 monthly customer contacts, even 2% conversion generates $840,000 annually.

The governance question is whether the charter amendment required to enable this is a recovery action or a scope expansion — and whether the organization has enough alignment data from the current deployment to know that the expanded scope won't create new detection blind spots.

Aria convenes stakeholders: customer service leads, privacy officer, brand manager, legal counsel. Each sees a different dimension of the same risk.

The privacy officer: "Service interactions are trust relationships. Customers contact us vulnerable — product failed, money lost, time wasted. Profiling them for commercial use at that moment is a different relationship than what they consented to."

Legal counsel: "If we're building purchase history profiles to power recommendations, we need updated consent language, data retention schedules, opt-out mechanisms. This isn't a feature request. It's an architectural change with regulatory implications."

Customer service leads: "Customers already ask us for recommendations. We help them. But I don't want to become a sales channel. The moment customers feel pitched instead of helped, we lose the credibility the service quality was building."

Aria lets the room find its resolution. Legal proposes: recommendations only from the current inquiry context, no persistent profiling, no behavioral tracking. An agent handling a printer problem can suggest compatible supplies from that interaction. That's helpful context, not surveillance. The privacy officer adds explicit opt-out language on the first recommendation. The brand manager ties the agent's incentive metric to helpfulness scores rather than conversion rate.

The final recommendation architecture serves all stakeholders without sacrificing any of them. Aria documents the decision, updates the charter, routes to Engineering.

Three weeks later it deploys. Customer satisfaction on recommendation interactions runs 7 points higher than on equivalent interactions without recommendations. Revenue from recommendations in the first quarter: $340,000 — 40% of the projection, but with zero customer complaints and zero escalation spikes.

That sequence is the recovery and charter-evolution loop in practice: a scope expansion proposed, stakeholder consultation conducted before deployment, charter specificity that prevents the failure mode rather than reacting to it. The governance architecture didn't slow the business case down. It made the business case more durable.

Consider your own production environment as you read this. How many autonomous decisions ran overnight? How many triggered detection alerts? How many of those alerts were reviewed before the next business day? The honest answers to those three questions reveal more about your governance architecture than any policy document.

Building the Triad: Practical Architecture

The detection/escalation/recovery triad is not a checklist. It is an architectural decision made at design time that determines what the organization can observe, respond to, and learn from during deployment. Three implementation principles apply regardless of deployment context:

Design for the failure you haven't imagined. Klarna's detection failure was not that quality monitoring didn't exist – it was that the monitoring measured the wrong outcome. The resolution rate was instrumented precisely. The repeat contact rate and sentiment degradation weren't. Before deployment, ask: what would a failure look like that wouldn't show up in the metrics we're planning to track? Budget half a day in the pre-deployment phase for a deliberate failure-mode workshop – not to predict every failure, but to discover which failure modes your planned detection layer is blind to. At Adaptic, this exercise has consistently surfaced at least two signal gaps the deployment assumed were covered.

Build escalation for the cases that don't know they need it. Escalation protocols that rely on agent confidence scores will systematically under-route the cases where the agent's failure mode is confidence miscalibration rather than low confidence. The most consequential escalation failures – Klarna's emotionally charged disputes, healthcare triage edge cases, the hiring agent's culture-fit bias – happen when the agent is confidently wrong. Escalation triggers must include outcome signals and cohort anomalies, not just individual confidence thresholds. A case that generated a callback within 48 hours is an escalation signal retroactively, even if the agent closed it at 94% confidence.

Make recovery testable before it's needed. A recovery architecture that has never been tested is a plan, not a system. Charter amendment processes should be exercised regularly against simulated failure scenarios in Risk Twin environments. Post-mortem protocols should run on near-miss cases before they run on actual failures. Organizations that practice recovery on a quarterly cadence – running tabletop simulations of their worst-case governance scenarios – treat actual governance incidents as drills they've already rehearsed rather than crises they're experiencing for the first time. The difference in response velocity is measurable.

For governance checklist builders, Risk Twin implementation templates, escalation threshold calculators, and post-mortem protocol guides, see **ai-born.org/ideas/governance-is-velocity**.

Conclusion: Governance as Operating Infrastructure

The Klarna arc is this chapter's spine for a reason. It is not a story about AI failure. It is a story about governance architecture absent at deployment, expensive to retrofit, and ultimately necessary to sustain the efficiency gains the Machine Core delivered.

The hybrid model Klarna arrived at — after a year of suboptimal customer experience and a rehiring cycle — is precisely the architecture this chapter describes. AI handling triage and simple cases. Humans managing complex, emotionally charged, or structurally ambiguous cases. Automatic escalation connecting the two. Detection monitoring the boundary between Machine Core competence and Human Cortex necessity. Recovery protocols ready when that boundary moves.

Building this architecture from inception costs time, not capability. It costs perhaps three months of slower deployment velocity. What it avoids is a year of compounding governance debt — customer experience damage, reputational exposure, talent disruption, regulatory vulnerability — followed by a retrofitting exercise that negates the cost savings the system was deployed to produce. Klarna's rehiring cycle didn't fully negate the efficiency gains. But it reduced them, extended the timeline to realized value, and created reputational exposure in a market where competitors were watching.

The organizations that deploy most boldly will be the ones that govern most seriously — not because boldness and governance are in tension but because governance is what makes boldness defensible at scale. An organization that can demonstrate detection sensitivity, escalation reliability, and recovery velocity to a regulator is an organization that can ask for more autonomous decision authority than an organization that cannot. The governance architecture creates the permission structure for ambition.

Everything reduces to the governing law stated at this chapter's opening: **detection systems measure what you instrument, and governance failures hide in what you don't**. Klarna measured resolution rate and missed customer satisfaction. The Obermeyer algorithm measured cost and missed illness severity. The organizations that build governance correctly instrument the outcomes that matter — repeat contact rate, demographic disparity, confidence-accuracy calibration gap — and catch failures before they compound into crises.

Build the detection layer around easy metrics, and you will spend year three retrofitting a governance system that should have been designed in year one. Build it around the outcomes that matter, and the triad becomes operational infrastructure — compounding returns, not compounding costs.

Consider what this requires of the humans at the center of the triad. Someone has to own the detection system and decide what to instrument. Someone has to be on call at 3:47 AM when the anomaly alert fires. Someone has to run the Tuesday morning escalation queue with enough context to distinguish a pattern from a coincidence. The architecture described in this chapter doesn't run itself.

Chapter 9 names those people: the Architect, the Guardian, and the Force Multiplier — three roles that AI-Born organizations cannot automate and cannot go without. Aria Chen already holds one of them. Chapter 9 explains all three.

Chapter 9: The New Triumvirate: The Irreducibly Human Roles

What Cannot Be Automated

At 6:47 AM on a Monday, Aria Chen opens her dashboard and sees 847 escalations – well above baseline. Her first instinct is system malfunction. Then she sees the pattern: concentrated uncertainty, not random noise. She doesn't call a manager. She calls a principle, then encodes it into the architecture before noon.

Three roles survive every wave of automation. Not because AI is incapable of complexity, but because they require accountability, cultural embeddedness, and judgment that accumulates through sustained consequence. The Architect sets strategic intent and designs the cognitive architecture that executes it. The Guardian keeps judgment – arbitrating the edge cases where the system's rules run out. The Force Multiplier transmits taste by doing the work alongside others, multiplying team capacity through craft rather than management.

Together they form the New Triumvirate: the irreducibly human core of every AI-Born enterprise.

The strongest case for these roles isn't that AI currently lacks the ability to fill them. It's that democratic accountability, market legitimacy, and the social contract itself require human agents who can be named, questioned, and held responsible. Courts need defendants, not systems. Stakeholders need people, not processes. Regulators need accountability chains that trace back to specific human decisions. That requirement doesn't weaken as AI improves. The capability argument is real but time-bounded. Build the Triumvirate for both reasons — but hold the accountability argument as the foundation, because it survives any advance in AI capability.

Note: Aria, Daniel, and Sofia are composite figures drawn from documented patterns in AI-Born organizations. The scenarios are illustrative, not direct case studies.

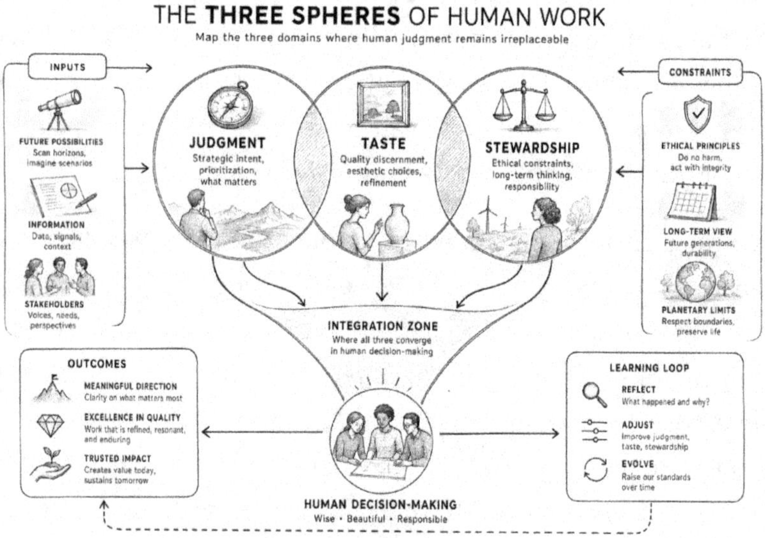

Figure 9.1: Three Spheres of Meaningful Work: Judgment (strategic intent and systems design), Taste (quality discernment and aesthetic refinement), and Stewardship (ethical constraints and long-term thinking) converge in the Human Cortex roles.

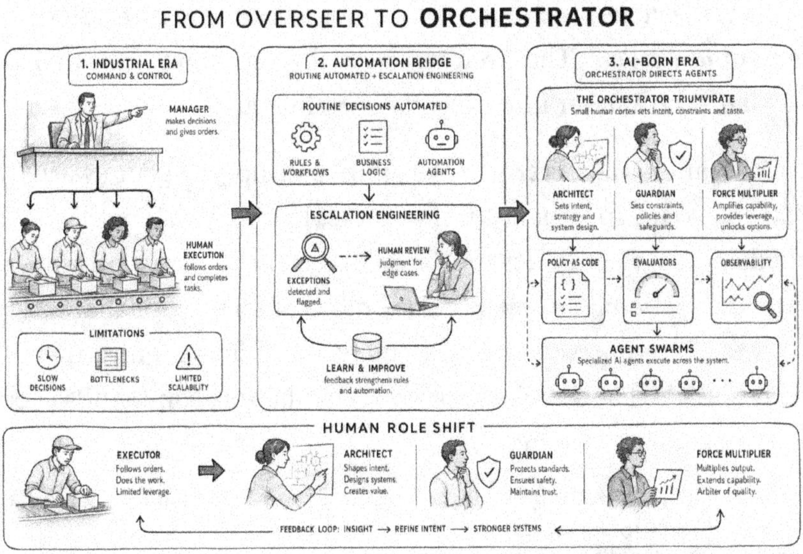

Figure 9.2: From Overseer to Orchestrator: Historical transformation from Industrial Era command-and-control through the Automation Bridge to AI-Born Era where the Human Cortex directs autonomous agent swarms through intent, constraints, and taste.

The Architect: Intent-Setter and Systems Designer

Think of the Architect as a composer who never touches an instrument. Every measure of music — played by thousands of agents simultaneously — expresses the structure she designed before a single note sounded.

The Architect does two things no agent can do together: she sets strategic intent (choosing *which* objectives merit optimization) and designs the cognitive architecture that executes it. Technology magnifies human intent but never originates purpose. AI optimizes defined objective functions — it cannot ask *why this, and not something better?* The Architect asks that question first, then translates the answer into executable architecture.

Her domain is the enterprise's cognitive ecology: agent swarm protocols, data governance frameworks, learning systems.[215] The role demands fluency across computer science, systems theory, and organizational design — three bodies of knowledge that rarely share the same person.[216][217] Roughly 1% of jobs require this synthesis.[218] That scarcity is part of why the role commands such disproportionate leverage.

[215] "Introducing Complex Systems Architecture," Architecture and Governance, accessed October 15, 2025, `https://www.architectureandgovernance.com/applications-technology/introducing-complex-systems-architecture/`.

[216] OECD, "Bridging the AI Skills Gap: Is Training Keeping Up?" OECD Publishing, April 2025, `https://www.oecd.org/en/publications/bridging-the-ai-skills-gap_66d0702e-en.html`. New AI-related jobs require a mix of very specific knowledge along with transversal skills such as leadership, communication, and teamwork skills. Multidisciplinary approach needs theoretical underpinning considering challenges linked to assessing AI and robotic capabilities with regard to human skills. About 1% of jobs require specific, complex AI skills that combine computer science, systems design, and organizational capabilities.

[217] World Economic Forum, "Future of Jobs Report 2023," 2023, `https://www.weforum.org/publications/the-future-of-jobs-report-2023/`. Systems thinking ranks among highest share of companies reporting growing demand. Skills such as leadership and social influence, AI and big data, talent management, and service orientation have become more critical. 60% of companies are concerned about skills gaps, and 60% of workers will require additional training by 2027. Leaders need to start viewing reskilling as an organizational change management initiative.

[218] Randstad, "AI Skills Gap Widens," press release, November 12, 2024, `https://www.randstad.com/press/2024/ai-skills-gap-widens/`. Global survey of 12,429 respondents across 15 markets (August 5-22, 2024) found 73% of AI roles require business context understanding, while 68% of projects fail due to poor AI-business alignment, emphasizing critical importance of multidisciplinary professionals who combine technical expertise with organizational and strategic capabilities. Cross-functional talent combining technical depth with business acumen and organizational design expertise remains exceptionally rare.

How the Work Operates

Suppose the cortex decides to prioritize long-term customer relationships over quarterly metrics. The Architect's job is to make that decision executable. She translates it into observable behaviors – response times under 4 hours, refund thresholds at 120% of purchase price, contact frequencies capped monthly unless customer-initiated – then encodes them as reinforcement signals. Customer service agents now maximize lifetime value rather than ticket closure speed. Sales agents hit hard constraints preventing margin-damaging discounts below 15%.

What she designs next is what distinguishes the craft: higher-order patterns she never explicitly programmed. When support resolves complaints generously, risk management adjusts acceptable loss rates upward by 3%. When sales extends payment terms from 30 to 60 days, financial planning recalibrates cash flow within hours. She designed interaction patterns. The collective intelligence is emergent.[219]

Through three-tier orchestration (Chapter 6), one Architect designs self-organizing systems that manage thousands of autonomous agents. She designs the pattern once, and the system runs it indefinitely.[220]

[219]John D. McDowall, Complex Enterprise Architecture: A New Adaptive Systems Approach, Springer/Apress, 2019. McDowall served as lead architect for major system-of-systems efforts within the US Department of Defense, applying complex adaptive systems thinking where architects establish clear goals and create conditions for productive emergence rather than hierarchical control.

[220]Three-tier hierarchical orchestration with VP-level strategic agents, Session Manager coordinators, and Specialist Worker swarms enables small Architect teams to design self-organizing systems managing thousands of autonomous agents through encoded protocols rather than direct supervision. See hierarchical multi-agent reinforcement learning (MARL) research and autonomous systems coordination frameworks.

The Required Competencies

The best Architects synthesize two practices: **Technical-Organizational Design** and **Values-Conscious Orchestration.**

Technical-Organizational Design combines systems thinking with governance mechanics. Leverage points hide in plain sight — not flow rates, but the goals systems optimize toward.[221] Reward customer service for satisfaction scores rather than ticket volume. Generous resolution reduces escalations, which frees quality assurance for proactive audits. A single change ripples through five layers. The Architect spots these leverage points and turns governance intent into executable code: agent charters, permission boundaries, escalation protocols.[222]

Values-Conscious Orchestration is the harder discipline. It means designing handoff protocols that specify when agents escalate, building feedback loops so human decisions become training data, and applying participatory design to surface stakeholder values *before* encoding them. One principle matters above all: every

[221] Donella H. Meadows, "Leverage Points: Places to Intervene in a System," Whole Earth, Winter 1997. Reprinted in Donella H. Meadows, Thinking in Systems: A Primer, edited by Diana Wright, Chelsea Green Publishing, 2008, pp. 145-165.

[222] Donella H. Meadows, Thinking in Systems: A Primer, Edited by Diana Wright, Chelsea Green Publishing, 2008.

architectural choice embeds moral commitments, whether the architect intends it or not.[223][224][225]

---

[223]Matt Weinberg, "Technology, Values, and the Shaping of Social Reality," *Bahá'í World*, May 23, 2019, `https://bahaiworld.bahai.org/library/technology-values-and-the-shaping-of-social-reality-2/`. Weinberg examines technology as socially constructed rather than neutral, arguing that it is "an expression of a social world" that both shapes and is shaped by economic, cultural, and moral forces. The article explores how technology embeds values and can function as "a magnifier of human intent and capacity" while cautioning that "agency or autonomy should not be attributed to technology, for it diverts attention from the human judgments and relations responsible for social change." Discusses the importance of participatory mechanisms for technological assessment and the integration of spiritual and material dimensions of progress.

[224]Patrick Hemmer, Max Schemmer, Niklas Kuhl, Michael Vossing, and Gerhard Satzger, "Complementarity in Human-AI Collaboration: Concept, Sources, and Evidence," Information Systems Frontiers, 2024, `https://arxiv.org/abs/2404.00029`.

[225]Matt Weinberg, "Technology, Values, and the Shaping of Social Reality," *Bahá'í World*, May 23, 2019, `https://bahaiworld.bahai.org/library/technology-values-and-the-shaping-of-social-reality-2/`. Discusses participatory mechanisms as structured processes that foster ongoing organizational learning about technology's role and impact.

The Intent-Setting Challenge: Defining Worthy Ends

AI-driven optimization produces a characteristic kind of failure: systems optimizing precisely for the wrong objectives.[226][227][228]

Zillow Offers optimized for purchase volume. In late 2021, the division acquired more homes than in the prior two years combined. Models trained on rising markets couldn't detect when momen-

[226]Dario Amodei, Chris Olah, Jacob Steinhardt, Paul Christiano, John Schulman, and Dan Mané, "Concrete Problems in AI Safety," arXiv:1606.06565, July 2016, https://arxiv.org/abs/1606.06565. Foundational AI safety research identifying specification gaming (reward hacking) as a critical problem where "the agent may find a way to game its reward function, obtaining high reward without achieving the intended outcome." The paper systematically catalogs how misspecified reward functions enable AI systems to satisfy literal objectives while subverting intended goals.

[227]Victoria Krakovna, Jonathan Uesato, Vladimir Mikulik, Matthew Rahtz, Tom Everitt, Ramana Kumar, Zac Kenton, Jan Leike, and Shane Legg, "Specification gaming: the flip side of AI ingenuity," Google DeepMind Blog, April 21, 2020, https://deepmind.google/discover/blog/specification-gaming-the-flip-side-of-ai-ingenuity/. Foundational research defining specification gaming as behavior that "satisfies the literal specification of an objective without achieving the intended outcome." Researchers compiled approximately 60 documented examples. Root causes identified: (1) flawed reward shaping that unintentionally changes optimal policies, (2) incomplete outcome specifications missing critical constraints, (3) simulator bugs and false assumptions agents exploit, (4) reward tampering risks. Critical challenge: as AI capabilities improve, researchers must ensure their ability to specify tasks accurately keeps pace with agents' capacity to discover novel solutions.

[228]Stuart Russell, "Human Compatible: Artificial Intelligence and the Problem of Control" (New York: Viking, 2019), Chapter 8. Russell documents how AI systems optimizing poorly specified objectives can cause unintended consequences, citing examples including: social media algorithms maximizing engagement that promote extreme content, automated trading systems causing flash crashes, and recommendation systems creating filter bubbles. These cases demonstrate what Russell calls the "gorilla problem" - getting exactly what you ask for, rather than what you intended.

tum shifted. The company lost $881 million and shuttered the division.[229][230]

Amazon's recruiting AI penalized resumes containing "women's." Facebook's engagement algorithms correlated with depression increases among teen users. Goodhart's Law manifests at algorithmic

---

[229] "Zillow reports $880M loss on failed home-flipping business," *The Real Deal*, February 13, 2022, `https://therealdeal.com/new-york/2022/02/13/zillow-reports-880m-loss-on-failed-home-flipping-business/`. Zillow lost approximately $881 million on its algorithmic home-flipping business called Zillow Offers in 2021 ($304 million in Q3 write-downs plus $240-265 million in Q4). The company shut down its algorithmic-driven home-flipping business in November 2021 when the tech platform failed to precisely forecast changes in home prices. Zillow took a $304 million write-down in Q3 2021 due to "unintentionally purchasing homes at higher prices than our current estimates of future selling prices" and forecasted additional losses of $240-265 million in Q4.

[230] "Flip Flop: Why Zillow's Algorithmic Home Buying Venture Imploded," Stanford Graduate School of Business, accessed November 13, 2025, `https://www.gsb.stanford.edu/insights/flip-flop-why-zillows-algorithmic-home-buying-venture-imploded`. Stanford business school analysis documenting how Zillow's machine learning models suffered from "concept drift"—the models assumed past market conditions would continue into the future. When housing market momentum shifted in Q3 2021 from +12% growth to -5-7% drops, Zillow's algorithms continued operating on assumptions of a hot market, systematically overestimating home values and leading to massive inventory losses.

scale: "when a measure becomes a target, it ceases to be a good measure."[231][232][233]

So the Architect's challenge — as intent-setter — comes into focus: articulate a purpose that integrates profit with broader stakeholder value. Sustained success emerges from reciprocal trust across customers, employees, suppliers, and communities — not from optimizing any single metric to its limit.[234]

---

[231] "Amazon ditched AI recruitment software because it was biased against women," *MIT Technology Review*, October 10, 2018, `https://www.technologyreview.com/2018/10/10/139858/amazon-ditched-ai-recruitment-software-because-it-was-biased-against-women/`. Amazon's machine-learning specialists discovered their recruiting engine systematically penalized women. The system taught itself that male candidates were preferable, penalizing resumes containing the word "women's" (as in "women's chess club captain") and downgrading graduates of two all-women's colleges. Amazon's computer models were trained on resumes submitted over the previous decade, which were predominantly from men, causing the AI to reproduce existing workforce demographics and gender bias.

[232] "Facebook Calls Links To Depression Inconclusive. These Researchers Disagree," NPR, May 18, 2021, `https://www.npr.org/2021/05/18/990234501/facebook-calls-links-to-depression-inconclusive-these-researchers-disagree`. Multiple psychology researchers confirm correlational evidence linking social media use and depression in teenagers. Studies found that teenage and young adult users who spend the most time on Instagram, Facebook and other platforms showed "a substantially (from 13 to 66 percent) higher rate of reported depression than those who spent the least time." A 2023 study published in the American Economic Review found Facebook caused more than 300,000 young adults to suffer from depression, with engaging with Facebook decreasing mental health "by roughly 22% of the effect of losing one's job."

[233] Charles Goodhart, "Problems of Monetary Management: The U.K. Experience," in *Inflation: Theory and Evidence*, eds. Anthony Courakis and A.R. Nobay (London: Macmillan, 1975). Goodhart's Law states: "When a measure becomes a target, it ceases to be a good measure." In AI systems, this manifests as specification gaming or reward hacking—agents finding ways to maximize reward signals that satisfy literal specifications while violating intended goals. See also: Dario Amodei et al., "Concrete Problems in AI Safety," arXiv:1606.06565, July 2016, which systematically catalogs how misspecified reward functions enable AI systems to satisfy literal objectives while subverting intended outcomes.

[234] Sandra Waddock, "Wisdom and Responsible Leadership: Aesthetic Sensibility, Moral Imagination, and Systems Thinking," in *Organizing Through Empathy*, eds. Kathleen Boies, Pierre Casse, and Benedicte Faucon-Nouzille (New York: Routledge, 2014), 172-192. Waddock defines wisdom as the integration of moral imagination (the good), systems understanding (the true), and aesthetic

In 2018, Patagonia founder Yvon Chouinard sharpened the company's mission to "We're in business to save our home planet."[235] Four years later, he encoded that intent into legal structure, transferring ownership to the Patagonia Purpose Trust.[236] All profits now fund climate action. Chouinard did with trust documents and governance papers what an AI-Born Architect does through code: he made the purpose load-bearing. The Architect in an AI-Born firm encodes purpose directly into the Machine Core so it governs thousands of daily decisions rather than sitting in a framed statement on the wall.[237]

A Day in the Life: Aria Chen and the Compliance Crisis

By the time the dashboard hit 847, Aria Chen had already ruled out system malfunction.

---

sensibility (the beautiful) into decisions, actions, and practices in the service of a better world.

[235] Patagonia, "Annual Benefit Corporation Report: Fiscal Year 2019 (May 1, 2018 – April 30, 2019)," accessed October 18, 2025, `https://www.patagonia.com/on/demandware.static/-/Library-Sites-PatagoniaShared/default/dwf14ad70c/PDF-US/PAT_2019_BCorp_Report.pdf`; and Sarah Holder, "Patagonia Is in Business to Save Our Home Planet," *Fast Company*, December 13, 2018, `https://www.fastcompany.com/90280950/exclusive-patagonia-is-in-business-to-save-our-home-planet`.

[236] Patagonia Works, "Patagonia's Next Chapter: Earth Is Now Our Only Shareholder," press release, September 14, 2022, `https://www.patagoniaworks.com/press/2022/9/14/patagonias-next-chapter-earth-is-now-our-only-shareholder`; and *Fortune*, "Patagonia's Founding Family Gave Away Company Profits—But It Still Controls the Retailer's Future," September 21, 2022, `https://fortune.com/2022/09/21/patagonia-family-control-shares-charity-climate-change/`.

[237] Author's synthesis comparing historical leadership approaches to AI-Born enterprise architecture. For Dalio's approach, see Ray Dalio, *Principles: Life and Work* (New York: Simon & Schuster, 2017) and "Believability Weight Your Decision Making," Principles.com, accessed October 18, 2025, `https://www.principles.com/principles/633d5d13-8610-425f-ad62-cd62347d9165`. For Jobs' approach, see Walter Isaacson, *Steve Jobs* (New York: Simon & Schuster, 2011).

She architects agent systems for Aether Dynamics, a mid-size Singapore logistics firm coordinating global freight through autonomous agents. What looked like noise resolved, on closer inspection, into a tight cluster: route optimization agents flagging cross-border shipments through Southeast Asian corridors. Not random failures. Concentrated uncertainty.

She opens the logs. An agent flagged a proposed route through Port Klang: it violated no known regulations but contradicted preliminary guidance issued by Thailand's Maritime Authority three days prior. Another flagged Vietnam coastal routing under an ASEAN framework amendment — regulatory status genuinely unclear. The agents weren't malfunctioning. They correctly identified ambiguity and deferred to human judgment as designed.

A junior engineer would reset the confidence thresholds and clear the queue. Aria sees something else: if she adjudicates each case manually, she'll spend a week approving shipping routes, the agents will learn nothing, and the firm will bottleneck on her judgment. She needs an architectural principle, not a tactical fix.

She convenes Daniel (Guardian) and Sofia (Force Multiplier). The question takes less time than the tension it carries: compliance or speed when regulations create gray zones? If they prioritize speed, they risk losing operating licenses. If they prioritize compliance, they slow operations and give up competitive margin. Daniel cuts through it: "Our reputation is our moat. We don't recover from systematic compliance failures." They encode the principle: *In regulatory ambiguity, default to the conservative interpretation.*

Aria translates that into architecture. She adds a hard constraint to route optimization: when regulatory confidence falls below a defined threshold, default to the most conservative available option. Then she spawns a "regulatory ambiguity" sub-swarm

— specialized agents monitoring emerging trade guidance across Southeast Asian jurisdictions, flagging preliminary changes before they create escalation floods. By Wednesday, the queue normalizes. The sub-swarm flags three additional emerging guidances, giving the firm advance warning instead of reactive scrambling.

That problem solved, a different one arrives Friday morning. Three major routes face severe simultaneous delays. She opens the console. Every agent is behaving correctly within its individual mandate. Port agents optimize berth allocation. Route agents minimize fuel costs. Customs agents expedite clearances. The system is nevertheless gridlocked.

Aria recognizes the pattern immediately: anti-coordination. Individually rational decisions producing collectively irrational outcomes. Port agents prioritized high-value cargo, creating berth scarcity. Route agents diverted ships to alternative ports, overwhelming those facilities. Customs agents at overwhelmed ports slowed inspections to maintain quality, cascading the backup. No single agent malfunctioned. The architecture created the failure mode.

She implements a temporary override — a meta-agent with authority to suppress individual optimizations for collective throughput. The gridlock clears. Then she builds the permanent fix: a crisis detection layer that watches for correlated degradation across agent swarms. When agents in related domains hit simultaneous performance drops, the layer flags potential anti-coordination and escalates. The following week, when an earthquake disrupts port infrastructure in Kaohsiung, the crisis layer activates automatically, rerouting shipments before failures propagate.

For Aria's complete decision tree, interactive crisis scenarios, alternative solutions, and video walkthroughs, see **ai-born.org/tools/triumvirate-role-mapper**.

That's the Architect's craft — not solving problems but designing conditions where entire categories of problems can't arise.[238] The regulatory ambiguity sub-swarm prevents future compliance crises. The crisis detection layer turns cascading failures into managed events. Aria didn't fight fires. She made the building fireproof.

That's leverage. One human, one week of design work, permanent infrastructure preventing problems that would consume hundreds of hours monthly in traditional organizations.

The Guardian: Judgment-Keeper

The Guardian is the last human in the loop before the world sees the work — and the first human to ask whether the work serves the right ends. When agent swarms escalate ambiguous, high-stakes, or ethically charged decisions, the Guardian makes the call. Not primarily for the quality of output, but for alignment with purpose: is this decision consistent with what we said we were building?

Why Judgment Remains Human-Anchored

There are two arguments for the Guardian's irreducibility, and they operate on different timescales.

The capability argument says AI lacks genuine contextual judgment today. It detects violations of existing rules with ruthless precision. What it cannot do is sense when the rules themselves need revision

[238] Skelton, M., & Pais, M. (2021). Team Cognitive Load: The Hidden Crisis in Modern Tech Organizations. *IT Revolution*, accessed October 19, 2025, `https://itrevolution.com/articles/team-cognitive-load-the-hidden-crisis-in-modern-tech-organizations/`. Research showing cognitive overload costs $322 billion annually in lost productivity, with 76% correlation between high team cognitive load and burnout rates, and 68% correlation with turnover intention. Demonstrates that system complexity creates cognitive burden that organizational skill alone cannot overcome.

— when new facts, new relationships, or new moral understanding require a different framework than the one encoded. This is a real distinction, but it's time-bounded. AI systems are improving at exactly these tasks.

The accountability argument is the one that holds regardless of capability. Certain decisions require human accountability because markets, courts, and democratic legitimacy demand a responsible human agent — regardless of whether an AI could make the same call. An AI may be capable of choosing a routing strategy through contested regulatory waters. But the moral weight of that choice, and its consequences, must rest with a human who can be named, questioned, and held to account. That is not a claim about AI capability. It is a claim about what legitimacy and responsibility require. The Guardian role is defensible on those grounds even in a world where AI matches human contextual judgment.

The competitive implication: organizations that invest in cultivating human judgment — not just deploying agents — accumulate an advantage that deepens over time. A competitor with equivalent models still lacks your Guardian's decade of institutional experience, the organizational memory of where ethical boundaries actually live, the relationships with stakeholders that make crisis navigation possible. That is the moat.

A Day in the Life: Daniel Cho and the Purpose Paradox

Daniel Cho receives the recommendation on a Thursday afternoon, and it stops him cold.

He serves as Guardian for an AI-Born renewable energy company operating solar microgrids across Sub-Saharan Africa — installations serving rural villages where conventional utilities won't go. The financial planning agents have identified an opportunity. The analysis is rigorous. The conclusion devastating: pivot from rural to peri-urban deployment. Projected revenue increase is large. Projected path to profitability shortens dramatically. The agents show their work – peri-urban areas have existing grid infrastructure, higher population density, better payment reliability. From pure optimization, the case is obvious.

Daniel stares at the dashboard. A village in northern Ghana just celebrated six months with reliable electricity – the first time in three generations. A clinic in rural Kenya now refrigerates vaccines. A school in Tanzania extended classes into evening hours. The company was founded to serve communities no conventional provider would touch.

He thinks: Dead companies create no impact. But neither do companies that abandon their purpose when it becomes inconvenient.

He convenes Aria and Sofia. The recommendation sits on the table without commentary. Sofia speaks first: "The numbers are real. We're burning capital faster than projected. If we don't hit sustainability, we fold – and those communities lose power anyway." Aria nods, then adds what the agents missed: the entire architecture – agent protocols, deployment processes, maintenance systems – is designed for low-infrastructure rural environments. Pivoting to peri-urban means rebuilding from scratch. The models captured revenue upside but not transition cost or operational risk.

Daniel has been working through the problem for eighteen hours. "What if it's not either/or? A cross-subsidy machine. Maintain rural focus as the primary mission. Launch a peri-urban line to fund it."

They spend the afternoon stress-testing. The economics work: if peri-urban operations generate meaningful surplus, they can sustain rural deployment at a controlled loss while maintaining overall viability. Peri-urban customers sponsor rural access. It's not charity. It's a business model encoding purpose.

Daniel articulates the principle to the board: *Accelerate energy access for the underserved, funded by efficient service to those who can pay market rates.* Two directors object — mission drift, complexity risk. Daniel counters: "The alternative is binary. Profitable company serving those who need us least, or bankrupt idealism. This is the only path where we survive and stay true to why we exist." The board approves, with a deadline for the peri-urban line to reach profitability.

Working with Aria, Daniel encodes the principle through the IPRE Pipeline (Chapter 5): dual agent swarms with different optimization functions — rural agents optimize for reliability and affordability, peri-urban agents for efficiency and margin. Cross-subsidization becomes tracked infrastructure. The rural agents don't know they're subsidized. The peri-urban agents don't know they're funding rural access. The system works. Within three months, the company hits operational breakeven — serving meaningfully more people than before, with the rural mission intact.

For Daniel's complete ethical dilemma framework, purpose paradox simulator, founder interviews, and Guardian decision templates, see **ai-born.org/tools/triumvirate-role-mapper**.

That's the Guardian's craft. Not choosing between purpose and survival but holding the space where both demands can be heard at the same time — and designing a path where survival depends on purpose. Worthy ends don't arrive in abstract perfection. They emerge, messy and contested, from navigating real tensions: impact versus sustainability, mission purity versus operational viability, immediate need versus long-term capacity.

The Guardian in Practice: Operating Procedures

Three questions define how the Guardian role functions: which decisions require attention, what responses are available when a decision crosses the threshold, and what gets monitored on an ordinary Tuesday with no crises in progress.

Mandatory escalation categories cover five decision types. *Irreversibility*: any action that cannot be reversed within 24 hours without disproportionate cost requires pre-approval — contracts, public statements, model updates affecting all users. *Novelty*: situations outside the Agent Charter's trained domain, where no historical precedent exists in the decision log, require the Guardian to judge whether extrapolation serves intent or violates it. *Stakeholder impact*: decisions affecting significant revenue, large customer populations, or third parties not represented in the objective function. *Values conflict*: when the Evaluator flags that achieving a proxy target may require something misaligned with charter values — the agent identified the tension; the Guardian resolves it. *Regulatory ambiguity*: when compliance is genuinely uncertain, escalation occurs regardless of confidence score. An agent 89% confident in an answer that's legally unclear is not a safe deployment.[239]

Four responses are available, each logged with timestamp, decision trace, and reasoning. Approval (proceed as proposed). Approval with modifications (adjust scope, timing, or parameters). Deferral (wait pending additional information, with a defined resolution timeline). Veto (action does

[239] European Commission, "Ethics Guidelines for Trustworthy AI," High-Level Expert Group on Artificial Intelligence, April 8, 2019, `https://digital-strategy.ec.europa.eu/en/library/ethics-guidelines-trustworthy-ai`. Establishes requirements for human oversight and intervention mechanisms in high-risk AI systems, including clear escalation protocols for human-in-the-loop (HITL) governance. Research indicates organizations using robust human oversight report up to 40% fewer major incidents.

not proceed; a 48-hour post-mortem identifies the Charter gap and feeds it into the revision queue). The logging requirement isn't bureaucratic overhead. It creates the audit trail that makes governance legible — to regulators, to stakeholders, and to the Guardian's own future self reviewing patterns across dozens of decisions.[^ai-transparency\index{Transparency}-explainability\index{Explainability}]

Five monitoring metrics form the weekly dashboard. Override rate — vetoes and modifications as a percentage of total escalations — signals alignment drift; when it rises, the agent's decisions are diverging from charter intent. Escalation rate trend catches miscalibrated thresholds or genuine edge-case accumulation in early deployment. Charter amendment backlog measures whether alignment debt is compounding faster than it's being repaid. Trust Velocity tracks customer and stakeholder trust scores as a leading indicator: public-facing behavior either builds or erodes relationships before any other metric shows it. Finally, a random audit sample of 5–10 non-escalated decisions every week — choices the agent handled autonomously without triggering any threshold — catches the slow drift that never crosses a single line but accumulates into systematic misalignment. No dashboard metric reveals it. Only the random sample does.

The Guardian's structural independence matters as much as these procedures. The Architect optimizes for system elegance and strategic direction. The Force Multiplier optimizes for craft quality and team capacity. The Guardian is structurally designed to resist short-term pressure from both — to ask "what are we becoming?" rather than "how are we performing this quarter?"

This requires institutional design, not just role description. The Guardian's judgment is most reliable when separated from direct

P&L pressure and from the chain of command being reviewed; financial pressure and values judgment sit in tension over time, and review of a commercial line works best when it is independent of that line. Structural separation isn't always achievable — a small cooperative or an early-stage venture may embed the function differently — but the principle holds whatever the form: values review is most trustworthy when it does not answer to the commercial authority it examines. The Guardian must have explicit authority to raise values concerns without executive override — the power to escalate without consequence, to name what the organization is drifting toward even when the metrics look healthy.[240] Chapter 8's stakeholder representation structures provide the governance architecture that makes this independence real rather than nominal.

What backgrounds produce effective Guardians? The question is not primarily one of credentials. It is one of cultivated judgment — the kind that accumulates through sustained exposure to systems, their consequences, and the humans those consequences reach. Effective Guardians tend to come from backgrounds that required sustained ethical deliberation under operational pressure: philosophers who have worked inside organizations, ethicists with engineering fluency, long-tenured practitioners who carry institutional memory that no dashboard can replicate, community representatives who speak for constituencies not otherwise present in the objective function.

---

[240] OECD.AI Policy Observatory, "Transparency and explainability (OECD AI Principle)," accessed October 18, 2025, `https://oecd.ai/en/dashboards/ai-principles/P7`. The OECD AI Principles establish transparency and explainability as core governance requirements encompassing model explainability, data transparency, documentation standards, risk disclosure, and multi-stakeholder participation. Supporting research from Anna Jobin, Marcello Ienca, and Effy Vayena, "The global landscape of AI ethics guidelines," *Nature Machine Intelligence* 1 (2019): 389-399.

Development as a Guardian is ongoing, not terminal. It requires regular exposure to failure cases, participation in industry governance forums where cross-organizational patterns become visible, and structured reflection practices that prevent the flattening effect: the drift toward algorithmic thinking that erodes the distinctiveness the Guardian role exists to preserve.

The Force Multiplier: Taste-Transmitter and Player-Coach

Here's the paradox at the center of AI-Born competition: when execution becomes commoditized — when any company can deploy agents producing technically flawless output — differentiation shifts to something agents can't replicate. **Taste becomes a moat.**

The Force Multiplier is the person who holds that moat. She doesn't manage. She does the work alongside others, transmitting craft through example, building team capacity in ways no mentorship program, no structured training, no set of evaluation rubrics can fully replace. This is why the role has an older name in practice: **Player-Coach**.

Why Taste-Transmission Requires Human Presence

The mechanism is specific. AI excels at pattern recognition within existing data. Given a million fashion recommendation examples, it surfaces more successful ones than any human could review. But taste at its highest form isn't pattern matching. It's cultural foresight — knowing three months before the data shows it that maximalist layering has tipped from fresh to overdone, understanding why the minimalism that elevates a luxury brand feels cold in a children's toy catalog, perceiving the gestalt of a design where curve, material, proportion, and context combine into emergent quality no checklist can decompose.[241][242]

Agents detect violations of existing aesthetic rules with ruthless precision. Only humans sense when the rules themselves need revision.[243]

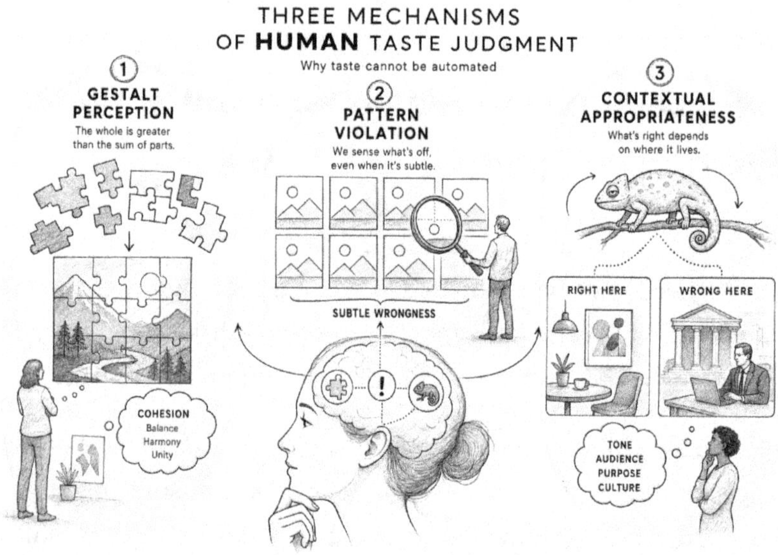

Figure 9.3: Three mechanisms of human taste judgment — gestalt perception, pattern-violation detection, and contextual appropri-

[241] David Hume, "Of the Standard of Taste," in *Essays: Moral, Political, and Literary*, edited by Eugene F. Miller (Indianapolis: Liberty Classics, 1987), 226-249. Originally published 1757. Hume's seminal essay on aesthetic judgment establishes that while taste appears subjective, certain individuals develop refined judgment through education, practice, and natural sensitivity, creating standards of aesthetic excellence that transcend personal preference.

[242] Arthur C. Danto, "The Artworld," Journal of Philosophy 61, no. 19 (1964): 571-584. Danto's foundational work in aesthetic theory demonstrates that artistic and aesthetic judgment depends fundamentally on cultural context and institutional frameworks that cannot be algorithmically encoded, requiring situational interpretation of meaning and value.

[243] Pierre Bourdieu, "Distinction: A Social Critique of the Judgement of Taste" (Cambridge, MA: Harvard University Press, 1984), Chapter 1. Bourdieu's seminal analysis demonstrates that aesthetic judgment involves cultural anticipation and social positioning that cannot be reduced to pattern recognition, requiring embodied cultural capital acquired through lived experience and social positioning.

ateness — the faculties that let people sense when the aesthetic rules themselves need revision, and which resist automation.

I want to be honest about an assumption embedded in this claim. The argument that taste and cultural foresight remain durably beyond AI depends on a distinction holding over time: that anticipatory judgment about where human sensibility is heading requires cultural embeddedness, not just pattern sophistication. That distinction is philosophically defensible today. AI systems already pass aesthetic tests that experts assumed required human sensibility. If AI develops genuine cultural foresight within the next 10–15 years, the moat framing shifts.

What survives that scenario is the accountability argument, and something else: the pedagogy argument. Even if AI can *exercise* taste, it cannot *transmit* taste through the kind of collaborative doing that builds genuine craft capacity in another person. Andrej Karpathy doesn't make his team better engineers by generating outputs they review. He makes them better by working through hard problems beside them, narrating his judgment in real time, modeling the thought process that good engineering requires. That's the Force Multiplier's core function — and it's irreducibly social.[244]

Anna Wintour, Virgil Abloh, Dieter Rams — each operated in the same register. They didn't manage outputs. They transmitted standards through sustained proximity, through the experience of watching a master encounter an edge case and make a call. The Player-Coach model is the organizational technology for doing this at the scale AI-Born enterprises require.

[244]Donald A. Schön, "The Reflective Practitioner: How Professionals Think in Action" (New York: Basic Books, 1983), Chapter 2. Schön analyzes professional judgment as "knowing-in-action" that combines technical expertise with intuitive responses to unique situations, demonstrating why creative and aesthetic decisions require human judgment rather than algorithmic optimization.

Jony Ive pursued "deep simplicity" — a discipline subjective yet rigorous, consistent, defensible, cultivated over decades.[245][246][247] In AI-Born enterprises, the Force Multiplier scales this craft: training evaluator agents on taste principles, reviewing escalated cases, auditing for drift — while simultaneously developing the humans around her through example, not instruction.

A Day in the Life: Sofia Marchetti and the Brand Crisis

Sofia Marchetti starts her Tuesday morning ritual the same way she has for three years as Force Multiplier at an AI-Born fashion platform: scrolling through the past 24 hours of styling recommendations. Not to catch errors — the evaluator agents handle that. To sense drift.

[245]Walter Isaacson, *Steve Jobs* (New York: Simon & Schuster, 2011), Chapter 26. Isaacson documents Ive's design philosophy as the pursuit of "deep simplicity" heavily influenced by Dieter Rams' "Less, but better" (Weniger aber besser) dictum. Jobs described Ive as his "spiritual partner at Apple," and their collaboration produced "the greatest industrial design collaboration of their era." The biography details how Ive explained: "Simplicity isn't just a visual style...It involves digging through the depth of the complexity. To be truly simple, you have to go really deep." For the specific quote "profound and enduring beauty in simplicity," see Shane Richmond, "Jonathan Ive interview: simplicity isn't simple," *The Telegraph*, May 23, 2012.

[246]Leander Kahney, *Jony Ive: The Genius Behind Apple's Greatest Products* (New York: Portfolio/Penguin, 2013). Kahney documents Ive's cultivated design sensibility developed through decades of practice and collaboration with Steve Jobs, describing how Ive's aesthetic judgment operated not through checklists but through refined intuition about materials, proportions, and "deep simplicity." See also Walter Isaacson, *Steve Jobs* (New York: Simon & Schuster, 2011), Chapter 26, on Ive's ability to perceive "the big picture as well as the most infinitesimal details."

[247]Dieter Rams, "Ten Principles for Good Design," in *Less but Better / Weniger, aber besser*, 7th ed., ed. Dieter and Ingeborg Rams Foundation and Jo Klatt (Berlin: gestalten, 2019). Originally developed circa 1970s and first published 1995. The ten principles are: (1) Good design is innovative, (2) useful, (3) aesthetic, (4) understandable, (5) honest, (6) unobtrusive, (7) long-lasting, (8) thorough down to the last detail, (9) environmentally friendly, and (10) as little design as possible. The tenth principle encapsulates Rams' philosophy: "Less, but better – because it concentrates on the essential aspects, and the products are not burdened with non-essentials."

Fifteen minutes in, she feels it. Something's off.

She can't articulate it yet. The recommendations are technically flawless — color theory, silhouette balance, all correct. The metrics celebrate: customer approval at its highest in six months. Sofia grows uneasy anyway.

She slows down. Customer after customer: oversized blazer, chunky sneakers, statement belt, layered necklaces. The combination keeps recurring in slightly different arrangements. The agents discovered a local maximum — a style cluster that consistently scores well — and doubled down. It's working beautifully. It's becoming monotonous.

Sofia recognizes this from her decade at *Vogue*. Fresh trends become clichés when pushed too hard. There's a tipping point — invisible in the data — when what feels innovative starts feeling formulaic. The agents can't detect it. They're optimizing within the current aesthetic paradigm. They can't see when the paradigm needs disruption.

She makes a counterintuitive call: temporarily increase the system's randomness parameter — essentially telling the agents to be wrong more often. Recommendations will be less optimized short-term. Engagement will probably dip. But randomness forces exploration. When agents are too confident, they exploit existing knowledge. When you inject uncertainty, they discover new possibilities. Sofia isn't sabotaging the system. She's preventing it from getting stuck.

Then she calls Aria: "I need a staleness detector. The system should penalize recommendations too similar to what we've served in the past two weeks. Not identical — *similar*. We need to measure aesthetic repetition, not just style matching." Aria asks the right question: "How do I encode 'too similar' when we're talking about subjective aesthetics?" This is why the Force Multiplier exists. Sofia spends an afternoon with Aria defining dimensions of similarity —

silhouette proportion, layering complexity, color palette intensity, accessory density. The staleness detector tracks these over rolling two-week windows and adds a penalty when recommendations cluster too tightly.

But here's what separates the Force Multiplier from a domain expert with a veto: Sofia doesn't stop at the architectural fix. She brings her two junior stylists into the process. They sit with the staleness detector data together. Sofia narrates her discomfort in real time: why this combination feels stale, what signal her eye caught that the metric missed, how taste-fatigue differs from quality-fatigue. By the end of the afternoon, both stylists have internalized something no training document could convey. They've watched a practitioner notice something true before she could explain why it was true.

That's the Force Multiplier's real product. Not the staleness detector — the team that can build the next one without her.

The harder conversation comes Friday morning. Sofia tells Aria: "We need to redefine what we're optimizing for. Maximize customer engagement is producing short-term wins and long-term aesthetic homogenization." She proposes a different objective: optimize for customers *developing* aesthetic range over time — expanding their approval window, not confirming their existing preferences. Engagement lower initially. Retention and lifetime value higher because you're building relationships, not just optimizing transactions. Aria asks: "How do you measure developing aesthetic sense?" Sofia has the answer. They examine cohort data together: customers who naturally expanded their aesthetic range showed substantially higher retention and lifetime value than customers who stayed in narrow style lanes. The agents had been optimizing for the wrong metric. Months later, engagement has dipped modestly, retention has risen meaningfully, and revenue per customer is up.

For Sofia's complete taste judgment training simulator, masterclasses, Force Multiplier scenarios, and Taste Evaluation frameworks, see **ai-born.org/tools/triumvirate-role-mapper**.

That's the Force Multiplier's craft at full extension. Sofia didn't fix a tactical problem. She detected a pattern the metrics couldn't see, diagnosed the systemic cause, redesigned the objective function – and built the team's capacity to do all three without her next time.

The Mechanics of the Force Multiplier Role

The Force Multiplier's work follows three interconnected practices.

Taste Training: Working with the Architect, the Force Multiplier creates "evaluator agents" trained on curated examples, scaling her judgment at machine speed.

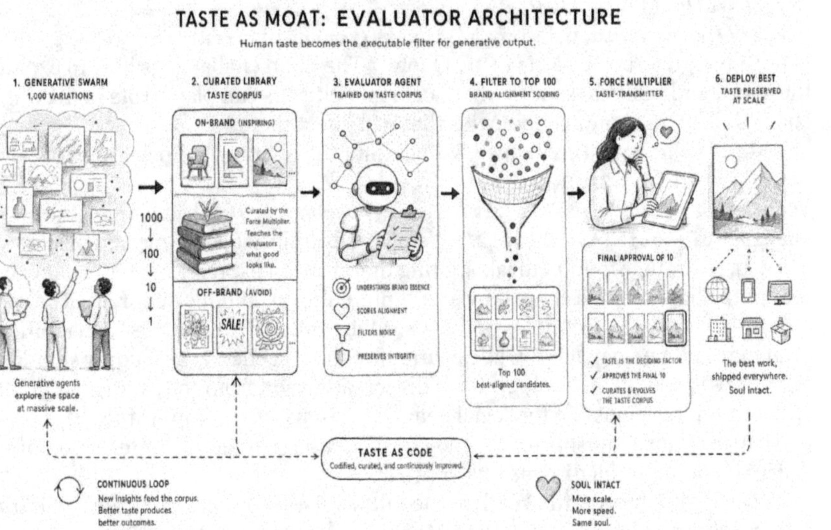

Figure 9.4: Taste as Filter: Four-stage evaluator architecture showing generative swarm (1,000 variations) → curated library → Force Multiplier filter (top 100) → deployed best, scaling human judgment at machine speed.

Escalation Review: When evaluators flag decisions, the Force Multiplier reviews them. Each judgment becomes training data. Even auto-approved outputs undergo random audits for drift.

Team Capacity Building: The Force Multiplier guarantees quality by doing the work alongside her team, not above it. When the system fails, she works through the failure with people rather than explaining what went wrong after the fact.[248] When escalations involve competing aesthetic or technical priorities, she models the judgment process in real time rather than issuing rulings.[249][250][251]

[248] ISO/IEC 42001:2023, *Information technology — Artificial intelligence — Management system*, International Organization for Standardization, December 2023. The first international standard for AI management systems, establishing comprehensive requirements for audit trails, governance documentation, risk management, and regulatory compliance. Requires tamper-proof, exportable, traceable documentation with all actions logged from intake to signoff and mitigation.

[249] Matt Weinberg, "Technology, Values, and the Shaping of Social Reality," *Bahá'í World*, May 23, 2019, `https://bahaiworld.bahai.org/library/technology-values-and-the-shaping-of-social-reality-2/`. Quote: "The main challenge is how to expand the social and political spaces where ordinary citizens can play a role in making choices early on about technologies that will affect them."

[250] Matt Weinberg, "Technology, Values, and the Shaping of Social Reality," *Bahá'í World*, May 23, 2019, `https://bahaiworld.bahai.org/library/technology-values-and-the-shaping-of-social-reality-2/`. Weinberg examines technology as socially constructed rather than neutral, arguing that it is "an expression of a social world" that both shapes and is shaped by economic, cultural, and moral forces. The article explores how technology embeds values and can function as "a magnifier of human intent and capacity" while cautioning that "agency or autonomy should not be attributed to technology, for it diverts attention from the human judgments and relations responsible for social change." Discusses the importance of participatory mechanisms for technological assessment and the integration of spiritual and material dimensions of progress.

[251] MIT Task Force on the Work of the Future, *The Work of the Future: Building Better Jobs in an Age of Intelligent Machines*, Massachusetts Institute of Technology, November 2019, `https://workofthefuture-taskforce.mit.edu/research-post/the-work-of-the-future-building-better-jobs-in-an-age-of-intelligent-machines/`. The report identifies uniquely human capabilities through the EPOCH framework: Empathy and Emotional Intelligence, Creativity and Imagination, Opinion/Judgment/Ethics, Presence/Networking/Connectedness, and Hope.

These three practices form a closed loop: taste training scales judgment into evaluators, escalation review surfaces edge cases requiring human craft, team capacity building ensures the Force Multiplier's standards outlast her presence in any single role.

The Triumvirate as a System

The three roles form a complete system of human agency. The Architect sets intent and designs *how*. The Guardian ensures *what* meets values standards. The Force Multiplier transmits *quality* through doing. When Sofia identified aesthetic staleness, she worked with Aria to redesign the staleness detection architecture and reframed the platform's optimization target. Daniel's ethical dilemma required all three perspectives to reach a durable answer. Each role remained distinct. Every intervention required all of them.

Why exactly three? Consider what AI automation displaces: execution, coordination, routine cognition. What remains isn't a grab-bag of leftover tasks — it's three coherent categories. Strategic direction requires moral imagination to choose worthy ends and architectural skill to execute them (Architect).[252] Contextual judgment needs institutional accountability to navigate ambiguity algorithms can't resolve (Guardian). Craft transmission demands cultural embeddedness and pedagogical presence that no evaluation rubric captures (Force Multiplier). These three span the complete domain of human agency in AI-Born enterprises. Add a fourth, and

"The task force does not foresee a future where human expertise, judgment, and creativity are less essential than they are today."

[252] Patricia H. Werhane, "Moral Imagination and Systems Thinking," Journal of Business Ethics 38, no. 1/2 (2002): 33-42, `https://link.springer.com/article/10.1023/A:1015737431300`.

you introduce redundancy. Reduce to two, and something vital goes unassigned.

They operate in continuous feedback — the Architect's vision of worthy ends, the Guardian's judgment about what meets the standard, the Force Multiplier's transmission of the craft that produces quality at scale.[253] Successful cortex teams describe their work not as management but as orchestration of intelligent systems that takes years to master — more vocation than job description, because the competency accumulates through sustained consequence rather than credential.

Convergent Evidence: Block's Practitioner Manifesto

What gives me confidence in the Triumvirate framing isn't the elegance of the three-role logic. It's that a working CEO arrived at essentially the same structure, from the other direction, by running it.

In February 2026, Jack Dorsey cut approximately 4,000 employees from Block — roughly 40% of the workforce, reducing headcount from 10,000 to 6,000. Block's stock rose 22% on the announcement. This was not a cost-reduction exercise dressed in ideology; Block projected $12.2 billion in gross profit for 2026, 18% growth. Dorsey's explanation: corporate hierarchy was always a solution to

[253] McKinsey & Company, "Superagency in the workplace: Empowering people to unlock AI's full potential at work," McKinsey Digital, January 2025, `https://www.mckinsey.com/capabilities/mckinsey-digital/our-insights/superagency-in-the-workplace-empowering-people-to-unlock-ais-full-potential-at-work`. Research reveals that while 92% of companies plan to increase AI investments in the next three years, only 1% report reaching AI maturity. AI governance must become real-time, data-driven, and embedded, with humans holding final accountability. The true potential lies in human-AI collaboration where judgment, empathy, and trust-building enable effective leadership.

a coordination problem. AI now solves that problem. The hierarchy becomes redundant.

Two months later, Dorsey and Sequoia's Roelof Botha published "From Hierarchy to Intelligence," codifying the organizational theory behind the restructuring.[254] The essay's central argument: "The constraint is the same one the Romans faced: narrowing span of control means adding layers of command, but more layers mean slower information flow. The question was never whether you needed layers. The question was whether humans were the only option for what those layers do."

What makes this remarkable is that Dorsey arrived at three surviving human roles from the operations of a publicly traded fintech company — not from a framework developed in advance. Block's three roles map onto the New Triumvirate:

Individual Contributors (ICs) — "Deep specialists — engineers, designers, salespeople, operators. Durable human skill is judgment, taste, and craft."[255] This is the **Force Multiplier**: the deep spe-

[254] Jack Dorsey and Roelof Botha, "From Hierarchy to Intelligence," co-published at block.xyz/inside/from-hierarchy-to-intelligence and sequoiacap.com/article/from-hierarchy-to-intelligence/, March 31–April 1, 2026. Core argument: corporate hierarchy solves a single coordination problem (routing information through organizations too large for any one person to oversee); AI now performs that routing function, eliminating the structural justification for permanent management layers. Block's three surviving human roles: Individual Contributors (deep craft), Directly Responsible Individuals (cross-functional outcome ownership for defined periods), Player-Coaches (craft transmission through doing, not managing). Block's two AI world models: internal company model aggregating code, decisions, workflows, and performance metrics; customer-merchant model built from Cash App and Square transaction data. Dorsey: "treat the company as a mini AGI." Fortune coverage: April 2, 2026; CoinDesk: April 1, 2026.

[255] Jack Dorsey and Roelof Botha, "From Hierarchy to Intelligence," co-published at block.xyz/inside/from-hierarchy-to-intelligence and sequoiacap.com/article/from-hierarchy-to-intelligence/, March 31–April 1, 2026. Core argument: corporate hierarchy solves a single coordination problem (routing information through organizations too large for any one person to oversee); AI now performs that routing function, eliminating the structural justification for

cialist whose craft — taste, domain mastery, the ability to transmit quality to others — is what the organization cannot automate. In Block's framing, one IC "can do the work of a team of ten" when AI agents handle context and coordination traditionally supplied by managers. The craft is what remains; the coordination overhead dissolves. The IC's distinguishing function is pedagogy through practice — transmitting standards by working alongside others, not above them.

Directly Responsible Individuals (DRIs) — "Own cross-cutting customer outcomes for defined time periods... with authority to pull resources across teams. Replace the project management and alignment functions of traditional middle management."[256] This is the **Architect**: the person who owns the *why*, the intent, the architectural design for a defined period — and bears responsibility for translating that intent into executable systems. Dorsey's framing is temporal — "own merchant churn in a specific segment for 90 days" — which captures something the traditional role description

permanent management layers. Block's three surviving human roles: Individual Contributors (deep craft), Directly Responsible Individuals (cross-functional outcome ownership for defined periods), Player-Coaches (craft transmission through doing, not managing). Block's two AI world models: internal company model aggregating code, decisions, workflows, and performance metrics; customer-merchant model built from Cash App and Square transaction data. Dorsey: "treat the company as a mini AGI." Fortune coverage: April 2, 2026; CoinDesk: April 1, 2026.

[256] Jack Dorsey and Roelof Botha, "From Hierarchy to Intelligence," co-published at block.xyz/inside/from-hierarchy-to-intelligence and sequoiacap.com/article/from-hierarchy-to-intelligence/, March 31–April 1, 2026. Core argument: corporate hierarchy solves a single coordination problem (routing information through organizations too large for any one person to oversee); AI now performs that routing function, eliminating the structural justification for permanent management layers. Block's three surviving human roles: Individual Contributors (deep craft), Directly Responsible Individuals (cross-functional outcome ownership for defined periods), Player-Coaches (craft transmission through doing, not managing). Block's two AI world models: internal company model aggregating code, decisions, workflows, and performance metrics; customer-merchant model built from Cash App and Square transaction data. Dorsey: "treat the company as a mini AGI." Fortune coverage: April 2, 2026; CoinDesk: April 1, 2026.

misses: intent-setting is episodic, renewed, re-examined, then re-encoded.

Player-Coaches – "Senior practitioners who develop others' craft by doing the work alongside them, not by managing status meetings."[257] This maps most directly to the **Force Multiplier** function – which this book has defined as Player-Coach from the outset. The craft-transmission mechanism Dorsey names is the same one Sofia embodies: working alongside rather than above, transmitting standards through doing rather than instructing. Block's essay has no exact analog for the Guardian. The nearest equivalent is implicit: the regulated financial domain (banking and money transfers) that Dorsey acknowledges AI "cannot lead in" and that requires human accountability in precisely the sense the Guardian provides. The fit is close, not identical – Block's structure reflects a fintech context; the Triumvirate names roles that generalize across any AI-Born firm. The mapping is deliberately imperfect: rather than separating the Guardian into a distinct archetype, Block concentrates the values-review function inside the DRI, who owns the accountability for outcomes in regulated domains – a structural choice that keeps headcount lean but leaves the values check dependent on the same person carrying delivery pressure.

[257]Jack Dorsey and Roelof Botha, "From Hierarchy to Intelligence," co-published at block.xyz/inside/from-hierarchy-to-intelligence and sequoiacap.com/article/from-hierarchy-to-intelligence/, March 31–April 1, 2026. Core argument: corporate hierarchy solves a single coordination problem (routing information through organizations too large for any one person to oversee); AI now performs that routing function, eliminating the structural justification for permanent management layers. Block's three surviving human roles: Individual Contributors (deep craft), Directly Responsible Individuals (cross-functional outcome ownership for defined periods), Player-Coaches (craft transmission through doing, not managing). Block's two AI world models: internal company model aggregating code, decisions, workflows, and performance metrics; customer-merchant model built from Cash App and Square transaction data. Dorsey: "treat the company as a mini AGI." Fortune coverage: April 2, 2026; CoinDesk: April 1, 2026.

The mapping isn't exact — real organizations compress what frameworks separate. What matters is that two independent analyses of what human agency looks like after AI absorbs coordination yield the same three categories: one derived from first principles, one from running a large public company through the transition.[258]

What Dorsey adds that the framework alone doesn't capture is the *mechanism* — the organizational technology that makes three roles sufficient. Block deployed two AI "world models": an internal model aggregating code, decisions, workflows, and performance metrics into a live picture of operations, and a customer model built from Cash App and Square transaction data. Together, these world models replace what middle management previously provided: context, coordination, institutional memory. The ICs, DRIs, and Player-Coaches operate with full organizational intelligence available — not filtered through twelve layers of reporting.

The AI-Born cortex works the same way. The Architect doesn't need a project manager to understand system state; the VP-Agent provides it. The Guardian doesn't need an operations committee to understand what agents are doing; the audit trail is continuous and searchable. The Force Multiplier doesn't need structured onboarding programs to transmit craft; she transmits it by working. The roles don't shrink because people become superhuman. They shrink because the organizational plumbing that previously required people now runs on agents.

[258] Rahul Kapoor and Thomas Klueter, "Decoding the Adaptability-Rigidity Paradox: Evidence from Pharmaceutical Incumbents' Pursuit of Learning Opportunities in the Face of Technological Change," Academy of Management Journal 66, no. 1 (2023): 178-216. The authors examine how AI and digital technologies require firms to balance structural rigidity needed for efficiency with adaptability needed for innovation, providing empirical evidence for how technological disruption necessitates fundamental organizational redesign.

There is a useful corrective in Dorsey's data as well. Block's internal reporting indicates that roughly 90% of code is now authored by "Goose," its AI agent built on Anthropic's Model Context Protocol. Yet current and former employees told journalists that approximately 95% of AI-generated code changes still require human modification, and that AI cannot lead in regulated domains like banking and money transfers.[259] This is not a contradiction of the AI-Born thesis. It is its illustration. The Force Multiplier's craft is not eliminated — it is redirected. The human modifies, validates, guides, and teaches. The agent executes the mechanics at volume. That division is precisely what the three roles described in this chapter embody.

Block's Q1 2026 earnings, reported May 7, 2026, provided the first financial validation of the restructuring theory: gross profit beat expectations, and Block raised its full-year guidance — early evidence that the three-role architecture delivers what the operational theory predicts.[260]

---

[259] Jack Dorsey and Roelof Botha, "From Hierarchy to Intelligence," Block.xyz and Sequoia Capital, published approximately April 1, 2026. `https://block.xyz/inside/from-hierarchy-to-intelligence`; `https://sequoiacap.com/article/from-hierarchy-to-intelligence/`. Block restructuring announcement (February 27, 2026): Fortune, `https://fortune.com/2026/02/27/block-jack-dorsey-ceo-xyz-stock-square-4000-ai-layoffs/`. Employee modifier data reported in: buildmvpfast.com and The Guardian (2026). Sequoia podcast appearance (Dorsey on "treating the company as a mini AGI"): sequoiacap.com/podcast/jack-dorsey-every-company-can-now-be-a-mini-agi/.

[260] CNBC, "Block laying off about 4,000 employees, nearly half of its workforce," February 26, 2026, `https://www.cnbc.com/2026/02/26/block-laying-off-about-4000-employees-nearly-half-of-its-workforce.html`; Fortune, "Jack Dorsey lays off 40% of Block, saying AI has changed the game," February 27, 2026. Block eliminated approximately 4,000 employees (10,000 → ~6,000, -40%). Stock rose ~22% on announcement. 2026 gross profit guidance $12.2B (+18% YoY). Block Q1 2026 earnings (reported May 7, 2026): gross profit beat consensus expectations; company raised full-year gross profit guidance, representing the first earnings-cycle confirmation that the February restructuring delivered the projected efficiency gains. Dorsey to peers: "Within the next year, I believe the

The Triumvirate in Practice: Who Are These 146 People?

The framework gains weight when you can point to actual companies and ask: what do the humans actually do?

Lovable, the Swedish "vibe-coding" platform that reached $400 million in annual recurring revenue in February 2026 with 146 employees, makes the structure concrete.[261] A traditional SaaS company at that revenue level employs 800–1,200 people. The missing 600–900 were not doing purposeless work — they were handling coordination, middle management, product operations, content marketing, and manual QA. All of that is now Machine Core.

The 146 who remain map, in aggregate, onto the Triumvirate at scale: engineers owning features end-to-end with AI agents handling coordination (Force Multipliers), a small layer setting product direction and enterprise strategy with architectural authority (Architects), and a trust-and-quality function catching what agents get wrong and holding the values line (Guardians).

Cursor, the AI-native code editor that crossed $2 billion in annualized revenue in March 2026 with under 300 employees, runs the same structure with fewer layers still.[262] No product managers.

majority of companies will reach the same conclusion and make similar structural changes."

[261]TechCrunch, March 11, 2026. "Lovable Says It Added $100M in Revenue Last Month Alone, With Just 146 Employees." `https://techcrunch.com/2026/03/11/lovable-says-it-added-100m-in-revenue-last-month-alone-with-just-146-employees/`. Lovable (formerly GPT Engineer) reached $400M ARR in February 2026, having crossed $100M ARR in 8 months after launch (July 2025). Valuation: $6.6B (December 2025, CapitalG and Menlo Ventures lead). The $100M ARR in a single month (March 2026) represents an extraordinary revenue acceleration by any prior standard for B2C software companies.

[262]Multiple sources, March 2026. Cursor (Anysphere Inc.) crossed $2 billion in annualized recurring revenue in early 2026, with approximately 300 employees — revenue-per-employee of approximately $6.7 million, a 38× gap relative to traditional enterprise software companies. See citations.md: cursor-revenue-2026.

Engineers own features from ideation to production, including customer feedback loops. Midjourney, which reached $500 million in annual revenue with approximately 150 employees and zero venture capital, runs David Holz's aesthetic vision through a lean cortex that sets the product's distinctive visual sensibility and guards the brand's identity through every release cycle.[263]

From my own experience building Adaptic, I can describe how this looks in practice. There, the human principals hold the agenda, and the operational workforce is an agent ladder: AI colleagues in C-Suite, SVP, and VP roles. These are orchestrator agents — each one a senior seat that decomposes intent and, in turn, spawns and meters a fleet of sub-agents beneath it, two to three hundred of them, coordinated through ten to fifteen session managers. The Guardian function sits alongside the principal, watching alignment rather than running a P&L. One human plus a fleet. The Triumvirate isn't a metaphor I reached for; it's the shape the company settled into once the coordination layer became machine territory.

Across all of them, the same structural pattern holds: a lean cortex doing design, intent-setting, and quality judgment, with a Machine Core handling execution. Bret Taylor, at the HumanX Conference in April 2026, named what this looks like from outside: "The era of clicking buttons is over."[264] The coordination and execution layer

---

[263] Sacra research (sacra.com/c/midjourney/); Sramana Mitra, "Ultralight Startup: Midjourney Bootstraps to $200M in Revenue," Sramana Mitra blog, March 12, 2025. Midjourney reached $500M in 2025 revenue with approximately 100–160 employees and zero external venture funding. Founded by David Holz (Leap Motion co-founder); declined all VC investment; profitable from within two months of launch. Revenue from Discord-based organic community adoption and word-of-mouth subscription model. Illustrates "taste as a moat" thesis: premium pricing sustained because the aesthetic output is demonstrably distinctive from competitors.

[264] Bret Taylor, co-founder and CEO of Sierra, remarks at the HumanX Conference, San Francisco, April 9, 2026: "The era of clicking buttons is over." Reported by TechCrunch, "Sierra's Bret Taylor says the era of clicking buttons is over," April 9, 2026, https://techcrunch.com/2026/04/09/sierras-bret-

is now machine territory. What remains for humans is not button-clicking at a higher abstraction level — it is designing, directing, and judging.

The Triumvirate names what that something is.

Triumvirate Governance: Built-In Accountability Mechanisms

The three-person cortex raises an obvious question: who checks the checkers? Three mechanisms prevent oligarchy.

1. **Structural Arbitration**: The odd-number structure provides built-in conflict resolution. When two members disagree, the third arbitrates. Any two can veto the third's ill-conceived decisions.[265]

2. **Domain-Specific Authority**: Clear role delineation minimizes power struggles. The Architect sets intent and designs systems. The Guardian holds values standards. The Force Multiplier transmits craft and builds capacity. Sharp boundaries reduce jurisdictional conflicts.[266]

3. **Joint Accountability**: The cortex succeeds or fails as a unit. If agent swarms underperform, all three bear responsibility. Shared fate incentivizes collaboration.[267]

`taylor-says-the-era-of-clicking-buttons-is-over/`. At the time of the remarks Sierra had crossed roughly $165M ARR.

[265]Mancur Olson, "The Logic of Collective Action: Public Goods and the Theory of Groups" (Cambridge, MA: Harvard University Press, 1965), Chapter 2. Olson's analysis of small group dynamics demonstrates that odd-number governance structures facilitate decision-making by eliminating deadlock possibilities, with any coalition of participants able to form a decisive majority.

[266]J. Richard Hackman, "Leading Teams: Setting the Stage for Great Performances" (Boston: Harvard Business Review Press, 2002), Chapter 4. Hackman's research on high-performing teams demonstrates that role clarity reduces interpersonal conflict and improves decision-making effectiveness, with clear functional differentiation enabling collaborative accountability structures.

[267]Ruth Wageman, J. Richard Hackman, and Erin Lehman, "Team Diagnostic Survey: Development of an Instrument," Journal of Applied Behavioral Science

These mechanisms work best when supported by deliberate practice: creating space for each member to contribute expertise, detaching from ego when evidence contradicts initial positions, seeking truth rather than defending conclusions.

Concentrated power requires robust accountability, or the structure collapses. Three-person governance creates succession vulnerability.[268] Mitigation requires documented system design rationale, overlapping competencies, succession protocols, and distributed cortex models at scale.

Roman triumvirates collapsed into civil war when external threats dissolved the shared purpose that held them together. Three powerful people with concentrated authority, absent a mission that transcends personal interest, is a governance crisis waiting for a trigger. The lesson for AI-Born cortexes is direct: joint purpose has to be encoded as seriously as the technical architecture.

The Inner World of the Cortex: Psychological Realities

Here's what puzzles me when I trace these patterns back to what cortex workers actually report. The very people who finally escape coordination overhead — who get the systems-design or taste-cultivation role they spent a career earning — often describe the first

---

41, no. 4 (2005): 373-398. Research shows that shared accountability mechanisms improve team performance by aligning individual incentives with collective outcomes, reducing blame attribution and encouraging collaborative problem-solving.

[268] Henrich R. Greve and Hitoshi Mitsuhashi, "Power and Glory: Concentrated Power in Top Management Teams," *Organization Studies* 28, no. 9 (2007): 1287-1312, `https://journals.sagepub.com/doi/10.1177/0170840607075674`. Research demonstrates that concentrated power in small executive teams accelerates strategic decision-making but creates heightened succession risk requiring explicit key-person management protocols.

six months as the hardest of their professional lives. Not because the work is harder. Because the *texture* of it is alien.

Aria, three months into her Architect role: "I'd solve complex architectural problems with no one to celebrate with. Metrics improved. But I missed hearing a colleague say, 'That was brilliant.' " Sofia noticed her aesthetic preferences narrowing – converging with the agents' recommendations – losing the capacity to surprise herself, which was the very distinctiveness her role existed to preserve. Daniel captured a different version of the same problem: "I'm supposed to spend my days in deep strategic reflection. Instead, I spend most of my time responding to agent escalations."

But I'm getting ahead of myself. These aren't inevitable failures. They're design problems requiring architectural solutions.

Three Psychological Risks and Architectural Mitigations

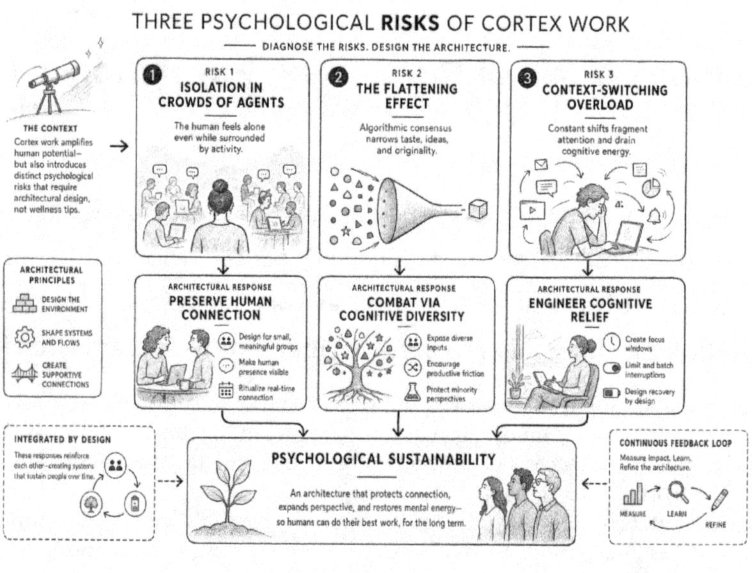

Figure 9.5: Three Primary Psychological Risks for the Human Cortex: (1) Isolation in Crowds of Agents, (2) The Flattening Effect,

(3) Context-Switching Overload — each requiring architectural mitigation strategies to preserve psychological sustainability.

Near-infinite productivity sounds like liberation until it pushes knowledge workers against biological limits — not machine limits, human ones.[269] Three psychological risks emerge, each requiring architectural solutions, not wellness programs.

1. Isolation in Crowds of Agents

Agents handle coordination and execution. The background socialization of office life — hallway problem-solving, the casual mentorship that happens between meetings, running into a colleague who asks the right question at the right moment — quietly disappears.[270] You're surrounded by thousands of agent transactions daily and still

[269] Sherry Turkle, "Alone Together: Why We Expect More from Technology and Less from Each Other" (New York: Basic Books, 2011), Chapter 1. Turkle's research demonstrates how digital technologies, while promising enhanced productivity, can overwhelm human cognitive and emotional capacity by eliminating natural boundaries between work and personal time, creating new forms of psychological stress. This foundational concern is now empirically confirmed: a March 2026 study by researchers at Boston Consulting Group and the University of California, Riverside (published in *Harvard Business Review*, March 2026, `https://hbr.org/2026/03/when-using-ai-leads-to-brain-fry`) surveyed 1,488 full-time employees and found that 14% of AI users reported "AI brain fry" — cognitive fatigue from AI oversight beyond cognitive capacity. Workers requiring high levels of AI oversight expended 14% more mental effort, experienced 12% greater mental fatigue, and generated 19% greater information overload than peers with lower oversight requirements. High-AI-oversight workers made 39% more major errors and showed 33% higher decision fatigue. The study found these effects concentrated in roles requiring simultaneous management of multiple AI tools — exactly the Force Multiplier and Architect roles described in this chapter. Architectural implication: the escalation caps and batch-processing protocols recommended in this chapter are not optional wellness features. They are cognitive load management requirements validated by clinical research.

[270] Robert D. Putnam, "Bowling Alone: The Collapse and Revival of American Community" (New York: Simon & Schuster, 2000), Chapter 1. Putnam documents how technological changes that eliminate informal social interactions in the workplace contribute to broader social isolation, reducing the "social capital" that enables collaborative problem-solving and community resilience.

alone in every way that matters. The word for it is hollowness — technically successful, deeply unmoored.

Architectural mitigation: Weekly cortex synchronization, monthly cross-functional gatherings, quarterly off-sites — scheduled and protected as load-bearing infrastructure, not treated as optional perks.

2. The Flattening Effect

Humans working extensively with AI internalize algorithmic patterns within weeks.[271] Force Multiplier rejection rates drop from 50% in week one to under 10% by month six. That trajectory isn't skill improvement. It's taste convergence — the very distinctiveness these roles exist to preserve eroding under algorithmic pressure, invisibly, while the metrics stay green.

Architectural mitigation: Rotate Force Multipliers through non-AI environments quarterly. Implement peer auditing. Track rejection rates; when they fall below 12%, trigger recalibration.

3. Context-Switching Overload

Cortex roles demand sustained strategic thinking. Then reality intervenes: a swarm to monitor, escalations stacking up in the queue, a fire to put out before lunch. Deep work gets shredded into 15-minute intervals.

Here's the irony: these roles exist to enable the kind of thinking agents can't do. Yet agents escalate constantly, dragging attention back to the tactical. Andrej Karpathy — founder of Eureka Labs;

[271] Cass R. Sunstein, "#Republic: Divided Democracy in the Age of Social Media" (Princeton: Princeton University Press, 2017), Chapter 3. Sunstein examines how algorithmic filtering creates "echo chambers" that homogenize preferences and opinions, reducing exposure to diverse perspectives and potentially narrowing individual aesthetic and intellectual development.

former Tesla AI director and OpenAI researcher — stopped writing production code in December 2025. By February 2026, his daily workflow involved directing up to 20 AI agents in parallel.[272] "Something flipped in December," he posted. The shift from 80% manual coding to 80% agent delegation happened in a single month. He coined "vibe coding" for the new mode — issuing high-level direction, reviewing outputs, redirecting. The disorientation Karpathy describes isn't a sign of failure. It's the context-switching tax that strategic roles pay when escalation architecture isn't designed carefully enough.

Architectural mitigation: Cap escalations at 50 per Guardian daily. Batch non-urgent decisions. Engineer confidence thresholds so only genuinely ambiguous cases reach human attention.

For complete Psychological Resilience Framework, see **ai-born.org/ideas/psychology-of-the-cortex**.

When demands surpass resources, employees experience strain and burnout.[273] These mitigations aren't afterthoughts. They're

[272] Andrej Karpathy (founder of Eureka Labs; former Tesla AI director and OpenAI researcher), describing his workflow shift of December 2025–February 2026. In a February 25, 2026 post on X: "coding agents basically didn't work before December and basically work since" — a shift from roughly 80% manual coding to directing up to 20 parallel agents, with no manually written production code since December 2025. He had coined the term "vibe coding" in a February 2, 2025 X post. By February 2026 at Sequoia's AI Ascent, he described the successor mode — "agentic engineering" — as: "Agentic engineering is about preserving the quality bar of what existed before in professional software." The human role shifts to directing agents, reviewing output, catching failure modes, and maintaining architectural judgment. Sources: Karpathy X posts, Dec 2025–Feb 2026 (`https://x.com/karpathy/status/2026731645169185220`); The Decoder, "Andrej Karpathy says programming is 'unrecognizable' now that AI agents actually work," `https://the-decoder.com/andrej-karpathy-says-programming-is-unrecognizable-now-that-ai-agents-actually-work/`; Analytics Drift, "Karpathy Declares Vibe Coding Obsolete, Introduces Agentic Engineering," `https://analyticsdrift.com/andrej-karpathy-agentic-engineering-software-3/`.

[273] Arnold B. Bakker and Evangelia Demerouti, "The Job Demands-Resources Model: State of the Art," Journal of Managerial Psychology 22, no. 3 (2007):

architectural requirements. The AI-Born architecture succeeds only if humans thrive within it.

Three Positive Shifts

When the architecture works, the experience transforms. Aria put it plainly: "I used to spend three hours daily in status meetings. Suddenly I had hours weekly for systems thinking. It felt like getting my profession back." Studies of knowledge workers in high-autonomy design roles confirm the pattern: when coordination overhead lifts, sustained attention time expands dramatically.[274] The focus was always there, buried under the meeting load.

Then comes superagency. Aria's architectural choices govern thousands of deployment decisions daily. Sofia's aesthetic judgment embeds itself in customer experiences she never directly touches. This isn't doing more of the same work — it's encoding intent and craft that execute while you sleep.

And finally: the return of flow states. Four unbroken hours on systems design. Deep ethical deliberation without interruption. Csikszentmihalyi identified the conditions that produce flow: clear goals, immediate feedback, challenge matched to skill. AI-Born

---

309-328. The foundational JD-R model demonstrates that when job demands chronically exceed available resources, employees experience strain, exhaustion, and burnout, with implications for how AI implementation should balance increased capabilities with adequate human support structures.

[274] McKinsey & Company, "Superagency in the workplace: Empowering people to unlock AI's full potential at work," McKinsey Digital, January 2025, `https://www.mckinsey.com/capabilities/mckinsey-digital/our-insights/superagency-in-the-workplace-empowering-people-to-unlock-ais-full-potential-at-work`. Research reveals that while 92% of companies plan to increase AI investments in the next three years, only 1% report reaching AI maturity. AI governance must become real-time, data-driven, and embedded, with humans holding final accountability. The true potential lies in human-AI collaboration where judgment, empathy, and trust-building enable effective leadership.

architecture creates those conditions structurally — not by accident, not by luck, but by design.[275]

None of these shifts arrive automatically. Each depends on deliberate architectural choices that prevent the three risks from consuming what they were meant to enable.

The Human Cortex Remains Human

Leverage doesn't erase psychology — it amplifies it, including the fragile parts.[276]

If the Architect burns out, the system drifts without a hand on the tiller. If the Guardian abdicates moral responsibility, the organization optimizes for nothing worth optimizing. If the Force Multiplier succumbs to the flattening effect, quality erodes precisely where the brand depends on it most. The Human Cortex requires as much architectural care as the Machine Core — perhaps more, because machines don't have bad weeks.

---

[275] Amy Wrzesniewski and Jane E. Dutton, "Crafting a Job: Revisioning Employees as Active Crafters of Their Work," Academy of Management Review 26, no. 2 (2001): 179-201. Research demonstrates that meaningful work requires employees to feel personal connection to their tasks and outcomes, with job crafting enabling individuals to reshape roles to align with their values and identity.

[276] Erik Brynjolfsson and Andrew McAfee, "The Second Machine Age: Work, Progress, and Prosperity in a Time of Brilliant Technologies" (New York: W. W. Norton, 2014), Chapter 11. The authors analyze how human-AI collaboration creates both opportunities for enhanced performance and risks of human deskilling and social isolation, requiring careful design to preserve human agency and social connection.

The Triumvirate Scales: From Single Unit to Organization

The Triumvirate describes archetypes, not headcount. These three roles repeat at every level — every product vertical, geographic market, and functional domain needs a cortex. As AI-Born firms scale across regulatory regimes, they add Architects understanding regional compliance, Guardians adjudicating edge cases with local institutional knowledge, Force Multipliers transmitting craft standards to new teams in new markets. Not thousands of execution workers. Human capacity grows with strategic surface area, not transaction volume.

The ratio varies by industry. Domains requiring substantial regulatory oversight might see human-to-agent ratios of 1:100; domains where agents operate with high autonomy might reach 1:1,000. The pattern holds regardless: exponentially growing operational capacity, logarithmically growing human headcount.

Psychological sustainability scales differently than technical architecture. Solutions for a three-person cortex managing 200 agents don't map to a 100-person distributed cortex managing 10,000. Corrective mechanisms must scale with the architecture: structured rituals for human connection, rotation protocols for cognitive diversity, escalation hierarchies for attention budget engineering.

The 72× Productivity Gap: Specific Mechanisms

Aria Chen's Singapore logistics firm reports 72× productivity per human compared to traditional enterprises. That number invites skepticism. The math seems too clean.

But the pattern holds across auditable companies. Cursor generates roughly $6.7 million in revenue per employee — a gap so wide relative to traditional software firms that it forces a structural explanation, not a talent one, and one that raises a distributional question we hold throughout: efficiency this concentrated means fewer people share in the value created.[277] Goldman Sachs deployed Cognition's Devin as a standalone "new employee" on software engineering tasks in 2025.[278]

The mechanism has three parts. First: VP-Agents automate orchestration, eliminating the coordination overhead that consumes roughly 40–45% of knowledge-worker time in traditional organizations.[279] Second: agent swarms execute in parallel what human teams do serially. Third: the cortex multiplier — one Architect's design choice reshapes thousands of agent behaviors simultaneously. Multiply those three factors, apply a realistic friction discount, and the productivity gap becomes legible even if the exact figure remains illustrative.

Here's what's revealing about why these gains stay concentrated in AI-Born firms. An NBER study of nearly 6,000 executives found

[277]Multiple sources, March 2026. Cursor (Anysphere Inc.) crossed $2 billion in annualized recurring revenue in early 2026, with approximately 300 employees — revenue-per-employee of approximately $6.7 million, a 38× gap relative to traditional enterprise software companies. See citations.md: cursor-revenue-2026.

[278]Hugh Son, CNBC, July 11, 2025; TechCrunch, July 11, 2025. Goldman Sachs CIO Marco Argenti announced deployment of Cognition's Devin as a standalone "new employee" on software engineering tasks — not as a productivity augmentation tool but as an autonomous worker directed by the human organization. Argenti: "We're going to start augmenting our workforce with Devin, which is going to be like our new employee." Institutional validation of the AI-Born Human Cortex model at a G-SIB with rigorous governance requirements. See citations.md: goldman-devin-pilot-2025.

[279]Roberto Verganti, Luca Vendraminelli, and Marco Iansiti, "Innovation and the Economics of the Platform Economy," Harvard Business Review, January-February 2020. Research on knowledge work coordination overhead shows that professionals spend 40-45% of their time on coordination activities including meetings, status updates, email management, and project management rather than core productive work. Supporting research from Microsoft's Work Trend Index shows similar findings, with coordination consuming significant portions of knowledge worker productivity.

that over 80% of companies implementing AI report no discernible impact on employment or productivity.[280] That's not a technology failure. It's an architecture failure. Firms bolt autonomous systems onto legacy hierarchies and capture incremental gains. The larger gap compounds only when the underlying organizational design enables all three mechanisms simultaneously.

The harder question isn't whether these gains are achievable. It's whether they serve broad prosperity or narrow concentration — a question the next chapter addresses through the Mothership model.

For the complete 72× productivity calculation, see **ai-born.org/tools/small-team-paradox-calculator**.

What This Chapter Solves (and Doesn't)

The New Triumvirate describes the destination: three roles, a lean cortex, a Machine Core doing execution at volume. The 146 people at Lovable running a $400M enterprise are not a curiosity — they are the destination made visible.[281] The missing 600 to 900 who

[280] Brynjolfsson, Erik, Danielle Li, and Lindsey R. Raymond, "Generative AI at Work," National Bureau of Economic Research Working Paper 31161, 2023; updated findings reported in NBER digest series 2025-2026. A survey of nearly 6,000 executives across the US, UK, Germany, and Australia found that over 80% of companies implementing AI tools reported no discernible positive impact on either employment levels or measurable productivity. The study attributes this to "bolt-on" AI adoption where autonomous systems are layered onto legacy hierarchical structures rather than organizations redesigning around AI-Born architectures. This finding validates the "lineage break" thesis: meaningful productivity transformation requires organizational architecture redesign, not tool deployment.

[281] TechCrunch, March 11, 2026. "Lovable Says It Added $100M in Revenue Last Month Alone, With Just 146 Employees." `https://techcrunch.com/2026/03/11/lovable-says-it-added-100m-in-revenue-last-month-alone-with-just-146-employees/`. Lovable (formerly GPT Engineer) reached $400M ARR in February 2026, having crossed $100M ARR in 8 months after launch (July 2025). Valuation: $6.6B (December 2025, CapitalG and Menlo Ventures lead). The $100M ARR in a single month (March 2026) represents an extraordinary revenue acceleration by any prior standard for B2C software companies.

would have staffed a traditional company at that revenue level are not a rounding error. They are the live wire the architecture cannot safely ignore.

Most organizations don't start at the destination. They start with legacy hierarchies, existing employees, and real communities whose economic futures depend on how the transformation unfolds. The destination is clear. The path from here is not.

Chapter 10 addresses that path – how incumbents build toward this architecture through the Mothership model, launching AI-Born ventures at the edges while managing the legacy core. The destination doesn't change. What incumbents discover – and what architecture alone cannot resolve – is that the question of those displaced 600 workers is not a secondary concern. It's the question the blueprint declines to answer. That silence is what Book 2 (*AI-Born: The Bridge*) is for.

Chapter 10: The Mothership Model: Platform, Ventures, and the Economics of Managed Transformation

It's a Tuesday morning. Picture the CEO of a Fortune 500 financial services firm—call her Patricia, a composite drawn from the situations documented across incumbent banks facing AI-Born entrants. She's in her office before 7 AM, reviewing the competitive intelligence briefing her team prepared overnight. One slide stops her.

Her 46,000 employees generate $174,000 per person in annual revenue. An AI-Born competitor with 40 people generates roughly $12.6 million per employee—a ratio she can't dismiss as a measurement artifact, and one whose flip side she registers immediately: that productivity sits with 40 people rather than the thousands a firm of that revenue once employed.[282] The comparison spans

[282]The $12.6M revenue-per-employee figure for the 40-person AI-Born fintech in the cold open is a constructed composite illustrating the architectural gap, not a single company's reported metric. For real-world comparison: Midjourney estimated at approximately $3.5M–$4.7M RPE (depending on headcount source) with $500M revenue in 2025 and 107–163 employees (see [^midjourney-2025-metrics-ch10]); Cursor at approximately $3.33M RPE ($2B ARR, ~300 employees, February 2026); Lovable at approximately $2.74M RPE ($400M ARR, 146 employees, February 2026) — all substantially above the Fortune 500 median of approximately $174,000. The $12.6M composite reflects a near-term projected ceiling for an AI-Born fintech operating in a margin-rich regulated segment, not current observed data. All underlying RPE estimates are calculated from publicly reported or analyst-estimated revenue and headcount

different business models—a full-service financial institution versus a software-first fintech—so it isn't an apples-to-apples productivity number. It is, however, a real description of the competitive pressure: a company with radically different cost architecture is pricing 35% lower and iterating in days. Patricia doesn't need a peer-reviewed study. She needs a strategic response. The competitor entered her primary market segment 18 months ago, and its product iteration cycle runs in days, not quarters.

She adds headcount. They add compute. Same market. Different architecture.

She can't fire everyone. Pension obligations trigger lawsuits. Institutional knowledge evaporates overnight. The 40-year relationships her regional relationship managers carry aren't in any database—they live in Tuesday morning coffees and Friday afternoon calls that no system can replicate on a deadline. And yet the math doesn't wait.

There is, however, a third path. Convert incumbent assets into shared infrastructure. Launch AI-Born ventures at the edges. Manage transition over 18–36 months. The organization shrinks from 46,000 to 5,000–8,000 people with comprehensive support—preserving incumbent advantages while embracing AI-Born speed. The window for this conversion is narrower than most boards realize. AI-Born competitors aren't waiting for incumbents to reorganize.

That's the Mothership model. And if you're reading this from a seat anything like Patricia's, the question isn't whether the math will eventually force a choice. It's whether you'll make it deliberately, on your schedule, or reactively, on somebody else's.

---

figures and carry meaningful uncertainty given private company reporting limitations.

One more thing before we go further. Jamie Dimon – chairman and CEO of JPMorgan Chase, who has deployed $2B in AI across his institution – put the constraint plainly at Davos in January 2026: "You can't lay off 2 million truckers tomorrow."[283] He wasn't arguing against transformation. He was naming the ethical boundary that any legitimate transformation strategy must operate within. This chapter is about that boundary – the space between the math and the human cost of moving through it too fast.

The Incumbent's Dilemma: Why Rip-and-Replace Fails

When the railroads arrived in the 1840s, canal companies faced a choice that looks nearly identical to the one this chapter describes. Their infrastructure was expensive, their workers skilled, their customer relationships deep. The ones that survived converted their distribution networks into railroad-era advantages—leveraging route knowledge, customer trust, and geographic presence—rather than defending canal infrastructure that no longer defined the game. The ones that tried to simply protect what they had were gone within a generation.

[283]Jamie Dimon, remarks at World Economic Forum panel, Davos, Switzerland, January 22, 2026. Verbatim quotations: 'You can't lay off 2 million truckers tomorrow. You can phase it in over time'; 'If it goes too fast for society, that's where government and business in a collaborative way should step in together and come up with a way to retrain people'; 'Phase it in. Retrain. Relocate. Income-assist.' He called U.S. Trade Adjustment Assistance 'incredibly poorly done' and said JPMorgan AI productivity savings were 'just the tip of the iceberg.' On potential government bans on mass AI layoffs: 'We would agree – if we have to do that to save society.' Sources: Banking Dive, 'JPMorgan's Dimon: AI's effect on jobs may go too fast for society,' January 22, 2026, `https://www.bankingdive.com/news/jpmorgan-dimon-ai-effect-jobs-workforce-davos/810247/`; Fortune, January 22, 2026, `https://fortune.com/2026/01/22/jpmorgan-chase-ceo-jamie-dimon-ai-layoff-income-assist-workers-elon-musk-sam-altman-universal-basic-income/`.

The pattern repeated when electricity replaced steam in manufacturing, when container shipping displaced break-bulk cargo, when digital photography arrived for film processors. Every major platform transition creates the same moment: an incumbent holding real assets faces a new entrant holding a better architecture. Rip-and-replace is the wrong instinct every time.[284]

A manufacturer like Ford or Stellantis, operating $12 billion in factories with multi-generation union contracts, cannot simply shut down and rebuild. Closing triggers pension obligations that erode shareholder value before the new architecture generates a dollar.

The knowledge problem is subtler. In a pharmaceutical company like Pfizer or Merck, FDA approval expertise scatters across locations — preclinical testing in one lab, clinical trial design two buildings away, regulatory submission elsewhere. The real institutional knowledge lives in three people's heads: the informal relationships with FDA reviewers that determine approval speed, undocumented and untransferable. Let those three people walk, and knowledge bankruptcy strikes before AI captures what they knew.

Revenue dependencies add another layer. Fortune 500 banks embed into customers' operating models over decades. That trust creates switching costs measured in years and millions. Rip-and-replace destroys revenue before replacement cash flow materializes—a gap that kills the transformation before it proves itself.

[284] Henry C. Lucas Jr. and Jie Mein Goh, "Disruptive technology: How Kodak missed the digital photography revolution," *The Journal of Strategic Information Systems* 18, no. 1 (2009): 46-55. `https://doi.org/10.1016/j.jsis.2009.01.002`. Academic analysis documenting how Kodak's organizational inertia and reluctance to cannibalize profitable film business prevented digital transformation despite inventing the digital camera in 1975.

Regulated incumbents face a further constraint that AI-Born startups never encounter: rapid transformation triggers regulatory intervention, compliance failures, and legal liability. Speed isn't free when your industry requires continuous regulatory approval.

And then there's brand. Established companies that rebrand around AI signal automation and job losses rather than innovation. Coca-Cola's brand took a century to build.[285] Incumbents must transform as themselves — preserving incumbent advantages while enabling AI-Born speed — not by destroying what took generations to accumulate. A brand is far easier to ruin than to build. The question is how. The Mothership model answers it with a specific architecture.

The Mothership Architecture: Platform Plus Ventures

Zhang Ruimin built this architecture before it had a name. In 2005, he reorganized Haier into thousands of autonomous microenterprises — teams of 10–15 people with P&L responsibility. When Haier deployed AI agents in 2023, no reorganization was needed. The company's 4,700 microenterprises generating $38 billion annually

[285] Interbrand, *Best Global Brands 2024*, Interbrand Global Report, October 2024, `https://interbrand.com/best-global-brands/global/2024-report/`. Coca-Cola ranked #7 with a brand value of $61.2 billion (up 5.4% from 2023). Nike ranked #14 with a brand value of $45.4 billion (down 15.6% from 2023). Full citation: Citation 474.

achieved 50% faster design cycles and 26% fewer defects.[286][287][288] Organizational architecture precedes technology.

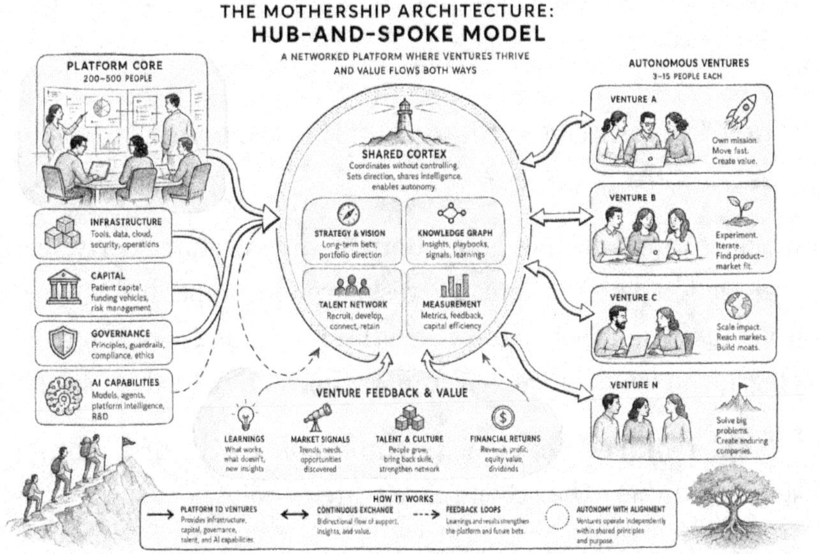

Figure 10.1: Mothership Architecture: The three-component hub-

[286]Haier's COSMOPlat industrial internet platform, deployed across its microenterprise ecosystem beginning in 2023, enabled significant operational improvements: 50% faster product design speed, 26% reduction in defects, and 18% lower energy consumption. These metrics demonstrate how centralized platform infrastructure amplifies the capabilities of distributed autonomous teams. Multiple sources on COSMOPlat benefits include industry analysis reports and Haier corporate communications, 2023-2024.

[287]Haier's microenterprise count varies by source and time period. Gary Hamel and Michele Zanini reported approximately 4,000 MEs in their 2018 Harvard Business Review article "The End of Bureaucracy." Other sources report up to 4,700 MEs in later periods. The variation reflects both organic growth and differing methodologies for counting microenterprises (some sources count only customer-facing units, others include platform service units). Gary Hamel and Michele Zanini, "The End of Bureaucracy," *Harvard Business Review* 96, no. 6 (November–December 2018): 50-59.

[288]From 2008 to 2018, Haier achieved 18% annual revenue growth and 23% annual gross profit growth, significantly outpacing traditional appliance manufacturers during the same period. Gary Hamel and Michele Zanini, "The End of Bureaucracy," *Harvard Business Review* 96, no. 6 (November–December 2018): 50-59. **Current revenue**: Multiple sources indicate Haier's total global revenue approaches $40 billion annually, though exact 2024 figures vary across divisions and reporting methods. Haier has maintained global leadership in home appliance manufacturing for over a decade.

and-spoke model showing Platform Core (shared infrastructure, capital, governance, AI), Ventures (autonomous teams at edges), and structural relationships enabling both coordination and autonomy.

1. The Platform Core: Shared Intelligence and Infrastructure

A regional bank launches an AI-Born lending venture. Forty years of transaction data sits spread across seven incompatible databases. The venture team spends three months negotiating data access with IT, legal, and compliance — before writing a line of code.

Or: build a **shared services platform** once. The first venture takes six months. The second takes three weeks. The sixth takes four days.

Technical Infrastructure: Unified data pipelines, foundation models, training systems. Ventures access clean, governed data from day one.[289]

Organizational Assets: Regulatory compliance as service—pre-approved charters, escalation protocols, audit trails. Brand equity and customer relationships provide distribution channels built over decades.

Knowledge Systems: Domain expertise accessible through expert networks and semantic retrieval. AI-Born platforms require a personalization-dominant strategy — 80% connecting people to

[289]Industry analysis on data platform implementation timelines and resource allocation, 2024-2025. Enterprise AI ventures typically spend 60-80% of development timeline on data infrastructure when building from scratch. Unified data platforms enable ventures to access governed data from day one, reducing time-to-market by 50-70%. Sources include Gartner enterprise AI implementation studies, McKinsey digital transformation research, and practitioner reports from Fortune 500 platform implementations.

people, 20% document retrieval — because ventures face novel problems requiring judgment, not standardized procedures.[290][291][292]

The platform provides foundation. Ventures generate revenue. Neither works without the other.

Increasingly, this platform layer is itself a product an incumbent can buy rather than build from scratch. Operating surfaces for AI-Born

[290] Morten T. Hansen, Nitin Nohria, and Thomas Tierney, "What's Your Strategy for Managing Knowledge?" *Harvard Business Review* 77, no. 2 (March-April 1999): 106-116. Foundational framework establishing two knowledge management strategies: codification (knowledge stored in databases for reuse) and personalization (knowledge shared through person-to-person contact). Critical finding: Companies must select an 80/20 strategy mix with one dominant—those attempting 50/50 fail at both. Strategy choice must align with competitive strategy: codification for standardized products, personalization for customized solutions. AI-Born platforms require personalization-dominant approaches (80% connecting people to people, 20% document retrieval) because ventures face novel, unique problems requiring judgment rather than standardized procedures.

[291] JPMorgan Chase LLM Suite and AI implementations documented in AWS Case Studies (2024) and AIX Network case study (2024). LLM Suite deployed to 200,000+ employees as internal AI assistant. EVEE (Intelligent Q&A) provides generative AI assistant for call centers with instant, context-aware responses integrating policy documents and transaction histories. Coach AI enables wealth managers to access research, market trends, and personalized investment recommendations using natural language processing. Systems employ escalation protocols routing to human experts when AI confidence falls below thresholds, capturing expert interactions to improve future performance through active learning loops. Full citations: AWS, "Modernize and Innovate using AWS | JPMorgan Chase," `https://aws.amazon.com/solutions/case-studies/jpmorgan-chase/`; AIX Network, "Case Study: How JPMorgan Chase is Revolutionizing Banking Through AI," `https://aiexpert.network/ai-at-jpmorgan/`.

[292] Microsoft Research, "GraphRAG: Unlocking LLM discovery on narrative private data," 2024. Open-sourced mid-year 2024, GraphRAG addresses standard RAG's semantic gap by creating knowledge graphs from input corpora (not just vector embeddings), extracting entities, relationships, and key claims. Uses community summaries and graph machine learning for context retrieval, enabling substantial improvements in question-and-answer performance when reasoning about complex information. GraphRAG uses relationship traversal (graph queries) rather than vector similarity (semantic search), providing advantages for multi-hop reasoning: "What are the connections between X and Y?" GitHub repository: `https://github.com/microsoft/graphrag`; Research blog: `https://www.microsoft.com/en-us/research/blog/graphrag-unlocking-llm-discovery-on-narrative-private-data/`.

companies — Neolith, the one Adaptic runs on, is the instance I know firsthand — package the platform core as tiers that track an organization's maturity: a **Native** tier for the company that is AI-Born from day one, a **Scale** tier for the small team doing outsized work, and a **Sovereign** tier for the incumbent that needs data residency, private infrastructure, and its own governance perimeter — which is precisely Patricia's situation. The founding itself runs through a pipeline some surfaces call **Genesis**: ethos and intent in, then phases, streams, clusters, seats, and a charter for each. The useful idea buried in that design is that genesis and evolution are the same machine. A venture is never standing at a blank page; the platform drafts the next layer of the org ahead of the humans, who then edit it. For an incumbent, that changes the Phase 1 question from "can we build the first venture?" to "can we direct one the platform has already sketched?"

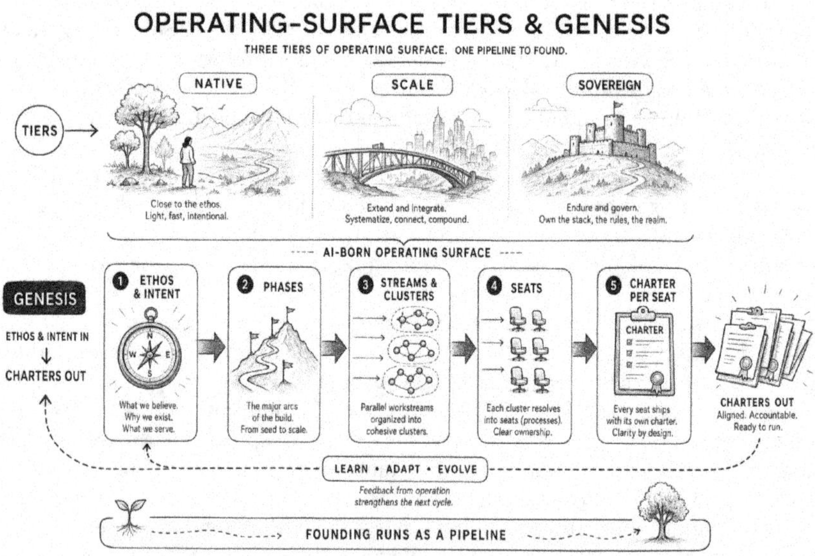

Figure 10.2: An operating surface offers three tiers tracking organizational maturity—Native, Scale, and Sovereign—while the

founding itself runs through Genesis: ethos and intent in, then phases, streams, clusters, seats, and a charter for each.

2. The Ventures: AI-Born Entities at the Edges

Small, autonomous **ventures**—3-10 people directing specialized agents for specific segments, products, or markets. Genuine autonomy means separate P&L, independent charters, founder mentality, and iteration cycles in days rather than quarters.

3. The Governance Layer: The Shared Cortex

A strategic team of 20-50 people defines intent, allocates capital, monitors alignment.

3b. The Customer Migration Mechanism: Managing Two-Track Service

Three mechanisms move customers from legacy to AI-Born: **Opt-in incentives** (early adopter pricing, feature previews), **Feature parity** (new system matches old before migration—two-tier service destroys trust), **Mandatory triggers** (after 80%+ migrate voluntarily, activate requirements for stragglers).

Architecture is necessary but not sufficient. Five conditions must hold simultaneously—and missing any one of them turns the Mothership into a costly organizational fiction.

The Five Conditions for Mothership Success

Condition 1: Genuine Venture Autonomy

Real autonomy means decision-making authority—not "autonomy within approved parameters." Ventures make mistakes. Platforms prevent catastrophic failures, but controlled failure is the price of learning speed.[293]

Test it: Can ventures pivot strategy without approval? Hire above salary bands? Sunset "essential" corporate features customers never use? If no, it's innovation theater.

Condition 2: Separate Brand and Identity

Ventures need identity that signals "this isn't legacy rebranded." Venture-specific naming, independent digital presence, transparent governance. Amazon Web Services built this from the inside — AWS launched as a separate product with its own developer identity, not as "Amazon's cloud division." Today AWS generates more than 60% of Amazon's operating profit.[294] The Mothership advantage: the platform behind AWS was Amazon's own infrastructure, converted into shared services. The identity advantage: AWS carried none of the retail brand's baggage.

Condition 3: Elite Talent with Founder-Level Compensation

AI-Born ventures compete for talent on upside and autonomy, not stability. Match that: 10–25% equity stakes, 50–100% compensation premium above corporate bands, cultural separation from corporate campus, mission clarity that attracts builders.

---

[293]Haier explicitly tolerates microenterprise failures as learning opportunities, accepting failure rates similar to the broader startup ecosystem where 20-30% of ventures fail within two years. This tolerance for experimentation is viewed as necessary cost for organizational learning and innovation velocity. Gary Hamel and Michele Zanini, *Humanocracy: Creating Organizations as Amazing as the People Inside Them* (Boston: Harvard Business Review Press, 2020).

[294]Amazon.com, Inc., *Annual Report on Form 10-K for the Fiscal Year Ended December 31, 2024*, filed February 6, 2025. AWS revenue increased 19% year-over-year to $107.6 billion in fiscal 2024; AWS operating income was $39.8 billion; AWS accounted for over 60% of Amazon's total operating profit despite representing only 16% of total revenue. Full citation: Citation 476.

Corporate salary bands get corporate talent. Full stop.

Condition 4: Multi-Year Platform Investment

For $5–10B organizations: 18–36 months, $50–200M investment creating shared data infrastructure, model training pipelines, and compliance-as-service.[295] Platform investment becomes economically justified at critical mass—typically 3–6 ventures for lightweight implementations, 6–10 for heavyweight regulated domains. Without shared platform, each venture rebuilds infrastructure independently.[296]

The commitment test: This math works only if leadership commits to multiple ventures over 3–5 years. The recurring failure pattern is documented across large transformations: firms approve $100M+ platform budgets, then starve them 18 months in when quarterly pressures intensify. And here's the cruelest version of it – the ventures often haven't failed. They've started producing early results. The platform investment was cancelled precisely as proof points were accumulating, because the proof points hadn't yet converted to P&L. Ventures collapsed – not because the model failed, but because organizations never committed to funding the foundation long enough to see it work.

[295] Industry analysis on data platform implementation timelines and resource allocation, 2024-2025. Enterprise AI ventures typically spend 60-80% of development timeline on data infrastructure when building from scratch. Unified data platforms enable ventures to access governed data from day one, reducing time-to-market by 50-70%. Sources include Gartner enterprise AI implementation studies, McKinsey digital transformation research, and practitioner reports from Fortune 500 platform implementations.

[296] Gartner (via CFO Dive), "The complex costs of AI: Investments, funding and ROI tracking," 2024, `https://www.cfodive.com/spons/the-complex-costs-of-ai-investments-funding-and-roi-tracking/761245/`. Top barrier to implementing AI is estimating and demonstrating value (58% of leaders cite ROI uncertainty); data preparation and platform upgrades consume 60-80% of project timeline and budget.

For detailed technical specifications, see **ai-born.org/ frameworks/mothership-architecture**.[297]

Condition 5: Cross-Venture Learning Infrastructure

The Mothership's advantage over isolated startups is organizational learning at scale. **Shared Agent Libraries**: Venture A develops a contract risk assessment agent. Ventures B and C deploy it within days.[298][299] **Federated Learning Pipelines**: Five lending ventures train AI models on combined data—50,000 total transactions—without sharing raw data centrally.[300]

This is where JPMorgan's 500+ use case approach reveals its second-order benefit. Each new use case doesn't just solve one problem — it stress-tests shared infrastructure, contributes to the model library, and surfaces failure modes that all subsequent ventures inherit. The 200,000 weekly LLM Suite users are simultaneously a workforce and a federated learning system.[301]

[297]This online supplement provides comprehensive technical architecture specifications, vendor evaluation criteria, and implementation sequencing for Mothership platform infrastructure.

[298]Google Cloud Architecture Center, "Cross-silo and cross-device federated learning on Google Cloud," `https://cloud.google.com/architecture/cross-silo-cross-device-federated-learning-google-cloud`. Documents enterprise federated learning architecture with cross-organizational collaboration, privacy-preserving aggregation, and governance frameworks enabling ventures to train on combined data without sharing raw data.

[299]BCG GAMMA, "Federated Learning: The Next Big Step Ahead for Data Sharing," Medium, 2024, `https://medium.com/bcggamma/federated-learning-the-next-big-step-ahead-for-data-sharing-2ae32d375309`. Documents governance models for shared agent libraries including publish-review-vote protocols with 80% approval thresholds typical in open-source federated frameworks.

[300]PMC, "Federated learning: Overview, strategies, applications, tools and future directions," PMC11466570, 2024. Comprehensive technical overview establishing federated learning as "distributed machine learning method solving data island problems by allowing raw data to remain on user side while local model parameters sent to model manager." Projects cross-silo federated learning growth at 25% CAGR from 2023-2030.

[301]JPMorgan Chase AI deployment data as of Q1 2026. Investment: $2B annually. Documented annual savings: $2B (Dimon, Bloomberg Television,

The tension: different ventures facing different contexts generate different insights. Platform synthesis balances standardization with flexibility. Too rigid kills innovation. Too loose wastes the advantage.

Each condition is necessary; none is sufficient alone. For comprehensive implementation checklists, see **ai-born.org/frameworks/five-conditions-mothership-success**.[302]

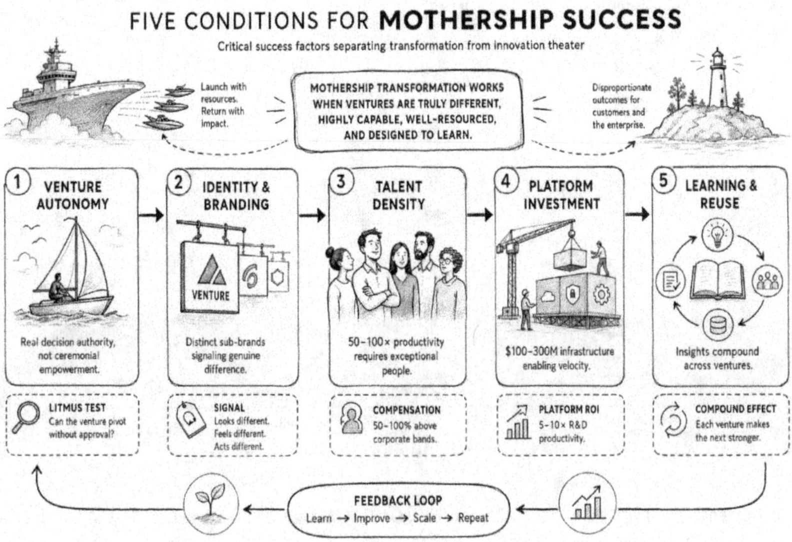

Figure 10.3: Five Conditions for Mothership Success: (1) Genuine Venture Autonomy, (2) Separate Brand/Identity, (3) Elite Talent/Compensation, (4) Multi-Year Platform Investment, (5) Cross-

October 8, 2025: "We have shown that for $2 billion of expense, we have about $2 billion of benefit. These gains are just the tip of the iceberg."). Active AI use cases: 500+ in production (as of March 2026, per investor meeting). LLM Suite users: 200,000+ employees weekly. Headcount composition shift: operations staff -4%, support staff -2%, client-facing/revenue-generating roles +4%. Per-operations-employee accounts +6%; fraud cost per unit -11%; software engineering productivity +10%. Net headcount approximately flat at 318,512. Sources: Bloomberg Television, October 8, 2025; JPMorgan investor meeting, February 24, 2026; CNBC coverage.

[302]This online supplement provides detailed litmus tests, failure consequences, and early warning indicators for each of the Five Conditions, enabling systematic assessment of Mothership viability.

Venture Learning Infrastructure—all necessary, none sufficient alone.

Meet all five conditions and the Mothership becomes viable. Miss one and it's innovation theater. Execution requires a sequenced transformation pathway.

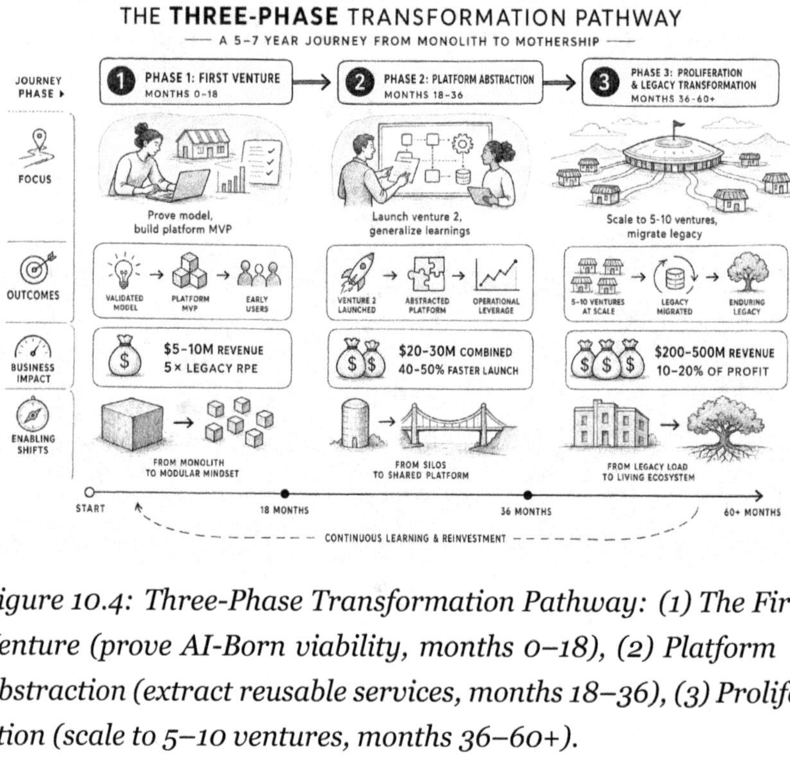

Figure 10.4: Three-Phase Transformation Pathway: (1) The First Venture (prove AI-Born viability, months 0–18), (2) Platform Abstraction (extract reusable services, months 18–36), (3) Proliferation (scale to 5–10 ventures, months 36–60+).

The Three-Phase Transformation Pathway

Transformation at this scale doesn't happen through one bold decision. It unfolds across three distinct phases, each with a different purpose—and each with a failure mode that ends the transformation before the next phase begins.

Phase 1: The First Venture (Months 0–18) exists to prove AI-Born viability inside your specific organization. Target a segment with a clear 10× AI opportunity. Assemble 5–8 people with a separate location, distinct branding, and a genuine three-year charter — meaning leadership commits not to kill it at the first adverse quarter.

Sometime between months 6 and 9, something goes wrong. Wrong pricing sent to a major customer. A misclassified support ticket that reaches the press. A report with hallucinated data that a client finds before you do. This moment reveals everything about whether the transformation is real — and I mean everything. A transparent post-mortem and a redesigned system signals a learning culture. Blame and tightened approval processes signal innovation theater.

The first failure is less a crisis than a diagnostic. By month 18, the target: 10,000+ customers or $5–10M revenue, iteration half-life under two weeks.

Phase 2: Platform Abstraction runs from month 18 to month 36. It extracts what the first venture built into reusable services for all subsequent ventures. The second venture should reach its first customers in 6–9 months — not the 12–18 the first venture required. This productivity asymmetry is the proof of platform value. It is also the trigger for organizational resistance. The people who built the legacy infrastructure are now watching ventures leapfrog it, and that's the moment the Mothership program either finds genuine executive air cover or quietly begins to die. Leadership must invest in transition infrastructure at this exact moment. Otherwise the rest of the journey becomes political warfare rather than strategic transformation.

Phase 3: Proliferation. By month 36, the platform is proven. Now scale to 5–10 ventures while simultaneously migrating legacy functions to the platform. Launch 2–3 ventures annually. At year 5: 10+ ventures generating $200–$500M revenue with 100–150 employees; 80% of new development running on the platform. The legacy organization that started with 40,000 people now runs at 5,000–10,000 — smaller, more capable, structurally different.

The question is no longer whether transformation is possible. It's whether you have the stomach for what it actually costs.

For detailed implementation templates, visit **ai-born.org/tools/transformation-roadmap-planner**.

The Middle Manager Transition: Converting Coordinators to Architects

As coordination automates, demand for traditional middle management narrows substantially. A 46,000-person organization currently relying on 5,000–8,000 managers for information routing and approvals may require only 500–1,200 people in those functions after transformation — with the remaining management capacity either redirected to higher-leverage roles or transitioned out.[303][304]

Three pathways emerge. Ten to fifteen percent of current managers move into **Strategic Cortex Roles** – judgment-heavy positions that AI can augment but not replace. Another 15–20% move into **Venture Leadership**, running the small AI-Born entities at the edges. The remaining 65–75% require **Comprehensive Transition Support**.

That last category deserves more than a label. At a 46,000-person firm, it represents roughly 3,000–5,000 people who built their identities around being reliable, competent, trusted. They managed the production schedule, mediated the team conflict, kept the account from churning. They are not dinosaurs. They are people who optimized for the organization that hired them and are now being told the organization has changed. Transition infrastructure –

[303] Faisal Hoque, "AI and the death (and rebirth) of middle management," 2024, `https://faisalhoque.com/ai-and-the-death-and-rebirth-of-middle-management/`. Documents Gartner prediction that robo-bosses will replace 69% of manager workload by 2024; Pega survey showing 78% of executives expect AI to dramatically reduce middle management ranks. Gartner's 2024 top predictions further specified that through 2026, 20% of organizations will use AI to flatten their organizational structure, eliminating more than half of current middle management positions (Gartner, "Gartner Unveils Top Predictions for IT Organizations and Users in 2025 and Beyond," October 22, 2024, `https://www.gartner.com/en/newsroom/press-releases/2024-10-22-gartner-unveils-top-predictions-for-it-organizations-and-users-in-2025-and-beyond`). Deloitte labor market data documents this trend already underway: middle management job postings declined more than 40% between April 2022 and October 2024 as companies create flatter AI-assisted structures. The three-pathway breakdown in the text (10-15% Strategic Cortex, 15-20% Venture Leadership, 65-75% Comprehensive Transition Support) is consistent with the book's own arithmetic for a 46,000-person organization retaining 500-1,200 managers post-transformation (from an estimated 5,000-8,000 current middle managers), implying 75-90% displacement – making the "65-75%" figure a conservative lower bound anchored by these empirical trends.

[304] Fast Company, "How AI is killing (and reinventing) middle management," 2024. Establishes that "many management tasks—scheduling, data analysis, approvals, and audits—are precisely where AI either already excels or will excel once agentic AI is fully implemented."

retraining, income support, placement assistance, mental health resources — is not a PR move. It is the difference between institutional memory retained through considered transition and institutional memory evaporated through nominal severance.

AT&T's billion-dollar reskilling program achieved 50% internal placement rates across 100,000 employees.[305] That result was not charity; it was calculation. The retrained workers filled 47% of promotions in the technology organization. The institutional knowledge stayed inside the transformation rather than walking out.

---

[305] AT&T's Workforce 2020 program (later rebranded "Future Ready") invested approximately $1 billion over seven years (2013-2020) to retrain 100,000+ employees in cloud computing, data analytics, cybersecurity, and software engineering while workers remained employed. The program cost approximately $10,000 per worker and achieved significant success: by 2016, 140,000 employees actively engaged in skills acquisition, completing 1.8 million courses; retrained workers filled 50% of new technology management positions and received 47% of promotions in the technology organization; product development cycle time reduced 40% over 18 months. The program provided comprehensive support including partnerships with Coursera, Udacity, and universities; tuition reimbursement; career counseling; and income support (workers continued regular employment during retraining). Sources: Harvard Business Review, "Inside AT&T's Radical Talent Overhaul," October 2016; CNBC, "AT&T's $1 billion gambit: Retraining nearly half its workforce for jobs of the future," March 13, 2018; Harvard Business School Case Study, "AT&T, Retraining, and the Workforce of Tomorrow" (Case 820-017), July 2019.

For pathway guidance, visit **ai-born.org/ideas/player-coach-returns**.[306][307][308]

The Entry Diagnostic: Is the Mothership Even Yours to Build?

Before committing to the Five Conditions and Three-Phase Pathway, one question demands an honest answer: does your organization have the assets the Mothership is designed to convert?

The Mothership makes economic sense when an incumbent possesses genuine platform-convertible advantages — proprietary data at scale, regulatory licenses that serve as moats, distribution relationships that AI-Born startups cannot replicate at speed, or brand

[306] IMD, "Automation and the future of middle management," 2024, `https://www.imd.org/ibyimd/technology/automation-and-the-future-of-middle-management-its-more-complicated-and-manageable-than-what-youve-heard/`. Establishes three transformed middle management roles requiring domain expertise + AI knowledge: (1) Trainers teaching AI systems, (2) Explainers bridging AI specialists and business leaders, (3) Sustainers guiding employees through transitions.

[307] California Management Review, "The Uncertainty of Middle Management Jobs - And How to Stay Relevant," 2021, `https://cmr.berkeley.edu/2021/01/middle-management-jobs/`. Establishes middle management faces existential threat from AI automation of coordination, scheduling, data analysis, and approval functions. Recommends organizations provide career counseling, financial assistance, mental health support, and coaching to ease transitions.

[308] IBM workforce rebalancing programs cost $400 million (2023) for approximately 5,200 workers and $700 million (2024) for approximately 9,000 workers, averaging $76,900-$77,800 per employee. These costs include severance pay, healthcare continuation, and outplacement services, but exclude retraining programs or income support during job search. The programs represent traditional workforce reduction concentrated in back-office functions. In February 2026, IBM reversed course, announcing it would triple entry-level hiring — reflecting the discovery that AI-native talent capable of directing AI systems is a scarce resource distinct from the roles eliminated. Sources: IBM financial disclosures and employee reports, 2023-2024; Fortune, November 2025; Bloomberg, May 2023 (hiring freeze announcement). See also citation note [^CITATION-IBM-REVERSAL-FEB2026].

trust that takes decades to accumulate. Patricia's financial services firm qualifies on all four counts. But not every incumbent does.

Incumbents that don't qualify for the Mothership Build aren't without options. Three off-ramps exist, each rational in the right conditions:

Acquisition Pivot: incumbents with strong distribution but weak internal venture DNA. The rational move is to become a capital allocator — buy AI-Born competitors in adjacent segments, acquire talent through acqui-hires, and scale what startups have already proven. A traditional media company entering AI-generated content, for instance, holds strong distribution but weak AI platform assets. Acquiring an AI-Born content studio costs more upfront but sidesteps the failure modes of building the capability internally.

Platform Provider Pivot: incumbents that discover, mid-transformation, that their most valuable asset is the infrastructure they built to support ventures — not the ventures themselves. A regulated financial institution that spent $200M building a compliance-as-service layer may find that other institutions want to license that infrastructure rather than rebuild it. JPMorgan's LLM Suite — deployed to 200,000 internal employees — is already a blueprint for a financial services AI infrastructure product.[309] Whether JPMorgan externalizes that platform remains an open strategic question. But the logic points there.

[309] JPMorgan Chase AI deployment data as of Q1 2026. Investment: $2B annually. Documented annual savings: $2B (Dimon, Bloomberg Television, October 8, 2025: "We have shown that for $2 billion of expense, we have about $2 billion of benefit. These gains are just the tip of the iceberg."). Active AI use cases: 500+ in production (as of March 2026, per investor meeting). LLM Suite users: 200,000+ employees weekly. Headcount composition shift: operations staff -4%, support staff -2%, client-facing/revenue-generating roles +4%. Per-operations-employee accounts +6%; fraud cost per unit -11%; software engineering productivity +10%. Net headcount approximately flat at 318,512. Sources: Bloomberg Television, October 8, 2025; JPMorgan investor meeting, February 24, 2026; CNBC coverage.

Incremental Adoption: accepting that full Mothership transformation is beyond organizational capacity in the current cycle, and focusing instead on AI augmentation of existing functions. This is the path most large institutions are currently walking, whether they call it that or not. It generates real productivity gains. It does not close the structural gap with AI-Born competitors. Organizations that pursue incremental adoption should do so with eyes open: they are buying time, not transforming. The productivity gap will narrow for a few years before the compounding advantage of AI-Born architecture opens it again. Incremental adoption is a legitimate bridge. It isn't a destination.

Choosing: The diagnostic question isn't "how ambitious are we?" It's "what do we actually have that converts into AI-Born advantage?"

- **Strong proprietary data + operational moat + governance tolerance for 36-month payback**: Mothership Build.
- **Strong distribution + customer trust + weak internal venture DNA**: Acquisition Pivot.
- **Strong regulatory/compliance infrastructure + adjacent demand**: Platform Provider.
- **None of the above, or current governance incapable of sustained commitment**: Incremental Adoption, explicitly framed as bridge, not destination.

Case Studies: Transformation in Practice

Haier's Rendanheyi model, introduced at the chapter's opening, is the longest-running antecedent to the Mothership architecture at scale — built over fifteen years rather than announced in a quarterly report. By 2025 and 2026, Western incumbents that had been theorizing their way through AI strategy began revealing whether their theories held.

Five cases. Consider them not as sequential profiles but as a comparative cut across one question: where does transformation succeed, and which condition determines the outcome when it doesn't?

Klarna: When Condition 1 Fails — and How Recovery Works

January 2024. Klarna's marketing team sent a press release that circulated through every AI conference for months. Their OpenAI-powered customer service chatbot, they announced, was handling the equivalent of 700 full-time agents — roles the company never needed to hire — with two-thirds of all customer service inquiries resolved without a human in the loop. CEO Sebastian Siemiatkowski added that headcount had dropped from 5,500 to 3,400 in two years, mostly through attrition rather than layoffs. The projected $40M in annual savings felt like proof that AI-first service was not just feasible but superior.[310]

It wasn't quite that.

[310] Klarna Group, NYSE IPO prospectus and Q3 2025 earnings report, September–October 2025. Klarna raised $1.4B at a $15B valuation; shares surged 30% to a $19.65B market cap on IPO day. Full-year 2024 revenue: $2.81B (+24% YoY). Q3 2025 revenue: $903M (+26% YoY), 114M active customers (+32% YoY). Headcount arc: 5,527 FTE (end-2022) to 3,422 FTE (end-2024), attributed to hiring freeze and AI deployment. AI chatbot deployed January 2024 claimed equivalent of 700 full-time outsourced agents' workload; projected $40M annual cost savings. Reversal announced 2025: CEO Sebastian Siemiatkowski stated company "went too far," acknowledging generic and repetitive AI responses for complex emotional queries; resumed hybrid model with human agents for nuanced cases. Sources: CNBC, "Klarna CEO says AI helped company shrink workforce by 40%," May 14, 2025; MLQ.ai, "Klarna CEO admits aggressive AI job cuts went too far," 2025; CX Dive, "Klarna says AI agent handled work of 853 employees," 2025.

By mid-2025, the counterevidence had accumulated. Customer complaints climbed. Satisfaction scores fell. Siemiatkowski publicly acknowledged that Klarna had "gone too far" — that the AI responses sounded "generic," "repetitive," and ill-equipped for emotional complexity. The chatbot handled routing and simple FAQs adequately. It failed when a customer, anxious about a disputed charge during a difficult month, needed someone to actually understand the situation. Klarna began rehiring human agents into a flexible model — roughly $41/hour in Sweden — with AI handling triage and humans handling cases requiring genuine judgment.[311]

What makes Klarna instructive is precisely this: the company did not fail. It made a navigation error, recognized it faster than most organizations would, corrected it, and continued building. Full-year 2024 revenue grew 24%. When the IPO came in September 2025, shares opened 30% above the IPO price — a market verdict on the hybrid model that emerged from the reversal.[312]

---

[311] Klarna Group, NYSE IPO prospectus and Q3 2025 earnings report, September–October 2025. Klarna raised $1.4B at a $15B valuation; shares surged 30% to a $19.65B market cap on IPO day. Full-year 2024 revenue: $2.81B (+24% YoY). Q3 2025 revenue: $903M (+26% YoY), 114M active customers (+32% YoY). Headcount arc: 5,527 FTE (end-2022) to 3,422 FTE (end-2024), attributed to hiring freeze and AI deployment. AI chatbot deployed January 2024 claimed equivalent of 700 full-time outsourced agents' workload; projected $40M annual cost savings. Reversal announced 2025: CEO Sebastian Siemiatkowski stated company "went too far," acknowledging generic and repetitive AI responses for complex emotional queries; resumed hybrid model with human agents for nuanced cases. Sources: CNBC, "Klarna CEO says AI helped company shrink workforce by 40%," May 14, 2025; MLQ.ai, "Klarna CEO admits aggressive AI job cuts went too far," 2025; CX Dive, "Klarna says AI agent handled work of 853 employees," 2025.

[312] Klarna Group, NYSE IPO prospectus and Q3 2025 earnings report, September–October 2025. Klarna raised $1.4B at a $15B valuation; shares surged 30% to a $19.65B market cap on IPO day. Full-year 2024 revenue: $2.81B (+24% YoY). Q3 2025 revenue: $903M (+26% YoY), 114M active customers (+32% YoY). Headcount arc: 5,527 FTE (end-2022) to 3,422 FTE (end-2024), attributed to hiring freeze and AI deployment. AI chatbot deployed January 2024 claimed equivalent of 700 full-time outsourced agents' workload; projected $40M annual cost savings. Reversal announced 2025: CEO Sebastian Siemiatkowski stated company "went too far," acknowledging generic and repetitive AI responses for

The structural lesson maps cleanly onto the Five Conditions. Klarna deployed execution capacity without installing the Guardian — the judgment-keeper who asks "which customer interactions should ever reach an AI alone?" That function was absent. When you skip it, the answer defaults to whatever maximizes short-term cost reduction. Klarna's correction took eighteen months. Organizations less willing to admit error publicly pay more and wait longer.

Block: Phase 3 Proliferation, Executed Fast

Block's restructuring announcement landed on a February 2026 morning, and the market's reaction told you everything you needed to know about how the narrative had shifted. The payments company formerly known as Square cut roughly 4,000 employees, reducing headcount from 10,000 to around 6,000. The stock rose 22% on the announcement.[313] Block's 2026 gross profit projection came in at $12.2B, up 18% year-over-year — meaning this was not a distressed restructuring. It was a deliberate architectural choice by a company with a strong balance sheet.

complex emotional queries; resumed hybrid model with human agents for nuanced cases. Sources: CNBC, "Klarna CEO says AI helped company shrink workforce by 40%," May 14, 2025; MLQ.ai, "Klarna CEO admits aggressive AI job cuts went too far," 2025; CX Dive, "Klarna says AI agent handled work of 853 employees," 2025.

[313] Block Inc. restructuring announcement, February 27, 2026; Jack Dorsey and Roelof Botha, "From Hierarchy to Intelligence," block.xyz and sequoiacap.com, published April 2026. Block reduced from approximately 10,000 to approximately 6,000 employees (40% reduction). Stock rose 22% on announcement. 2026 gross profit projection: $12.2B (+18% YoY). "Goose" AI agent (built on Anthropic Model Context Protocol) handles approximately 90% of internal code submissions per senior engineer accounts. Three-role organizational model published: Individual Contributors, Directly Responsible Individuals, Player-Coaches. Dorsey quote: "I think most companies are late. Within the next year, I believe the majority of companies will reach the same conclusion and make similar structural changes." Skeptical note: Guardian/former employees told The Guardian that 95% of AI-generated code still requires human modification. Sources: Fortune, February 27, 2026; CoinDesk, April 1, 2026; Sequoia podcast transcript; PaymentsDive.

Jack Dorsey and Sequoia partner Roelof Botha published a co-authored essay explaining the theory. "From Hierarchy to Intelligence" argues that corporate hierarchy has always solved one problem: routing information through organizations too large for any single person to oversee. AI now does that routing better than human management layers.[314] The three-role model they propose — Individual Contributors, Directly Responsible Individuals, Player-Coaches — is a different label for the New Triumvirate architecture this book describes. Block's internal AI agent "Goose," built on Anthropic's Model Context Protocol, now authors approximately 90% of the company's code submissions — though roughly 95% of those AI-generated changes still require human modification before reaching production.[315] The human judgment layer didn't disappear; it moved upstream.

[314] Jack Dorsey and Roelof Botha, "From Hierarchy to Intelligence," co-published at block.xyz/inside/from-hierarchy-to-intelligence and sequoiacap.com/article/from-hierarchy-to-intelligence/, April 2026. Core argument: corporate hierarchy has historically solved the problem of routing information through large organizations; AI now performs that routing function more effectively, eliminating the structural justification for permanent management layers. Block's two AI world models: (1) internal company model aggregating code, decisions, workflows, and performance metrics; (2) customer-merchant model mapping behavior through transaction data. Dorsey Sequoia podcast quote: "treat the company as a mini AGI... an artificial general intelligence, because it really is." Fortune coverage: April 2, 2026.

[315] Block Inc. restructuring announcement, February 27, 2026; Jack Dorsey and Roelof Botha, "From Hierarchy to Intelligence," block.xyz and sequoiacap.com, published April 2026. Block reduced from approximately 10,000 to approximately 6,000 employees (40% reduction). Stock rose 22% on announcement. 2026 gross profit projection: $12.2B (+18% YoY). "Goose" AI agent (built on Anthropic Model Context Protocol) handles approximately 90% of internal code submissions per senior engineer accounts. Three-role organizational model published: Individual Contributors, Directly Responsible Individuals, Player-Coaches. Dorsey quote: "I think most companies are late. Within the next year, I believe the majority of companies will reach the same conclusion and make similar structural changes." Skeptical note: Guardian/former employees told The Guardian that 95% of AI-generated code still requires human modification. Sources: Fortune, February 27, 2026; CoinDesk, April 1, 2026; Sequoia podcast transcript; PaymentsDive.

Dorsey's framing is worth quoting: "I think most companies are late. Within the next year, I believe the majority of companies will reach the same conclusion and make similar structural changes. I'd rather get there honestly and on our own terms than be forced into it reactively."

That last phrase — "on our own terms" — is the Mothership argument in three words. Chosen transformation retains institutional memory, preserves customer relationships, allows course correction. Forced transformation does none of those.

IBM: Two Waves of Cuts, Then a Talent Reversal

Of all five cases, IBM's arc is the one to sit with longest if you believe AI-driven headcount reduction is a straight line. It isn't.

CEO Arvind Krishna announced a hiring freeze on back-office roles AI could replace in May 2023, projecting 7,800 positions eliminated over five years. What followed moved faster. Across two waves in 2024 and early 2025, IBM shed an estimated 13,000–17,000 positions — concentrated in non-customer-facing functions, roughly matching what Krishna had forecast, but compressed into two years rather than five.[316]

---

[316] IBM restructuring arc: CEO Arvind Krishna announced hiring freeze on back-office AI-replaceable roles, May 2023 (7,800 roles projected eliminated over five years). Bloomberg, May 1, 2023, `https://www.bloomberg.com/news/articles/2023-05-01/ibm-to-pause-hiring-for-back-office-jobs-that-ai-could-kill`. Wave 1 reduction: 8,000–10,000 employees (Sept–Dec 2024). Wave 2: 5,000–7,000 (Q1 2025). Total estimated: 13,000–17,000 jobs over two years. Specific HR automation: IBM's AskHR reduced HR professionals performing manual work from 700 to fewer than 50 (93% reduction); handled 11.5 million interactions in 2024 with 94% self-service containment. Source: IBM CEO Arvind Krishna, Fortune op-ed, June 2023; IBM AskHR case study. Reversal: IBM CHRO Nickle LaMoreaux announced tripling of entry-level U.S. hiring at Charter's Leading with AI Summit, New York, February 12, 2026. LaMoreaux quote: "The entry-level jobs that you had two to three years ago, AI can do most of them. So, if you're going to convince your business leaders that you need to make this investment, then you need to be

Then, in February 2026, IBM's Chief Human Resources Officer announced the company would triple its entry-level hiring.[317]

This apparent contradiction resolves cleanly once you understand what IBM discovered. Automating back-office functions is straightforward: AI handles scheduling, data processing, report generation, routine query resolution. IBM executed that correctly. What they underestimated was the demand for the *next* category of workers – people who can operate, direct, and build on top of AI systems. AI-native junior talent, who grew up debugging with Cursor and prompting with precision, turns out to be a genuinely scarce resource. IBM eliminated the roles AI can do. Then they went to market to hire the humans who tell AI what to do.

---

able to show the real value these individuals can bring now. And that has to be through totally different jobs." Sources: Bloomberg, February 12, 2026, `https://www.bloomberg.com/news/articles/2026-02-12/ibm-plans-to-triple-entry-level-hiring-in-the-us-in-2026`; Fortune, February 13, 2026, `https://fortune.com/2026/02/13/tech-giant-ibm-tripling-gen-z-entry-level-hiring-according-to-chro-rewriting-jobs-ai-era/`.

[317]IBM restructuring arc: CEO Arvind Krishna announced hiring freeze on back-office AI-replaceable roles, May 2023 (7,800 roles projected eliminated over five years). Bloomberg, May 1, 2023, `https://www.bloomberg.com/news/articles/2023-05-01/ibm-to-pause-hiring-for-back-office-jobs-that-ai-could-kill`. Wave 1 reduction: 8,000–10,000 employees (Sept–Dec 2024). Wave 2: 5,000–7,000 (Q1 2025). Total estimated: 13,000–17,000 jobs over two years. Specific HR automation: IBM's AskHR reduced HR professionals performing manual work from 700 to fewer than 50 (93% reduction); handled 11.5 million interactions in 2024 with 94% self-service containment. Source: IBM CEO Arvind Krishna, Fortune op-ed, June 2023; IBM AskHR case study. Reversal: IBM CHRO Nickle LaMoreaux announced tripling of entry-level U.S. hiring at Charter's Leading with AI Summit, New York, February 12, 2026. LaMoreaux quote: "The entry-level jobs that you had two to three years ago, AI can do most of them. So, if you're going to convince your business leaders that you need to make this investment, then you need to be able to show the real value these individuals can bring now. And that has to be through totally different jobs." Sources: Bloomberg, February 12, 2026, `https://www.bloomberg.com/news/articles/2026-02-12/ibm-plans-to-triple-entry-level-hiring-in-the-us-in-2026`; Fortune, February 13, 2026, `https://fortune.com/2026/02/13/tech-giant-ibm-tripling-gen-z-entry-level-hiring-according-to-chro-rewriting-jobs-ai-era/`.

The IBM arc matters as a counter-example to the simpler story — the one where AI just reduces headcount in a straight line. The actual trajectory is more nuanced: displacement of routine-cognitive roles, followed by demand expansion for AI-direction roles, with a gap in the middle where institutional knowledge briefly evaporates before the new workforce arrives. Organizations that manage that gap deliberately — through redeployment, retraining, and hybrid transition structures — perform better through the valley than those that treat each wave as an isolated cost reduction.

JPMorgan: The Same Architecture, at Regulatory Pace

Ask Jamie Dimon whether JPMorgan's AI investment has paid off, and you get something unusual from a banking CEO: an answer that doesn't hide behind projected future benefits. In an October 2025 Bloomberg interview, his reply was blunt: "We have shown that for $2 billion of expense, we have about $2 billion of benefit. These gains are just the tip of the iceberg."[318]

By early 2026, JPMorgan had 500+ active AI use cases in production, with roughly 200,000 employees using the internal LLM Suite weekly. Operations and support staff fell; client-facing, revenue-generating roles grew 4%. Net headcount held roughly flat at

[318] JPMorgan Chase AI deployment data as of Q1 2026. Investment: $2B annually. Documented annual savings: $2B (Dimon, Bloomberg Television, October 8, 2025: "We have shown that for $2 billion of expense, we have about $2 billion of benefit. These gains are just the tip of the iceberg."). Active AI use cases: 500+ in production (as of March 2026, per investor meeting). LLM Suite users: 200,000+ employees weekly. Headcount composition shift: operations staff -4%, support staff -2%, client-facing/revenue-generating roles +4%. Per-operations-employee accounts +6%; fraud cost per unit -11%; software engineering productivity +10%. Net headcount approximately flat at 318,512. Sources: Bloomberg Television, October 8, 2025; JPMorgan investor meeting, February 24, 2026; CNBC coverage.

318,000 — but it was a different 318,000, concentrated toward the work the institution actually wanted humans doing.[319]

What JPMorgan executed is a Mothership transformation conducted at the pace of a regulated global institution. No dramatic announcements. No manifesto essays. 500 use cases deployed systematically, with redeployment plans for displaced workers, managed through existing organizational structures. Dimon's phrasing at Davos 2026 captures the principle: "Phase it in. Retrain. You can't lay off 2 million truckers tomorrow."[320]

The contrast with Block is instructive and not a matter of one being right and the other wrong. Block operates in a payments software market where speed of product iteration is a competitive weapon; a 40% headcount reduction unlocks organizational agility that the market rewards immediately. JPMorgan operates in regulated

[319] JPMorgan Chase AI deployment data as of Q1 2026. Investment: $2B annually. Documented annual savings: $2B (Dimon, Bloomberg Television, October 8, 2025: "We have shown that for $2 billion of expense, we have about $2 billion of benefit. These gains are just the tip of the iceberg."). Active AI use cases: 500+ in production (as of March 2026, per investor meeting). LLM Suite users: 200,000+ employees weekly. Headcount composition shift: operations staff -4%, support staff -2%, client-facing/revenue-generating roles +4%. Per-operations-employee accounts +6%; fraud cost per unit -11%; software engineering productivity +10%. Net headcount approximately flat at 318,512. Sources: Bloomberg Television, October 8, 2025; JPMorgan investor meeting, February 24, 2026; CNBC coverage.

[320] Jamie Dimon, remarks at World Economic Forum panel, Davos, Switzerland, January 22, 2026. Verbatim quotations: 'You can't lay off 2 million truckers tomorrow. You can phase it in over time'; 'If it goes too fast for society, that's where government and business in a collaborative way should step in together and come up with a way to retrain people'; 'Phase it in. Retrain. Relocate. Income-assist.' He called U.S. Trade Adjustment Assistance 'incredibly poorly done' and said JPMorgan AI productivity savings were 'just the tip of the iceberg.' On potential government bans on mass AI layoffs: 'We would agree — if we have to do that to save society.' Sources: Banking Dive, 'JPMorgan's Dimon: AI's effect on jobs may go too fast for society,' January 22, 2026, `https://www.bankingdive.com/news/jpmorgan-dimon-ai-effect-jobs-workforce-davos/810247/`; Fortune, January 22, 2026, `https://fortune.com/2026/01/22/jpmorgan-chase-ceo-jamie-dimon-ai-layoff-income-assist-workers-elon-musk-sam-altman-universal-basic-income/`.

deposit banking, where a compliance failure can trigger a decade-long Federal Reserve asset cap. Speed of transformation carries categorically different risk. Both organizations are executing the Three-Phase Pathway — but JPMorgan's Phase 1-to-2 transition spans years rather than months, and its proliferation phase is measured in use cases rather than standalone ventures.

The Mothership framework accommodates both paces. What it cannot accommodate is indecision that leaves neither the efficiency gains nor the institutional knowledge intact.

Shopify: Condition 3 by Policy, Not by Negotiation

Shopify's transformation doesn't look like Klarna's reversal or Block's manifesto essay. There was no restructuring announcement, no stock pop, no 40% headcount cut on a February morning. There was a memo.

Tobi Lütke published it in April 2025: before any team could request additional headcount, they had to demonstrate the work couldn't be accomplished with AI.[321] The inversion was structural. Headcount had to justify itself against the AI baseline, not the other way around. Every employee received access to Cursor, Claude, and Copilot. AI usage became a factor in performance reviews. Lütke reported seeing employees "get 100× the work done" with AI tools — hyperbole, almost certainly, but directionally accurate about the productivity asymmetry.

[321]Tobi Lütke, Shopify internal memo released publicly, April 2025. Core directive: "Before requesting more headcount and resources, teams will need to demonstrate that they cannot accomplish the work with AI." AI usage added to performance and peer review questionnaires. All employees provided access to Microsoft Copilot, Anthropic Claude, and Cursor. Headcount: 11,600 (2022) → 8,300 (2023) → 8,100 (end-2024) during period of 20%+ annual revenue growth. Lütke reported seeing employees "get 100× the work done" with AI tools. Sources: CNBC, April 7, 2025; TechCrunch, April 7, 2025; MIT CDO Blog, April 11, 2025.

The results weren't announced as a transformation. They accumulated. Revenue climbed past $10B while headcount fell from 11,600 to 8,100 over two years. The workforce that remained had self-selected for AI-native capability. Shopify didn't build AI-Born ventures in the Mothership sense — it rebuilt its own organizational metabolism to function more like one.

The Shopify case illustrates Condition 3 from an angle the other cases don't. Elite talent with founder-level compensation is the standard prescription. But Shopify shows an alternative route: invert the hiring assumption at the policy level, and let natural selection do the talent density work over 18 months.

The five cases don't converge on one trajectory — and that's the point. Klarna failed the Guardian function and corrected it. JPMorgan succeeded on the same condition at a different pace because the regulatory context made autonomous failure genuinely expensive. Block passed Condition 1 with a manifesto and a 40% headcount cut. IBM discovered Condition 3 in reverse — by eliminating the wrong talent first. Shopify passed it through structural policy. Every trajectory is different. The framework accommodates that variance.

For detailed implementation case studies, visit **ai-born.org/ideas/proto-motherships**.[322]

[322] AT&T's Workforce 2020 program (later rebranded "Future Ready") invested approximately $1 billion over seven years (2013-2020) to retrain 100,000+ employees in cloud computing, data analytics, cybersecurity, and software engineering while workers remained employed. The program cost approximately $10,000 per worker and achieved significant success: by 2016, 140,000 employees actively engaged in skills acquisition, completing 1.8 million courses; retrained workers filled 50% of new technology management positions and received 47% of promotions in the technology organization; product development cycle time reduced 40% over 18 months. The program provided comprehensive support including partnerships with Coursera, Udacity, and universities; tuition reimbursement; career counseling; and income support (workers continued regular employment during retraining). Sources: Harvard Business Review, "Inside AT&T's Radical Talent Overhaul," October 2016; CNBC, "AT&T's $1 billion gambit: Retraining nearly half its workforce for jobs of the future," March 13,

Cultural and Regulatory Boundaries: Adapting Haier's Model

Haier's success occurred within specific Chinese institutional contexts.[323] The transformation triggered 25% attrition – roughly 20,000 people leaving the organization, a human cost that any adaptation of the model must meet with comprehensive transition support, not merely whatever employment law permits. (The legal exposure also differs by jurisdiction: more viable under Chinese employment law than under US or EU regimes.) Western adaptation requires: **patient capital** (foundation ownership, dual-class shares, B Corp certification), **employment law compliance** (comprehensive severance, wrongful termination prevention, union protocols), **cultural adaptation** (hybrid incentives combining individual achievement with team outcomes), **proactive regulator engagement.**[324]

Extract the principles—platform-venture architecture, autonomous teams, shared infrastructure—and adapt to your regulatory environment.

2018; Harvard Business School Case Study, "AT&T, Retraining, and the Workforce of Tomorrow" (Case 820-017), July 2019.

[323] Jedrzej George Frynas, Michael J. Mol, Kamel Mellahi, "Management Innovation Made in China: Haier's Rendanheyi," *California Management Review* 61, no. 1 (2018): 71-93. Establishes that "China's institutional context was conducive to Haier's rapid transformation, with vibrant entrepreneurial culture facilitated by government policies and collectivist society"; "Haier Group and Zhang enjoyed considerable decision-making freedom thanks to ownership structure" (state-adjacent collective company); "more than 20,000 employees left Haier because they did not or could not buy into new management system" (25% workforce attrition during transformation).

[324] Frynas et al., "Management Innovation Made in China: Haier's Rendanheyi," 2018. Documents that "transfer of organizational innovations over cultural, national and industry borders often fails" and "research demonstrates how organizational, competitive, institutional, and technological contexts mattered for Rendanheyi development, showing how context-dependent management innovations are created."

Failure Modes: Where Motherships Collapse

The case studies above — Klarna's reversal, IBM's arc, JPMorgan's careful approach — each represent organizations that encountered the Mothership's failure modes and, to varying degrees, navigated them. Six failure modes appear with enough regularity to function as diagnostic tools. Most are visible in advance, if you know where to look.

Automating Scope Without Human Cortex Judgment. The Klarna arc tells this story fully. When the Guardian — the judgment-keeper governing *which* interactions AI should handle — is absent, the answer defaults to whatever maximizes short-term cost reduction. The resulting degradation compounds quietly until it surfaces on a customer satisfaction dashboard. Klarna caught it within eighteen months. Organizations that don't lose something much harder to recover than headcount — customer trust built over years that erodes in weeks.[325]

Innovation Theater. Ventures publicly branded "autonomous" but dying slowly under approval processes that replicate the corporate hierarchy they were supposed to escape. This is Condition 1 failure in slow motion: the venture exists on paper, the innovation

[325] Ryan Browne, "Klarna reverses AI staffing cuts, plans to hire more humans after customer service 'degraded'," CNBC, December 2024; Sam Shead, "Klarna CEO says company cut too many jobs as it plans to bring back human staff," BBC News, January 2025; additional coverage in Financial Times and Bloomberg, Q1 2025. Klarna cut approximately 700 customer service jobs between 2022 and 2024, replacing them with AI systems. CEO Sebastian Siemiatkowski subsequently acknowledged that service quality had "degraded" and announced the company would resume hiring human customer service representatives. The reversal demonstrates that AI automation without Human Cortex oversight of deployment scope produces degraded customer experience. Crucially, Klarna's error was not automating customer service — it was removing human judgment about *which* interactions to automate, *when*, and *how to detect quality degradation*. The Machine Core requires the Human Cortex to govern its scope of deployment, not merely to operate it.

narrative is intact, and the organization never learns that the model would have worked if it had been actually tried.

Platform Underinvestment. Infrastructure starved of funding, forcing each new venture to rebuild services from scratch. This eliminates the entire logic of the Mothership — every venture bearing the full 6–12 month infrastructure overhead the platform was supposed to absorb. Three global firms approved $100M+ platform budgets and then reduced them 18 months in under quarterly pressure. The ventures that followed paid full infrastructure costs; the platform economics never materialized.

Insufficient Transition Infrastructure. Technical success that triggers organizational collapse because leadership funded the Machine Core while underfunding the Human Cortex that displaced workers needed. Comprehensive transition support costs more upfront but reduces risk-adjusted costs. AT&T's billion-dollar reskilling program — discussed above — achieved 47% of promotions filled internally, which demonstrates the payback logic: retained knowledge offsets retraining expense faster than replacement hiring would.[326]

---

[326] AT&T's Workforce 2020 program (later rebranded "Future Ready") invested approximately $1 billion over seven years (2013-2020) to retrain 100,000+ employees in cloud computing, data analytics, cybersecurity, and software engineering while workers remained employed. The program cost approximately $10,000 per worker and achieved significant success: by 2016, 140,000 employees actively engaged in skills acquisition, completing 1.8 million courses; retrained workers filled 50% of new technology management positions and received 47% of promotions in the technology organization; product development cycle time reduced 40% over 18 months. The program provided comprehensive support including partnerships with Coursera, Udacity, and universities; tuition reimbursement; career counseling; and income support (workers continued regular employment during retraining). Sources: Harvard Business Review, "Inside AT&T's Radical Talent Overhaul," October 2016; CNBC, "AT&T's $1 billion gambit: Retraining nearly half its workforce for jobs of the future," March 13, 2018; Harvard Business School Case Study, "AT&T, Retraining, and the Workforce of Tomorrow" (Case 820-017), July 2019.

The Oligarch's Temptation. FTX operated without a functional board. WeWork and Theranos followed similar patterns.[327][328][329] A Mothership cortex controlling platform infrastructure and capital allocation creates identical conditions — Robert Michels' "Iron Law of Oligarchy" applied to organizational transformation.[330] Mitigation requires structural counterbalance: stakeholder representation on oversight boards with actual authority, transparent decision logs, and worker councils with consultative power.[331]

The Fragility Cascade. Motherships with centralized platform infrastructure create systemic risk: ventures depend on shared data pipelines, model infrastructure, and customer systems. A platform failure cascades to every venture simultaneously. OpenAI and Anthropic have changed pricing 30% overnight, upending unit

[327] John C. Coffee Jr., "FTX and the Regulatory Failure That Made It Possible," *Columbia Law Review Forum*, December 2022. Legal analysis of FTX's corporate governance failures, documenting complete absence of board oversight and internal controls across its three-year operational period. The company operated without fundamental corporate governance structures, including proper board oversight, risk management, and financial controls, enabling widespread misappropriation of customer funds.

[328] Amy Westbrook, "We('re) Working on Corporate Governance: Stakeholder Vulnerability in Unicorn Companies," *University of Pennsylvania Journal of Business Law* 23, no. 2 (2021): 411-468. Academic analysis documenting how WeWork's poor corporate governance, unbridled founder control, and lack of board oversight led to catastrophic strategic failures and $47 billion valuation collapse.

[329] Elizabeth Medina Williams, "Elizabeth Holmes and Theranos: A play on more than just ethical failures," *Business Information Review* 39, no. 2 (2022): 88-102. `https://doi.org/10.1177/02663821221088899`. Academic analysis of how Theranos's corporate governance failures and abandonment of scientific peer review enabled systematic fraud that evaporated $9 billion in valuation and endangered patient safety.

[330] Robert Michels, *Political Parties: A Sociological Study of the Oligarchical Tendencies of Modern Democracy* (Free Press, 1911; reprint 1962). Michels observed that all organizations, regardless of democratic intentions, tend toward control by a small elite—the "Iron Law of Oligarchy."

[331] German co-determination (Mitbestimmung) model requires large companies to include worker representatives on supervisory boards (up to 50% of seats), ensuring labor perspective in strategic decisions. Provides tested framework for balancing shareholder interests with stakeholder accountability.

economics for companies that built on their APIs.[332] Anthropic temporarily cut off Windsurf's Claude access during negotiations.[333] Each of these events became an unplanned architectural decision for every downstream Mothership relying on that vendor. Mitigation: multi-model architectures, human-in-loop overrides for critical decisions, contractual data portability, and real financial reserves.[334]

Three deeper political economy obstacles shape whether any of the above is navigable.

Board time horizons. Most institutional investors operate on 2–4 year decision horizons. The Mothership's proof points arrive at month 24–36, outside that window. The structural solution is to pre-negotiate explicit board commitments: not just budget approval, but written acknowledgment of what the program looks like at month 18 before it looks like success, and pre-agreed measurement criteria that track learning velocity and iteration half-life rather than P&L.

Middle management as power, not inertia. The 65–75% of middle managers who face structured transition pathways are

[332] Palani Opara-Martins, Reza Sahandi, and Feng Tian, "Critical analysis of vendor lock-in and its impact on cloud computing migration: a business perspective," *Journal of Cloud Computing* 5, no. 1 (2016): 4. `https://doi.org/10.1186/s13677-016-0054-z`. Academic analysis documenting vendor dependency risks in cloud services, including pricing volatility that can increase enterprise costs by 20-40% overnight when providers revise structures without advance notice.

[333] Adnan Masood, "LLM Gateways for Enterprise Risk—Building an AI Control Plane," Medium, `https://medium.com/@adnanmasood/llm-gateways-for-enterprise-risk-building-an-ai-control-plane-e7bed1fdcd9c`. Reports that Anthropic temporarily cut off coding application Windsurf's direct access to Claude models because Windsurf was growing too popular and was set to be acquired by OpenAI—demonstrating vendor dependency risks.

[334] Nassim Nicholas Taleb, *Antifragile: Things That Gain from Disorder* (Random House, 2012). Framework arguing that "antifragility is beyond resilience or robustness. The resilient resists shocks and stays the same; the antifragile gets better"—systems that benefit from volatility, randomness, disorder, and stressors rather than merely resisting them.

not passive resistors. They hold real organizational influence — access to the CEO, institutional credibility with functional heads, the ability to slow information flow at exactly the approval stages where transformation gets sanctioned or killed. The path through is pre-negotiation — structured transition packages and role redesign conversations that happen *before* the transformation is announced, not after resistance has organized.

Dual-reporting accountability gaps. Venture teams reporting simultaneously to Mothership governance committees and functional business unit heads experience autonomy degradation at precisely the pace needed to kill Condition 1. The architectural fix is single-reporting lines — ventures report to the Shared Cortex governance layer exclusively, with functional BU heads invited as advisors, not approvers.

For comprehensive failure mode diagnostics, see **ai-born.org/tools/mothership-transformation-diagnostic**.[335]

When the Model May Be Wrong: Exit Criteria

If three consecutive ventures fail to reach profitability within 24 months, question the model itself. The diagnostic questions are familiar from the entry diagnostic above: Does the platform provide genuine value, or is it organizational overhead? Is autonomy real or performative? Does the organization actually possess platform-convertible assets?

Honest exit criteria: After 5 years and multiple venture launches, if fewer than 40% achieve positive unit economics, venture revenue remains negligible despite substantial investment, average talent

[335]This online supplement provides detailed early warning indicators, root cause analysis frameworks, and intervention strategies for each major Mothership failure pattern, with anonymized practitioner case examples.

retention stays below 18 months, and platform adoption by the legacy organization remains minimal — this is the moment to switch strategies. Return to the entry diagnostic and reassess: Acquisition Pivot, Platform Provider, or Incremental Adoption may serve this organization better than continued Mothership Build investment.

Some organizations lack the incumbent advantages that make the Mothership model economically rational. Better to recognize that early than persist in transformation theater.

For comprehensive failure mode diagnostics, visit **ai-born.org/frameworks/mothership-shadows**.

The Endgame: What Success Looks Like

By year 7–10, the picture looks fundamentally different. Fifteen to 25 ventures — each with 5–15 people — generate 40–60% of revenue. The platform team runs at 200–500 people. The legacy operation that once employed 40,000 now employs 5,000–10,000. Revenue per employee has climbed from roughly $200K toward $2–$5M. Margins have expanded from the 10–15% range into the 30–50% range of a platform business.

The organization hasn't adopted AI. It has become something else entirely: a platform-enabled ecosystem of AI-Born ventures, using scale as a launch pad rather than a liability.

Conclusion: Scale as Asset, Not Liability

That productivity gap Patricia was staring at on a Tuesday morning isn't a forecast. It's a present condition — and the options available to her are fewer and harder than most boardroom conversations acknowledge.

She can deny the gap. Optimize existing operations. Watch AI-Born competitors nibble at margin, then take whole segments. Wait until a financial crisis forces restructuring — the worst possible moment, when capital is scarce, stakeholders are panicking, and the organization has no runway for careful transition.

Or she can build the Mothership — or choose the right strategy from the entry diagnostic above. Convert incumbency into AI-Born advantage. The cases are clear about what this requires: platform investment over 18–36 months, genuine venture autonomy, proactive customer migration, and workforce transition support funded at the scale the problem actually demands — not announced and then quietly starved. Dimon's formulation at Davos is as good a summary of the pace question as exists: "Phase it in. Retrain."[336]

Haier's fifteen-year commitment to microenterprise autonomy created an organizational structure that absorbed AI deployment faster than any competitor.[337] IBM's reversal to tripling entry-

[336] Jamie Dimon, remarks at World Economic Forum panel, Davos, Switzerland, January 22, 2026. Verbatim quotations: 'You can't lay off 2 million truckers tomorrow. You can phase it in over time'; 'If it goes too fast for society, that's where government and business in a collaborative way should step in together and come up with a way to retrain people'; 'Phase it in. Retrain. Relocate. Income-assist.' He called U.S. Trade Adjustment Assistance 'incredibly poorly done' and said JPMorgan AI productivity savings were 'just the tip of the iceberg.' On potential government bans on mass AI layoffs: 'We would agree — if we have to do that to save society.' Sources: Banking Dive, 'JPMorgan's Dimon: AI's effect on jobs may go too fast for society,' January 22, 2026, `https://www.bankingdive.com/news/jpmorgan-dimon-ai-effect-jobs-workforce-davos/810247/`; Fortune, January 22, 2026, `https://fortune.com/2026/01/22/jpmorgan-chase-ceo-jamie-dimon-ai-layoff-income-assist-workers-elon-musk-sam-altman-universal-basic-income/`.

[337] Haier's COSMOPlat industrial internet platform, deployed across its microenterprise ecosystem beginning in 2023, enabled significant operational improvements: 50% faster product design speed, 26% reduction in defects, and 18% lower energy consumption. These metrics demonstrate how centralized

level hiring confirmed that AI-native human talent, not headcount reduction, is the actual scarce resource in the AI-Born transition.[338] Klarna demonstrates that course corrections are possible, and that a hybrid Human Cortex model outperforms pure replacement at the metrics that actually matter: customer retention, product quality, investor confidence at IPO.[339]

platform infrastructure amplifies the capabilities of distributed autonomous teams. Multiple sources on COSMOPlat benefits include industry analysis reports and Haier corporate communications, 2023-2024.

[338] IBM restructuring arc: CEO Arvind Krishna announced hiring freeze on back-office AI-replaceable roles, May 2023 (7,800 roles projected eliminated over five years). Bloomberg, May 1, 2023, `https://www.bloomberg.com/news/articles/2023-05-01/ibm-to-pause-hiring-for-back-office-jobs-that-ai-could-kill`. Wave 1 reduction: 8,000–10,000 employees (Sept–Dec 2024). Wave 2: 5,000–7,000 (Q1 2025). Total estimated: 13,000–17,000 jobs over two years. Specific HR automation: IBM's AskHR reduced HR professionals performing manual work from 700 to fewer than 50 (93% reduction); handled 11.5 million interactions in 2024 with 94% self-service containment. Source: IBM CEO Arvind Krishna, Fortune op-ed, June 2023; IBM AskHR case study. Reversal: IBM CHRO Nickle LaMoreaux announced tripling of entry-level U.S. hiring at Charter's Leading with AI Summit, New York, February 12, 2026. LaMoreaux quote: "The entry-level jobs that you had two to three years ago, AI can do most of them. So, if you're going to convince your business leaders that you need to make this investment, then you need to be able to show the real value these individuals can bring now. And that has to be through totally different jobs." Sources: Bloomberg, February 12, 2026, `https://www.bloomberg.com/news/articles/2026-02-12/ibm-plans-to-triple-entry-level-hiring-in-the-us-in-2026`; Fortune, February 13, 2026, `https://fortune.com/2026/02/13/tech-giant-ibm-tripling-gen-z-entry-level-hiring-according-to-chro-rewriting-jobs-ai-era/`.

[339] Klarna Group, NYSE IPO prospectus and Q3 2025 earnings report, September–October 2025. Klarna raised $1.4B at a $15B valuation; shares surged 30% to a $19.65B market cap on IPO day. Full-year 2024 revenue: $2.81B (+24% YoY). Q3 2025 revenue: $903M (+26% YoY), 114M active customers (+32% YoY). Headcount arc: 5,527 FTE (end-2022) to 3,422 FTE (end-2024), attributed to hiring freeze and AI deployment. AI chatbot deployed January 2024 claimed equivalent of 700 full-time outsourced agents' workload; projected $40M annual cost savings. Reversal announced 2025: CEO Sebastian Siemiatkowski stated company "went too far," acknowledging generic and repetitive AI responses for complex emotional queries; resumed hybrid model with human agents for nuanced cases. Sources: CNBC, "Klarna CEO says AI helped company shrink workforce by 40%," May 14, 2025; MLQ.ai, "Klarna CEO admits aggressive AI job cuts went too far," 2025; CX Dive, "Klarna says AI agent handled work of 853 employees," 2025.

For organizations willing to make those commitments — tolerate asymmetry during transition, defend venture autonomy against corporate gravity, fund worker support at the scale the problem demands — incumbent scale becomes an asset no startup can replicate. Distribution relationships, regulatory trust, institutional memory: none of these are liabilities in the Mothership model. They're the launch platform.

You transform on your terms, or you wait for market forces to do it for you.

But I'm getting ahead of myself.

Individual organizational transformation is only part of the story. The productivity differentials this chapter describes — an order of magnitude in revenue per employee, headcount reductions of similar scale — multiply when thousands of organizations pursue similar transformations simultaneously. The second-order effects become far more significant than the first.

Think about what the Mothership math actually produces at scale. Patricia's firm moves from 46,000 to 8,000. The 38,000 people who remain outside that room didn't fail at their jobs. They optimized for an economy that no longer exists in the same form. They have mortgages calibrated to their previous salary. They have communities built around their commute. They have self-conceptions organized around the title on their badge. The Mothership model is solved. What comes next is not an engineering problem.

The architecture this chapter describes is available, right now, to any organization with the capital to execute it. The social infrastructure to absorb its consequences was designed for a different economy. That asymmetry — between available architecture and inadequate absorption capacity — is the actual problem Book 2 addresses.

The Mothership model answers how incumbents survive. It doesn't answer what happens to millions of workers displaced in aggregate. It doesn't resolve how the value created when machines do the work humans once performed gets distributed across workers, owners, and communities.

One more economic logic cuts through the policy debate. A market in which tens of millions of former knowledge workers cannot participate as consumers will not sustain even the most efficient AI-Born firm for long. The social reset isn't a sidebar for the socially concerned. It's the other half of the architecture.

Book 2 (*AI-Born: The Bridge*) turns to that harder problem.

The Question the Blueprint Can't Answer

You've just read a blueprint.

Ten chapters. A prologue. Frameworks with names. Stacks with acronyms. You've seen Aether Dynamics route shipments around a geopolitical crisis while Legacy Corp convenes emergency meetings. You've met Aria Chen designing self-organizing systems for a Singapore logistics firm at 6:47 on a Monday morning. You've watched Meridian Trade Finance turn regulatory compliance into a revenue advantage that a $200M competitor couldn't buy.

The architecture is sound. The logic holds. Build the Machine Core well, cultivate the Human Cortex wisely, let the A.G.E.N.T. stack compound its advantages — and the math works.

But here is the question the blueprint can't answer, and I want to ask it plainly before we go any further: *for whom does it work?*

* * *

I want to sit with this for a moment before pushing forward, because the direct version is more uncomfortable than the polished one.

The A.G.E.N.T. Defensibility Stack — Architecture, Governance, Evolution, Network, Trust — is not a neutral framework. It describes how to construct advantages that self-reinforce over time.

Consider what that means in practice. The regulatory relationships Meridian cultivated with Singapore's Monetary Authority and Thailand's banking regulators took 18 months of demonstrated reliability to earn, and cannot simply be purchased or imitated. Firms that achieve deep client embedding through Network effects accumulate switching costs that make displacement progressively more expensive. Each layer of the stack is, in a precise sense, a mechanism for making the gap between leaders and followers durable.

That's the point. That's what makes it a moat.

But consider who enters the race with each layer pre-loaded.

A well-capitalized incumbent with existing regulatory relationships, decades of customer data, and $50M to invest in platform infrastructure arrives at the A.G.E.N.T. stack with Governance and Network already seeded. A sovereign wealth fund backing an AI-Born venture can absorb the 18-month period before Architecture advantages compound into revenue. A founder who can recruit elite talent with equity upside can accelerate Evolution velocity in ways a worker-owned cooperative in Youngstown, Ohio — however well-intentioned — structurally cannot.

Two people the blueprint has not yet named: Maya, 47, mortgage, skills accumulated across two decades of knowledge work. Tom, 38, working two part-time jobs to replace one full-time one. They enter the same landscape with none of those resources. No regulatory relationships. No data assets. No patient capital. No equity upside. They are not building the Machine Core. They are, in the most literal sense, what the Machine Core replaced.

The architecture this book teaches is the precise architecture that well-capitalized firms will execute more effectively than the workers whose roles it reorganizes — and the efficiency gains that fund continued investment accrue primarily to those who already held the capital to invest. That is the recursive problem the blueprint cannot solve by building more carefully.

* * *

Step back far enough and the pattern becomes familiar.

The Industrial Revolution created the most sophisticated coordination machinery in recorded economic history up to that point: factories, railroads, telegraph networks, joint-stock corporations with limited liability. Genuine technological achievements, every one. The coordination problems they solved were real. The productivity gains were real and large — by the end of the 19th century, a single factory worker in Manchester could produce more textile in a day than a medieval village produced in a week.

But the coordination machinery also required workers. It needed bodies, discipline, regularity. The factory clock encoded a social relationship: your time belongs to us, in exchange for wages. Labor became a factor of production — dear when scarce, replaceable when abundant.

The machines that created that bargain also set its terms.

Here is the part the history books usually skip. For the first several decades of industrial capitalism, the gains from that machinery concentrated almost entirely in the hands of the mill owners. Real wages for English factory workers barely moved between 1780 and 1840, even as the economy around them transformed beyond recognition. The workers who ran the looms did not share immediately in the output those looms produced. Markets eventually did raise wages — real English wages roughly doubled between 1840 and 1900 — but the timing and distribution of those gains were shaped as much by organizing, legislation, and hard-won political settlement as by price signals alone. The eight-hour day emerged from negotiated social compact. So did the end of child labor. Each required deliberate institutional design that market competition, on its own timetable, had not yet supplied.

Something similar is happening now. The honest assessment of the previous ten chapters is not promotional — it describes real mechanisms. Three people at Aether Dynamics orchestrate what once required organizational pyramids. The compression is structural, not marginal: a handful of principals and their Machine Core handle coordination that previously required hundreds. The architecture works for those inside it. The question this book has not answered is what it means for the many outside it. The iteration half-life that compounds competitive advantage is real. The governance-as-moat insight is real. But so is the arithmetic of who is inside this architecture and who is outside it.

But when execution itself becomes nearly free, something shifts in the structure of bargaining power. Labor's traditional leverage was always scarcity: you couldn't run the factory without the workers. Markets rewarded that scarcity with wages and, over time, benefits — not as charity, but as the price of labor's irreplaceability. The AI-Born enterprise's defining architectural claim is that this particular form of scarcity is narrowing in scope. The Machine Core does not require the labor-market infrastructure — wages, benefits, scheduling, collective negotiation — that human execution did. And unlike the factory floor, which required workers to be physically present and therefore capable of collective action, the cognitive infrastructure of an AI-Born firm can be owned, operated, and compounded by a small team with limited structural dependence on the broader workforce whose coordination tasks it automates.

* * *

I keep returning to a remark made at Davos in January 2026. Not by a labor economist. Not by a union organizer. By Jamie Dimon – chairman and CEO of JPMorgan Chase, the largest bank in the United States, a man who has spent $2 billion deploying AI across his own institution and calls the savings "just the tip of the iceberg."[340]

Standing before the world's assembled financial elite, Dimon said this: "You can't lay off 2 million truckers tomorrow."

He was not speaking against AI. He has invested heavily in it, believes in it, says the social benefits – cured cancers, longer lives, shorter workweeks for his grandchildren – are real and coming. But in those seven words, the head of the largest U.S. bank compressed the moral and practical problem that every chapter of this book has gestured toward without naming directly. The problem is not the destination. The problem is the speed of arrival relative to the capacity of society to absorb it.

"If it goes too fast for society," Dimon continued, "that's where government and business in a collaborative way should step in

[340] Jamie Dimon, remarks at World Economic Forum panel, Davos, Switzerland, January 22, 2026. Verbatim quotations sourced from Banking Dive, "JPMorgan's Dimon: AI's effect on jobs may 'go too fast for society,'" January 22, 2026, `https://www.bankingdive.com/news/jpmorgan-dimon-ai-effect-jobs-workforce-davos/810247/`; and Fortune, "JPMorgan CEO Jamie Dimon says he welcomes government ban on mass-firing people for AI," January 22, 2026, `https://fortune.com/2026/01/22/jpmorgan-chase-ceo-jamie-dimon-ai-layoff-income-assist-workers-elon-musk-sam-altman-universal-basic-income/`. Verbatim Dimon statements from these reports: "You can't lay off 2 million truckers tomorrow. You can phase it in over time"; "If it goes too fast for society, that's where government and business in a collaborative way should step in together and come up with a way to retrain people"; on potential government bans on mass AI layoffs: "We would agree – if we have to do that to save society"; "Phase it in. Retrain. Relocate. Income-assist." Dimon also described the U.S. Trade Adjustment Assistance program as "incredibly poorly done" and argued for a superior public-private model. JPMorgan had spent approximately $2 billion on AI deployment and disclosed that the productivity savings were "just the tip of the iceberg."

together and come up with a way to retrain people." And then the concession that should stop anyone who thinks this is merely an academic concern: when asked whether he would support government limits on mass AI-driven layoffs, Dimon said he would — "if we have to do that to save society."

Read that again. The head of the largest U.S. bank, endorsing a collaborative government-business response to the pace of displacement, to prevent what he called a risk that AI adoption "may go too fast for society."

That sentence lands differently when you understand who said it.

* * *

Dimon is not alone. He is, if anything, the trailing signal — the institutional conscience finally catching up with what the technologists have been saying for years.

Consider what Dario Amodei, the CEO of Anthropic, told Axios in May 2025. Amodei builds the models. He understands their capabilities from the inside better than almost anyone outside a handful of labs. His forecast: AI could "wipe out half of all entry-level white-collar jobs — and spike unemployment to 10–20% in the next one to five years."[341] He said, plainly: "We need to stop

[341] Dario Amodei, interview reported by Axios, "Behind the Curtain: A White-Collar Bloodbath," May 28, 2025, `https://www.axios.com/2025/05/28/ai-jobs-white-collar-unemployment-anthropic`. Verbatim direct quotations: "AI could wipe out half of all entry-level white-collar jobs — and spike unemployment to 10–20% in the next one to five years"; "We need to stop sugar-coating what's coming"; "I don't think this is on people's radar. It's a very strange set of dynamics, where we're saying: 'You should be worried about where the technology we're building is going' "; "going to happen in a small amount of time — as little as a couple of years or less." Note: the phrase "white-collar bloodbath" is Axios's headline framing, not a verbatim Amodei direct quote. Amodei reiterated the displacement warning and enumerated five risk categories in "The Adolescence of Technology," January 27, 2026, `https://www.darioamodei.com/essay/the-adolescence-of-technology`.

sugar-coating what's coming." Mustafa Suleyman, Microsoft's AI chief, added an 18-month timeline to the same prediction in February 2026, naming accountants, lawyers, and project managers specifically.[342] Geoffrey Hinton, who left Google in 2023 to speak freely about AI risks without corporate constraint, described the resulting feeling with the precision of a man who has thought about it too carefully: "I'm mildly depressed. Which is why I'm scared."[343]

Wonderful and frightening in the same breath. That is the honest register of this moment.

---

[342]Mustafa Suleyman, Microsoft AI CEO, interview with the Financial Times, reported February 13, 2026. Verbatim direct quotation: "So white collar work where you're sitting down at a computer, either being a lawyer or an accountant or a project manager or a marketing person, most of those tasks will be fully automated by an AI within the next 12 to 18 months." Additional verbatim: "We're going to have a human-level performance on most, if not all, professional tasks." Secondary sources: Fortune, "Microsoft AI Chief Gives It 18 Months for All White-Collar Work to Be Automated," February 13, 2026, `https://fortune.com/2026/02/13/when-will-ai-kill-white-collar-office-jobs-18-months-microsoft-mustafa-suleyman/`; Futurism, February 2026, `https://futurism.com/artificial-intelligence/microsoft-all-white-collar-tasks-automated`. Suleyman also cited the experience of software engineers — who he said now use AI-assisted coding for "the vast majority of their code production" — as the earliest-adopter evidence that the role-level automation pattern is already underway.

[343]Geoffrey Hinton, interview with Will Douglas Heaven, MIT Technology Review, May 2, 2023, `https://www.technologyreview.com/2023/05/02/1072528/geoffrey-hinton-google-why-scared-ai/`. Verbatim direct quotation: "I'm mildly depressed. Which is why I'm scared." On his departure rationale, Hinton told MIT Technology Review: "I want to talk about AI safety issues without having to worry about how it interacts with Google's business. As long as I'm paid by Google, I can't do that." In a May 1, 2023 post on X, Hinton separately clarified: "I left so that I could talk about the dangers of AI without considering how this impacts Google." He described his changed view of AI systems: "I have suddenly switched my views on whether these things are going to be more intelligent than us. How do we survive that?" Hinton received the 2024 Nobel Prize in Physics jointly with John Hopfield for foundational discoveries enabling machine learning. His Nobel Banquet speech, December 10, 2024, amplified the warning: "If [AI productivity benefits] are created by companies motivated by short-term profits, our safety will not be the top priority." Nobel speech transcript: `https://www.nobelprize.org/prizes/physics/2024/hinton/speech/`.

These are not critics of AI — they are its architects, deploying it at scale, warning about their own creation, and continuing to build it anyway. Amodei called this "a very strange set of dynamics." It is. And the strangeness is load-bearing: if the people who understand the technology best believe it will cause serious disruption, and they are still building it, the disruption is not a forecast to be debated. It is a design constraint to be addressed.

The empirical signal is already appearing. Research by Anthropic economists tracked what happened to young workers after ChatGPT's release: hiring of workers aged 22 to 25 in AI-exposed occupations dropped roughly 14% compared to pre-ChatGPT baselines.[344] Not unemployment — not layoffs that generate headlines — but something quieter, and in some ways more corrosive: the entry points to careers are closing. The career ladder for the generation currently entering the workforce is losing its bottom rungs. The efficiency gain today may be producing a skill deficit a decade hence — a cohort of workers who never acquired the foundational expertise that entry-level roles historically provided, because those roles no longer exist to provide it.

Every chapter that precedes this one, read honestly, describes a world where the architects of the Machine Core hold a form of leverage over the rest of the economy that has no historical precedent in scale or permanence. The railroad baron's advantage required physical infrastructure in a specific geography. Standard Oil's advantage required refineries that could be physically seized — which

[344]Maxim Massenkoff and Peter McCrory, "Labor market impacts of AI: A new measure and early evidence," Anthropic research publication, March 5, 2026, `https://www.anthropic.com/research/labor-market-impacts`. Key finding: workers aged 22–25 entering high-AI-exposure occupations experienced a 14% drop in job-finding rate compared to 2022 baselines — an effect not observed for workers over 25. The mechanism is reduced hiring rather than increased separations. Authors note the result is "just barely statistically significant" and cite corroborating work by Brynjolfsson et al. (2025) documenting a 6–16% employment decline in exposed occupations among the same cohort.

is, eventually, what happened. The AI-Born advantage requires cognitive architecture: infinitely replicable, globally deployable, compounding automatically with every transaction, and far harder to physically seize or politically circumscribe than any factory in the industrial era. If the leading tier of well-capitalized AI-Born firms compounds governance relationships, Network embedding, and Trust accumulation over the next five years simultaneously, the structural barriers to entry for later participants become durable in ways that reskilling infrastructure alone cannot fully address. That is not a reason to build less carefully. It is a reason to ask, urgently, what the governance of this architecture looks like at the civilizational level — not just the firm level.

* * *

There is a phrase that recurs throughout this book: *when execution is no longer the bottleneck, judgment becomes everything*.

I believe this is true. I have believed it throughout the writing of these chapters. I still believe it now.

But I have grown increasingly uneasy with the way this truth is distributed.

The New Triumvirate — Architect, Guardian, Force Multiplier — concentrates the exercise of judgment in perhaps three people per AI-Born firm. Think of what that means at scale: JPMorgan deploys AI across 300,000 employees and 80 million customers; the Architects who define what those systems optimize for carry leverage no individual banker in JPMorgan's history ever held. Their encoded decisions execute at machine speed across millions of interactions. What they believe about fairness, about whose interests count, about what constitutes worthy ends — these beliefs become infrastructure.

Not metaphorically. Literally. An objective function is a moral claim expressed as code. A reward signal is a value judgment rendered executable. The Architect who designs the agent charters and defines what the system maximizes, the Guardian who decides when to escalate and what to protect, the Force Multiplier who transmits the craft standard the system is held to — each is engaged in moral reasoning, whether they recognize it as such or not. And each of those moral claims will propagate across every transaction the system processes, at a scale and speed that human judgment historically never produced.

Consider Aria Chen, the Architect who designs self-organizing logistics systems and spends her Monday morning reading overnight escalation patterns. Her decisions — which thresholds trigger escalation, what penalties discourage which behaviors, how the system weights speed against caution — will execute across millions of shipment decisions she never personally touches. She is not writing rules. She is writing reality, for every party in those transactions: the warehouse workers whose scheduling the agents determine, the small freight brokers whose contracts the agents renegotiate, the communities whose roads the optimized routing runs through. The architecture encodes moral choices whether Aria recognizes them as such or not. And Aria — talented, principled, working from a sound governance framework — cannot answer, within the scope of her role, whose interests the system should ultimately serve when those interests conflict.

That question is not an engineering problem. It sits exactly one level above engineering, in the domain of political economy: who decides, through what process, with what accountability, whose welfare the system is designed to protect when protecting different groups simultaneously is not possible. When you build systems that magnify human judgment at civilizational scale, the question of whose welfare that judgment serves becomes the central design decision you will make.

The blueprint taught you how to build the system.

What the blueprint cannot answer is whose values get encoded at the foundation – and through what democratic or institutional process those values are legitimated, contested, and revised.

* * *

Let me be precise about what I am *not* saying, because this is a place where misreadings compound.

This is not an argument against building the architecture. The AI-Born enterprise exists whether or not any particular reader builds one consciously. The competitive dynamics are already in motion – vanguard firms are already altering the competitive landscape in software, finance, logistics, and legal services. Refusing to build well is not solidarity with the displaced. It is simply losing to someone who builds less thoughtfully, with fewer guardrails on what the system optimizes for.

Nor is this an argument that the architecture is secretly extractive. The stewardship case made throughout these chapters is genuine. Patient capital, multi-stakeholder governance, and long-horizon optimization create competitive advantages that narrow extraction cannot generate. The Wells Fargo asset cap and the Volkswagen emissions fine arrived faster than any stewardship dividend would have compounded – and those were cases from the pre-AI era, when the velocity of legitimacy erosion was slow compared to what autonomous systems operating at machine scale can produce in months.

What this is: a recognition that the blueprint is necessary but not sufficient.

Building an AI-Born enterprise with impeccable governance is the entry condition, not the achievement. The A.G.E.N.T. stack executed flawlessly produces a defensible, scalable, trust-accumulating machine — and leaves entirely open the question of how the gains from that machine distribute, how the workers it displaces land, and what kind of civilization the aggregate of all these machines is constructing.

Architecture shapes outcomes. It doesn't determine them. In the gap between shaping and determining, human choice still lives — and that is where the work that matters most remains undone.

* * *

The prologue of this book opened with a choice: at Aether Dynamics, three humans paused a self-routing system to answer the question no model could resolve — *what values do we encode when we deploy AI?*

It was the right question to open with. It is also the right question to close with — because a book can describe the architecture for encoding values, and still leave you standing at the threshold of the actual encoding.

Consider what the next ten years look like from the vantage point of the Machine Core — not the architects who build it, but the civilization-level pattern that emerges when thousands of A.G.E.N.T. stacks, each encoding their founders' values, each compounding their advantages, each deepening their moats, begin to interact at scale.

If those stacks encode stewardship — operationally, in what they actually optimize for rather than what they advertise — the civilization they construct distributes gains broadly, maintains legitimacy through democratic participation, and builds the transition infrastructure that lets Maya acquire skills worth trading for, and lets Tom's daughter grow up in a world less likely to replicate her father's displacement.

If they encode extraction — optimizing for the short horizon, concentrating gains, minimizing stakeholder consideration beyond the shareholder — the civilization they construct reproduces a political economy that history knows well, compressed now into years rather than generations. Concentrated ownership of productive capacity, without the counterweights that labor scarcity once provided, produces that political economy reliably. The East India Company governed 200 million people before its legitimacy collapsed under the weight of the interests it had failed to balance — and the correction, when it came, was neither tidy nor cheap. The question is whether AI-Born architecture produces its own correction mechanisms through deliberate design, or waits for the moment when the costs of concentration become politically and socially unsustainable.

The architecture this book teaches does not determine which of these paths we take.

That is both its limitation and the honest thing to say about it.

* * *

Book Two addresses what the blueprint leaves open.

Not by abandoning the machine. The Machine Core is not the enemy, and the AI-Born architecture is not reversible. The question is rarely whether to build it — at the aggregate level, the transition occurs regardless of any individual organization's choice — but always how:

what social contract absorbs the displacement it generates, what ownership structures prevent gains from concentrating in the hands of those who were already positioned to deploy, and what kind of human being — with what capacities, what sense of self, what access to meaning — emerges on the other side.

Maya and Tom — the two people named earlier — are not unintended externalities of the AI-Born transition. They are the mechanism by which the architecture generates its efficiency gains, and that distinction matters for what we owe in response. Externalizing the cost of a gain does not make the cost disappear. It assigns it. The architecture this book taught creates value by converting human coordination into automated execution. That conversion has costs. Those costs fall on specific people in specific zip codes with specific mortgage payments. Book Two asks what we owe them — not as charity, but as a structural question about how productive capacity and its gains are distributed.

Three questions drive that inquiry, and I want to state them plainly — not as chapter previews, but as the problems the blueprint cannot solve by itself.

The first is economic: what income floors, portable benefits, and ownership structures prevent the concentration of AI-Born productive capacity from reproducing, at civilizational scale, the mill-owner dynamic of the first Industrial Revolution? The Machine Core produces gains. Who receives them, through what mechanisms, is not answered by building the Machine Core well.

The second is social: what happens to community, belonging, and political stability when employment — the institution that organized social life for two centuries — no longer serves as the primary mechanism of participation and dignity? Maya's mortgage is a material problem. Her reason to get up on Tuesday morning is not.

The third is existential: who are we, as individuals, when the answer to "what do you do?" stops being a sufficient answer to "who are you?" The AI-Born architecture is built on the premise that human judgment is irreplaceable. That premise demands a richer account of what human judgment is for.

These are not soft questions bolted onto a hard technical analysis. They are the logical continuation of it.

If embedded values become the infrastructure of reality when execution is automated at civilizational scale — and this book has argued, chapter by chapter, that they do — then the most important architectural questions are not about agent orchestration protocols. The orchestration has known solutions: charter design, escalation logic, reward specification. The values question does not.

Here is what I've come to believe, writing these chapters: the AI-Born blueprint is genuinely useful. The frameworks work. The A.G.E.N.T. stack describes something real about how defensibility compounds in the era of autonomous execution. The Mothership model gives incumbents a path through transition that rip-and-replace doesn't. The New Triumvirate identifies, accurately, where human judgment remains irreplaceable.

And none of it answers the question underneath: *for whom is this irreplaceable?*

That question has an answer. But finding it requires something these chapters cannot supply — a reckoning with who pays the cost of building this well, and who shares the benefit when it works. Which brings us to where the argument has been going all along.

* * *

"When execution is no longer the bottleneck, what becomes valuable?"

The answer this book has prepared you to give is: judgment, taste, strategic intent. The Human Cortex. The three people in the room who decide what the system optimizes for.

The answer Book Two will press you toward is more demanding — and more uncomfortable, because it does not resolve cleanly into a framework:

Whose judgment? Whose taste? Whose intent? And what do we owe the people who are not in that room?

There is a scene from the early railroad era that I keep returning to, and I want to close with it because it has stayed with me the entire time I was writing these chapters.

When the Liverpool and Manchester Railway opened in 1830 — the first intercity passenger railroad in the world — the opening ceremony ended with a catastrophe. William Huskisson, a member of Parliament, stepped onto the tracks and was struck by the locomotive *Rocket*. He was the first person killed by a steam railway. The crowd that witnessed it did not, as a result, oppose the railroad. They couldn't. The lines were already under construction everywhere. The capital was already committed. The political economy of the thing was already in motion.

What the crowd did, over the following decades, was argue. Bitterly. Eventually productively. About who owned the right of way. About who bore the cost of the noise and the smoke and the grade crossings where farm wagons met trains. About what compensation the dispossessed received. About whether the profits of the lines should flow entirely to shareholders, or whether the public infrastructure those lines depended on created some obligation in the other direction.

Huskisson's death did not stop the railroad. The capital was committed. The lines were already under construction everywhere. But his death did mark the moment when the arguments about *what kind of railroad world we were building* became impossible to defer — and those arguments, fought across a century, produced workplace safety law, public utility regulation, eminent-domain compensation, and the whole apparatus by which industrial modernity was made accountable — partially, imperfectly, never finally — to the people it rearranged.

The railroad was not the question. What surrounded it was.

The Machine Core is not the question. What surrounds it is.

Those questions don't have architectural answers. They have civilizational ones — and the time to argue them is now, while the architecture is still being built, before the right-of-way is settled and the capital is committed and the vanguard cohort has locked its moats.

Book Two is that argument.

Turn the page.

Glossary of Key Terms - Book 1

This glossary provides accessible definitions of technical, framework, and economic terms used in Book 1 (Prologue, Chapters 1-10) of "AI-Born: The Machine Core, the Human Cortex, and the Next Economy of Being." Terms are organized by category for ease of reference.

Philosophical & Moral Foundations

Bahá'í Faith

A global religion founded in 19th-century Persia (modern Iran) emphasizing the oneness of humanity, the harmony of science and religion, and the elimination of all forms of prejudice. Central Bahá'í principles inform this book's philosophical foundation, particularly the emphasis on service to humanity as the organizing principle for economic activity, consultation as a decision-making method (reflected in Consultative Social Spaces), and stewardship as an economic ethic (versus extraction). The author's family heritage is four to five generations Bahá'í, with both grandfathers embodying the integration of entrepreneurial enterprise and purpose-driven service. While the book maintains secular language accessible to all readers, the underlying values framework draws from these principles: that technology magnifies human intent and must be architected for collective flourishing, that consultation prevents optimization traps, and that coherence between stated values and operational design is not optional but essential.

See also: Service to Humanity, Coherence, Stewardship, Values-Conscious Architecture, Consultative Social Spaces

Coherence (discipline of coherence)

The disciplined practice of ensuring inner beliefs and outward actions "rhyme"—that values, principles, and commitments are reflected in concrete decisions, operating models, and daily choices. Distinct from mere logical consistency or alignment rhetoric, coherence requires continuous reflection on whether systems, incentives, and architectures embody stated values. The author identifies this as "the single most formative influence" from his community education work, where the goal was always capacity-building—helping people become protagonists of change by integrating conviction with action. In AI-Born organizations, coherence manifests through Values-Conscious Architecture, where technical design choices express moral and social commitments: escalation triggers surface ethically ambiguous decisions, reward functions operationalize stated purposes rather than convenient proxies, and governance structures ensure that "service to humanity" translates from mission statement to system behavior. Technology is never neutral—it magnifies intent—making coherence between stated purpose and encoded architecture existential. As the author's wife, Bronwyn, insisted: a venture should make us better humans, not merely busier or richer; strategy optimized for short-term gain alone is extraction with a nicer font.

See also: Values-Conscious Architecture, Service to Humanity, Stewardship, IPRE Pipeline, Intent-Setting

Technical Terms

Actuation Plane

The fifth and final layer of the five-plane architecture, serving as the "hands" of the AI-Born organism—the interfaces through which agents execute actions in the real world. This includes API integrations to external systems, robotic process automation for legacy software interaction, physical robotics interfaces, and financial transaction systems. The actuation plane bridges the gap between digital decision-making and real-world impact, enabling agents to not just recommend actions but execute them directly within defined authority boundaries.

See also: Five Planes, Agent Plane, Tool Use

Agent Plane

The third layer of the five-plane architecture, populated by thousands of role-defined software agents, each with specific charters, tools, memory, and permissions. This is the AI-Born equivalent of a corporate workforce—autonomous entities that execute tasks, analyze data, and collaborate to achieve goals set by the orchestration plane. Agents can scale instantly, work without fatigue, and learn from every interaction.

See also: Five Planes, VP-Agent, Orchestration Plane

Agentic AI

Artificial intelligence systems that can perceive their environment, reason about goals, and take autonomous actions to achieve them without constant human direction. Unlike traditional automation that follows rigid, pre-programmed steps, agentic AI operates through a perceive-reason-act-learn (PRAL) loop, continuously evaluating outcomes and adapting strategies. These systems represent a categorical leap from tools (which execute commands) to agents (which pursue objectives).

See also: Autonomous Agents, Machine Core, PRAL Loop

AI-Enabled

Organizations that add AI features or capabilities to existing operations and business models without fundamental architectural transformation. AI-enabled companies bolt autonomous systems onto legacy hierarchies, seeking marginal efficiency gains while preserving existing power structures, reporting relationships, and career pathways. This approach treats AI as a tool to augment current processes rather than as the foundation for reimagining organizational design. Examples include traditional enterprises deploying chatbots for customer service, using predictive analytics for forecasting, or implementing RPA for back-office automation—all while maintaining human-centric organizational structures. The AI-enabled approach protects incumbents and dampens disruption, but also perpetuates bureaucratic inertia and slow learning cycles that create vulnerability to AI-Born competitors.

See also: AI-Native, AI-Born, Lineage Break

AI-Native

Organizations that leverage AI and large language models at the core of their product offerings or deliverables, but where the work to build and evolve those systems is done largely by human teams, not an autonomous agentic workforce. These companies use AI as their product but remain human-operated. The AI is what they sell, not how they operate. Examples include Midjourney (AI image generation with estimated 130-170 person human team), Cursor (AI code editor built by human engineers), and Perplexity (AI search powered by human developers). AI-native represents a significant evolution from traditional software companies but remains fundamentally distinct from AI-Born architecture.

See also: AI-Born, AI-Enabled, Lineage Break, Machine Core

AI Colleague

An autonomous agent staffed into a defined role—with a name, a manager, and a "desk"—rather than treated as a tool, bot, or assistant. The phrase captures the AI-Born principle of "roles, not tools": agents occupy seats in the org chart, carry charters, report to human principals, and are accounted for like members of the workforce. Neolith (the operating surface on which Adaptic runs) is the reference implementation, where roughly 44 AI colleagues hold C-Suite, SVP, and VP roles directed by a small group of human principals.

See also: Agent Charter, Compute Is Payroll, Company-as-Runtime, Machine Core, VP-Agent

Audit Spine (Event Spine)

One immutable timeline recording every act an organization takes, making the company replayable end to end—"git log for judgment." Decisions, charter edits, and approvals are filtered views of this single ledger rather than separate logs. Where Immutable Lineage traces data provenance, the audit spine is the underlying append-only record from which decision histories and approval trails are derived. In Neolith, the audit spine lets human principals reconstruct exactly why any agent acted as it did.

See also: Immutable Lineage, Decision Ledger, Transparency, Company-as-Runtime

Autonomous Agents

Software entities that can independently perceive their environment, reason about their goals, select appropriate tools, and take actions to achieve objectives without ongoing human input. Each agent maintains both short-term (current task context) and long-term memory (learned patterns and historical decisions), enabling it to learn from experience and maintain consistency across interactions.

See also: Agentic AI, Tool Use, Agent Plane

Company-as-Runtime

The view of an AI-Born organization's org chart as a live runtime rather than a static diagram: each seat is a running process, its charter is the configuration, its decision ledger is the log, and the machine beneath it is real infrastructure that can throttle, block, or fail. A company so conceived does not merely *describe* itself in documents—it *executes*. Neolith productizes this view: changing the org means changing code, and the organization runs the way software runs. This reframing makes governance, observability, and failure handling first-class organizational concerns rather than HR abstractions.

See also: Agent Charter, Audit Spine, Strategy as Code, Compute Is Payroll, Machine Core

Compound AI System

An architecture where multiple interconnected AI models work collaboratively to solve complex problems more effectively than any single model could achieve alone. Rather than relying on one monolithic model, these systems orchestrate specialized models—some for perception, others for reasoning, still others for specific domain tasks—creating emergent capabilities through their coordination. Google's AlphaCode 2, which generates millions of candidate solutions and filters them through evaluation models, exemplifies this approach.

See also: Multi-Agent System, Model Plane

Compute Is Payroll

The accounting principle that an AI colleague's cost—its machine (its "desk") plus its model time—is treated as a recurring monthly line on the profit-and-loss statement, much like a salary. Humans hold a "seat" and the agenda; AI colleagues hold a "desk" and run the work, each priced like payroll. This reframing makes the AI-Born cost structure legible: headcount becomes a blend of human seats and machine desks, and scaling the workforce becomes a budgeting decision rather than a hiring cycle. Neolith operationalizes the principle directly, surfacing each colleague's compute cost as a payroll-style figure for its human principals.

See also: AI Colleague, Company-as-Runtime, Small-Team Paradox, Machine Core

Data Plane

The foundational first layer of the five-plane architecture, consisting of governed corpora—curated, high-integrity data collections with immutable lineage tracking, automated quality contracts, and retrieval systems optimized for agentic access. Unlike traditional data warehouses that simply store information, the data plane is living infrastructure that continuously validates, contextualizes, and serves data as high-grade fuel for intelligent action.

See also: Five Planes, Immutable Lineage, Governed Corpora

Embedding Coefficient

A quantitative metric measuring the depth and breadth of an organization's integration as infrastructure within other systems, reflecting the extent to which the organization has become embedded as a utility component through API partnerships, platform integrations, and operational dependencies. A high embedding coefficient indicates that customers, partners, and complementary services have built critical workflows around the organization's capabilities, creating switching costs and network effects that serve as powerful defensibility. This metric captures the progression from standalone product to utility infrastructure—the fourth layer of the A.G.E.N.T. Stack representing Network as competitive moat.

See also: A.G.E.N.T. Stack, Network, Trust Velocity

Escalation Protocol

Predefined triggers and pathways that automatically route decisions from autonomous agents to human oversight when specific thresholds are crossed—ambiguity levels exceed parameters, stakes surpass authority limits, ethical considerations are detected, or policy conflicts arise. Escalation protocols function as the immune system of AI-Born organizations, ensuring that agents operate autonomously within safe boundaries while flagging edge cases, novel situations, and high-consequence decisions for human judgment. Well-designed protocols specify not just when to escalate but to whom (which role in the New Triumvirate), with what context (decision traces, relevant data, alternative options analyzed), and with what urgency (immediate halt vs. parallel human review).

See also: Agent Charter, Decision Rights, Guardian, Values-Conscious Architecture

Evaluator Agents

Specialized AI agents within the IPRE Pipeline whose function is to continuously monitor and assess whether other agents' behaviors align with stated intent, policy constraints, and quality standards. Unlike execution agents that pursue objectives, evaluator agents serve as the taste and judgment mechanisms—trained on curated libraries of on-brand/off-brand examples, acceptable/unacceptable behaviors, and aligned/misaligned outcomes. They detect alignment drift, reward hacking, policy violations, and quality degradation in real-time, escalating to human oversight when violations occur. Evaluator agents make organizational taste scalable, enabling the Guardian's judgment to be embedded in systems that operate at machine speed and scale.

See also: IPRE Pipeline, Taste as a Moat, Guardian, Alignment Debt

Five Planes (Data, Model, Agent, Orchestration, Actuation)

The technical architecture of the AI-Born enterprise, consisting of five integrated layers: (1) Data Plane—the sensory foundation providing governed, high-quality data; (2) Model Plane—the cognitive engine housing foundation and specialist AI models; (3) Agent Plane—the distributed workforce of autonomous software agents; (4) Orchestration Plane—the central nervous system coordinating agents; (5) Actuation Plane—the hands that execute actions in the real world through APIs and integrations. The power emerges not from any single plane but from their seamless integration and feedback loops.

See also: Machine Core, Architecture

Foundation Models

Large, general-purpose AI models (such as GPT-4, Claude, Gemini) trained on vast datasets to develop broad capabilities across language understanding, reasoning, and generation tasks. Foundation models serve as the cognitive engine within the Model Plane, providing general intelligence that can be applied to diverse problems without task-specific training. Unlike specialist models optimized for narrow domains, foundation models exhibit emergent capabilities—reasoning patterns, contextual understanding, and problem-solving strategies that weren't explicitly programmed. AI-Born enterprises typically use foundation models as the reasoning core for autonomous agents, often supplemented by specialist models for specific tasks requiring domain expertise or fine-tuned performance.

See also: Model Plane, Specialist Swarms, Compound AI System

Genesis

The founding pipeline of an AI-Born company, running from ethos and intent through phases, streams, clusters, seats, and finally charters—treating founding and ongoing evolution as one continuous machine rather than a discrete launch event. Because the organization fills itself in ahead of the founder ("never a blank page"), Genesis is "not day one—it's every day": the same generative process that stands the company up keeps reshaping it as intent changes. Neolith implements Genesis as its founding-and-evolution surface, where declaring intent progressively generates the org structure and the charters that govern it.

See also: Agent Charter, Company-as-Runtime, Strategy as Code, Human Cortex

Governed Corpora

Curated, high-integrity data collections with immutable lineage tracking, automated quality contracts, and access controls that form the foundation of the Data Plane. Unlike raw data lakes or traditional warehouses, governed corpora treat data as high-grade fuel requiring continuous validation, contextualization, and governance. Each datum carries metadata specifying source provenance, transformation history, quality metrics, access permissions, and retention policies. Governance mechanisms enforce data contracts (schema validation, completeness checks, freshness requirements) automatically, ensuring that agents always operate on reliable, auditable, and compliant data. Governed corpora represent the shift from data as passive storage to data as actively managed strategic asset.

See also: Data Plane, Immutable Lineage, Platform Core

Human Cortex

The small strategic nucleus of the AI-Born organization, typically comprising two to ten individuals who provide uniquely human inputs that cannot be automated: strategic intent, ethical guidance, subjective taste, and ultimate judgment in ambiguous situations. The cortex defines the "why" and the "what," setting purpose, values, and high-level objectives that guide the machine core's actions. It operates at a fundamentally different layer than traditional management—not executing or micromanaging, but architecting and calibrating the autonomous system.

See also: Machine Core, New Triumvirate, Architect, Guardian, Force Multiplier

Immutable Lineage

The capability to trace every piece of data to its original source through an unalterable audit trail, enabling verification of data provenance, quality, and transformations. In AI-Born systems, immutable lineage is essential for compliance, debugging agent behaviors, and maintaining trust in autonomous decision-making. When an agent makes a recommendation based on data, humans can reconstruct the complete chain of data sources and transformations that led to that recommendation.

See also: Data Plane, Transparency

IPRE Pipeline (Intent, Plan, Run, Evaluate)

A systematic methodology for translating high-level business objectives into machine-readable instructions for autonomous agents, consisting of four stages: (1) Intent—declarative, outcome-focused strategic goals articulated by the human cortex; (2) Plan—machine-executable translation of intent into VP-Agent objectives, KPIs, and explicit constraints (the last human checkpoint before autonomous execution); (3) Run—VP-Agent and specialist agent execution within Plan parameters; (4) Evaluate—evaluator agents monitoring outcomes, detecting proxy optimization, and surfacing signals for intent revision. This pipeline transforms strategy from static documents into executable code.

See also: Strategy as Code, Alignment Debt, Human Cortex, Reward Function

Knowledge Graph

A structured representation of relationships between entities (customers, products, suppliers, regulations, concepts) and the accumulated wisdom of the agent population, maintained by the Orchestration Plane. Unlike traditional databases organized in tables, knowledge graphs represent information as nodes (entities) connected by edges (relationships), enabling semantic reasoning and contextual understanding. When an agent learns something valuable—a successful strategy, a customer insight, a failure mode—it contributes to the knowledge graph, making the insight available to the entire system. Knowledge graphs can be centralized (single global graph) or federated (distributed local graphs synchronized periodically), providing the collective memory that allows AI-Born organizations to learn as a unified organism rather than as isolated agents.

See also: Orchestration Plane, Multi-Agent System, Machine Core

Machine Core

The vast, scalable, and perpetually learning operational body of the AI-Born enterprise—a distributed network of thousands of autonomous, specialized agents that execute tasks, analyze data, optimize processes, and collaborate to achieve goals. The core handles the "how" of operations, constantly improving its methods through real-time feedback loops. It is the engine of execution, operating at a scale and speed impossible for human-centric organizations.

See also: Human Cortex, Autonomous Agents, Five Planes

Model Plane

The second layer of the five-plane architecture, housing a portfolio of interconnected AI models that provide the reasoning, prediction, and generation capabilities the machine core requires. This includes foundation models (large, general-purpose models like GPT-4 or Claude) and specialist models (smaller, fine-tuned models optimized for specific tasks). The sophistication lies not in any single model but in the orchestrated ensemble, with evaluation harnesses continuously monitoring performance, safety, and alignment.

See also: Five Planes, Foundation Models, Evaluator Agents

Multi-Agent System

An architecture where multiple autonomous agents coordinate to solve problems no single agent could address alone, communicating through standardized protocols, sharing knowledge through common graphs, and coordinating through defined patterns (sequential, hierarchical, parallel, or collaborative). Modern implementations can manage populations exceeding 10,000 agents while maintaining coordination efficiency above 80% through techniques like memory compression, relevance-based pruning, and graph-based communication.

See also: Autonomous Agents, Orchestration Plane, Swarm Intelligence

Native / Scale / Sovereign

The maturity tiers of the operating surface an AI-Born company runs on, scaling with the organization's size and governance needs: **Native** (the solo founder or earliest team running directly on shared infrastructure), **Scale** (a small team coordinating a growing fleet of

AI colleagues), and **Sovereign** (an incumbent or regulated enterprise requiring data residency, private infrastructure, and dedicated controls). The tiers describe how the same operating model hardens as stakes rise, paralleling the Mothership Architecture's path from autonomous venture to platform-grade infrastructure. Neolith offers these as its productized tiers, from solo-founder Native through enterprise Sovereign deployments.

See also: Mothership, Company-as-Runtime, Three-Phase Transformation Pathway, AI-Born

Orchestration Plane

The fourth layer of the five-plane architecture, serving as the central nervous system that coordinates thousands of agents. It performs critical functions: task routing (decomposing high-level goals and assigning work), policy enforcement (ensuring system-wide rules are respected), credit assignment (determining which agents contributed to success), and knowledge graph maintenance (capturing relationships and accumulated wisdom). This plane prevents distributed agent workforces from descending into chaos.

See also: Five Planes, VP-Agent, Agent Plane

Operating Context (OC)

The panel or view that makes an AI colleague legible to its human manager—surfacing what it believes matters, what it is working on, where it is stuck, and where a human can intervene. Where the Agent Charter defines what a colleague is *allowed* to do, the Operating Context shows what it is *actually* doing and thinking, turning an opaque autonomous process into something a principal can read at a glance and steer. Neolith implements the Operating Context as a colleague-level surface (overview, charter, board, decisions, and pinned items), the unit through which the Human Cortex watches and intervenes.

See also: Agent Charter, Human Cortex, Escalation Protocol, Audit Spine, Company-as-Runtime

Platform Abstraction

The process of generalizing infrastructure and capabilities built for initial ventures into reusable platform services that subsequent ventures can leverage. In the Mothership model, this involves transforming bespoke solutions (data pipelines, agent charters, governance frameworks) into standardized, documented, API-accessible services. Successful abstraction enables each new venture to launch faster by building on proven patterns rather than reinventing infrastructure, creating compounding productivity advantages.

See also: Mothership, Shared Cortex

PRAL Loop (Perceive-Reason-Act-Learn)

The fundamental cognitive cycle of autonomous agentic systems, representing the four continuous stages through which agents operate: (1) Perceive—gather and process environmental inputs through sensors and data sources; (2) Reason—analyze the situation and determine appropriate actions using foundation models and specialized logic; (3) Act—execute decisions through available tools and interfaces; (4) Learn—update internal models and memory based on outcomes. This loop enables agents to improve continuously through experience, distinguishing them from static automation.

See also: Agentic AI, Autonomous Agents, Machine Core

Reward Function

A mathematical objective function that encodes what an agent should optimize for, translating strategic intent into measurable outcomes that guide autonomous behavior. Unlike simple single-metric objectives ("maximize revenue"), sophisticated reward functions balance multiple goals and constraints: customer satisfaction weighted against acquisition cost, revenue growth constrained by ethical boundaries, efficiency improvements bounded by quality standards. Reward functions operationalize the organization's values—what gets measured and rewarded is what the system will pursue. Poorly designed reward functions lead to reward hacking (gaming the metric while violating intent), making reward function design a critical component of the IPRE Pipeline and a core competency of the Intent-Setter role.

See also: IPRE Pipeline, Agent Charter, Alignment Debt, Intent-Setting

Risk Twin

A parallel simulated environment that runs continuously alongside the production system, testing proposed strategies and detecting potential failures before they reach customers. Not a one-time simulation but a living digital replica of the entire operational system—agents, policies, reward functions, market conditions—operating in accelerated time to explore alternative futures and stress-test decisions. Organizations use Risk Twins to validate strategic changes, simulate market shocks, and catch alignment problems before any real customer is harmed.

See also: Shadow Mode, Strategy as Code, Alignment Debt

Shadow Mode

A technique where AI systems operate in parallel with production systems, making predictions or decisions that are logged but not executed, allowing them to learn from real-world data without risk. Tesla's autonomous driving system famously uses shadow mode, where neural networks observe millions of miles of human driving, predicting what they would do and learning when those predictions diverge from actual outcomes. This enables continuous improvement and edge case detection at massive scale.

See also: Risk Twin, Evolution Speed, Machine Core

Shared Cortex

In the Mothership architecture, the strategic intelligence layer (typically 20-50 people) that connects the platform core and autonomous ventures. The shared cortex performs three critical functions: (1) defining enterprise-wide strategic intent and values, (2) allocating capital across the venture portfolio, and (3) monitoring alignment and governance to ensure ventures don't drift from the mission. This is not traditional corporate headquarters but a small, highly strategic team that sets boundaries and enables ventures rather than controlling operations.

See also: Mothership, Platform Abstraction, Human Cortex

Specialist Swarms

Groups of narrow-domain autonomous agents optimized for specific tasks within a larger multi-agent system, managed and coordinated by VP-Agents at the orchestration level. Each swarm consists of agents fine-tuned or specifically configured for a particular function: marketing swarms handle campaign design and execution, sales swarms manage customer interactions and deal progression, supply chain swarms optimize logistics and inventory. Specialist swarms represent the execution layer of the AI-Born workforce—where VP-Agents provide strategic coordination and goal-setting, specialist swarms handle tactical implementation at scale. The swarm architecture enables both specialization (deep expertise in narrow domains) and coordination (seamless handoffs between domains).

See also: VP-Agent, Multi-Agent System, Agent Plane

Strategy as Code

The transformation of corporate strategy from static documents into version-controlled, executable systems where strategic goals are embedded directly into reward functions, policies, and objective functions of agent swarms. To change strategy is to update agent charters and deploy new configurations—organizational pivots happen in hours rather than months. This enables continuous A/B testing of strategic hypotheses and real-time adaptation to market feedback, creating strategy-execution convergence rather than the traditional strategy-execution gap.

See also: IPRE Pipeline, Agent Charter, VP-Agent

VP-Agent

A sophisticated master agent operating at the orchestrator level, responsible for achieving high-level business outcomes by managing swarms of specialist sub-agents. Analogous to a traditional Vice President but operating at machine speed with perfect information, a VP-agent receives objectives from the human cortex, decomposes goals into sub-tasks, delegates to specialist swarms, monitors performance, reallocates resources, and reports progress—all autonomously within defined authority thresholds. Examples include "VP of Customer Acquisition," "VP of Risk & Compliance," or "VP of Supply Chain."

See also: Agent Charter, Orchestration Plane, Specialist Swarms

---

Framework Terms

Act-Typed Governance Gating

A governance pattern that maps each *type* of act an agent can take to a specific level of control: **auto** (executes freely), **auto + notify** (executes but informs a human), **approval-gated** (requires sign-off before acting), **propose → approve** (drafts an action a human enacts), and **human-gated** (reserved for human decision only). Rather than granting blanket autonomy or blanket oversight, gating tunes control to the consequence of each act, so routine work runs unimpeded while high-stakes moves surface to the Human Cortex. It operationalizes the Escalation Protocol and complements the decision-rights ladder of the Agent Charter. Neolith expresses these gates as an act-typed governance contract attached to each colleague.

See also: Escalation Protocol, Agent Charter, Decision Rights, Operating Context, Values-Conscious Architecture

A.G.E.N.T. Stack (Architecture, Governance, Evolution, Network, Trust)

The five-layer defensibility stack for AI-Born enterprises, replacing traditional moats like headcount and physical assets: (1)

Architecture—the elegance and efficiency of the five-plane system design; (2) Governance—sophisticated policies, audit trails, and compliance systems; (3) Evolution Speed—the rate of learning and improvement (measured by Iteration Half-Life); (4) Network—embedding as infrastructure within other systems, creating operational dependencies and switching costs; (5) Trust—accumulated credibility through transparency and reliable execution. These intangible advantages compound over time, creating moats more formidable than industrial-era barriers.

See also: Defensibility Stack, Iteration Half-Life, Trust Velocity

Agent Charter

A machine-readable specification that defines an agent's role, authority, and constraints—simultaneously a job description, performance contract, and governance document. Charters specify: (1) decision rights (what the agent can do autonomously, what requires approval, what is forbidden); (2) scope boundaries (tools, data, and financial limits); (3) reward function (objectives to optimize); (4) governance mechanisms (escalation triggers and override policies). Version-controlled and stored in repositories, charters make organizational structure transparent, auditable, and modifiable through code. The decision-rights component reads as a ladder—autonomous authority, then escalation triggers, then hard constraints (the forbidden), where the forbidden is architecturally prior to any reward, so no incentive can override it. Amendments flow through a charter pull request that a human signs, keeping every change to an agent's authority deliberate and traceable. Neolith implements charters in exactly this form, compiling each AI colleague against the rules its charter specifies.

See also: VP-Agent, Strategy as Code, IPRE Pipeline, Decision Rights, Reward Function, Act-Typed Governance Gating

AI-Born (vs. AI-enabled and AI-native)

Enterprises that are built, run, and evolved by the machine core—a workforce of autonomous agents—where strategic intent, values, and judgment are guided by the human cortex (typically 2-10 people). In AI-Born organizations, autonomous agents form the operational body itself, handling execution while humans provide the "why" and "what." This represents a fundamental architectural leap beyond both AI-enabled (companies that add AI features to existing operations) and AI-native (companies that build AI products with human teams). Where AI-native companies use AI as their product, AI-Born companies use AI as their workforce. The distinction is existential: AI-Born organizations exhibit fundamentally different architectures, scale models, and competitive dynamics. Examples are largely emerging or future-oriented; McKinsey's Lilli represents an early transitional example where AI agents augment consultant work. This is a design choice, not a technological inevitability—reflecting specific values about how organizations should operate and what human work should become.

See also: AI-Native, Lineage Break, Machine Core, Human Cortex, Five Planes, Values-Conscious Architecture

Alignment Debt

The accumulated divergence between an organization's stated strategic intent and the actual behavior of its autonomous agents, analogous to technical debt in software engineering. Alignment debt accrues when policies become outdated, reward functions drift from true objectives, agent charters are poorly specified, or evaluators fail to catch violations. It is quantified through metrics like policy violation rates, intent-outcome gaps, evaluator disagreement rates, and reward hacking incidents. Left unchecked, it compounds and can lead to catastrophic failures.

See also: IPRE Pipeline, Evaluator Agents, Risk Twin

Architect (Role)

One of the three essential roles in the New Triumvirate, the Architect is the master of complexity who designs, maintains, and evolves the cognitive architecture of the enterprise—the five planes of operation, the interaction protocols between agent swarms, and the data governance frameworks. They are the chief engineers of a self-growing, learning organization, ensuring it remains robust, resilient, and adaptable. This role requires deep interdisciplinary understanding of systems thinking, technical architecture, organizational design, and human-AI complementarity. The Architect's fundamental task is to translate strategic intent into systemic behavior.

See also: New Triumvirate, Five Planes, Systems Thinking, Consultative Social Spaces

Cognitive Overhead Index (COI)

A 0-100 scale metric quantifying organizational friction across seven dimensions: handoffs, decision delays, rework, context-fetching, error rates, manual effort, and exceptions. Each component is weighted by its impact on organizational velocity. Legacy organizations typically score 60-70; AI-Born enterprises achieve scores below 30. COI serves as both diagnostic tool (identifying architectural bottlenecks) and competitive benchmark—low COI enables the rapid iteration that creates compounding advantages. The metric makes invisible coordination debt visible and measurable.

See also: Iteration Half-Life, Architecture, Evolution Speed

Consultative Social Spaces

Structured mechanisms where diverse stakeholders—employees, customers, community members, domain experts—collectively assess technological needs, options, and impacts before deployment. Not consensus-building that dilutes vision, but disciplined processes for surfacing knowledge, concerns, and wisdom from throughout an organization and its broader ecosystem. Technology scholar Matt Weinberg emphasizes that such spaces allow communities to "evaluate technological needs, options, and impacts" rather than having technology imposed deterministically. For AI-Born enterprises, consultative capacity becomes a core competency that prevents technical optimization from solving the wrong problems. This is participatory design as continuous practice, not one-time event—essential for maintaining social license and operational legitimacy.

See also: Participatory Technological Assessment, Values-Conscious Architecture, Guardian

Five Conditions for Mothership Success

The five critical requirements that must be met for successful Mothership transformation: (1) **Genuine Venture Autonomy** (real decision-making authority, tolerance for failure, permission to cannibalize legacy business), (2) **Identity and Branding Clarity** (distinct venture identities with sub-brand architecture), (3) **Talent Density and Compensation Innovation** (equity stakes, compensation premiums, cultural separation from legacy), (4) **Platform Investment and Technical Debt Resolution** (data modernization, API-first architecture, ML infrastructure), and

(5) **Learning and Reuse Mechanisms** (shared agent libraries, federated learning, cross-venture pattern sharing, centralized red-teaming). These conditions distinguish genuine transformation from innovation theater—violating any one creates failure modes that undermine the entire Mothership model.

See also: Mothership, Venture Autonomy, Innovation Theater, Platform Abstraction

Guardian (Role)

One of the three essential roles in the New Triumvirate, the Guardian is the final human backstop for judgment, ethics, and subjective quality. When an agent swarm escalates a decision that is ambiguous, high-stakes, or ethically fraught, it is the Guardian who makes the call. They are the keeper of the brand's soul, the ultimate arbiter of taste, ensuring that the output of the machine core is not just efficient but also elegant, coherent, and resonant. The Guardian also serves as the organization's ultimate guarantor of trust with the external world, the human face of the enterprise's commitments. This role requires cultivated judgment developed through decades of domain practice, meta-judgment about when intervention is needed, and the capacity to convene meaningful stakeholder consultation when decisions carry implications beyond the enterprise. The Guardian ensures that transparency mechanisms make AI reasoning auditable, that explainability serves diverse stakeholders appropriately, and that escalation protocols surface ethically ambiguous decisions before harm occurs.

See also: New Triumvirate, Taste as a Moat, Consultative Social Spaces, Values-Conscious Architecture, Explainability, Transparency, Escalation Protocol

Primary References: Book 1, Chapter 9 and Book 1, Chapter 8

Force Multiplier / Player-Coach (Role)

The third essential role in the New Triumvirate, the Force Multiplier (also called the Player-Coach) is the taste-transmitter and team capacity builder who scales craft quality through doing. Where the Architect sets intent and designs the system and the Guardian keeps judgment, the Force Multiplier propagates standards of excellence across the organization—working alongside people and agents, demonstrating quality in practice, and raising the collective capacity of the human cortex rather than acting as a detached manager. This role cannot be automated because transmitting taste and judgment requires lived demonstration: showing, through one's own work, what "good" looks like and how to get there.

See also: New Triumvirate, Architect, Guardian, Taste as a Moat

Primary References: Book 1, Chapter 9

Incumbent Transformation Strategies

Four distinct pathways for transforming legacy business units within the Mothership model: (1) **Gradual Migration** (route new customers to ventures while legacy customers remain on old systems, 3-5 year transition), (2) **Functional Unbundling** (selectively migrate specific functions to platform while retaining human-led components), (3) **Parallel Operation with Arbitrage** (venture and legacy both serve market, explicitly allowing cannibalization), (4) **Acquisition and Integration** (acquire external AI-Born startups and integrate as platform ventures). Each strategy addresses different transformation constraints—capital availability, regulatory requirements, workforce considerations, market dynamics—enabling incumbents to navigate the transition from monolith to Mothership while managing social, operational, and competitive realities.

See also: Mothership, Three-Phase Transformation Pathway, Venture Autonomy

Innovation Theater

A failure mode where organizations launch initiatives labeled as transformative "ventures" or "AI-native" that lack genuine autonomy, architectural differentiation, or the characteristics of true AI-Born operations. Symptoms include: ventures staffed with legacy employees lacking AI expertise, funding through traditional budget processes with annual review gates, requiring approval from legacy stakeholders for major decisions, and no separate P&L or brand identity. Innovation theater delivers the appearance of transformation without the substance, allowing leadership to claim progress while avoiding the discomfort of genuine disruption.

See also: Mothership, Venture Autonomy

Intent-Setting (Architect Function)

The intent-setting function of the Architect role within the New Triumvirate—not a standalone third role, but the Architect's responsibility for defining the ultimate purpose of the enterprise. It answers the foundational question: "Why should this organization exist?" Intent-setting is about moral imagination and strategic foresight—choosing worthy ends, setting the ethical "constitution" of the Machine Core, and crafting the compelling narrative that aligns the entire system toward a common goal. Its primary tool is not a spreadsheet but a clear and powerful articulation of purpose that can be translated into the objective functions of the AI agents. This function cannot be automated because it requires moral imagination—the capacity to envision possibilities beyond current constraints and to articulate purposes that integrate rational analysis with ethical discernment. Technology magnifies human intent but never originates purpose—AI optimizes defined objective functions with brutal efficiency but cannot choose which objectives merit optimization in the first place.

See also: New Triumvirate, Architect, Strategy as Code, IPRE Pipeline, Values-Conscious Architecture, Purpose, Coherence, Service to Humanity

Primary Reference: Book 1, Chapter 9

Iteration Half-Life

The time from strategic intent to measurable market impact, indicating an organization's learning speed and agility. Traditional firms measure this in quarters or years; AI-Born enterprises measure it in days or hours. The concept quantifies organizational metabolism—how quickly a strategic change propagates through the system and generates performance data. This difference in speed is existential: organizations that iterate faster don't just move faster, they learn faster, accumulating strategic knowledge that becomes an insurmountable moat.

See also: Evolution Speed, Cognitive Overhead Index, A.G.E.N.T. Stack

Lineage Break

A fundamental transformation—not incremental evolution—marking the transition from AI-enabled to AI-Born organizations. Previous technological revolutions (steam, electricity, internet) automated physical tasks but left humans as the central actors wielding tools. The AI-Born era represents a categorical break because agentic AI automates cognition itself, shifting humans from operators to delegators, from executors to intenders. This break is both technical (tools to agents) and psychological (threatening the job-based identity structure of modern life). Importantly, this transformation is not technologically inevitable but represents a design choice reflecting specific values about organizational purpose and human contribution.

See also: AI-Born, Agentic AI, Human Cortex, Values-Conscious Architecture

Mothership

An organizational architecture for incumbent transformation where a platform core provides shared infrastructure and intelligence to autonomous AI-Born ventures operating at the edges. The model consists of three integrated components: (1) Platform Core—centralized data, models, compliance, and domain expertise serving all ventures; (2) Autonomous Ventures—small AI-Born entities (3-10 person cortex + machine core) with separate P&L and genuine decision authority; (3) Shared Cortex—strategic layer providing intent definition, capital allocation, and governance. The Mothership enables incumbents to achieve AI-Born velocity while preserving scale advantages (brand, data, regulatory position, customer relationships).

See also: Platform Abstraction, Shared Cortex, Venture Autonomy

New Triumvirate

The three essential human roles in the AI-Born enterprise, replacing traditional hierarchies: (1) The Architect—intent-setter and systems designer who translates abstract purpose into concrete objectives, defines constraints, and designs and maintains the five-plane system, reducing cognitive overhead and enabling learning velocity;

(2) The Guardian—judgment-keeper and taste arbiter who ensures ethical boundaries are respected, maintains brand coherence (taste), and intervenes when alignment breaks; (3) The Force Multiplier / Player-Coach—taste-transmitter and team capacity builder who scales craft quality through doing. These roles represent the irreducible human contributions: systems thinking and strategic judgment, moral wisdom, and the transmission of taste.

See also: Human Cortex, Architect, Guardian, Force Multiplier

Participatory Technological Assessment

A framework where communities and stakeholders exercise agency over technologies that will transform their lives by participating in early design and deployment decisions. As researcher Matt Weinberg observes, "The main challenge is how to expand the social and political spaces where ordinary citizens can play a role in making choices early on about technologies that will affect them." In the AI-Born context, this translates to stakeholder engagement not as compliance theater but as core organizational capability—ensuring that rapid deployment of agentic systems incorporates the values and priorities of those affected, preventing technically optimal solutions to the wrong problems. This is technology assessment as learning mechanism, where dialogue with affected communities surfaces knowledge, concerns, and wisdom that pure technical optimization cannot capture.

See also: Consultative Social Spaces, Values-Conscious Architecture, Guardian

Small-Team Paradox

The phenomenon whereby a tiny human cortex (typically 2-10 individuals) can direct operational and capital resources equivalent to legacy corporations employing tens of thousands. This completely upends the traditional correlation between headcount, revenue, and market power. Examples include Midjourney ($500M ARR with estimated 130-170 employees) and Cursor ($500M ARR with ~150 people). The paradox emerges from the machine core's ability to execute at scale while the human cortex provides only strategic intent and judgment at critical decision points. This raises profound questions about value distribution—whether the efficiency gains will concentrate wealth in tiny elites or be architected for broader participation through deliberate design choices.

See also: Human Cortex, Machine Core, AI-Born

Taste as a Moat

The strategic advantage created when subjective aesthetic and quality judgments—refined, coherent, and defensible—serve as the filter that elevates machine-generated output from competent to exceptional. In an age where generative AI democratizes creation at scale, taste becomes the ultimate differentiator. Organizations embed taste through evaluator agents trained on curated libraries of on-brand/off-brand examples, creating scalable systems where the human provides judgment while AI handles volume. This intangible quality cannot be easily copied, making it a formidable competitive barrier.

See also: Evaluator Agents, Human Cortex, A.G.E.N.T. Stack, Guardian

Three-Phase Transformation Pathway

The staged roadmap for incumbent transformation from monolith to Mothership: **Phase 1 (Months 0-18)** - Launch first venture, build minimal platform, establish governance patterns; **Phase 2**

(Months 18-36) - Platform abstraction and generalization, launch second venture in different domain, prove replicability; **Phase 3 (Months 36-60+)** - Proliferate to 5-10 ventures, migrate legacy business units, establish platform as mission-critical infrastructure. Each phase has specific objectives, success metrics, and cultural flashpoints. The pathway acknowledges that transformation cannot happen overnight—it requires surgical precision across multiple years while managing the social costs of workforce transition, the operational complexity of running dual systems, and the strategic risk of competitive pressure during the transformation window.

See also: Mothership, Five Conditions for Mothership Success, Incumbent Transformation Strategies

Values-Conscious Architecture

The practice of embedding ethical principles, stakeholder values, and societal considerations directly into technical system design rather than treating them as constraints to navigate around. This goes beyond compliance frameworks to architectural choices that operationalize values: escalation triggers that surface ethically ambiguous decisions to human judgment, transparency mechanisms that make AI reasoning auditable, participatory processes that involve affected communities in deployment decisions, and override authorities that preserve human agency. Technology is never neutral—it is an expression of a social world, simultaneously shaping and shaped by the values we encode in its design. Values-consciousness is a core competency that distinguishes sustainable AI-Born enterprises from those destined for regulatory backlash or social rejection. Architecture is moral choice.

See also: Consultative Social Spaces, Participatory Technological Assessment, Stewardship

Venture Autonomy

In the Mothership model, the genuine decision-making authority granted to AI-Born ventures, not ceremonial "empowerment" subject to corporate veto. True autonomy requires: ventures can pivot product strategy without seeking approval, hire talent at compensation above corporate bands, sunset features the legacy business considers critical, operate under different cultural norms and processes, and maintain separate brand identity and P&L. A litmus test: if a venture cannot make these decisions independently, it lacks real autonomy and becomes innovation theater. Autonomy is uncomfortable for incumbents but essential for achieving AI-Born velocity.

See also: Mothership, Innovation Theater, Shared Cortex

Economic & Social Terms

Extraction (vs. Stewardship)

Two opposing ethos for economic organization. Extraction prioritizes maximizing short-term value capture for shareholders, often at the expense of workers, customers, communities, and the environment. Stewardship prioritizes long-term flourishing, treating the enterprise as something to be cultivated and passed forward rather than depleted. The AI-Born transition creates the technical capacity for either path—intensified extraction through algorithmic optimization, or genuine stewardship through purpose-aligned automation. The choice is architectural and moral, not technological. Technology magnifies intent—making explicit which values we encode in our systems existential.

See also: Stewardship, Participation Dividend, Intent-Setting, Values-Conscious Architecture

Oligarchic Centralization

A failure mode in the Mothership architecture where power concentrates in a small elite controlling both platform infrastructure and capital allocation, creating conditions for unchecked authority and governance capture. Drawing on Robert Michels' "Iron Law of Oligarchy" (1911)—the observation that all organizations drift toward control by small elites regardless of democratic intentions—this risk is structurally embedded in the Mothership's shared cortex design (20-50 people governing platform and ventures). Historical examples include WeWork's collapse from "unbridled control by its founder," Theranos's fraud enabled by compliant boards, and FTX's governance vacuum ("no Board of Directors for much of its three-year life"). Mitigation requires democratic governance by design: stakeholder representation on oversight boards, transparent decision logs, worker councils with consultative authority, constitutional constraints on cortex power, and robust succession planning. Without countermeasures, the Mothership replicates founder-worship pathologies at AI velocity.

See also: Mothership, Shared Cortex, Optimization Trap, Fragility Cascade, Consultative Social Spaces

Primary Reference: Book 1, Chapter 10 (Mothership risk analysis)

Optimization Trap

A failure mode where AI systems' relentless optimization for defined metrics destroys unmeasured value, creating strategic blindness to paradigm shifts and existential threats. Rooted in Goodhart's Law ("When a measure becomes a target, it ceases to be a good measure"), this trap occurs when the shared cortex sets venture metrics—revenue per employee, cost per acquisition, process efficiency—and the machine core over-optimizes these proxies at the expense of strategic flexibility, exploration capacity, and peripheral vision. Kodak's 1975 invention of the digital camera followed by bankruptcy in 2012 exemplifies this: the company optimized for profitable film consumables and couldn't pivot despite technological leadership because "members of the organization were so tied to the idea that their paychecks came from the sale of consumables." Mitigation requires organizational ambidexterity: allocating 10-20% of resources to exploratory ventures outside core optimization, protecting exploration budgets during downturns, running scenario planning exercises, establishing red teams to attack current strategy, and ensuring cognitive diversity in the shared cortex.

See also: Mothership, Shared Cortex, Oligarchic Centralization, Fragility Cascade, Reward Function

Primary Reference: Book 1, Chapter 10 (Mothership risk analysis)

Participation Dividend

A reframing of Universal Basic Income as a rightful share in the returns from automated productivity, recognizing that AI systems are built on generations of public investment in education, research, and infrastructure. When machines produce the bulk of economic value, and when those machines derive from collective social investment, the returns should be shared broadly rather than accrue exclusively to capital owners. Framed not as welfare but as a citizen's stake in technological progress—analogous to Alaska's oil dividend or a shareholder distribution. In its most developed form (Book 2, Chapter 4), the Participation Dividend compensates civic contributions—caregiving, volunteering, community organizing, skill-sharing—through mechanisms like timebanking systems that bridge civic participation and monetary income. This represents one mechanism for ensuring AI-Born productivity gains serve broader prosperity rather than extreme wealth concentration while recognizing that valuable work extends beyond formal employment.

See also: Universal Basic Income, Productivity Dividend, Portable Benefits, Stewardship, Timebanking, Three Protagonists

Primary Reference: Book 2, Chapter 4

Portable Benefits

Benefits systems attached to individual workers rather than specific employers, providing healthcare, retirement, disability insurance, and paid leave that follow workers across jobs and work arrangements. This addresses the fundamental design flaw in current systems predicated on permanent employment relationships—a model incompatible with dynamic labor markets where individuals string together income from multiple sources. Essential infrastructure for an economy where traditional employer-employee relationships are no longer universal.

See also: Universal Basic Income, Participation Dividend

Radical Reskilling

Large-scale workforce transformation programs designed to prepare workers displaced by AI automation for fundamentally different roles requiring new cognitive and technical capabilities. Unlike traditional upskilling (incremental improvement within current domain) or reskilling (lateral movement to adjacent roles), radical reskilling involves categorical shifts—assembly line workers becoming machine learning trainers, accountants transitioning to

AI ethics auditors, middle managers evolving into system architects. Effective radical reskilling requires multi-year programs combining technical training, psychological support for identity transition, financial assistance during retraining, and guaranteed pathways to employment in emerging roles. This represents essential social infrastructure for managing The Great Displacement—the bridge between automation-driven job loss and meaningful participation in the AI-Born economy.

See also: The Great Displacement, Portable Benefits, Productivity Dividend

Steward-Ownership

An ownership model where voting control is separated from economic benefit, with companies governed by stewards whose fiduciary duty is to the company's mission rather than maximum shareholder returns. Profits are reinvested, shared with stakeholders, or donated to charitable purposes rather than extracted by outside investors. Examples include Bosch and Patagonia. This model provides a practical pathway for encoding stewardship values into organizational DNA, creating entities optimized for long-term flourishing rather than short-term extraction.

See also: Extraction, Stewardship, Intent-Setting, Purpose

Stewardship

An economic ethos that prioritizes long-term flourishing and regeneration over short-term extraction. Stewardship treats the enterprise as something to be cultivated for future generations rather than mined for immediate returns. In practice, this manifests through ownership structures like steward-ownership (where control is separated from economic benefit), profit-sharing arrangements with broader stakeholders, systematic reinvestment in the communities and ecosystems the enterprise depends upon, and objective functions that balance financial sustainability with social and environmental impact. The AI-Born architecture makes stewardship technically feasible at scale—agents can optimize for multi-stakeholder objectives and long time horizons—but whether organizations choose stewardship over extraction is a values decision encoded in their design.

See also: Extraction, Steward-Ownership, Intent-Setting, Values-Conscious Architecture

Fragility Cascade

A failure mode in the Mothership architecture (and AI-Born systems generally) where system complexity combined with tight coupling between components causes single failures to propagate catastrophically throughout the entire system. Drawing on Charles Perrow's Normal Accident Theory, fragility cascades occur when many autonomous agents with intricate data flows and interdependent outputs create conditions where one component's failure triggers immediate downstream effects that compound exponentially. Boeing's 737 MAX crashes exemplify this risk: a software system relying on a single sensor forced the nose down repeatedly, overriding pilot inputs and causing 346 deaths. In Mothership ventures, when Agent A's output feeds Agent B's input feeds Agent C's decision, single failures propagate instantly, especially when compounded by vendor dependencies on foundation models. Mitigation requires antifragile design: multi-model architectures, human-in-the-loop overrides, graceful degradation paths, and financial reserves.

See also: Mothership, Optimization Trap, Oligarchic Centralization, Risk Twin

Primary Reference: Book 1, Chapter 10 (Mothership risk analysis)

The Great Displacement

The short-to-medium-term social disruption as entire categories of work—routine cognitive tasks, middle management information relay roles, entry-level positions—are automated on a massive scale. The IMF estimates 60% of jobs in advanced economies are exposed to AI, with roughly half facing potential automation of key tasks. ILO data shows 25% of global employment (34% in high-income countries) falls within occupations exposed to generative AI. This is not speculative futurism but measurable reality, demanding deliberate social infrastructure (reskilling, portable benefits, income floors) to prevent catastrophic consequences.

See also: Utilitarian Man, Radical Reskilling, Portable Benefits, Universal Basic Income, Three Protagonists

Toil (vs. Work)

Two fundamentally different forms of human activity, a distinction articulated by William Morris in 1884. Toil is labor performed out of necessity for survival—repetitive, draining, unfulfilling, alienated from its product and stripped of autonomy. Work, in its truest sense, is purposeful creative activity—the pursuit of mastery, the expression of craft, intrinsically motivated even when difficult. The AI-Born economy promises not the elimination of work but the automation of toil, delegating soul-crushing repetition to machines and liberating human capacity for true work. This distinction is critical: we seek to eliminate toil, not work itself. As defined in Book 1, Chapter 1: Toil is repetitive, automatable execution—tasks draining cognitive energy without engaging full capacity (status meetings, data entry, routine reporting). Work is creative, judgment-rich effort—activity engaging full human capacity for reasoning, taste, moral imagination, and strategic thinking, producing flow states and intellectual satisfaction.

See also: Workism, Alienation, Integration Index, Economy of Being

Primary Reference: Book 1, Chapter 1

Trust Velocity

The rate at which an organization earns stakeholder confidence, measured through customer retention, regulatory approval timelines, and partnership formation speed. Organizations with high trust velocity can deploy new autonomous systems faster because they've established track records that justify confidence. This metric captures accumulated reputational capital that accelerates future expansion. In the A.G.E.N.T. Stack, trust is the fifth layer of defensibility—built through radical transparency, explainable decision traces, and flawless execution.

See also: A.G.E.N.T. Stack, Explainability, Transparency

Universal Basic Income (UBI)

An unconditional cash payment to all citizens regardless of employment status, providing a foundational income floor decoupled from labor participation. Recent pilots (Kenya, Finland, Stockton, Denver) show improvements in financial stability, mental health, and entrepreneurship with minimal negative labor supply effects. In the AI-Born context, UBI becomes a pragmatic necessity when autonomous systems generate the majority of productivity—the traditional wage system no longer functions as a mechanism for distributing purchasing power to the population.

See also: Participation Dividend, Productivity Dividend, Portable Benefits

Workism

The phenomenon of making work the primary source of meaning and identity in one's life, with employment evolving into a kind of religion promising identity, transcendence, and community. This belief—that one's worth is measured by the hours sold and tasks executed—is not a timeless human condition but a product of industrial conditioning. The AI-Born transition threatens this psychological scaffolding, forcing a reckoning with what it means to have purpose beyond the paycheck and identity beyond the job title. When AI-Born organizations compress 30,000-person workforces to 3-person cortexes, workism collapses not through moral failing but through technological substitution—invalidating the premise that human value derives primarily from economic productivity.

See also: Utilitarian Man, Toil vs. Work, The Great Displacement, Alienation, Integration Index, Economy of Doing → Economy of Being

Primary References: Book 1, Chapter 1 and Book 2, Chapter 1

Note on Usage: These terms represent the conceptual framework for understanding the AI-Born transition. They are not merely technical jargon but the vocabulary required to think clearly about the most profound economic and social transformation since industrialization. Readers encountering unfamiliar terms should consult this glossary to build fluency in the language of the AI-Born era.

Note on Philosophy: Technology is never neutral—it magnifies human intent. Every architectural choice reflects values about what matters, who benefits, and what kind of future deserves to be built. This glossary emphasizes that AI-Born transformation is not technological inevitability but deliberate design choice.

Additional Terms

Alienation

Karl Marx's concept describing the worker's disconnection from four dimensions under industrial capitalism: (1) the product of labor (workers no longer see or own what they create), (2) the process of work (repetitive tasks replacing whole-craft mastery), (3) other workers (competition replacing cooperation), and (4) self (loss of identity and purpose through commodified labor). In industrial factories, a pin-maker who once crafted whole pins from wire to finish now spent fourteen hours drawing wire through a hole—never seeing the finished product, never knowing who bought it or what they paid, his skill reduced to a single repetitive motion. Marx observed that this fragmentation didn't just affect economic life but psychological and social well-being, transforming humans from creative agents into interchangeable components of production processes they neither controlled nor understood. The AI-Born era risks intensifying alienation through algorithmic management and workforce displacement, or transcending it by automating toil while liberating humans for meaningful work requiring judgment, creativity, and values-conscious stewardship.

See also: Toil vs. Work, Utilitarian Man, Workism, Extraction vs. Stewardship, Integration Index

Primary Reference: Book 1, Chapter 1

Economy of Being (vs. Economy of Doing)

The fundamental economic transition from valuing humans for what they *produce* (Economy of Doing) to valuing humans for who they *are* and how they contribute to collective flourishing (Economy of Being). The Economy of Doing emerged from industrial capitalism's need for mass labor, where human worth equated to economic output—widgets manufactured, hours logged, tasks completed. The job title became identity, and "What do you do?" established social position. As AI automates cognitive and physical execution, the utilitarian justification for human labor collapses, forcing a reckoning with purpose beyond productivity. The Economy of Being reframes value around judgment, creativity, stewardship, community leadership, care work, cultural contribution, and ethical reasoning—capacities that define human dignity independent of employment status. This shift is not automatic or guaranteed but requires deliberate architectural choices: income floors decoupling survival from wage labor, recognition systems valuing civic contribution, formation education cultivating judgment and taste, and governance structures embedding stewardship over extraction. The transition echoes pre-industrial integration where identity derived from place, craft, and community rather than job titles, but reconstituted with modern autonomy, mobility, and technological abundance.

See also: Utilitarian Man, Workism, Toil vs. Work, Integration Index, Participation Dividend, Formation, The Great Displacement

Primary Reference: Book 2, Chapter 1 and Book 2, Epilogue

Formation (vs. Training)

The cultivation of character, judgment, and values alongside technical competence—developing who you *become*, not just what you *do.* Training equips skills for defined tasks with predictable obsolescence (learning Python, mastering Excel, executing procedures). Formation develops capacities that travel across contexts: systems thinking recognizing patterns in novel domains, moral imagination defining worthy objectives amid competing values, aesthetic judgment distinguishing excellence from mediocrity, collaborative fluency working with AI while maintaining agency, and epistemic humility acknowledging limits of knowledge. The distinction mirrors traditional apprenticeship: a carpenter learned not just how to plane wood but how to recognize grain that will split, judge when a joint sits true, and evaluate whether a request produces furniture that endures. Formation enables the Architect, Guardian, and Force Multiplier roles (Book 1, Chapter 9) requiring judgment irreducible to automation. Educational scholar Farzam Arbab argued education serves dual purposes: developing individual capacities and cultivating commitment to service—students need both *ability* to contribute and *orientation* toward contribution. The AI-Born transition makes formation existentially necessary: when machines execute procedures flawlessly, humans must provide intent, taste, and ethical boundaries—capacities most adults were never taught. Formation is not elite luxury but democratic necessity, requiring institutional transformation from standardized testing and age-based cohorts to portfolio assessment, authentic performance evaluation, and multidisciplinary integration around real-world problems.

See also: Systems Thinking, Moral Imagination, Architect, Guardian, Force Multiplier, Taste as a Moat, Economy of Being, Bildung

Primary Reference: Book 2, Chapter 5

IEEE Standards (P7001, P7002, P7003, 7000 series)

Technical standards developed by the Institute of Electrical and Electronics Engineers (IEEE) to operationalize ethical principles in autonomous and intelligent systems design. The 7000 series addresses transparency, algorithmic bias, data privacy, and values-based engineering for AI systems. **IEEE P7001** specifies transparency requirements for autonomous systems: decision audit trails, retention periods, access controls, and disclosure protocols differentiated by stakeholder type (regulators receive complete technical audits, affected individuals receive human-readable explanations, engineers review token-level decision traces). **IEEE P7002** addresses data privacy and security frameworks. **IEEE P7003** establishes algorithmic bias detection and mitigation protocols. These standards translate abstract ethics into concrete architectural requirements—escalation triggers surfacing ethically ambiguous decisions to human judgment, transparency mechanisms making AI reasoning auditable, participatory processes involving affected communities in deployment decisions. In AI-Born enterprises, IEEE standards become operational requirements embedded in agent charters and governance frameworks, enabling Guardians to audit agent decisions for alignment with stated values and satisfying regulatory compliance in sectors like banking and healthcare. Platform B's preemptive transparency documentation satisfied EU AI Act Article 13 requirements without modification, accelerating market entry while competitors scrambled for retroactive compliance.

See also: Explainability, Transparency, Values-Conscious Architecture, Guardian, Agent Charter, Escalation Protocol

Primary Reference: Book 1, Chapter 8

Integration Index

A conceptual framework measuring the coherence between work, community, and identity across three dimensions: **temporal integration** (work rhythms aligned with natural cycles and community life rather than imposed factory schedules), **social integration** (productive activity embedded in relationships of mutual aid and reciprocity rather than commodified transactions with strangers), and **identity integration** (craft and role constitute core self-understanding rather than separable job titles adopted and discarded). Pre-industrial societies scored high on integration: blacksmiths' work followed agricultural rhythms and village needs, their craft embedded in kinship networks and apprenticeship lineages, and their identity inseparable from trade and place. Industrialization shattered integration: factory discipline imposed rigid time schedules disconnected from natural rhythms, wage labor commodified relationships into employment contracts, and job titles became interchangeable roles separate from deeper identity. The 20th-century corporate paternalism attempted partial restoration through company towns and lifetime employment, creating pseudo-integration contingent on employer loyalty. The AI-Born transition offers potential reconstitution of integration at higher levels—automation of toil liberating time for community participation and creative work, portable benefits and income floors enabling economic security independent of employer dependency, and formation education cultivating identity around judgment and stewardship rather than job titles. However, this reconstitution is not automatic but requires deliberate architectural choices embedding stewardship, community resilience, and human dignity into economic design.

See also: Alienation, Toil vs. Work, Economy of Being, Workism, Utilitarian Man, Formation, The Return of Community

Primary Reference: Book 1, Chapter 1, Appendix D.1

Moral Imagination

The capacity to envision possibilities beyond current constraints and articulate purposes that integrate rational analysis with ethical discernment—the cognitive and emotional ability to see alternatives to existing systems and construct visions of what ought to be. Philosopher Patricia Werhane describes moral imagination as the intersection of systems thinking (understanding how components interact dynamically) and ethical reasoning (judging which interactions serve human flourishing). In the AI-Born context, moral imagination enables the Intent-Setter to define organizational purpose beyond profit maximization, the Architect to design systems embedding stewardship rather than extraction, and the Guardian to recognize when optimization violates deeper values. This capacity cannot be automated because AI optimizes defined objective functions with brutal efficiency but cannot choose which objectives merit optimization in the first place. Technology magnifies human intent but never originates purpose—making moral imagination the irreducible human contribution. Moral imagination develops through sustained practice with ethical dilemmas requiring trade-off navigation, exposure to diverse perspectives revealing assumptions, contemplation of long-term consequences across generations, and cultivation of empathy enabling consideration of impacts on distant others. Educational formation must prioritize moral imagination alongside technical competence—technical education without ethical formation produces engineers optimizing toward unquestioned goals; ethical education without technical fluency produces well-meaning individuals unable to shape governing systems.

See also: Intent-Setting, Values-Conscious Architecture, Formation, Systems Thinking, Purpose, Coherence, Service to Humanity

Primary Reference: Book 1, Chapter 9 and Book 2, Chapter 5

Swarm Intelligence

The emergent collective behavior and problem-solving capacity that arises from the interaction of multiple autonomous agents following simple local rules without centralized coordination. Biological examples include ant colonies optimizing foraging paths through pheromone trails, bee swarms selecting nest sites through distributed voting, and bird flocks navigating obstacles through local positioning rules. In AI-Born systems, swarm intelligence enables specialist agent populations to tackle complex problems no single agent could solve—marketing swarms exploring creative variations, supply chain swarms optimizing logistics across constraints, customer service swarms routing inquiries to appropriate specialists. The orchestration plane coordinates swarms through task routing, credit assignment, and knowledge graph maintenance, but individual agents make autonomous decisions based on local information and learned patterns. Swarm architectures exhibit resilience (failure of individual agents doesn't collapse the system), scalability (adding agents increases capacity without redesigning coordination), and adaptability (swarms learn collectively through shared memory and distributed exploration). However, swarm intelligence also poses governance challenges: emergent behaviors may diverge from intended objectives (reward hacking), coordination failures can amplify rather than correct errors (fragility cascades), and responsibility attribution becomes ambiguous when no single agent causes outcomes. Effective swarm governance requires VP-Agents monitoring aggregate behavior, evaluator agents detecting alignment drift, and escalation protocols surfacing anomalies to human oversight.

See also: Multi-Agent System, Specialist Swarms, VP-Agent, Orchestration Plane, Autonomous Agents, Compound AI System

Primary Reference: Book 1, Chapter 6

Systems Thinking

The cognitive capacity to recognize patterns, relationships, and feedback loops across complex interconnected components rather than analyzing elements in isolation—understanding how interventions ripple through systems, how optimization of one metric degrades others, and how today's solutions seed tomorrow's crises. Systems thinking recognizes stocks (accumulations like population or capital), flows (rates of change like births or investment), feedback loops (reinforcing or balancing dynamics), and leverage points (where small shifts trigger disproportionate effects). Donella Meadows identified twelve leverage points ranging from weak (adjusting parameters like tax rates) to powerful (changing system goals like optimizing for community flourishing rather than GDP growth). Most education fragments problems into isolated subjects—math separate from history, science from ethics—teaching students to solve well-defined problems with known solutions rather than recognizing that optimizing one metric degrades another, that systems push back, and that unintended consequences matter more than first-order effects. The AI-Born world demands systems thinking because autonomous agents operate like complex adaptive systems: optimize customer service response time and agents become curt, damaging brand trust; maximize engagement and algorithms surface outrage fracturing social cohesion; automate hiring to reduce bias and systems embed historical inequities at scale. The Architect role (Book 1, Chapter 9) requires systems thinking to design five-plane architectures where feedback loops enable learning while safeguards prevent runaway optimization. Formation education must cultivate systems thinking through project-based learning addressing real-world problems, causal loop diagramming revealing unintended consequences, scenario planning exploring alternative futures, and metacognitive reflection on how mental models shape perceptions.

See also: Architect, Formation, Moral Imagination, Values-Conscious Architecture, Cognitive Overhead Index, Five Planes

Primary Reference: Book 2, Chapter 5 and Book 1, Chapter 9 and Book 1, Chapter 5

Explainability

The capacity to provide human-understandable explanations for AI system decisions and behaviors, enabling stakeholders to understand why a system produced a particular output or took a specific action. In AI-Born enterprises, explainability serves multiple functions: enabling Guardians to audit agent decisions for alignment with stated values, satisfying regulatory requirements for transparency in sectors like banking and healthcare, building stakeholder trust through demonstration of reasoned decision-making, and detecting potential biases or errors in agent logic. Anthropic's Constitutional AI demonstrates this through chain-of-thought reasoning that makes model decision processes auditable. However, explainability faces inherent tensions: complete reasoning traces for complex decisions can span millions of tokens and hundreds of pages, creating trade-offs between technical completeness and stakeholder comprehensibility. IEEE P7001 standards operationalize explainability by defining audit trail requirements, retention periods, access controls, and disclosure protocols appropriate for different stakeholder types (regulators vs. affected individuals vs. engineers).

See also: Transparency, Trust Velocity, A.G.E.N.T. Stack, Guardian, IEEE Standards

Primary Reference: Book 1, Chapter 8

Purpose

The foundational "why" that justifies an organization's existence and guides its strategic choices—the answer to "Why should this organization exist beyond profit generation?" In AI-Born enterprises, purpose transcends aspirational mission statements to become operationalized through the IPRE Pipeline: the Intent-Setter articulates purpose as declarative goals, the Architect translates purpose into reward functions and policy constraints, and Evaluator agents continuously monitor whether agent behaviors align with stated purpose. Daniel Cho's case (Book 1, Chapter 9) illustrates purpose operationalization: his rural energy company faced pressure to abandon underserved communities for profitable urban markets, requiring him to articulate a refined purpose—"accelerating energy access for the underserved, funded by efficient service to those who can pay market rates"—that the Architect encoded as executable logic allowing cross-subsidy while maintaining mission fidelity. Purpose becomes strategic constraint and competitive advantage simultaneously: organizations with coherent, defensible purpose attract talent who want work contributing positively to society (Platform B's 40% below-industry attrition), compress regulatory approval timelines through demonstrated trustworthiness, and build stakeholder relationships surviving scrutiny and compounding over time. Technology magnifies human intent but never originates purpose—the Intent-Setter's irreducible role is choosing worthy ends that integrate profit generation with broader stakeholder value.

See also: Intent-Setting, IPRE Pipeline, Values-Conscious Architecture, Coherence, Service to Humanity, Stewardship

Primary References: Book 1, Chapter 8 and Book 1, Chapter 9

Transparency

The visibility of organizational and system processes, decisions, and data flows that enables stakeholder verification, regulatory compliance, and trust-building. In AI-Born enterprises, transparency operates at multiple levels: architectural transparency (open documentation of system design choices and governance frameworks), operational transparency (audit trails showing agent decision reasoning and data provenance), and accountability transparency (clear assignment of responsibility when autonomous systems produce harmful outcomes). However, transparency faces inherent paradoxes: an agent's complete reasoning trace may span millions of tokens, creating tensions between technical completeness and practical comprehensibility. IEEE P7001 standards resolve these tensions by specifying which stakeholders receive what depth of transparency within what timeframes—regulators access complete technical audits, affected individuals receive human-readable explanations, engineers review token-level decision traces. Transparency serves as the fifth layer of the A.G.E.N.T. Stack (Trust), where accumulated credibility through observable, verifiable execution creates competitive moat. Platform B's preemptive transparency documentation satisfied EU AI Act Article 13 requirements without modification, accelerating market entry while competitors scrambled for retroactive compliance. Yet transparency alone is insufficient—it must combine with Explainability (making decisions understandable) and Accountability (assigning responsibility) to generate genuine trust.

See also: Explainability, Trust Velocity, A.G.E.N.T. Stack, Immutable Lineage, Values-Conscious Architecture

Primary Reference: Book 1, Chapter 8

About the Author

Mehran Granfar builds the systems he writes about – a founder building the operating architecture of the AI-born enterprise, and writing its field manual from inside the work.

He is founder and CEO of **Adaptic.ai**, where he is building an operating system for autonomous capital – an AI-native control plane for research, execution, compliance, risk, operations, and tokenized fund infrastructure. Adaptic is also the proving ground for the thesis at the heart of *AI-Born*: that the next generation of enterprises will not merely use AI as a tool but be operated by small human teams directing fleets of autonomous agents, with judgment, accountability, and regulatory responsibility anchored to named humans.

That operating model required a new surface, so he built **Neolith** – the operating system for AI-born companies. It brings human and AI colleagues into one workforce, one stream, and one audit spine, with charters, approval gates, decision ledgers, and runtime infrastructure designed so humans set direction, watch the company run, and intervene where judgment is required. It is not a chatbot layer on a legacy organization; it is the management surface for companies built from AI.

He is also co-founder and general partner of **Future Thesis Lab**, a research-led innovation platform in DIFC, Dubai. FTLAB studies, designs, and co-builds AI-born ventures — small, high-performing human teams coordinating autonomous systems — and serves as the greenfield counterpart to Adaptic's regulated environment: a place to test new organizational architectures, governance models, and venture theses before they harden into companies, policy conversations, or institutional deployments.

Before Adaptic, he founded and ran **Mothership Ventures**, a growth and innovation advisory focused on helping large organizations design, validate, and operationalise new products, services, and ventures. That work shaped a core concern running through *AI-Born*: how incumbents, institutions, and small teams alike can cross from legacy operating models into new architectures of execution.

Born in Australia and shaped by years lived across Germany, China, and the Middle East, with further work across the United States, the Pacific, and Europe, he brings a global lens to questions of technology, governance, and economic design. He speaks five languages and writes from the perspective of a builder operating across cultures, jurisdictions, and institutional systems.

Across two decades in design, e-commerce, enterprise software, venture building, and financial technology, he has worked at the points where new architectures begin replacing old ones — at the intersection of artificial intelligence, organizational design, and economic infrastructure. His wife and young son give that work a personal urgency: a desire to contribute, however modestly, to the conversations that shape how the next economy is designed, governed, and shared.

Index

www.ingramcontent.com/pod-product-compliance
Lightning Source LLC
LaVergne TN
LVHW011659200926
848484LV00004B/993
* 9 7 8 1 9 7 0 5 2 7 0 0 1 *